INTRODUCING THE CHARACTERS

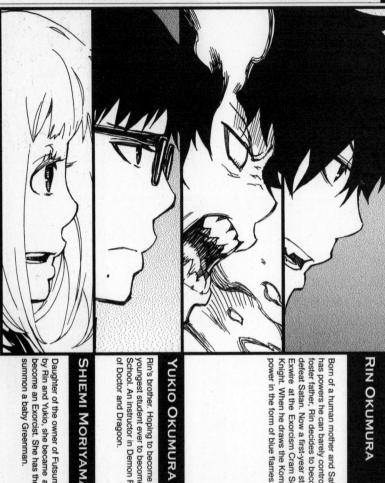

RIN OKUMURA

Born of a human mother and Satan, the God of Demons, Rin Okumura has powers he can barely control. After Satan kills Father Fujimoto, Rin's foster father, Rin decides to become an Exorcist so he can someday defeat Satan. Now a first-year student at True Cross Academy and an Exwire at the Exorcism Cram School, he hopes to someday become a Knight. When he draws the Koma Sword, he manifests his infernal power in the form of blue flames.

YUKIO OKUMURA

Rin's brother. Hoping to become a doctor, he's a genius who is the youngest student ever to become an instructor at the Exorcism Cram School. An instructor in Demon Pharmaceuticals, he possesses the titles of Doctor and Dragoon.

SHIEMI MORIYAMA

Daughter of the owner of Futsumaya, an exorcist supply shop. Inspired by Rin and Yukio, she became an Exwire and hopes to someday become an Exorcist. She has the ability to become a Tamer and can summon a baby Greenman.

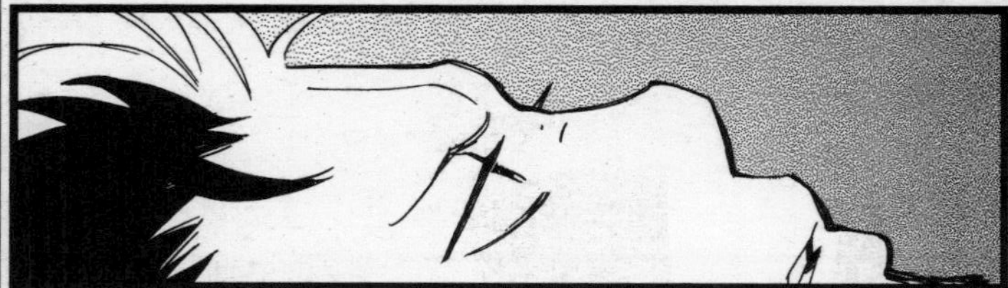

Ryuji Suguro

Heir to a venerable temple in Kyoto. After the Blue Night, he became an Exwire and hopes to become an Exorcist someday. He wants to achieve the titles of Dragoon and Aria.

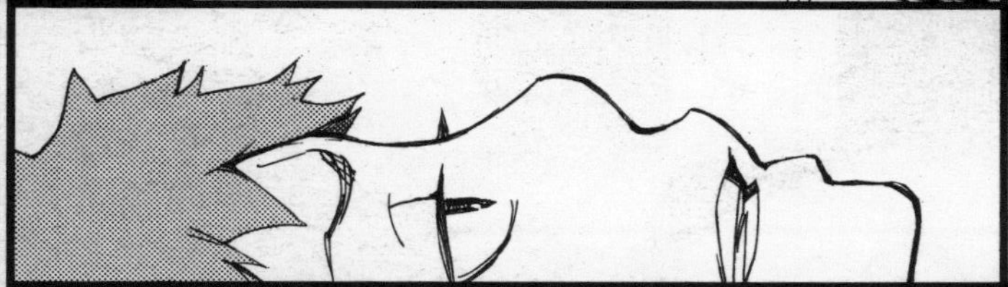

Renzo Shima

Once a pupil of Suguro's father and now Suguro's friend. He's an Exwire who wants to become an Aria. He has an easygoing personality and is totally girl-crazy.

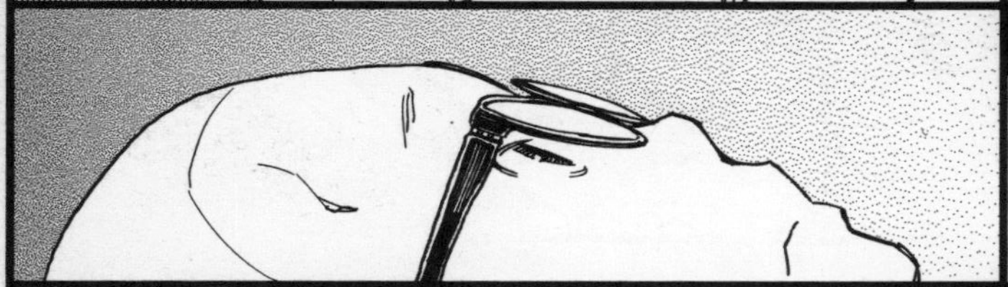

Konekomaru Miwa

Like Shima, he was once a pupil of Suguro's father and is now Suguro's friend. He's an Exwire who hopes to become an Aria someday. He is small in size and has a quiet and composed personality.

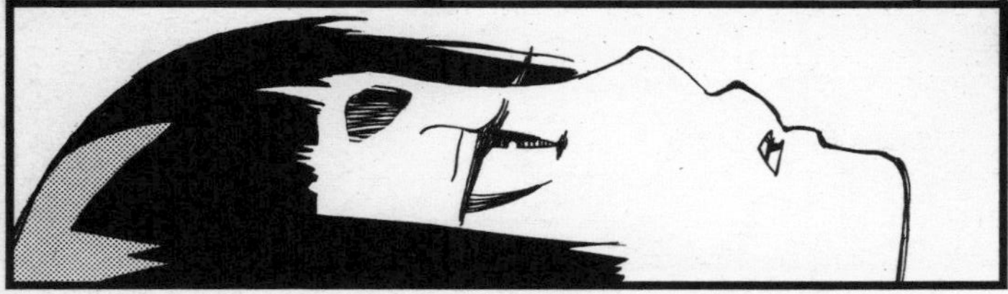

Izumo Kamiki

An Exwire with the blood of shrine maidens. She has the ability to become a Tamer and can summon two white foxes. Her friend Paku quit school, but she has continued attending.

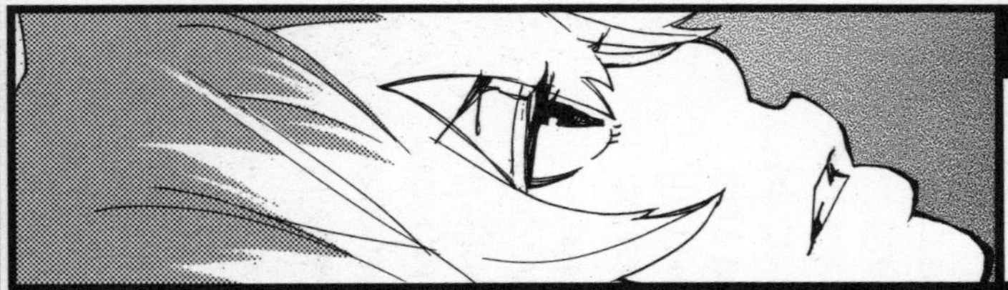

SHURA KIRIGAKURE

An upper-rank special investigator dispatched by Vatican Headquarters to True Cross Academy. A Senior Exorcist First Class who holds the titles of Knight, Tamer, Doctor and Aria. She was once Father Fujimoto's pupil and he asked her to teach swordsmanship to Rin.

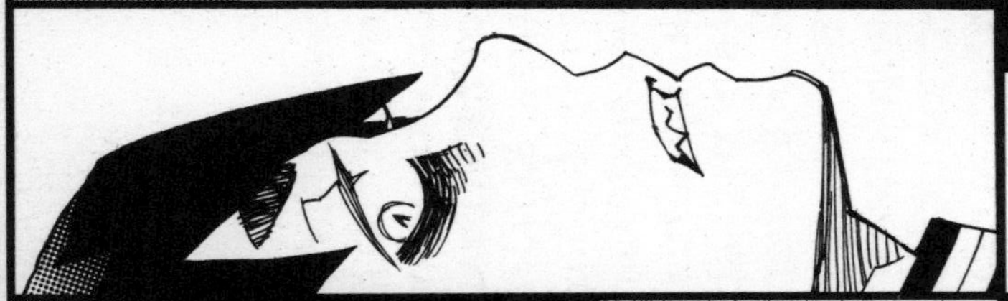

AMAIMON

Mephisto Pheles's younger brother. Mephisto ordered him to come to True Cross Academy. Little else is known about him.

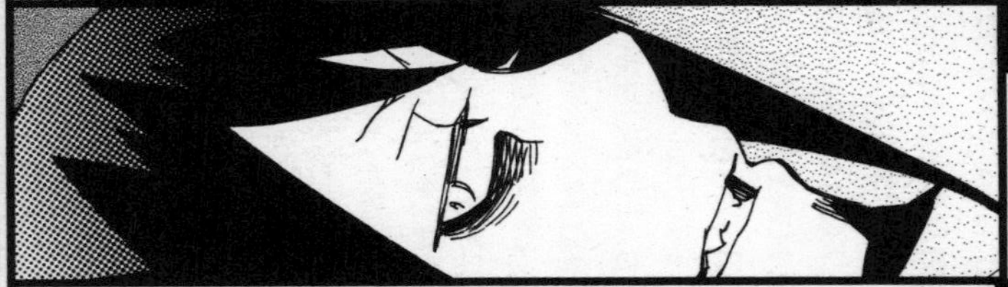

MEPHISTO PHELES

President of True Cross Academy and head of the Exorcism Cram School. He was Father Fujimoto's friend, and now he is Rin and Yukio's guardian. His behavior is suspicious and his goals are a mystery.

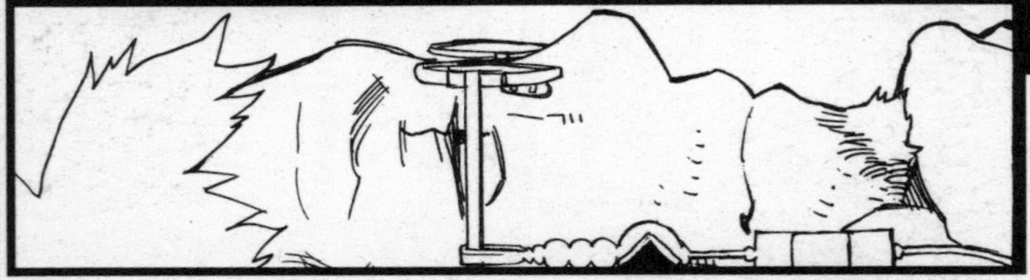

SHIRO FUJIMOTO

The man who raised Rin and Yukio. He was a priest at True Cross Church. He held the rank of Paladin and once taught Demon Pharmaceuticals. Satan possessed him and he gave his life defending Rin.

⚘ THE ACTION SO FAR ⚘

UNKNOWN TO RIN OKUMURA, BOTH HUMAN AND DEMON BLOOD RUNS IN HIS VEINS. IN AN ARGUMENT WITH HIS FOSTER FATHER, FATHER FUJIMOTO, RIN LEARNS THAT SATAN IS HIS TRUE FATHER. SATAN SUDDENLY APPEARS AND TRIES TO DRAG RIN DOWN TO GEHENNA BECAUSE RIN HAS INHERITED HIS POWER. FATHER FUJIMOTO FIGHTS TO DEFEND RIN, BUT DIES IN THE PROCESS. RIN DECIDES TO BECOME AN EXORCIST SO HE CAN SOMEDAY DEFEAT SATAN AND BEGINS STUDYING AT THE EXORCISM CRAM SCHOOL UNDER THE INSTRUCTION OF HIS TWIN BROTHER YUKIO, WHO IS ALREADY AN EXORCIST.

THE CRAM SCHOOL STUDENTS PASS THE EXWIRE CERTIFICATION EXAM AND BECOME EXWIRES. ONE DAY, THEY GO TO INVESTIGATE A GHOST THAT HAS BEEN APPEARING AT AN AMUSEMENT PARK ON SCHOOL GROUNDS. AMAIMON, KING OF EARTH, ATTACKS RIN AND STEALS THE KOMA SWORD, CAUSING RIN'S FLAME TO BLAZE OUT OF CONTROL. SHURA KIRIGAKURE, SENT BY THE KNIGHTS OF THE TRUE CROSS'S VATICAN HEADQUARTERS, STEPS IN TO SAVE RIN WHEN HE BURNS OUT HIS UNSTABLE POWER.

◉ THE ACTION SO FAR ◉

SHURA, WHO WAS ONCE SHIRO'S PUPIL, TELLS RIN THAT SHIRO WAS THE PALADIN, AND RIN DECLARES THAT HE HIMSELF WILL BECOME PALADIN IN ORDER TO PROVE THAT SHIRO WAS RIGHT TO RAISE HIM. WITH NEW DETERMINATION, RIN TACKLES HIS LESSONS MORE SERIOUSLY THAN BEFORE.

—SUMMER BREAK—

THE EXWIRES GO TO THE ACADEMY'S FOREST DISTRICT FOR A THREE-DAY TRAINING CAMP. PART OF THE CAMP IS A TEST TO SELECT WHO WILL GAIN THE RIGHT TO GO ON A REAL MISSION. THE STUDENTS MUST FIND LAMPS HIDDEN IN THE FOREST, LIGHT THEM, AND BRING THEM BACK TO CAMP. SHURA WARNS RIN NOT TO USE HIS POWER, BUT WHEN HE SEES SHIEMI ATTACKED BY DEMONS, HE FLARES UP—AND SUGURO SEES IT HAPPEN!

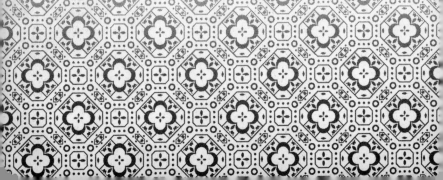

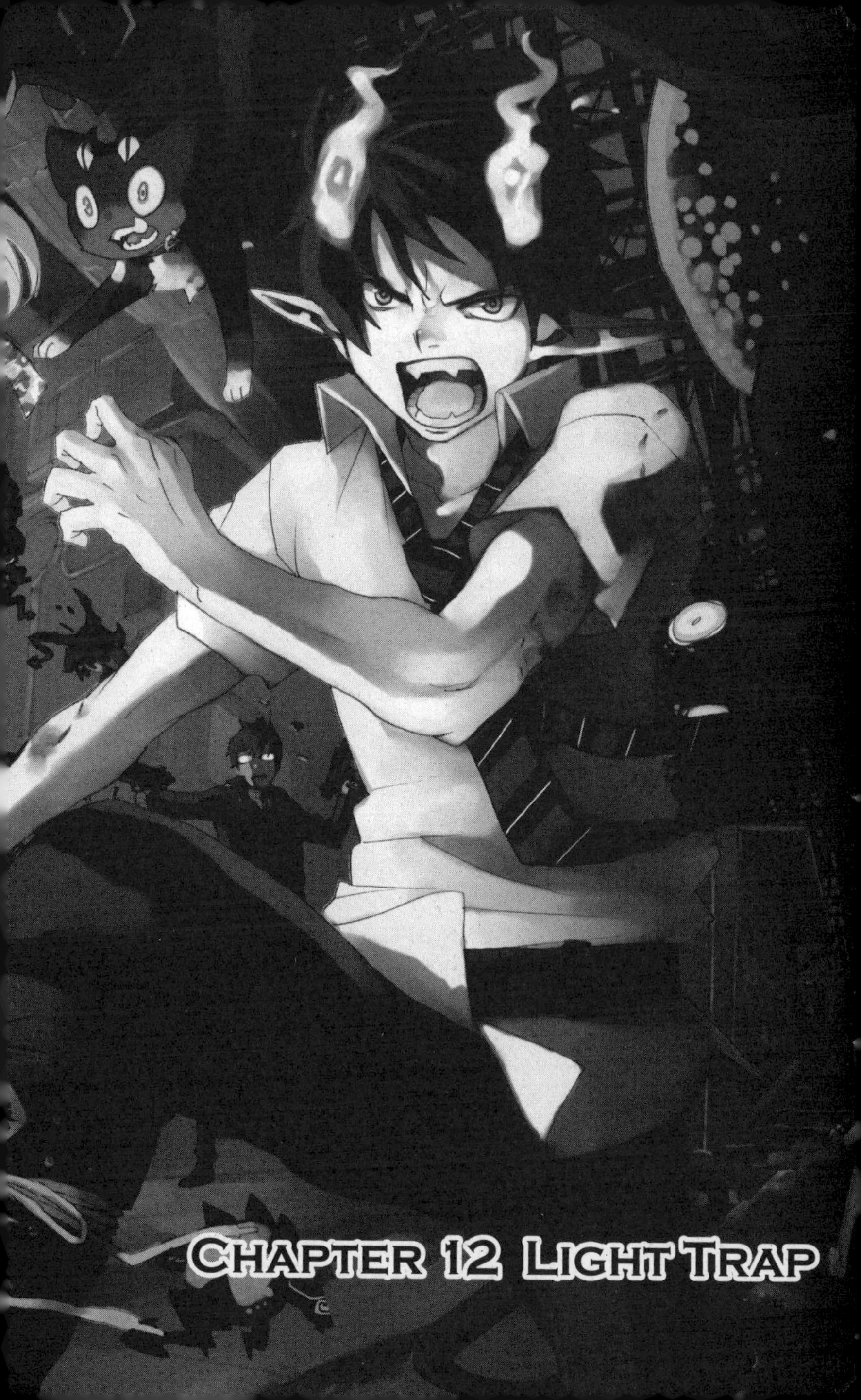
Chapter 12 Light Trap

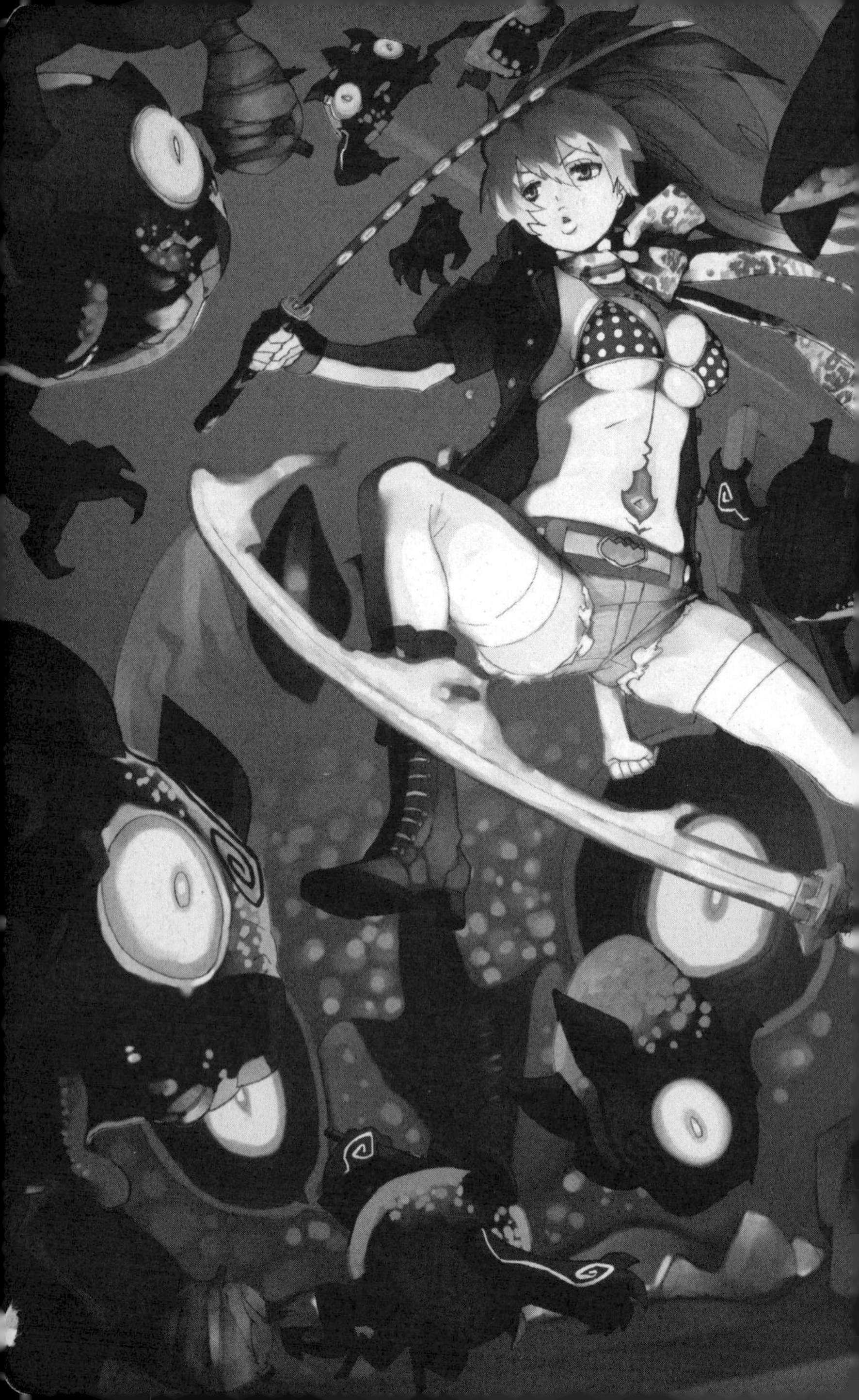

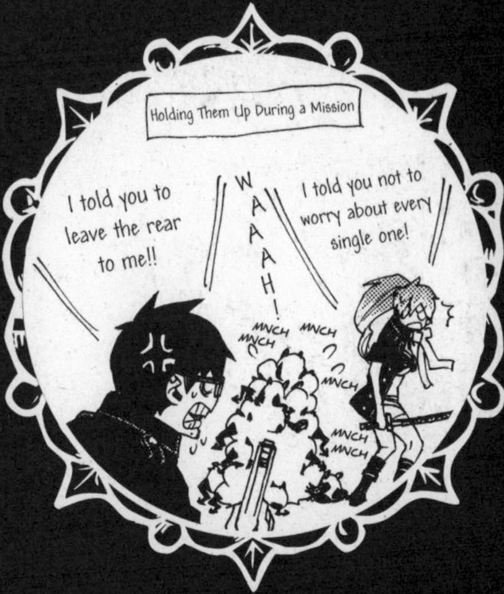
Holding Them Up During a Mission
I told you not to worry about every single one!
WAAAH!
I told you to leave the rear to me!!
MNCH MNCH
MNCH
MNCH
MNCH MNCH

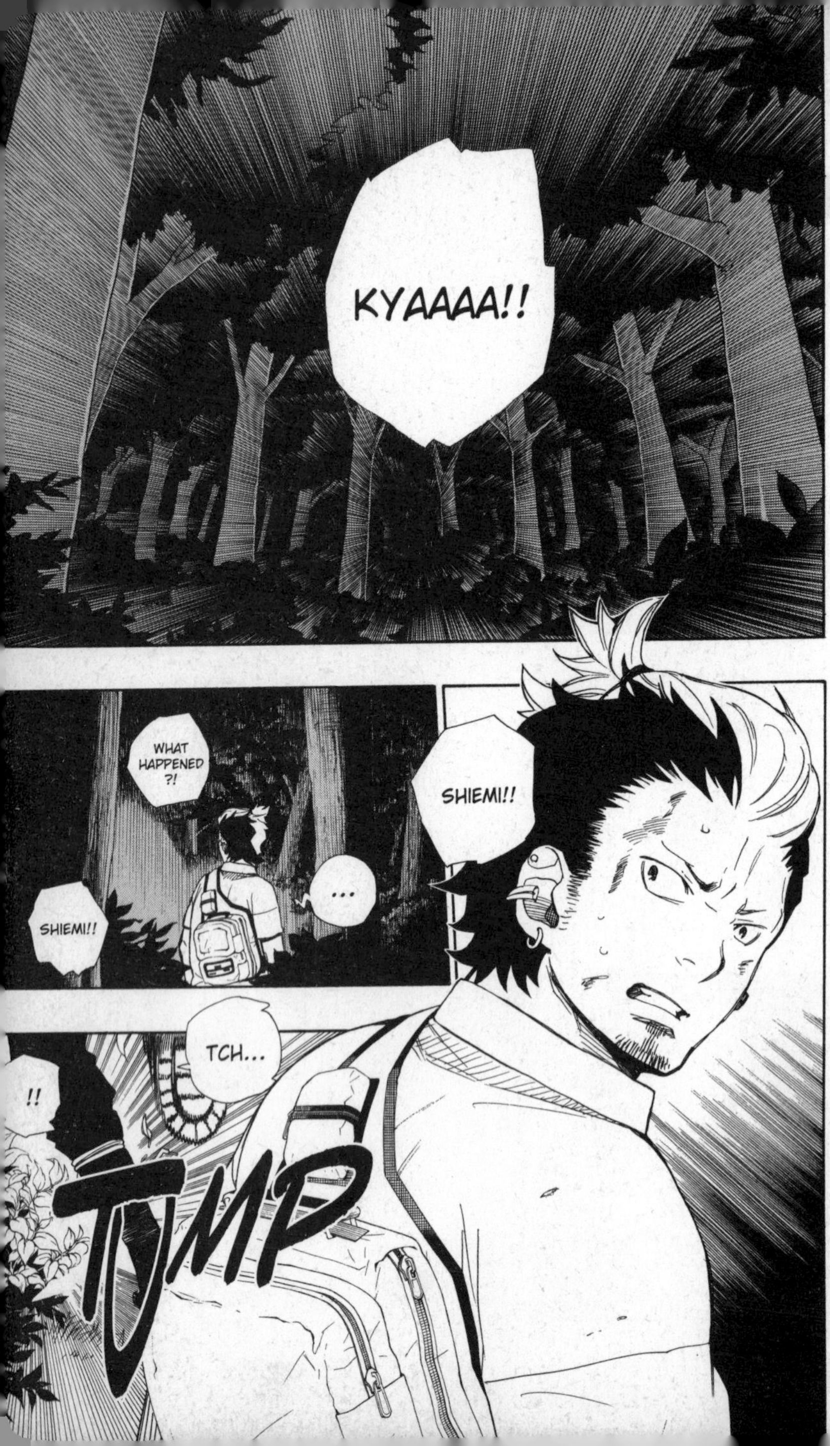
KYAAAA!!
SHIEMI!!
WHAT HAPPENED?!
...
SHIEMI!!
TCH...
!!
TUMP

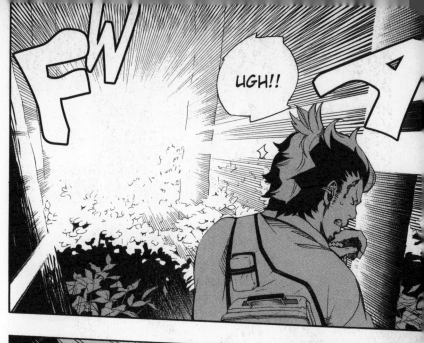

UGH!!

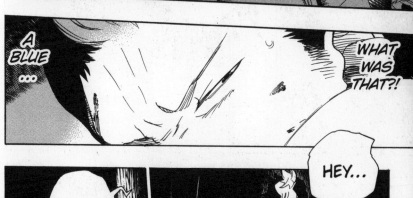

A BLUE...

WHAT WAS THAT?!

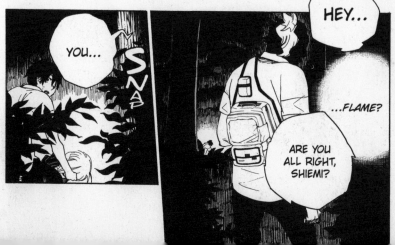

YOU...

SNAP

HEY...

...FLAME?

ARE YOU ALL RIGHT, SHIEMI?

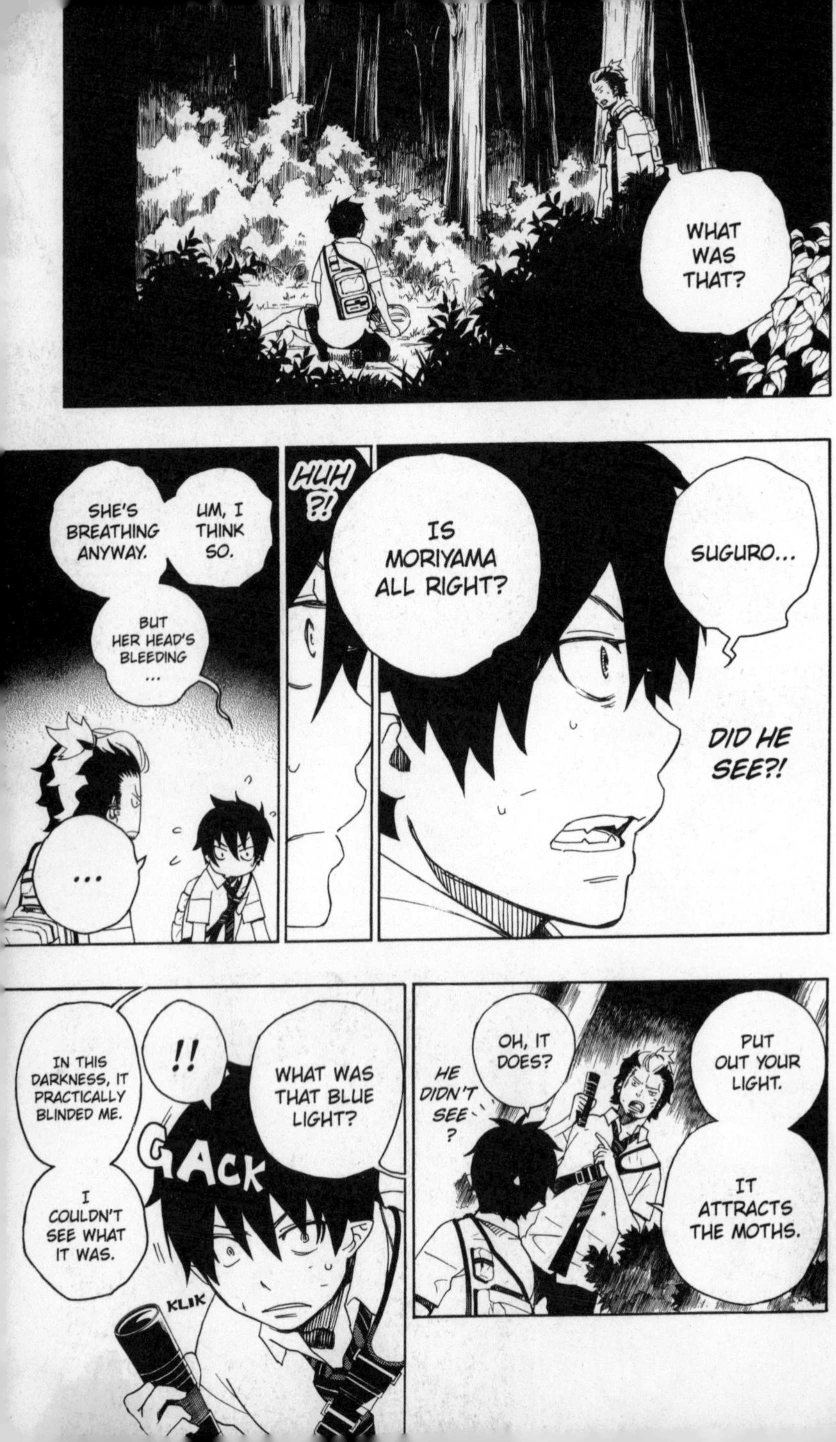
WHAT WAS THAT?
SUGURO...
IS MORIYAMA ALL RIGHT?
HUH ?!
DID HE SEE?!
UM, I THINK SO.
SHE'S BREATHING ANYWAY.
BUT HER HEAD'S BLEEDING ...
...
PUT OUT YOUR LIGHT.
IT ATTRACTS THE MOTHS.
OH, IT DOES?
HE DIDN'T SEE ?
WHAT WAS THAT BLUE LIGHT?
!!
IN THIS DARKNESS, IT PRACTICALLY BLINDED ME.
I COULDN'T SEE WHAT IT WAS.
GACK
KLIK

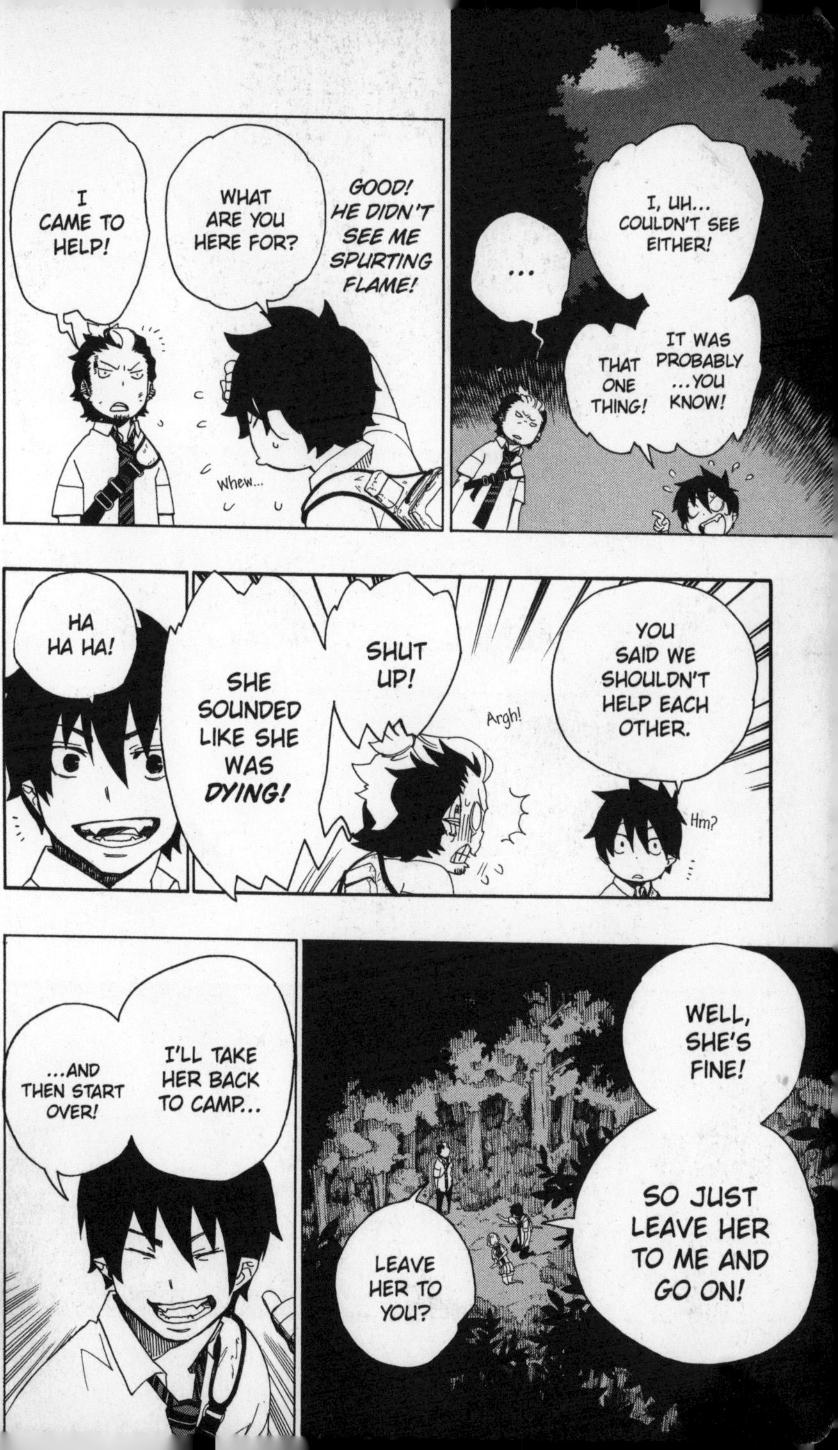
I, UH... COULDN'T SEE EITHER!
IT WAS PROBABLY ...YOU KNOW!
THAT ONE THING!
...
GOOD! HE DIDN'T SEE ME SPURTING FLAME!
WHAT ARE YOU HERE FOR?
I CAME TO HELP!
Whew...
YOU SAID WE SHOULDN'T HELP EACH OTHER.
Hm?
SHUT UP!
Argh!
SHE SOUNDED LIKE SHE WAS DYING!
HA HA HA!
WELL, SHE'S FINE!
SO JUST LEAVE HER TO ME AND GO ON!
LEAVE HER TO YOU?
I'LL TAKE HER BACK TO CAMP...
...AND THEN START OVER!

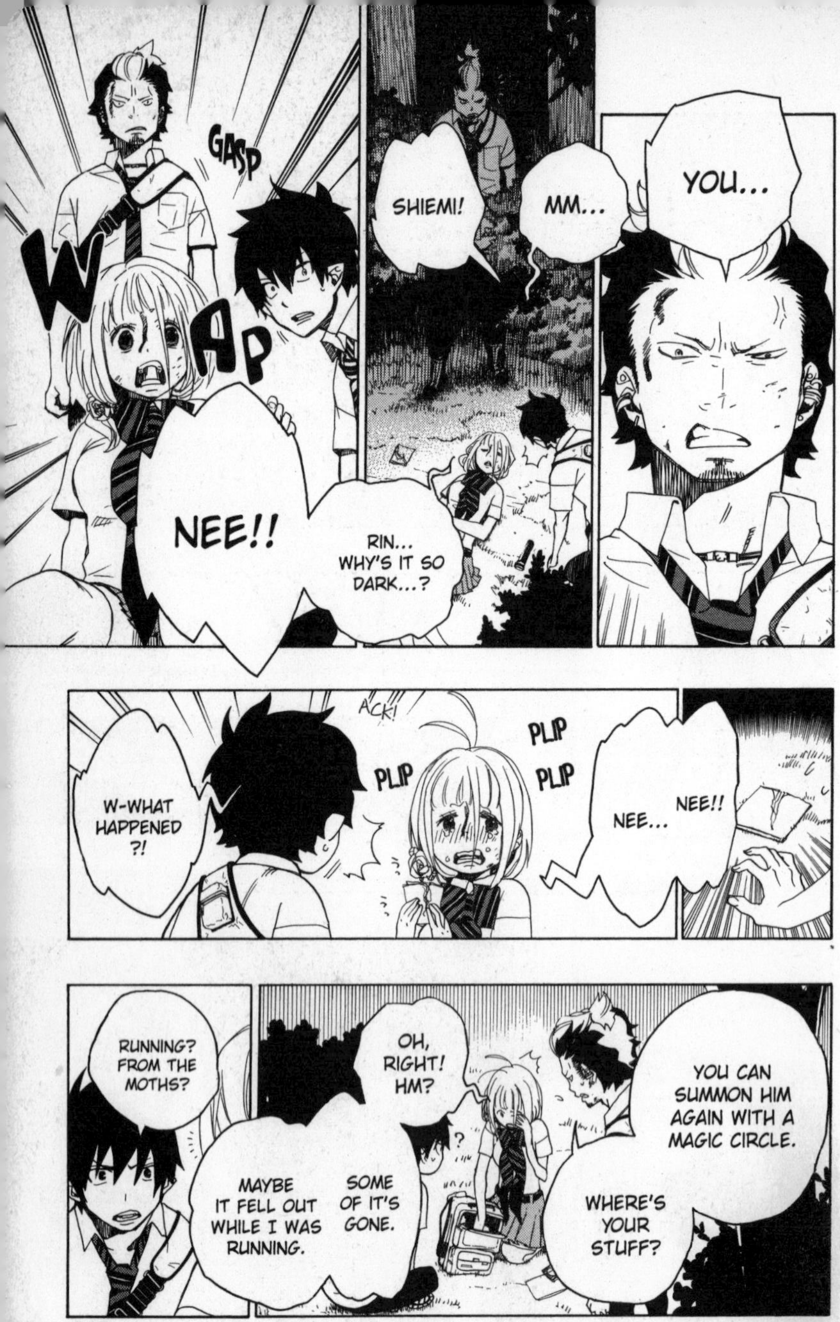
YOU...
MM...
SHIEMI!
RIN... WHY'S IT SO DARK...?
GASP
WAP
NEE!!
NEE... NEE!!
PLIP
PLIP
PLIP
ACK!
W-WHAT HAPPENED?!
YOU CAN SUMMON HIM AGAIN WITH A MAGIC CIRCLE.
WHERE'S YOUR STUFF?
OH, RIGHT! HM?
SOME OF IT'S GONE.
MAYBE IT FELL OUT WHILE I WAS RUNNING.
RUNNING? FROM THE MOTHS?

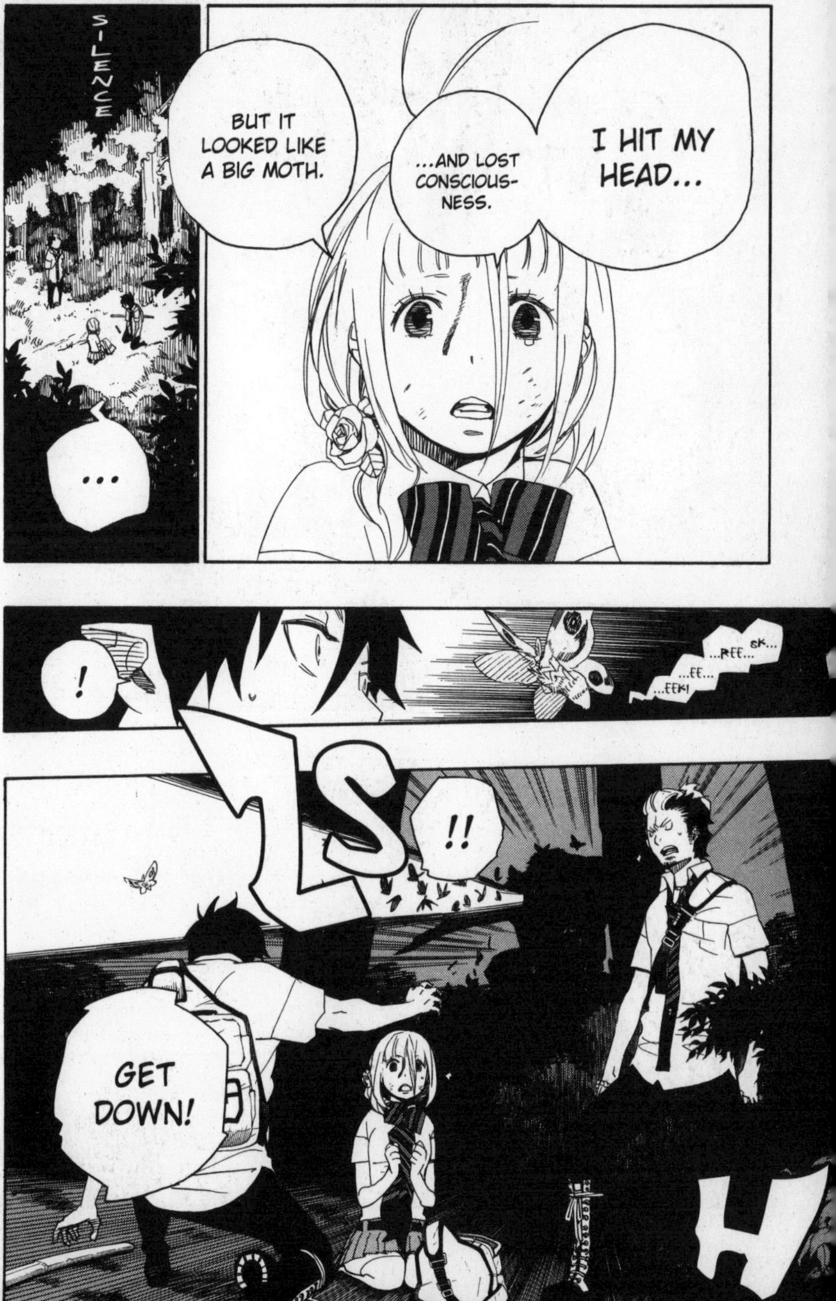
I HIT MY HEAD...
...AND LOST CONSCIOUS-NESS.
BUT IT LOOKED LIKE A BIG MOTH.
SILENCE
...
SK... ...REE... ...EE... ...EEK!
!
!!
GET DOWN!

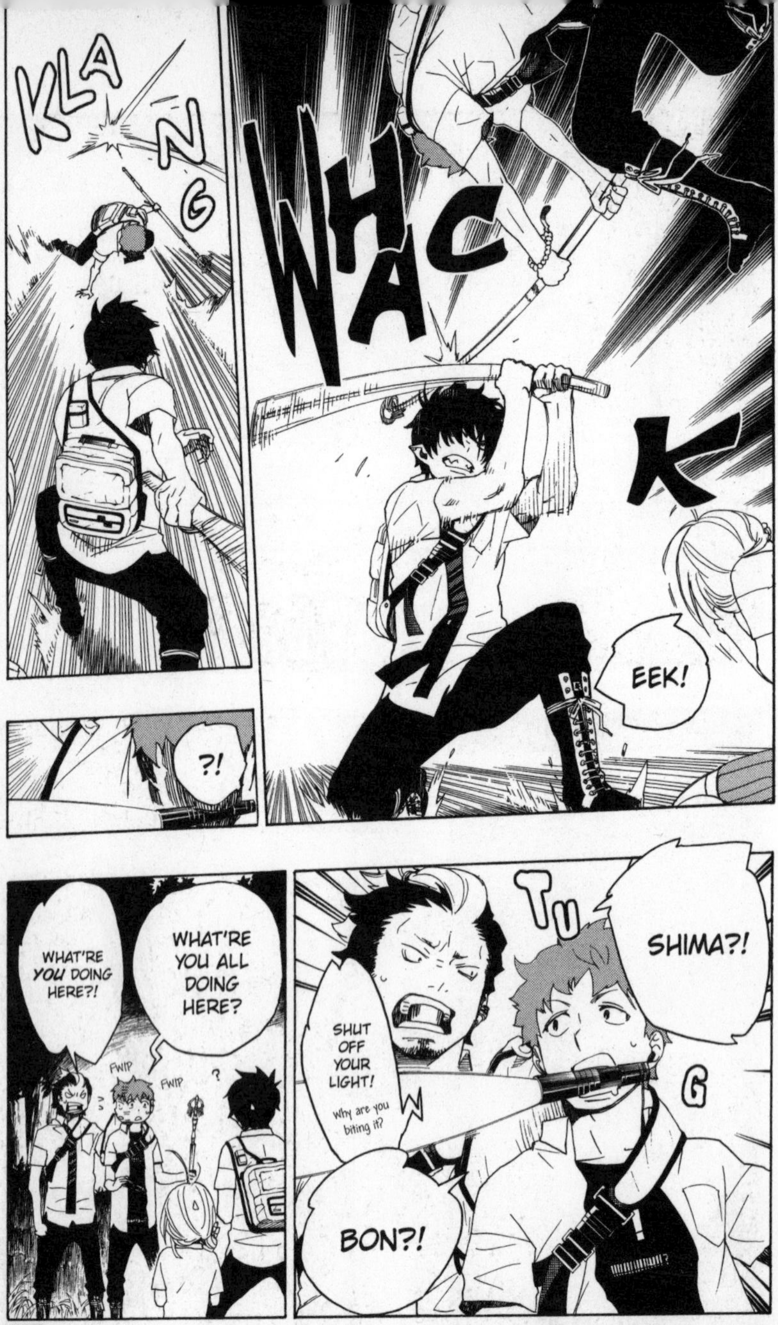
WHACK
K
EEK!
KLANG
?!
SHIMA?!
TUG
SHUT OFF YOUR LIGHT!
Why are you biting it?
BON?!
WHAT'RE YOU ALL DOING HERE?
WHAT'RE YOU DOING HERE?!
FWIP
FWIP
?

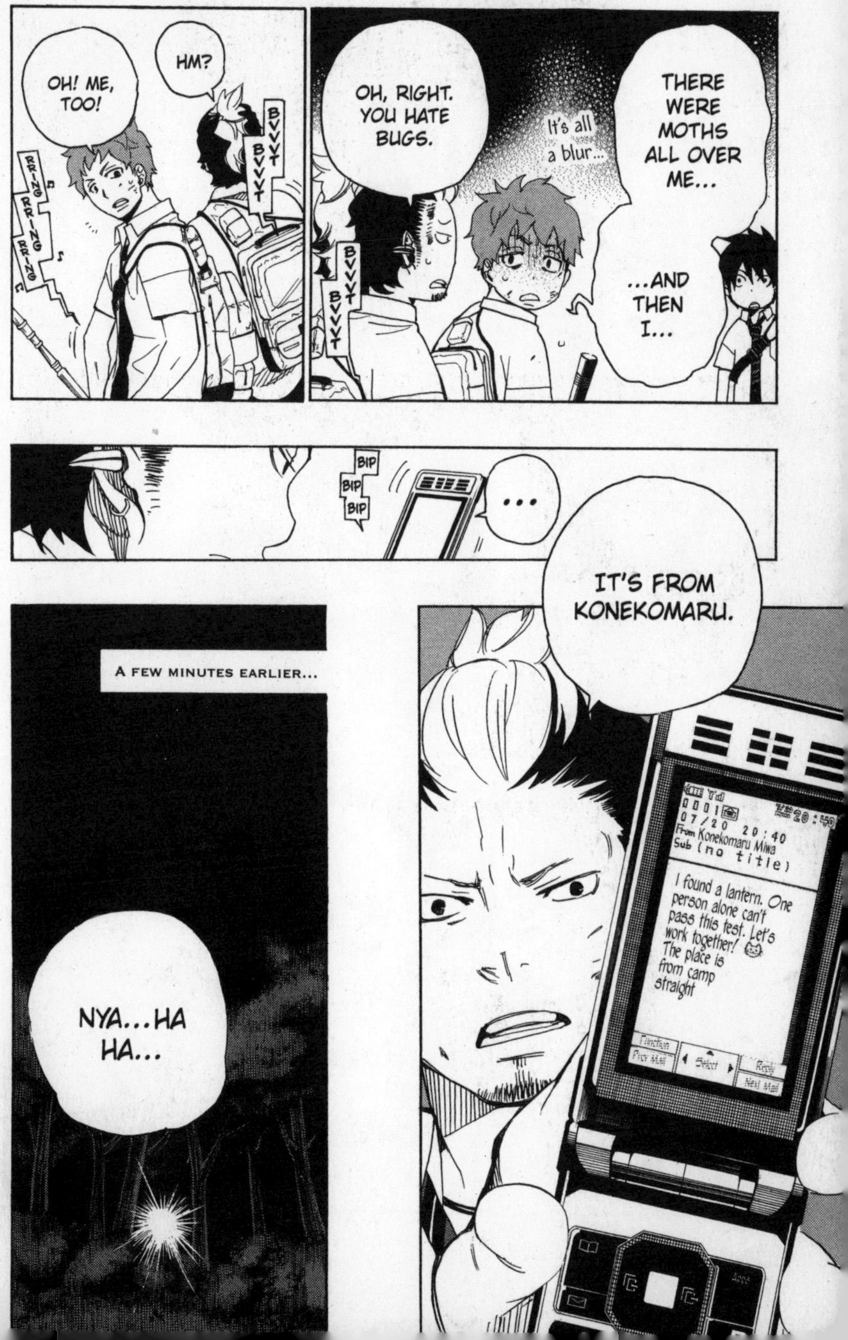
THERE WERE MOTHS ALL OVER ME...
It's all a blur...
...AND THEN I...
OH, RIGHT. YOU HATE BUGS.
BVVVT BVVVT
HM?
BVVVT BVVVT
OH! ME, TOO!
RRING RRING RRING
BIP BIP BIP
...
IT'S FROM KONEKOMARU.
07/20 20:40
From Konekomaru Miwa
Sub (no title)
I found a lantern. One person alone can't pass this test. Let's work together! The place is from camp straight
Select
Reply
Next Mail
Prev Mail
A FEW MINUTES EARLIER...
NYA...HA HA...

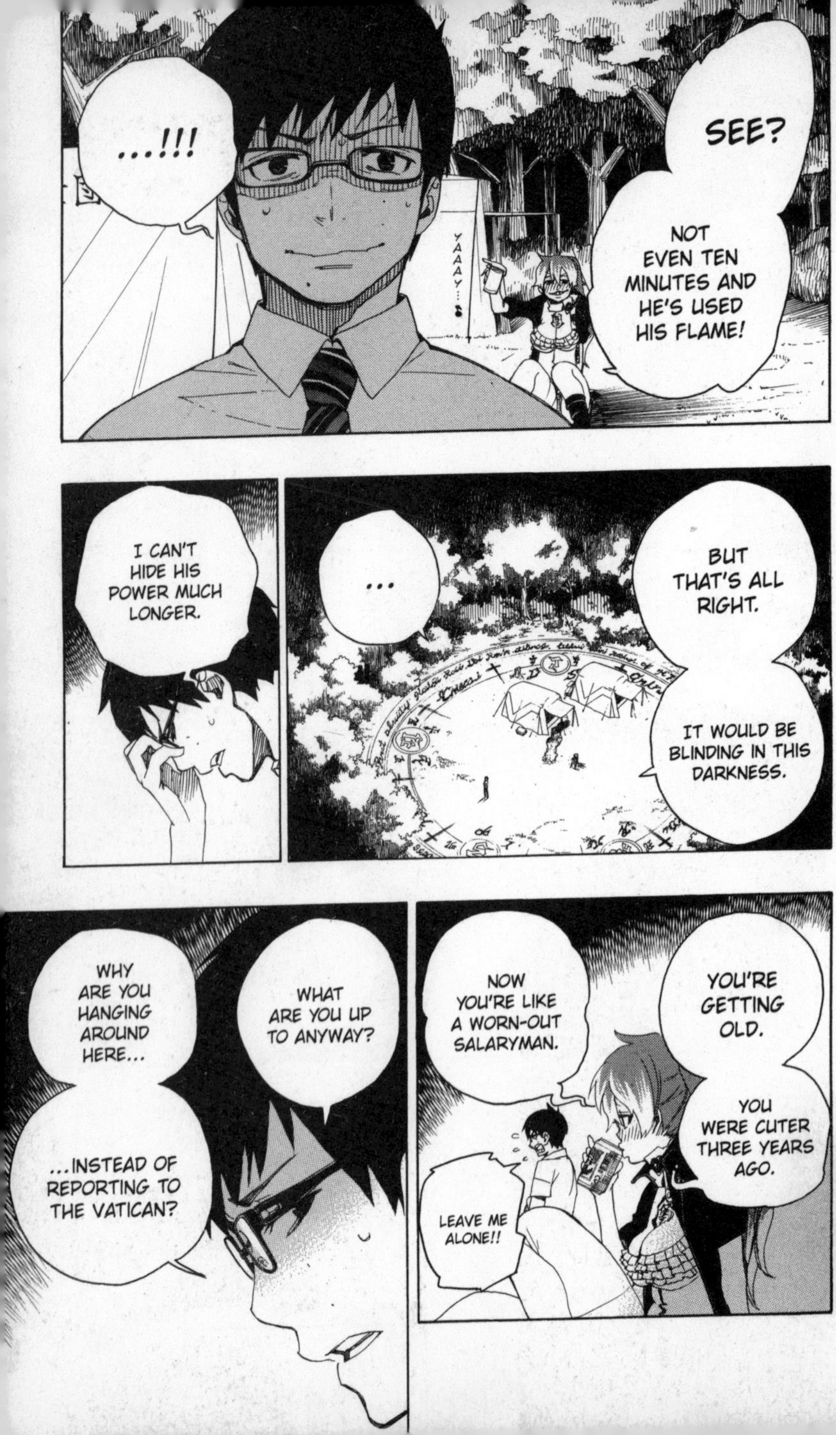
SEE?
NOT EVEN TEN MINUTES AND HE'S USED HIS FLAME!
YAAAY...
...!!!
BUT THAT'S ALL RIGHT.
IT WOULD BE BLINDING IN THIS DARKNESS.
...
I CAN'T HIDE HIS POWER MUCH LONGER.
YOU'RE GETTING OLD.
NOW YOU'RE LIKE A WORN-OUT SALARYMAN.
YOU WERE CUTER THREE YEARS AGO.
LEAVE ME ALONE!!
WHAT ARE YOU UP TO ANYWAY?
WHY ARE YOU HANGING AROUND HERE...
...INSTEAD OF REPORTING TO THE VATICAN?

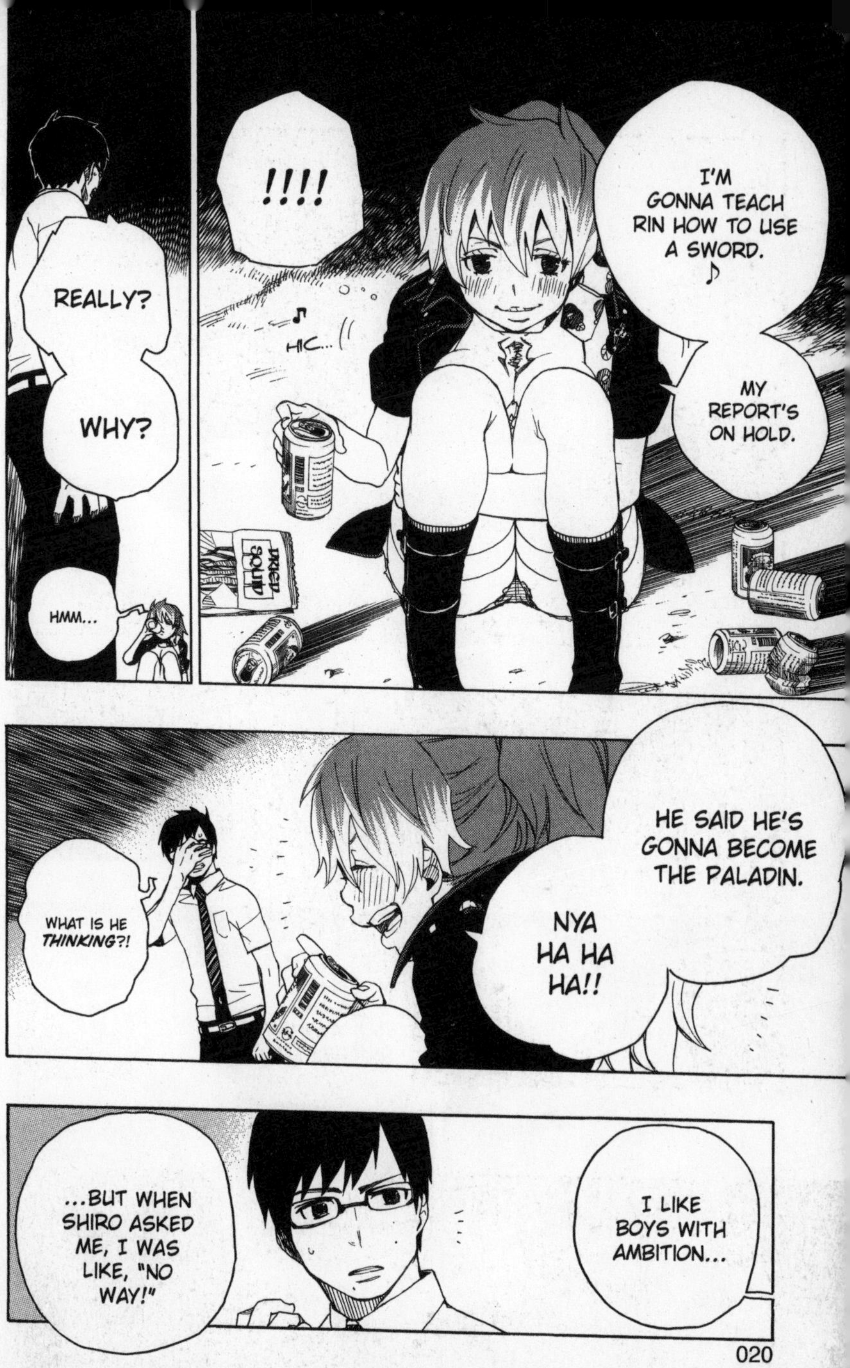
I'M GONNA TEACH RIN HOW TO USE A SWORD. ♪
!!!!
♪ HIC...
MY REPORT'S ON HOLD.
REALLY?
WHY?
HMM...
DRIED SQUID
HE SAID HE'S GONNA BECOME THE PALADIN.
NYA HA HA HA!!
WHAT IS HE *THINKING*?!
I LIKE BOYS WITH AMBITION...
...BUT WHEN SHIRO ASKED ME, I WAS LIKE, "NO WAY!"

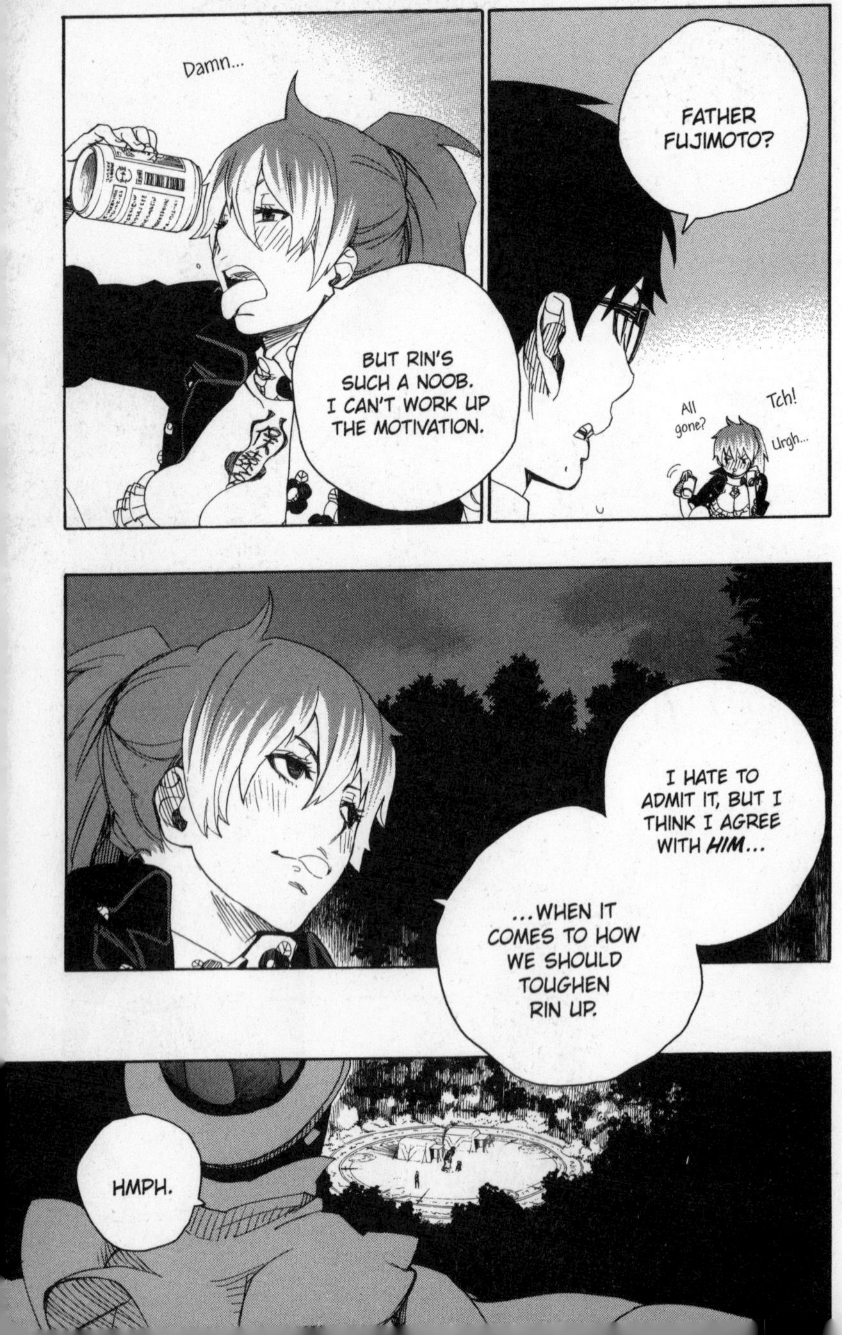
FATHER FUJIMOTO?
Tch!
Urgh...
All gone?
Damn...
BUT RIN'S SUCH A NOOB. I CAN'T WORK UP THE MOTIVATION.
I HATE TO ADMIT IT, BUT I THINK I AGREE WITH ***HIM***...
...WHEN IT COMES TO HOW WE SHOULD TOUGHEN RIN UP.
HMPH.

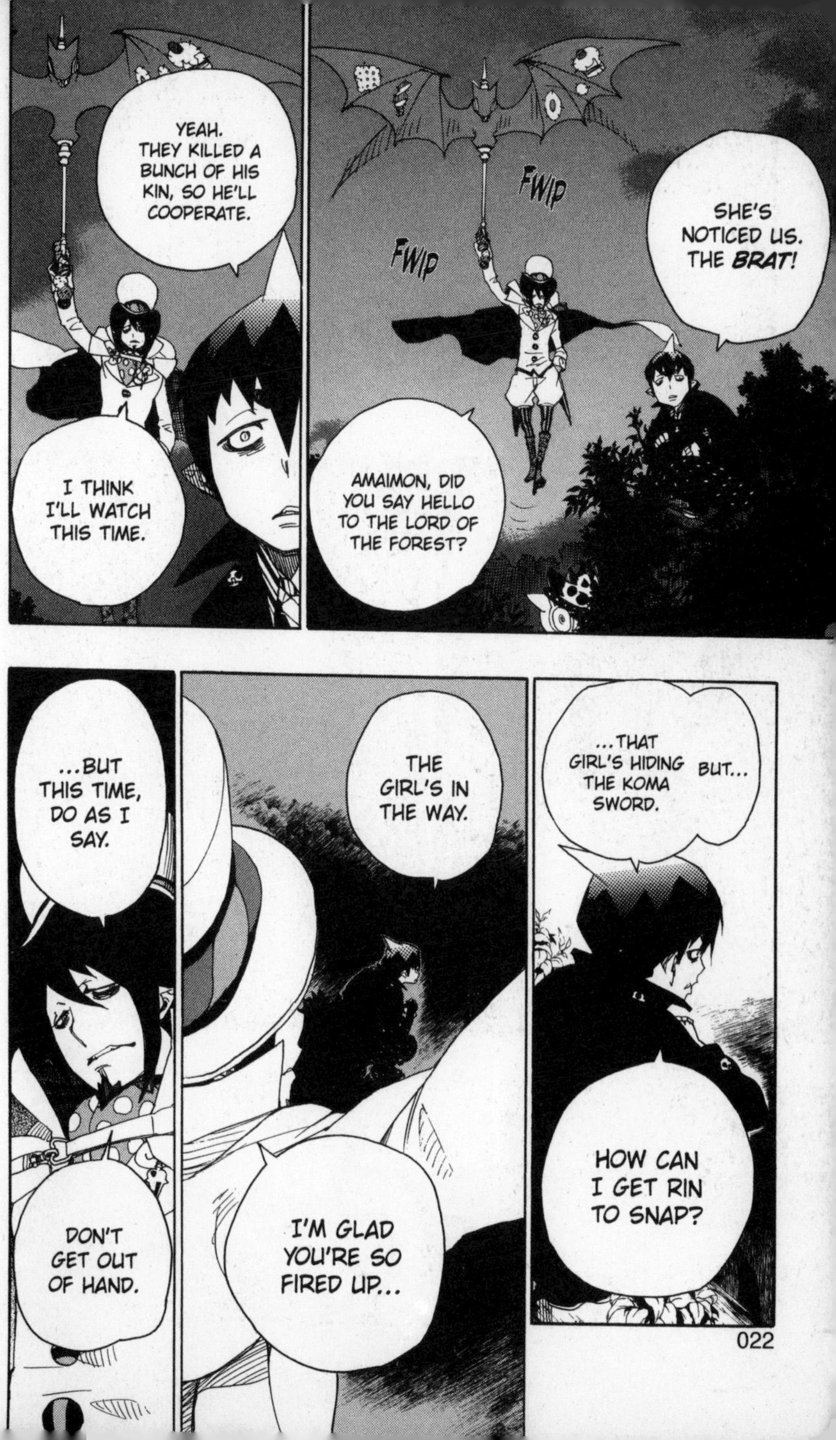
SHE'S NOTICED US. THE BRAT!
FWIP
FWIP
AMAIMON, DID YOU SAY HELLO TO THE LORD OF THE FOREST?
YEAH. THEY KILLED A BUNCH OF HIS KIN, SO HE'LL COOPERATE.
I THINK I'LL WATCH THIS TIME.
BUT...
...THAT GIRL'S HIDING THE KOMA SWORD.
HOW CAN I GET RIN TO SNAP?
THE GIRL'S IN THE WAY.
I'M GLAD YOU'RE SO FIRED UP...
...BUT THIS TIME, DO AS I SAY.
DON'T GET OUT OF HAND.

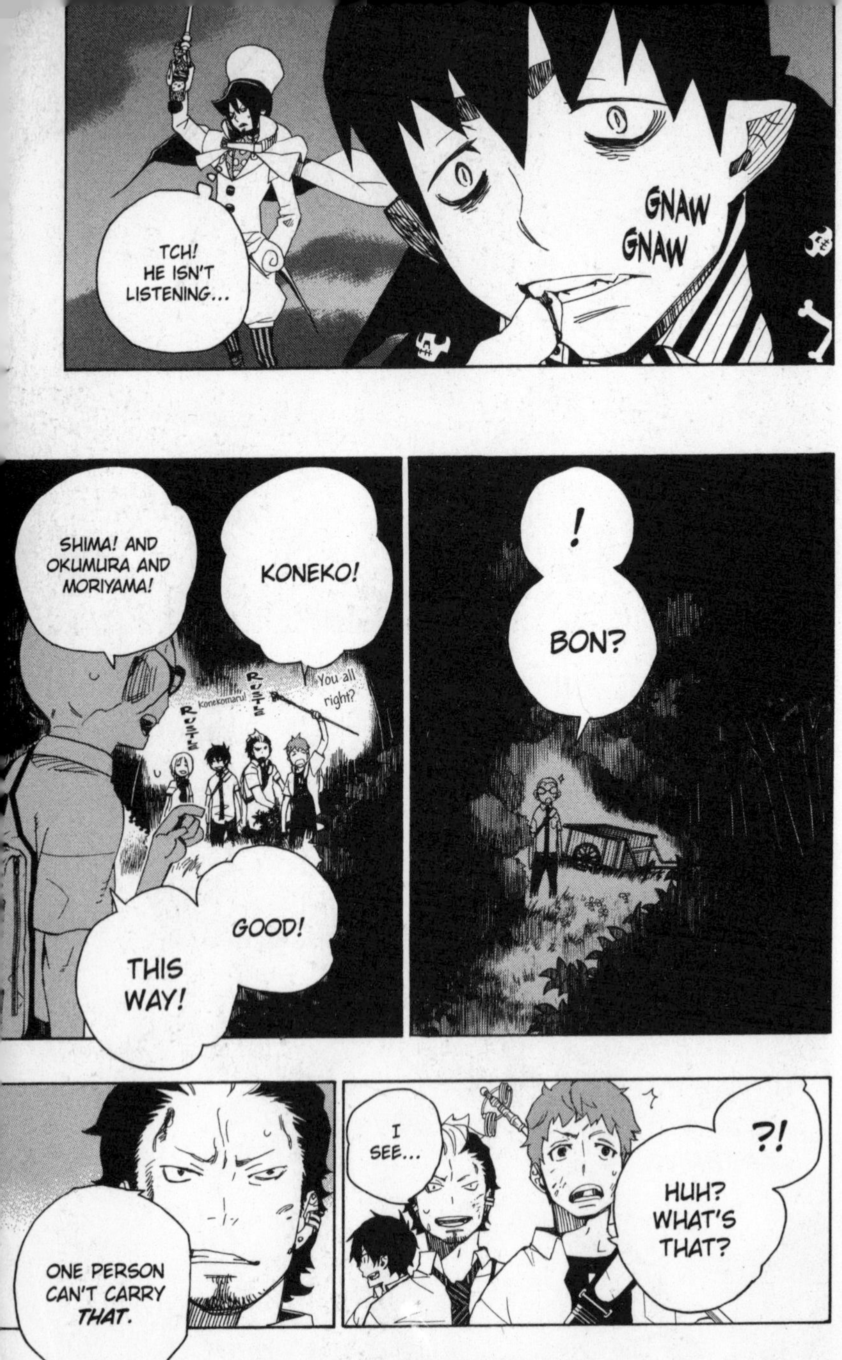
GNAW GNAW
TCH! HE ISN'T LISTENING...
!
BON?
KONEKO!
SHIMA! AND OKUMURA AND MORIYAMA!
You all right?
RUSTLE
Konekomaru!
RUSTLE
GOOD!
THIS WAY!
?!
HUH? WHAT'S THAT?
I SEE...
ONE PERSON CAN'T CARRY THAT.

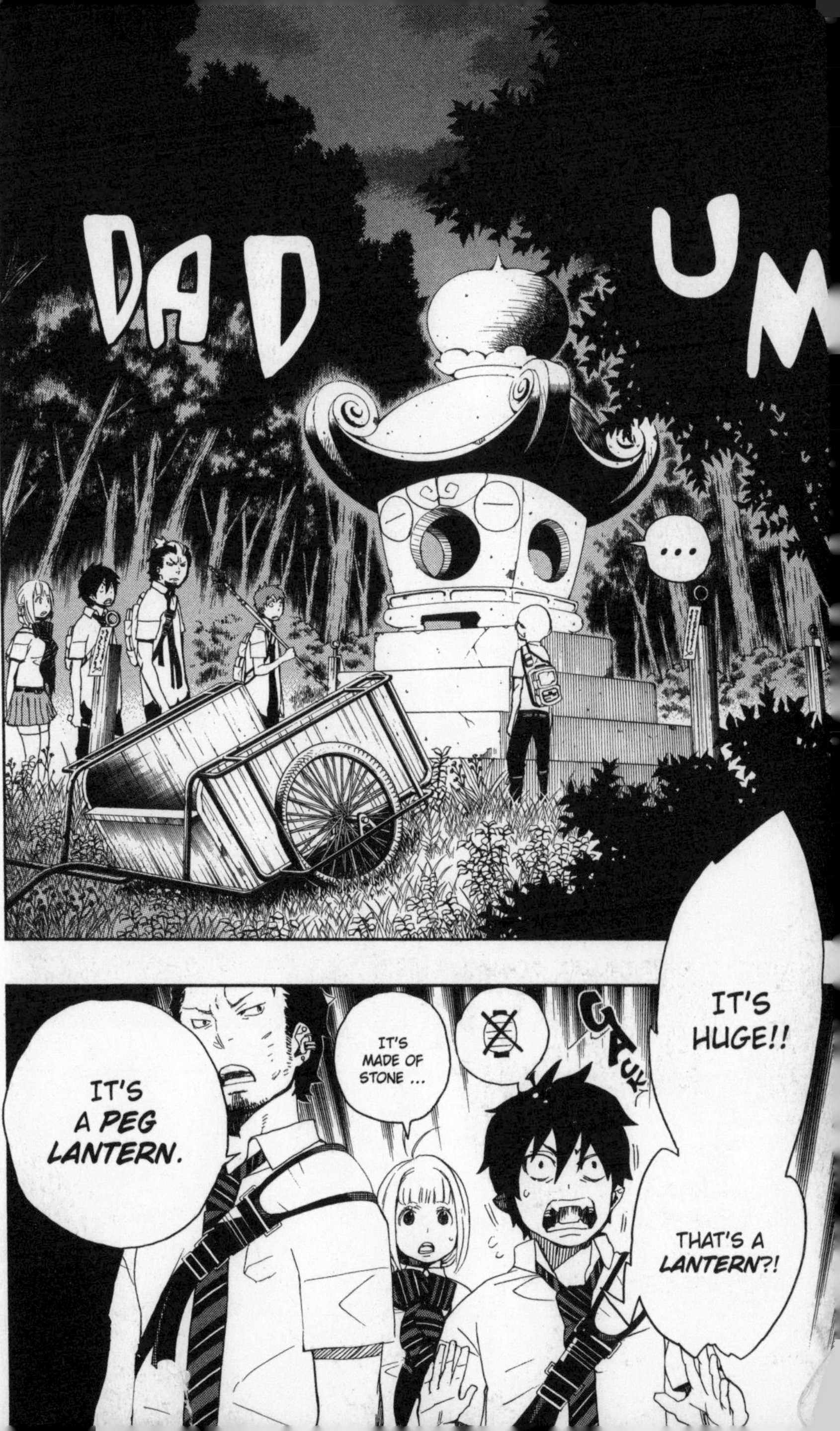
DADUM
...
IT'S HUGE!!
GACK
THAT'S A LANTERN?!
IT'S MADE OF STONE ...
IT'S A PEG LANTERN.

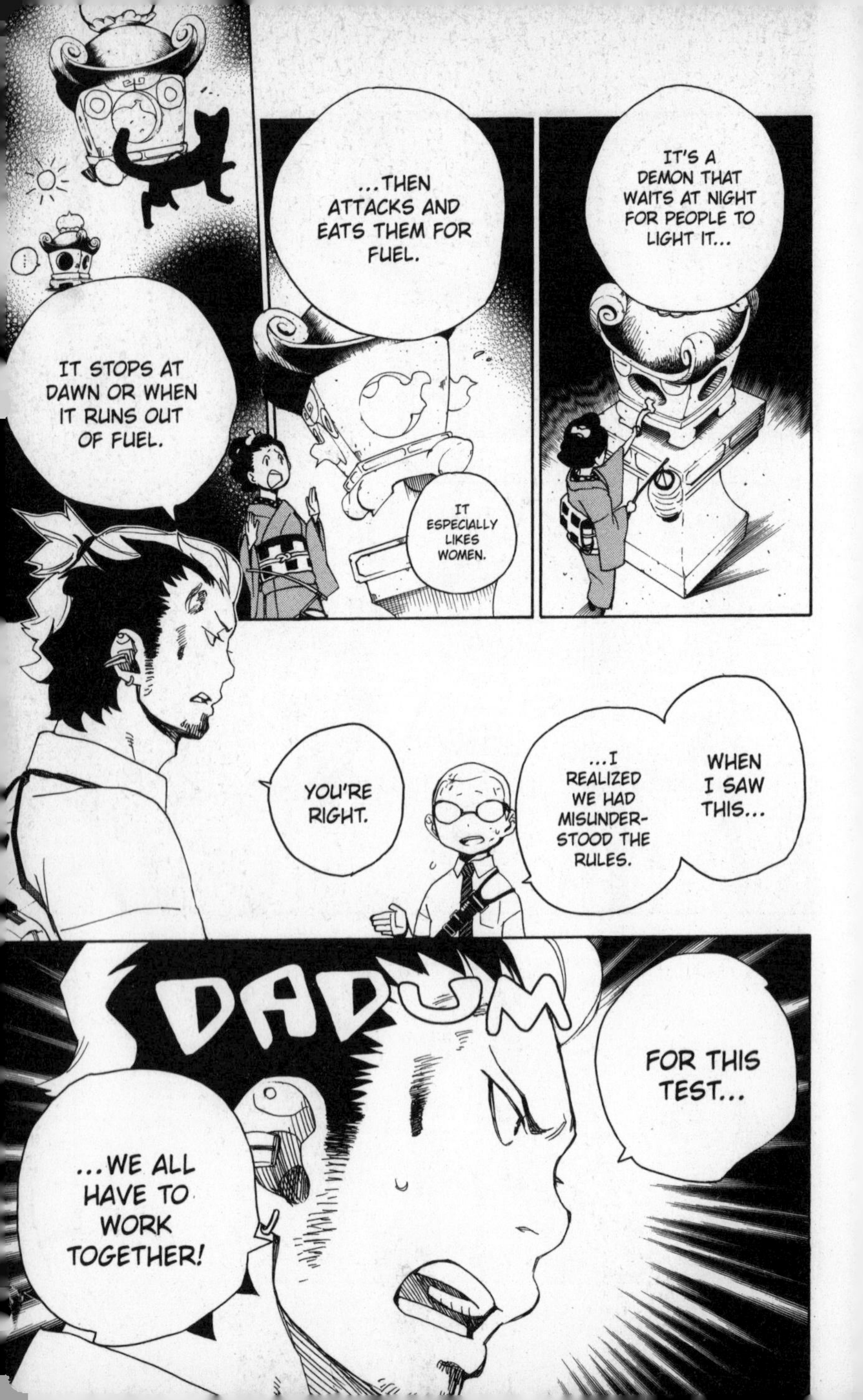
IT'S A DEMON THAT WAITS AT NIGHT FOR PEOPLE TO LIGHT IT...
...THEN ATTACKS AND EATS THEM FOR FUEL.
IT ESPECIALLY LIKES WOMEN.
IT STOPS AT DAWN OR WHEN IT RUNS OUT OF FUEL.
WHEN I SAW THIS...
...I REALIZED WE HAD MISUNDERSTOOD THE RULES.
YOU'RE RIGHT.
DADUM
FOR THIS TEST...
...WE ALL HAVE TO WORK TOGETHER!

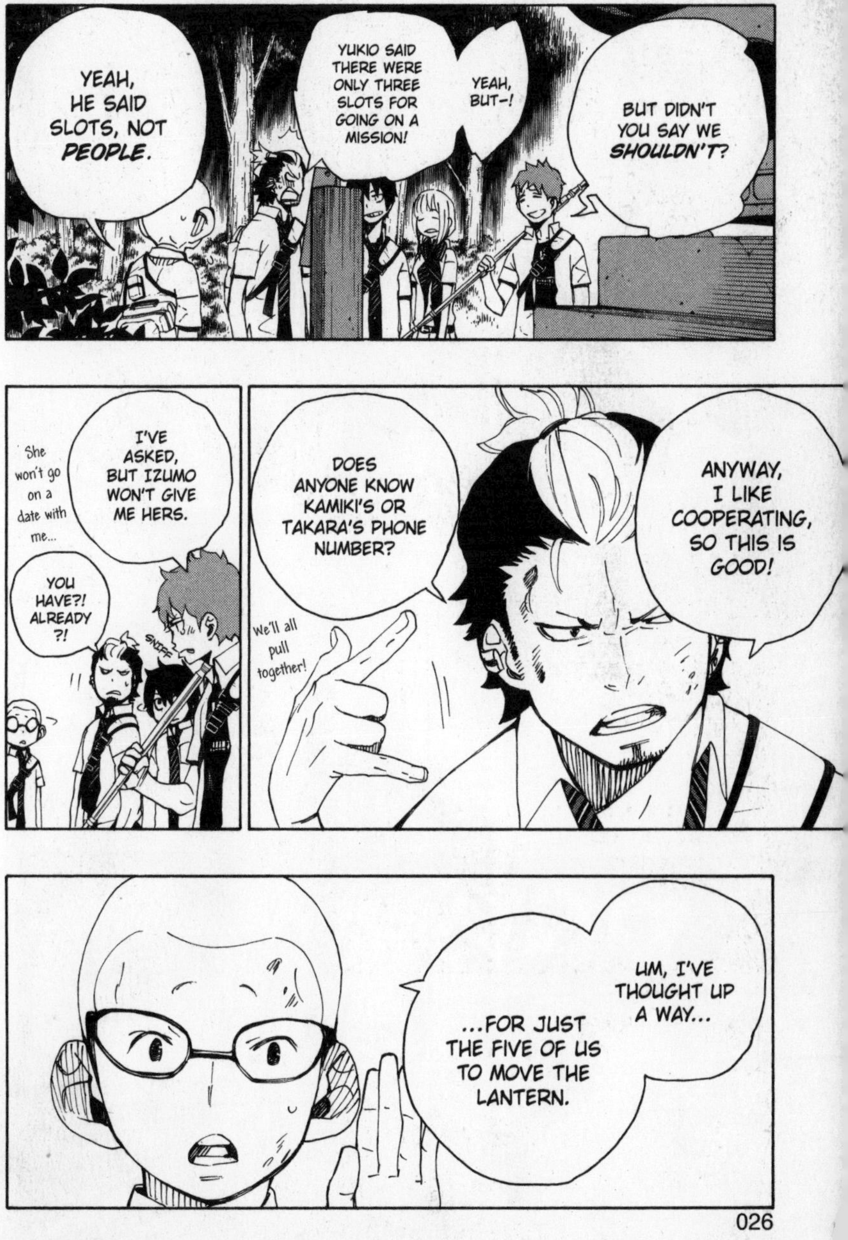
BUT DIDN'T YOU SAY WE *SHOULDN'T*?
YEAH, BUT–!
YUKIO SAID THERE WERE ONLY THREE SLOTS FOR GOING ON A MISSION!
YEAH, HE SAID SLOTS, NOT *PEOPLE*.
ANYWAY, I LIKE COOPERATING, SO THIS IS GOOD!
DOES ANYONE KNOW KAMIKI'S OR TAKARA'S PHONE NUMBER?
We'll all pull together!
I'VE ASKED, BUT IZUMO WON'T GIVE ME HERS.
She won't go on a date with me...
YOU HAVE?! ALREADY?!
SNIFF
UM, I'VE THOUGHT UP A WAY...
...FOR JUST THE FIVE OF US TO MOVE THE LANTERN.

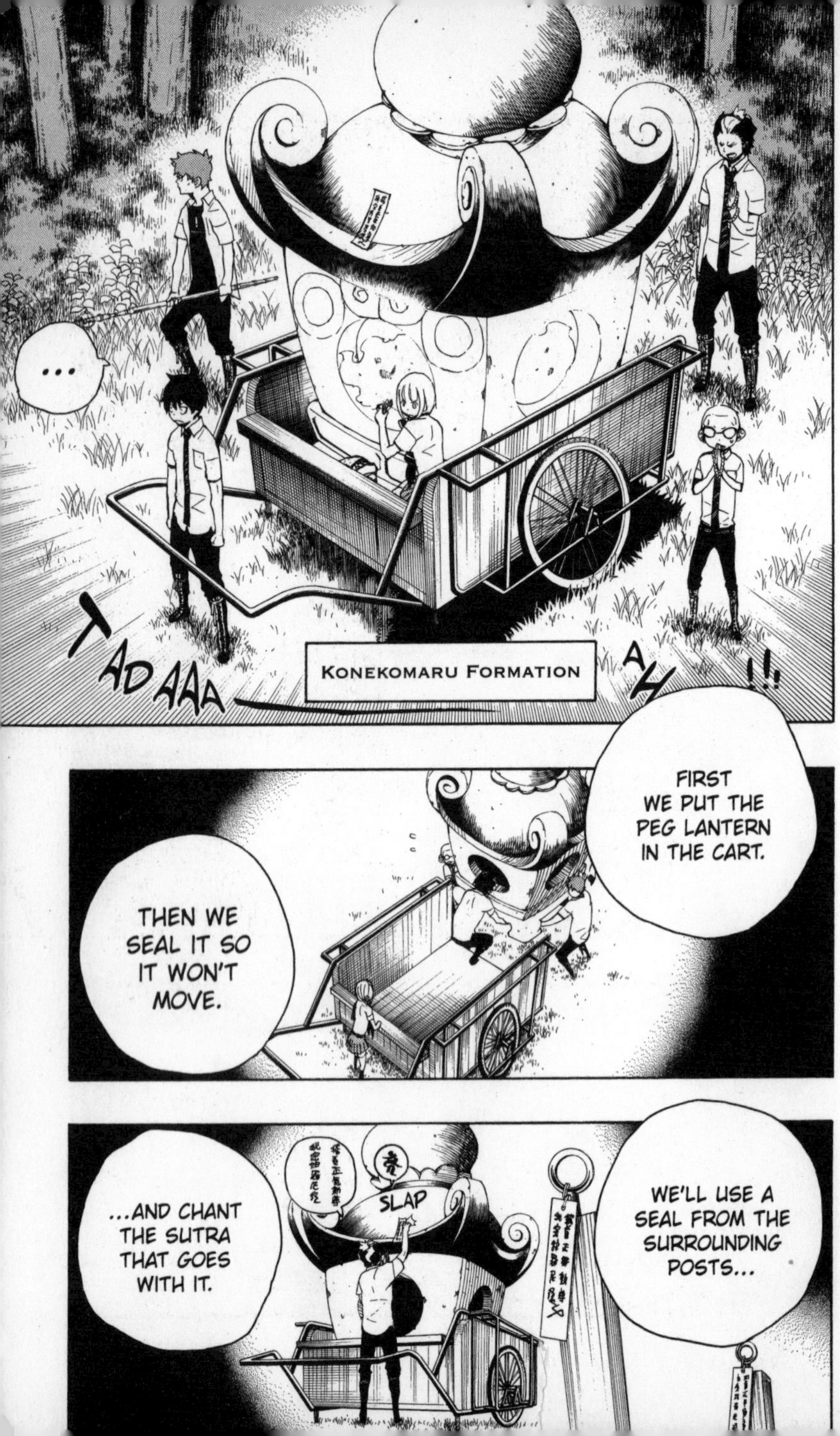
AH !!!
KONEKOMARU FORMATION
TADAAA
...
FIRST WE PUT THE PEG LANTERN IN THE CART.
THEN WE SEAL IT SO IT WON'T MOVE.
WE'LL USE A SEAL FROM THE SURROUNDING POSTS...
SLAP
...AND CHANT THE SUTRA THAT GOES WITH IT.

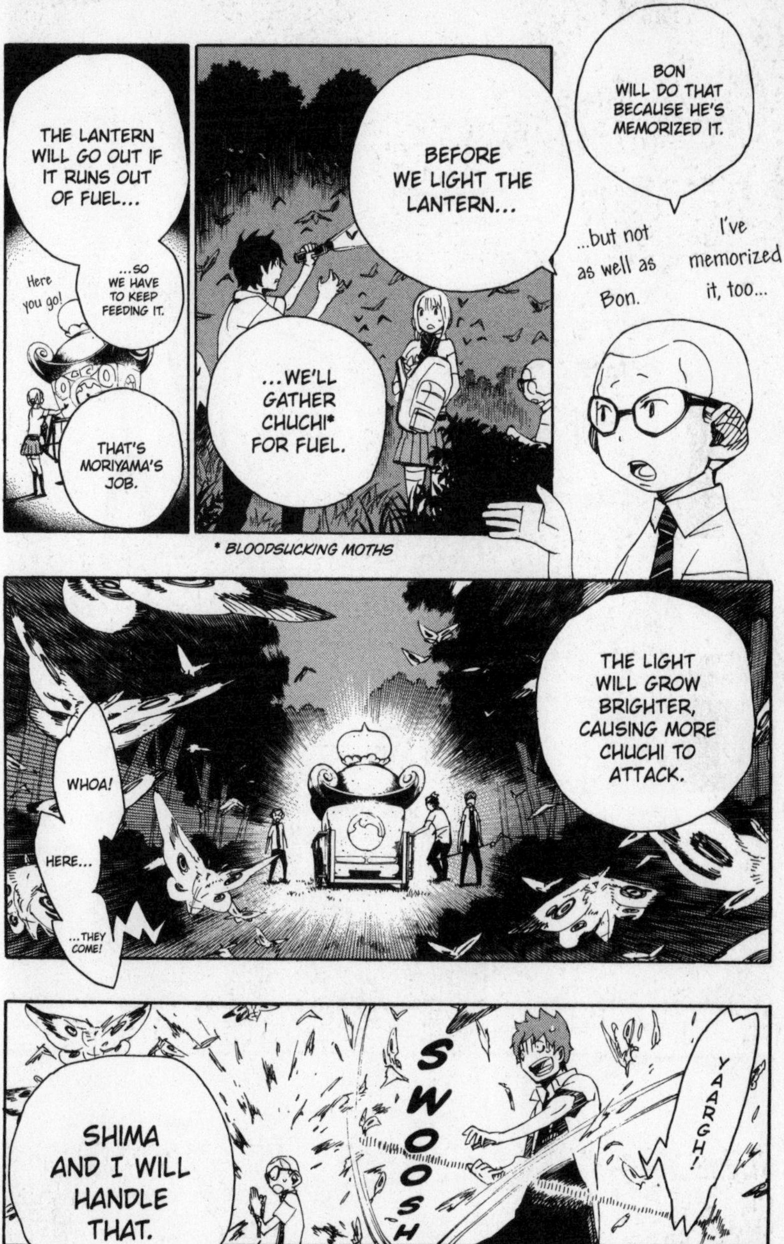
BON WILL DO THAT BECAUSE HE'S MEMORIZED IT.
I've memorized it, too...
...but not as well as Bon.
BEFORE WE LIGHT THE LANTERN...
...WE'LL GATHER CHUCHI* FOR FUEL.
THE LANTERN WILL GO OUT IF IT RUNS OUT OF FUEL...
...SO WE HAVE TO KEEP FEEDING IT.
Here you go!
THAT'S MORIYAMA'S JOB.
* BLOODSUCKING MOTHS
THE LIGHT WILL GROW BRIGHTER, CAUSING MORE CHUCHI TO ATTACK.
WHOA!
HERE...
...THEY COME!
YAARGH!
SWOOSH
SHIMA AND I WILL HANDLE THAT.

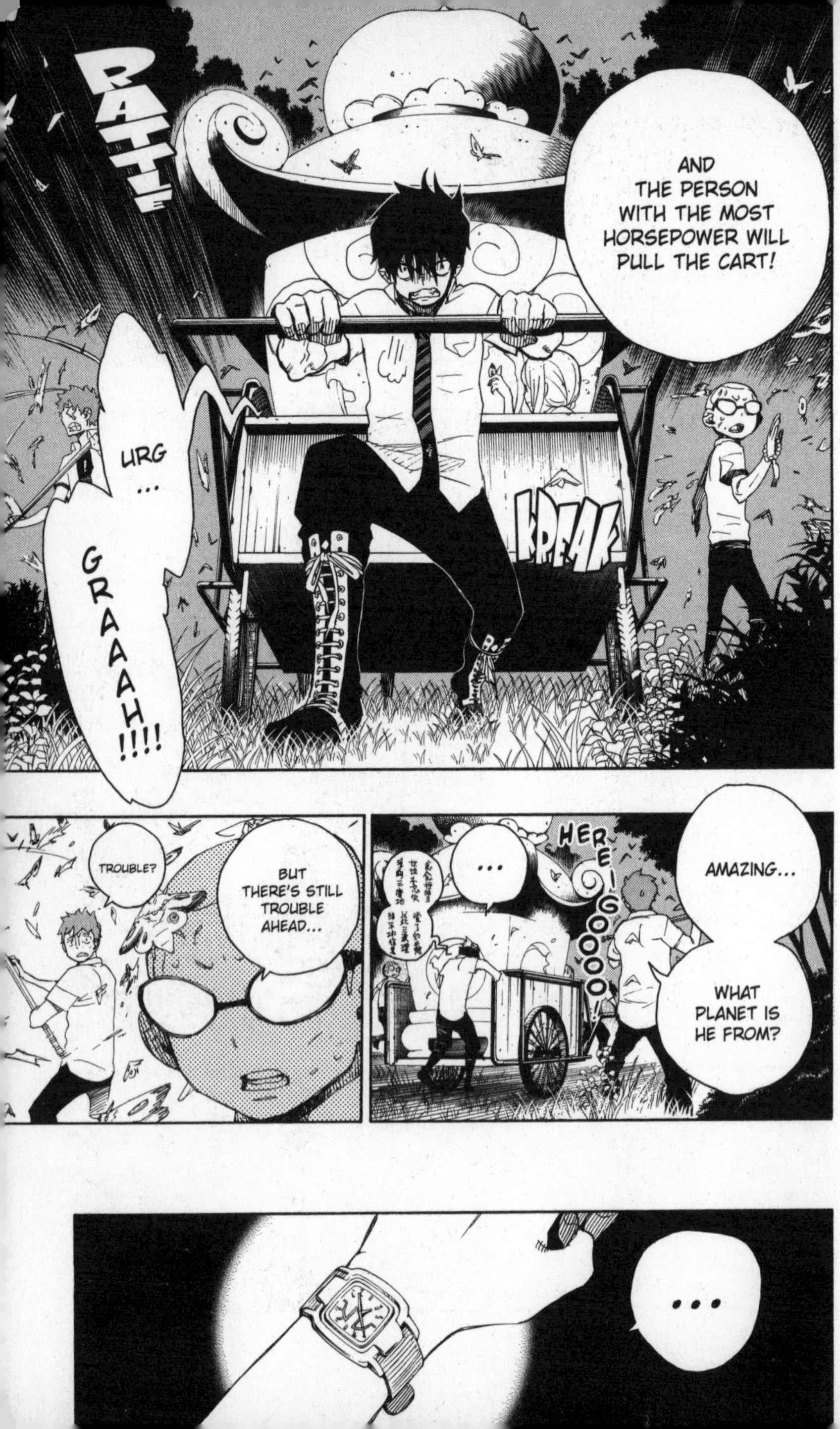
AND THE PERSON WITH THE MOST HORSEPOWER WILL PULL THE CART!
RATTLE
KREAK
URG... GRAAAAH!!!!
AMAZING...
WHAT PLANET IS HE FROM?
HERE I GOOOOO!
...
BUT THERE'S STILL TROUBLE AHEAD...
TROUBLE?
...

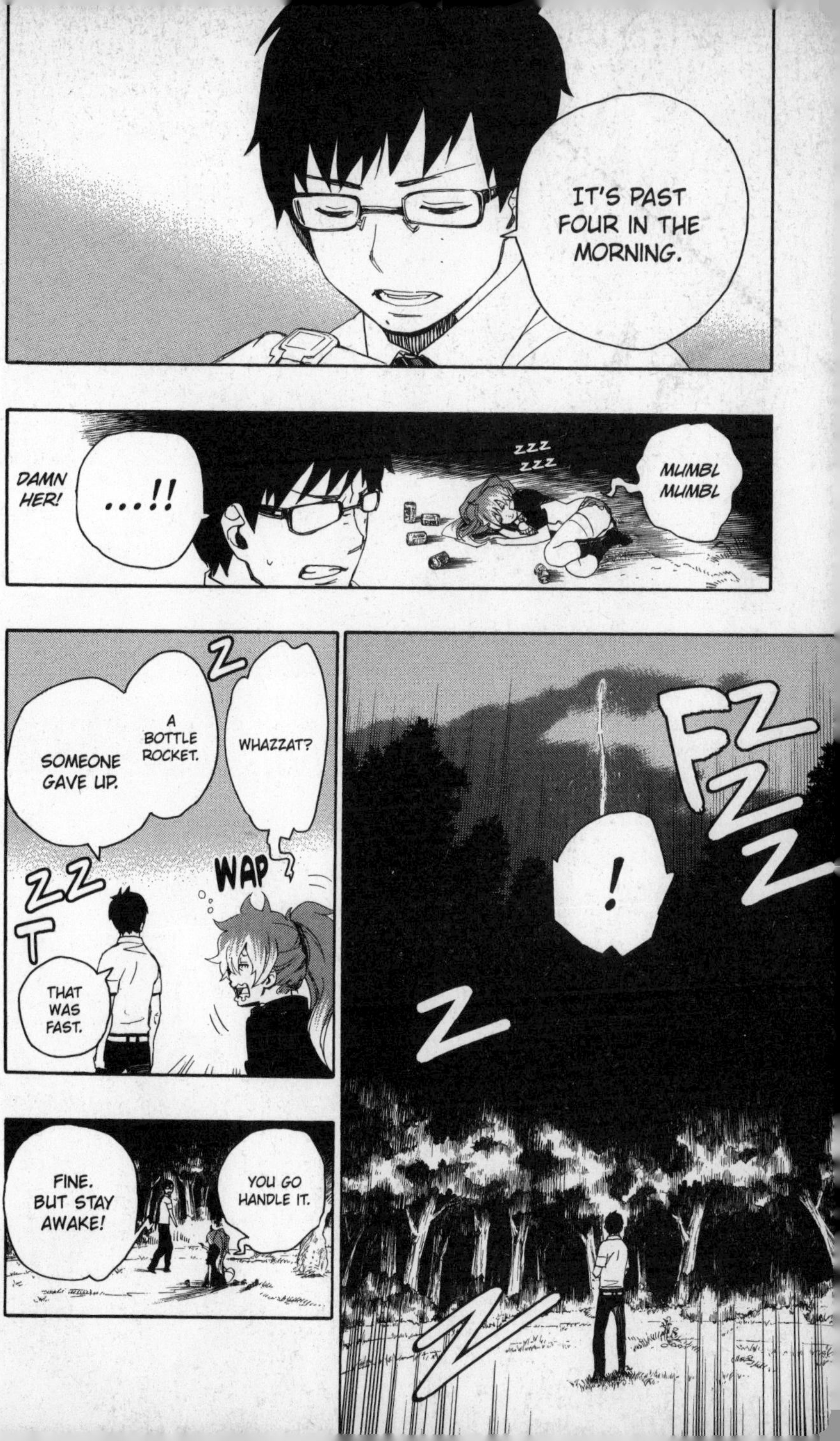
IT'S PAST FOUR IN THE MORNING.
ZZZ ZZZ
MUMBL MUMBL
...!!
DAMN HER!
FZZZZ
!
Z
Z
Z
WHAZZAT?
A BOTTLE ROCKET.
SOMEONE GAVE UP.
WAP
ZZT
THAT WAS FAST.
YOU GO HANDLE IT.
FINE. BUT STAY AWAKE!

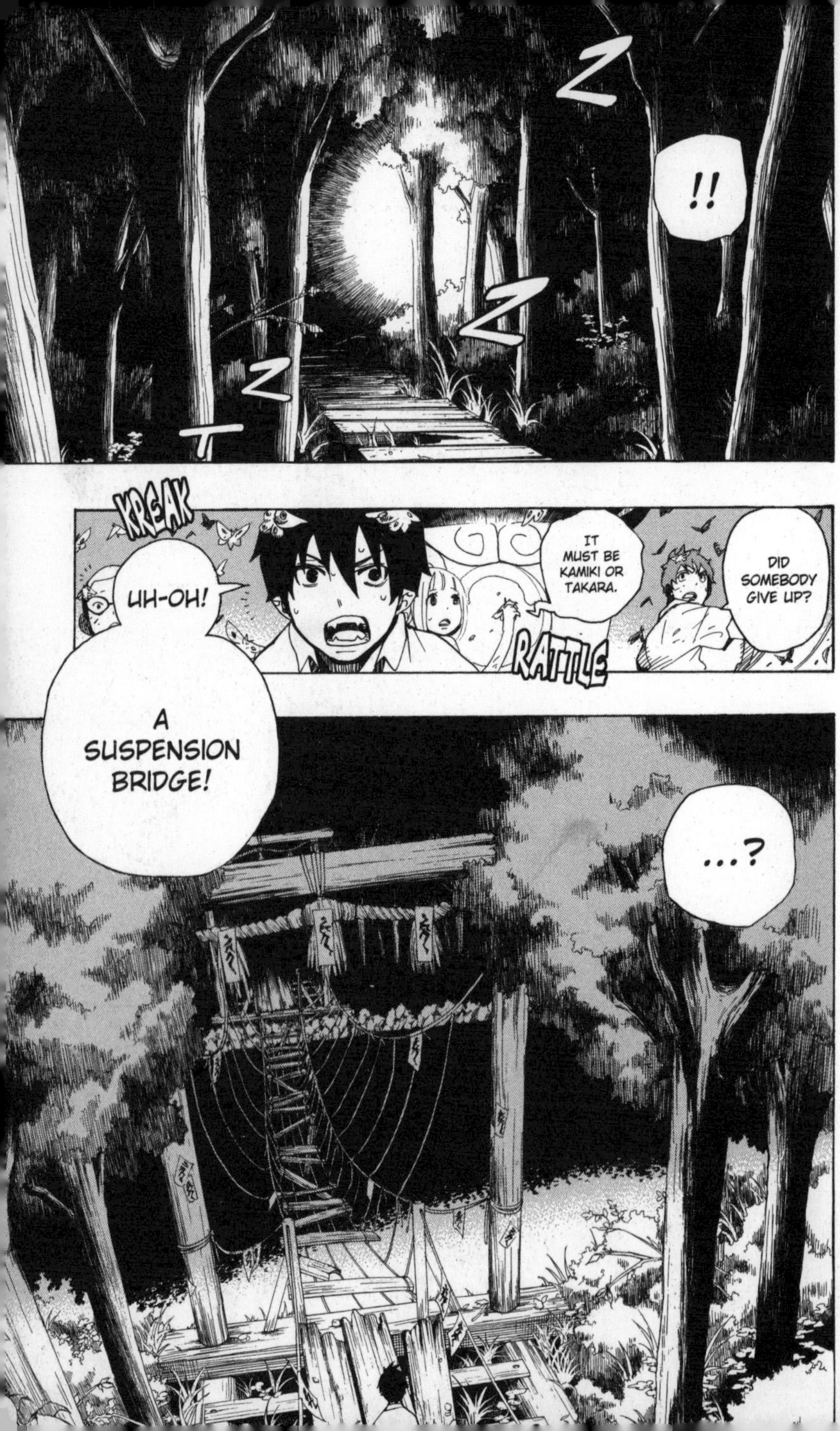

ZZZT
!!
DID SOMEBODY GIVE UP?
IT MUST BE KAMIKI OR TAKARA.
RATTLE
UH-OH!
KREAK
A SUSPENSION BRIDGE!
...?

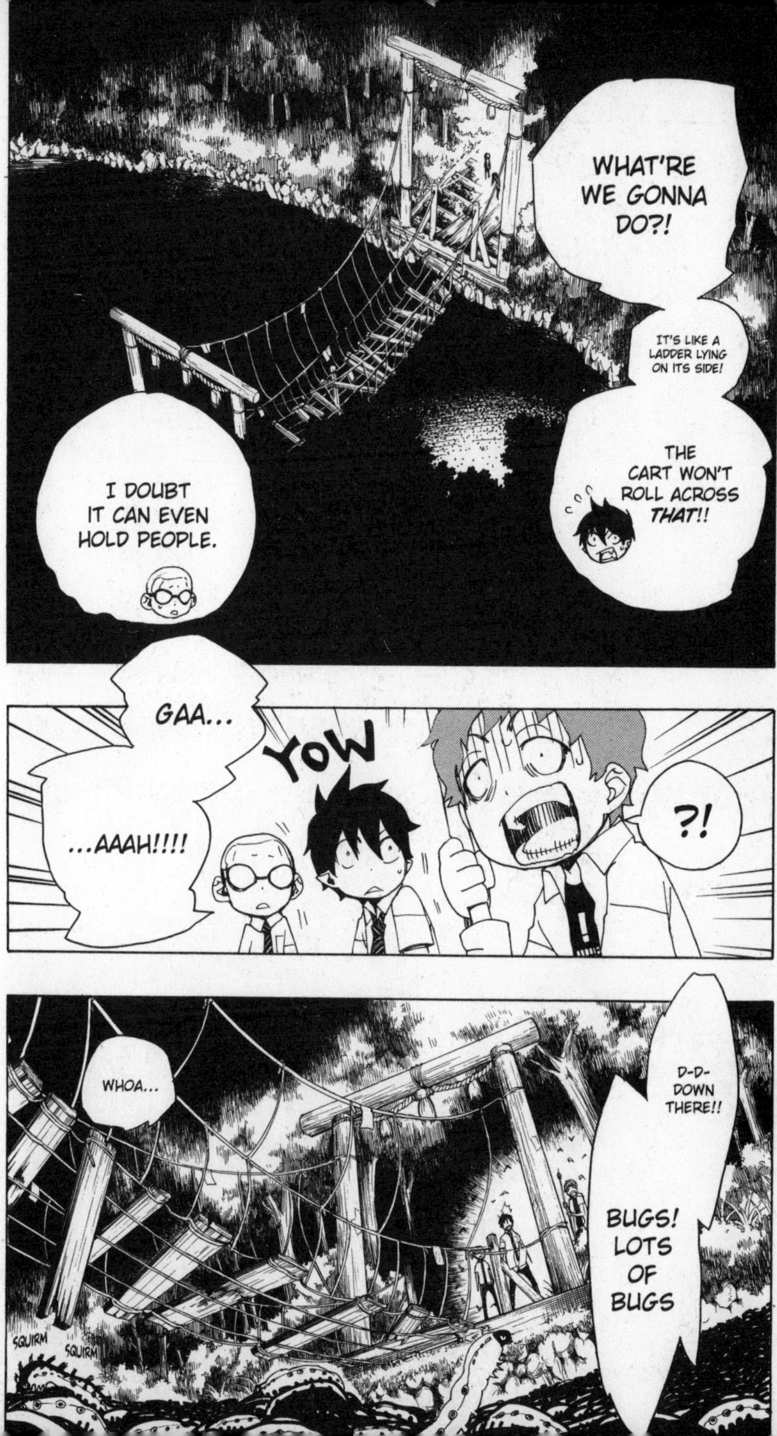
WHAT'RE WE GONNA DO?!
IT'S LIKE A LADDER LYING ON ITS SIDE!
THE CART WON'T ROLL ACROSS *THAT*!!
I DOUBT IT CAN EVEN HOLD PEOPLE.
?!
YOW
GAA...
...AAAH!!!!
D-D-DOWN THERE!!
BUGS! LOTS OF BUGS
WHOA...
SQUIRM
SQUIRM

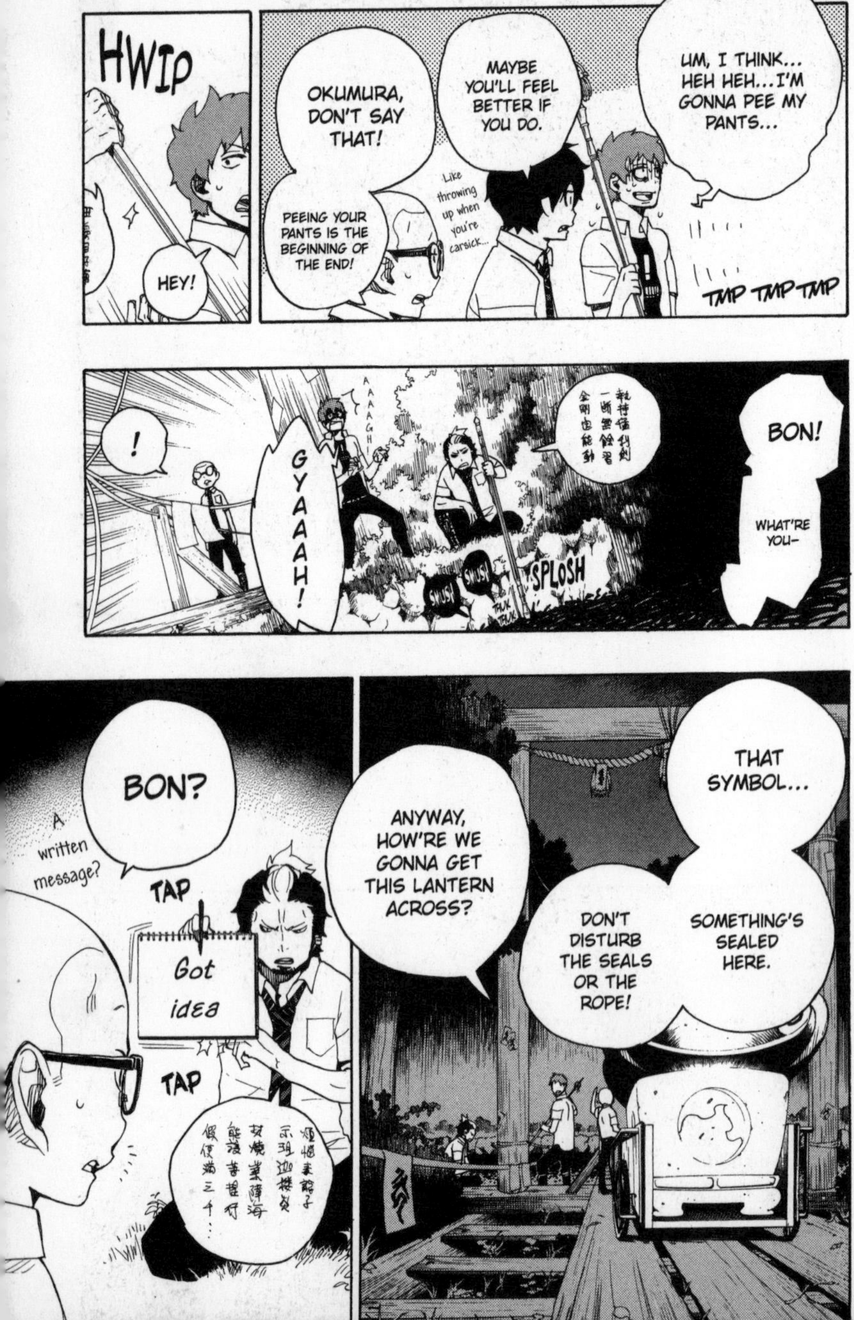
UM, I THINK... HEH HEH...I'M GONNA PEE MY PANTS...
TMP TMP TMP
MAYBE YOU'LL FEEL BETTER IF YOU DO.
Like throwing up when you're carsick...
OKUMURA, DON'T SAY THAT!
PEEING YOUR PANTS IS THE BEGINNING OF THE END!
HWIP
HEY!
BON!
WHAT'RE YOU–
SPLOSH
SMUSH
SMUSH
AAAAGH!
GYAAAAH!
!
THAT SYMBOL...
SOMETHING'S SEALED HERE.
DON'T DISTURB THE SEALS OR THE ROPE!
ANYWAY, HOW'RE WE GONNA GET THIS LANTERN ACROSS?
BON?
A written message?
TAP
Got idea
TAP

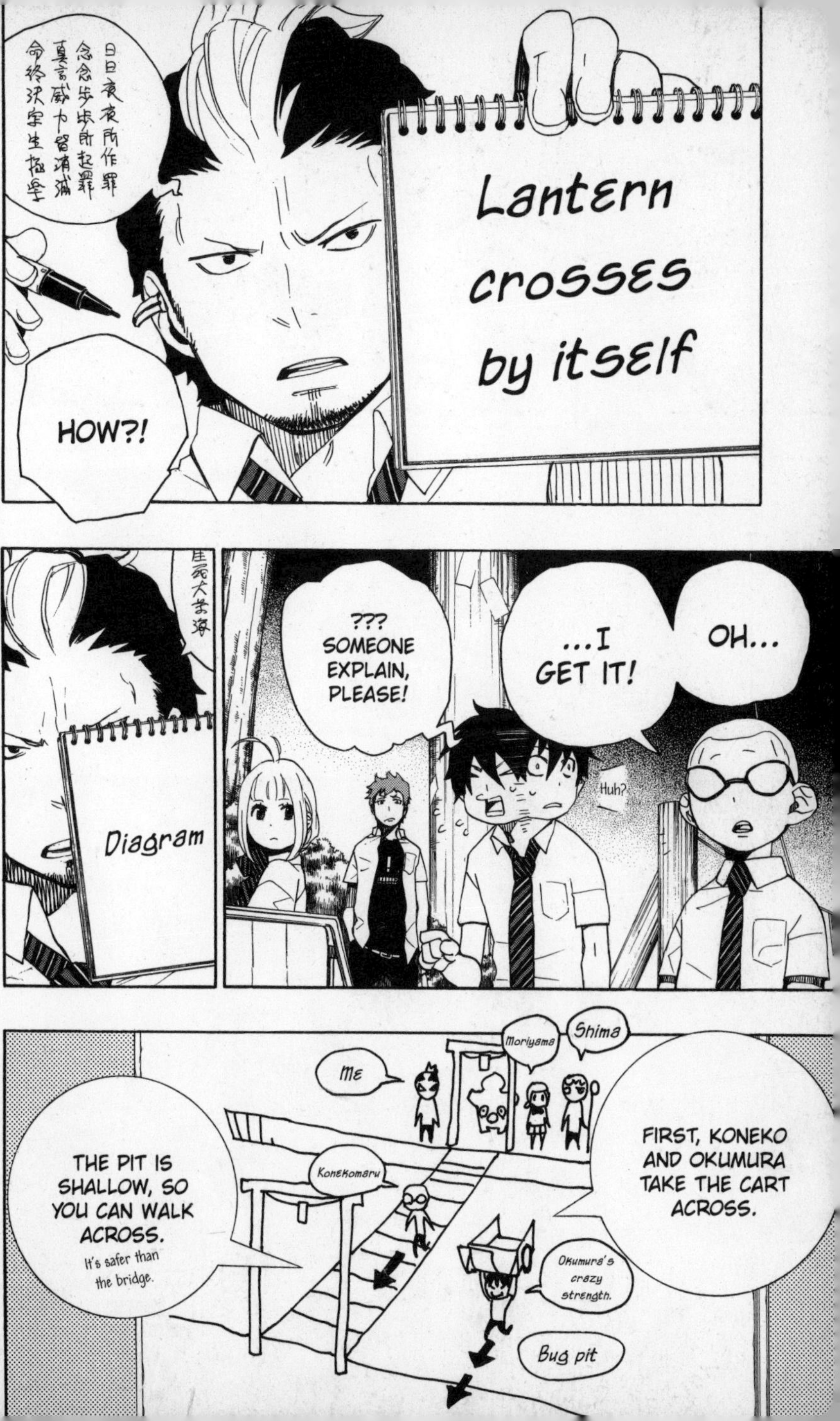
Lantern crosses by itself
日日夜夜所作罪
念念歩歩所起罪
真言威力皆消滅
命終決定生極楽
HOW?!
OH...
...I GET IT!
??? SOMEONE EXPLAIN, PLEASE!
Huh?
Diagram
FIRST, KONEKO AND OKUMURA TAKE THE CART ACROSS.
Shima
Moriyama
Me
Konekomaru
Okumura's crazy strength.
THE PIT IS SHALLOW, SO YOU CAN WALK ACROSS.
It's safer than the bridge.
Bug pit

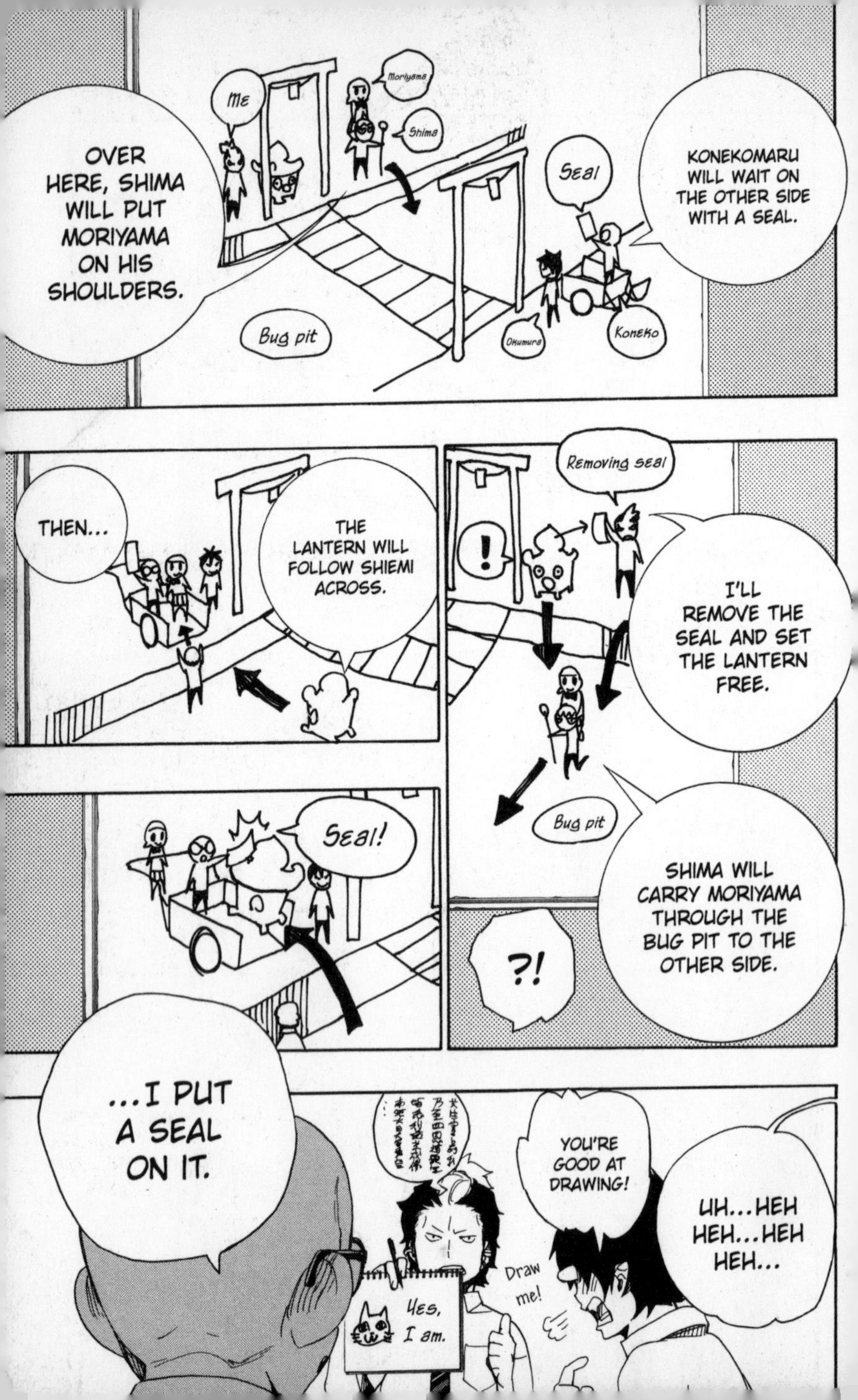
KONEKOMARU WILL WAIT ON THE OTHER SIDE WITH A SEAL.
Moriyama
Seal
Shima
Me
OVER HERE, SHIMA WILL PUT MORIYAMA ON HIS SHOULDERS.
Koneko
Okumura
Bug pit
Removing seal
I'LL REMOVE THE SEAL AND SET THE LANTERN FREE.
!
Bug pit
SHIMA WILL CARRY MORIYAMA THROUGH THE BUG PIT TO THE OTHER SIDE.
?!
THEN...
THE LANTERN WILL FOLLOW SHIEMI ACROSS.
Seal!
UH...HEH HEH...HEH HEH...
YOU'RE GOOD AT DRAWING!
Draw me!
Yes, I am.
...I PUT A SEAL ON IT.

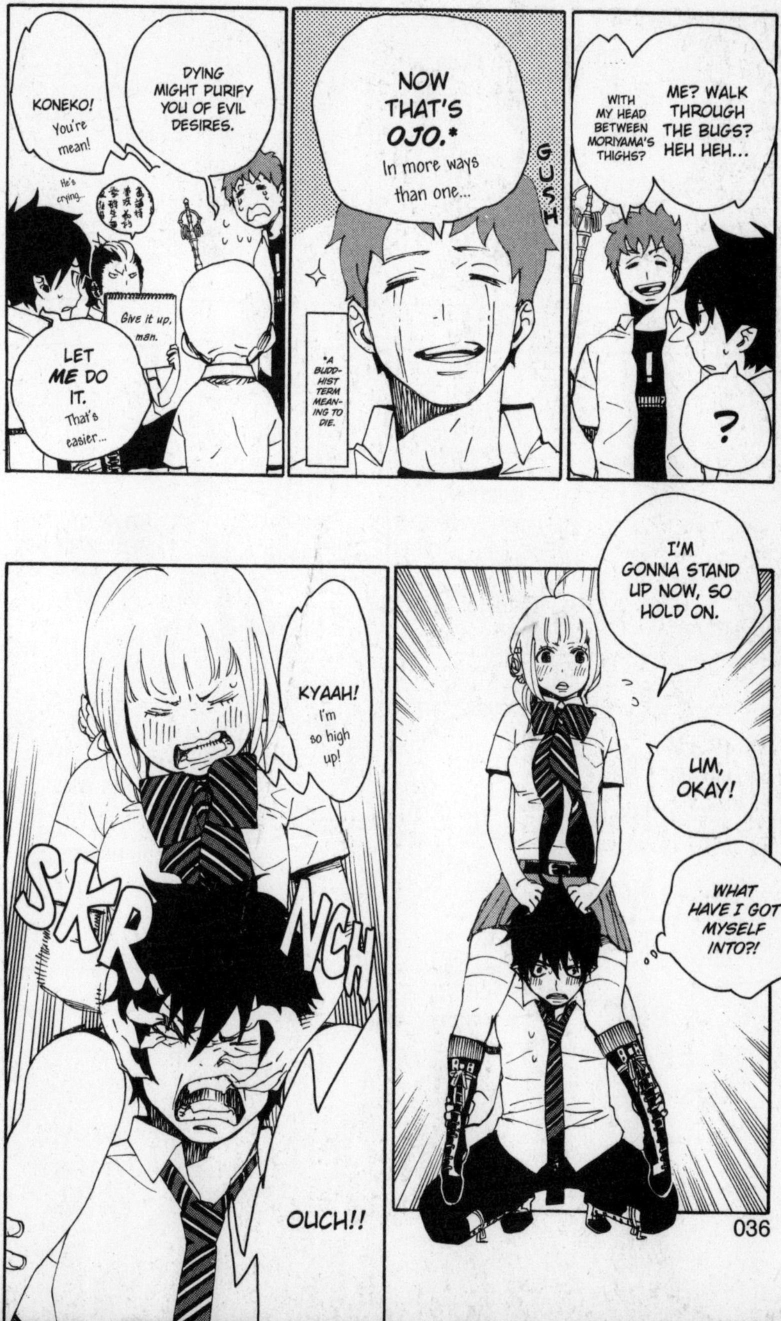
ME? WALK THROUGH THE BUGS? HEH HEH...
WITH MY HEAD BETWEEN MORIYAMA'S THIGHS?
?
NOW THAT'S OJO.* In more ways than one...
GUSH
*A BUDDHIST TERM MEANING TO DIE.
DYING MIGHT PURIFY YOU OF EVIL DESIRES.
KONEKO! You're mean!
He's crying...
Give it up, man.
LET ME DO IT. That's easier...
I'M GONNA STAND UP NOW, SO HOLD ON.
UM, OKAY!
WHAT HAVE I GOT MYSELF INTO?!
KYAAH! I'm so high up!
SKRNCH
OUCH!!

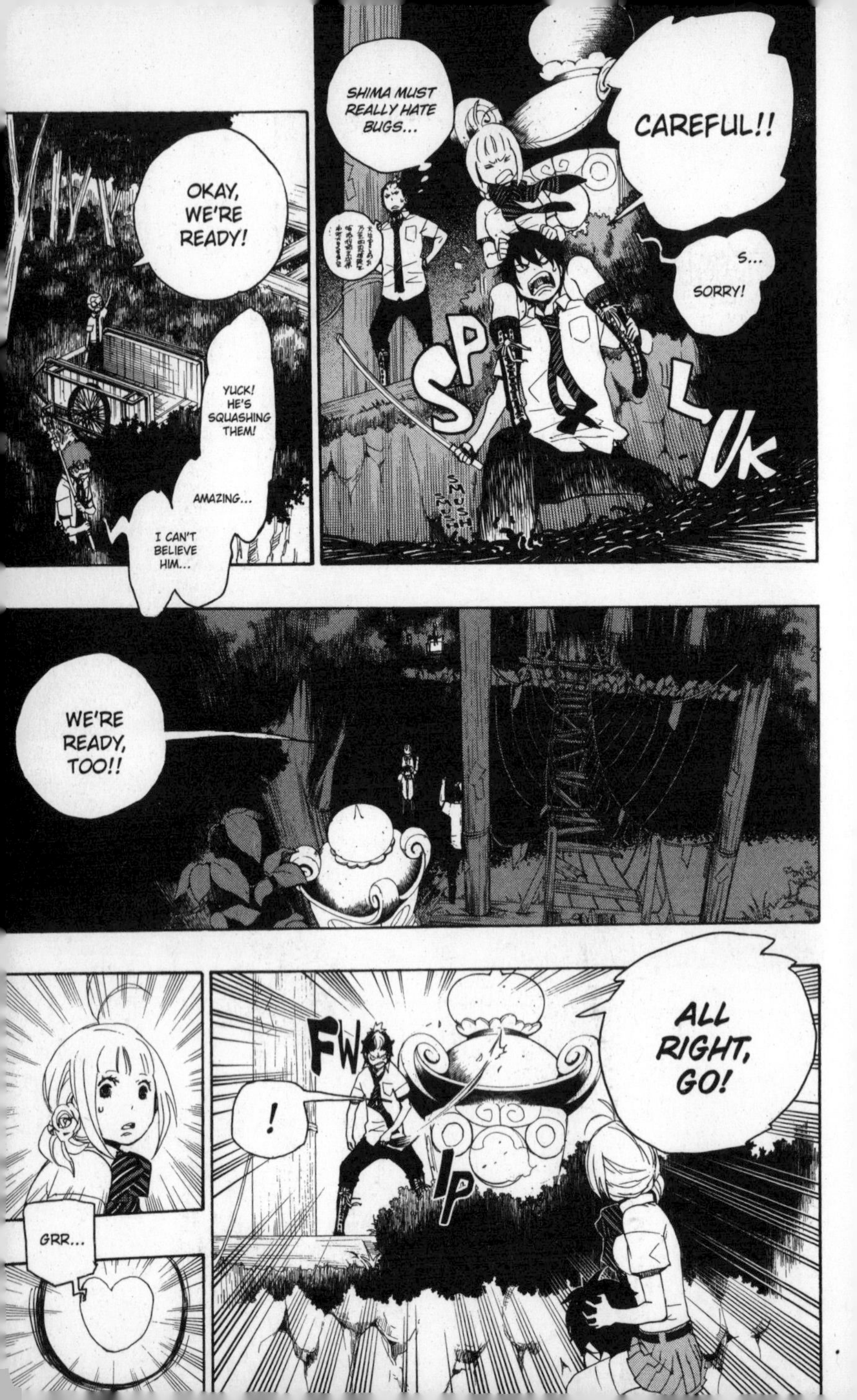
CAREFUL!!
S... SORRY!
SHIMA MUST REALLY HATE BUGS...
SPLUK
SMUSH SMUSH
OKAY, WE'RE READY!
YUCK! HE'S SQUASHING THEM!
AMAZING...
I CAN'T BELIEVE HIM...
WE'RE READY, TOO!!
ALL RIGHT, GO!
FWIP
!
GRR...

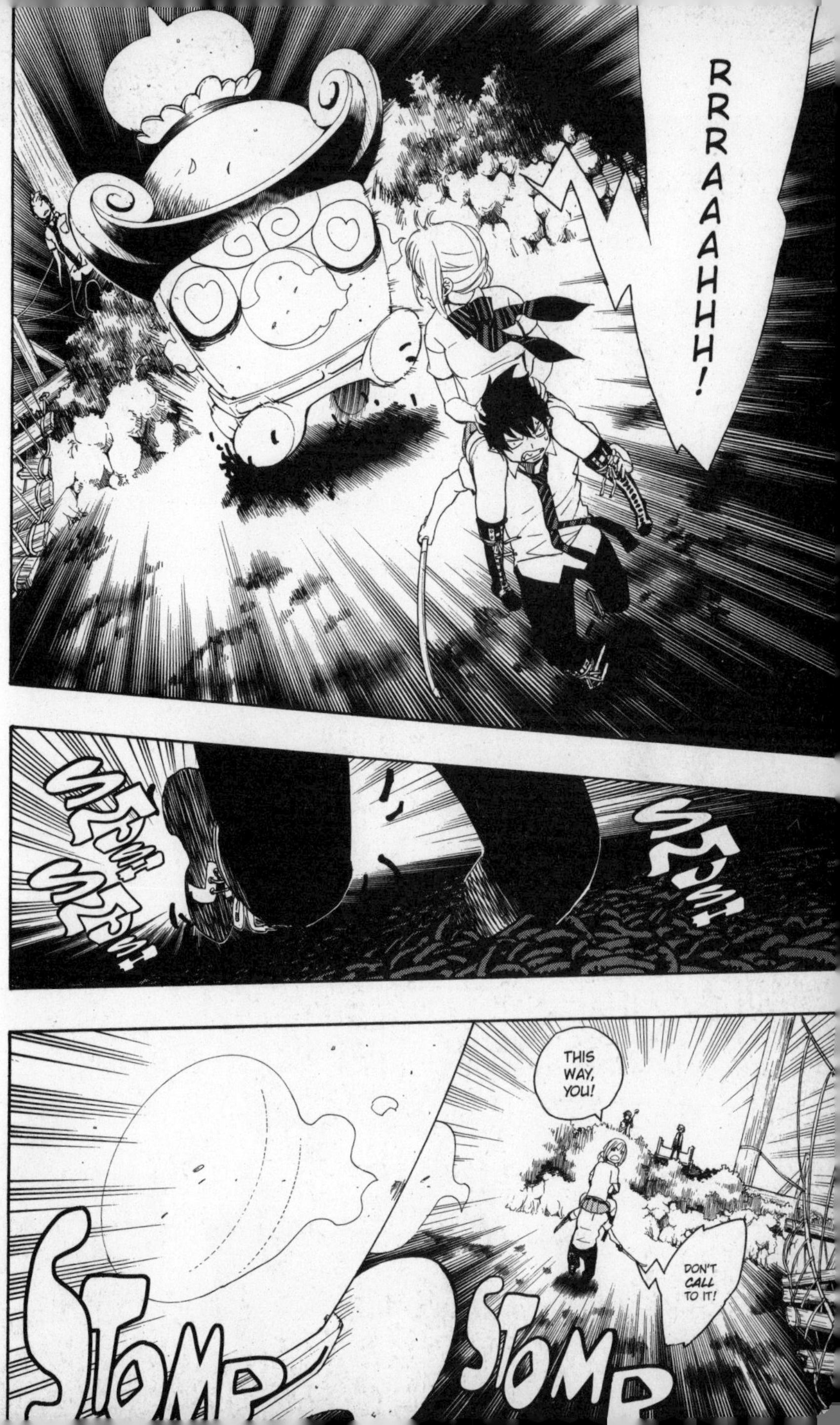
RRRAAAHHH!
THIS WAY, YOU!
DON'T CALL TO IT!
STOMP
STOMP

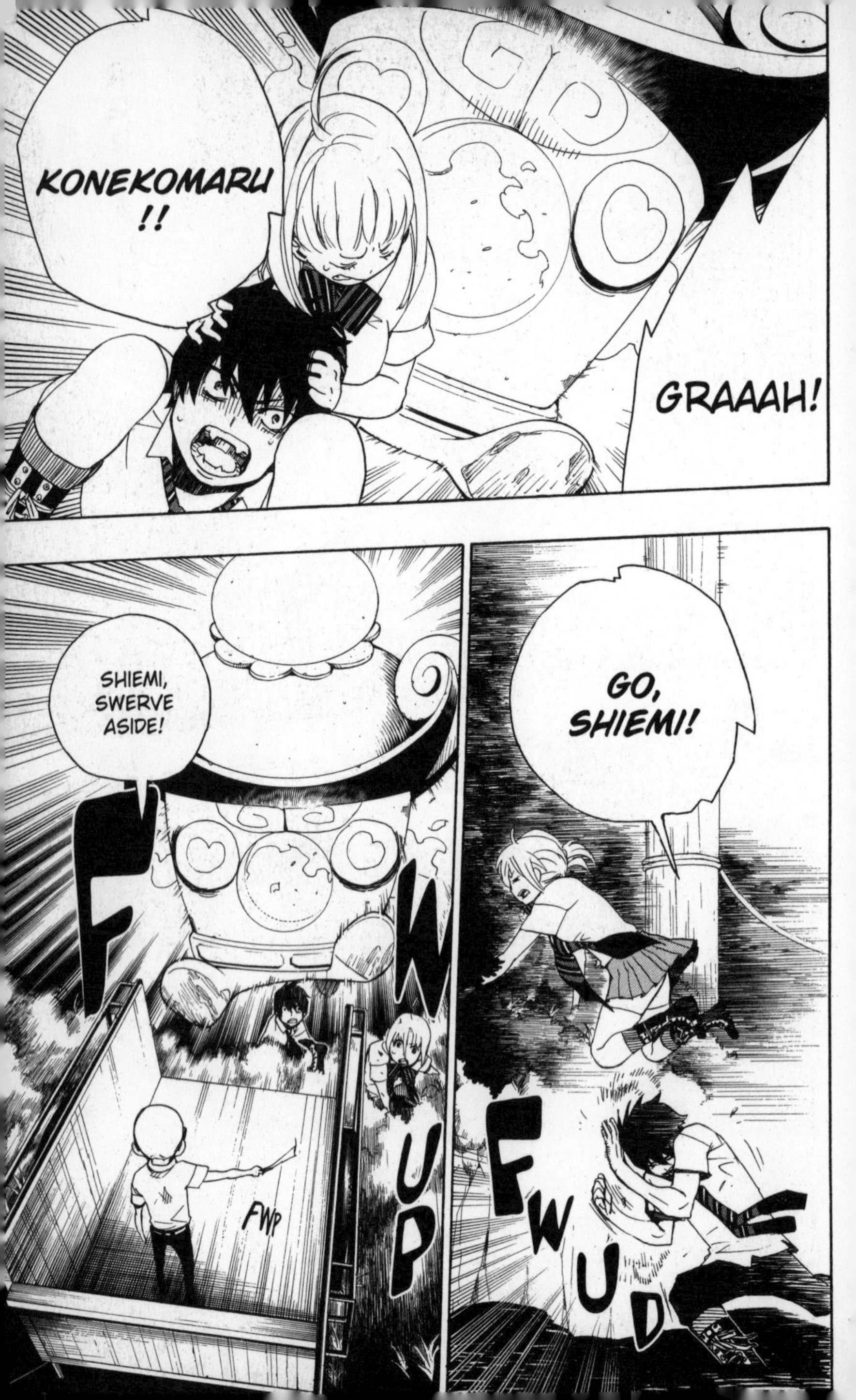
KONEKOMARU!!
GRAAAH!
GO, SHIEMI!
FWUD
SHIEMI, SWERVE ASIDE!
FWUP
FWP

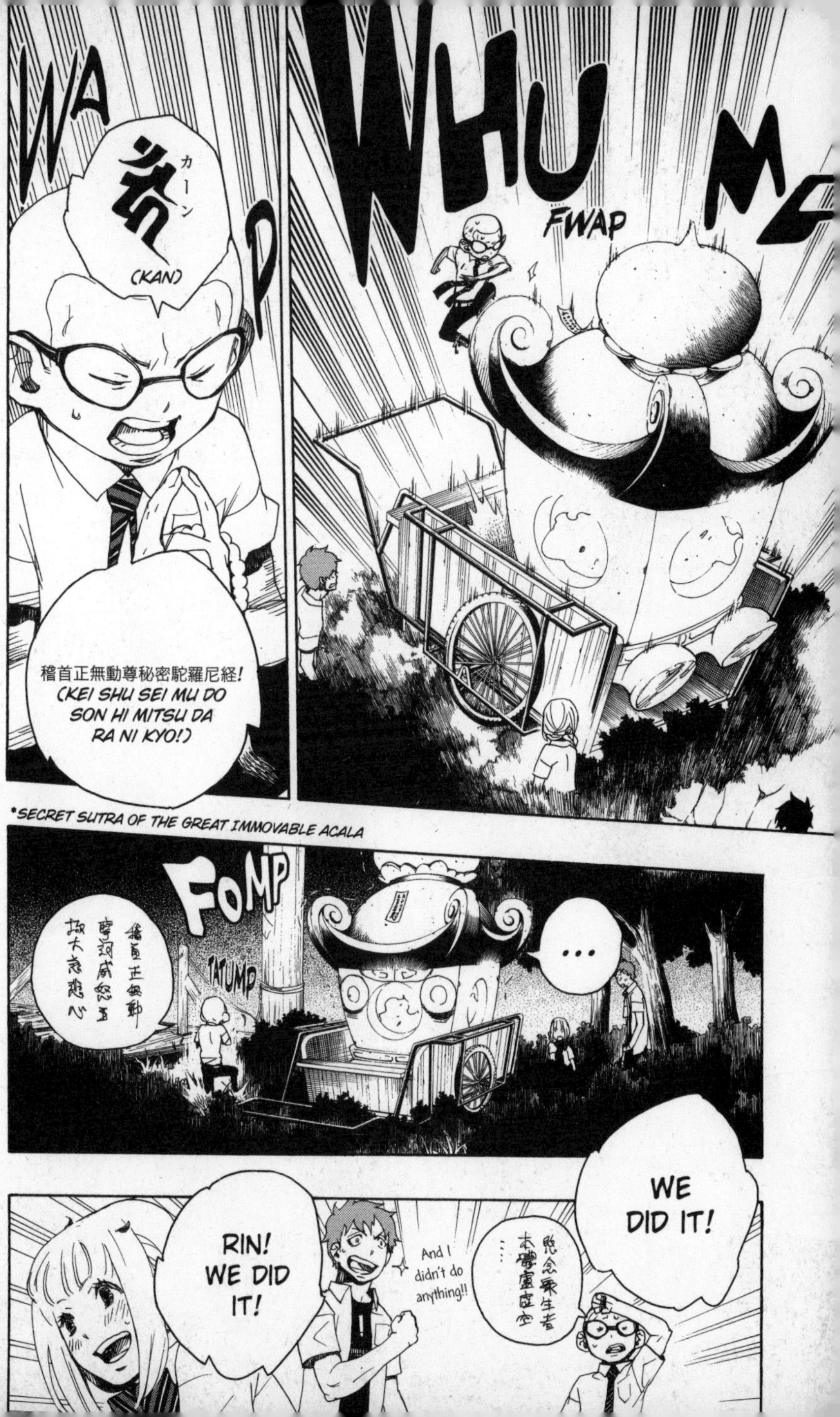
WHUMP
FWAP
WAP
カーン
(KAN)
稽首正無動尊秘密駝羅尼経!
(KEI SHU SEI MU DO SON HI MITSU DA RA NI KYO!)
*SECRET SUTRA OF THE GREAT IMMOVABLE ACALA
...
FOMP
稽首正無動
摩訶威怒王
救大慈悲心
TATUMP
WE DID IT!
愍念衆生者
本體盧虛空
…
And I didn't do anything!!
RIN! WE DID IT!

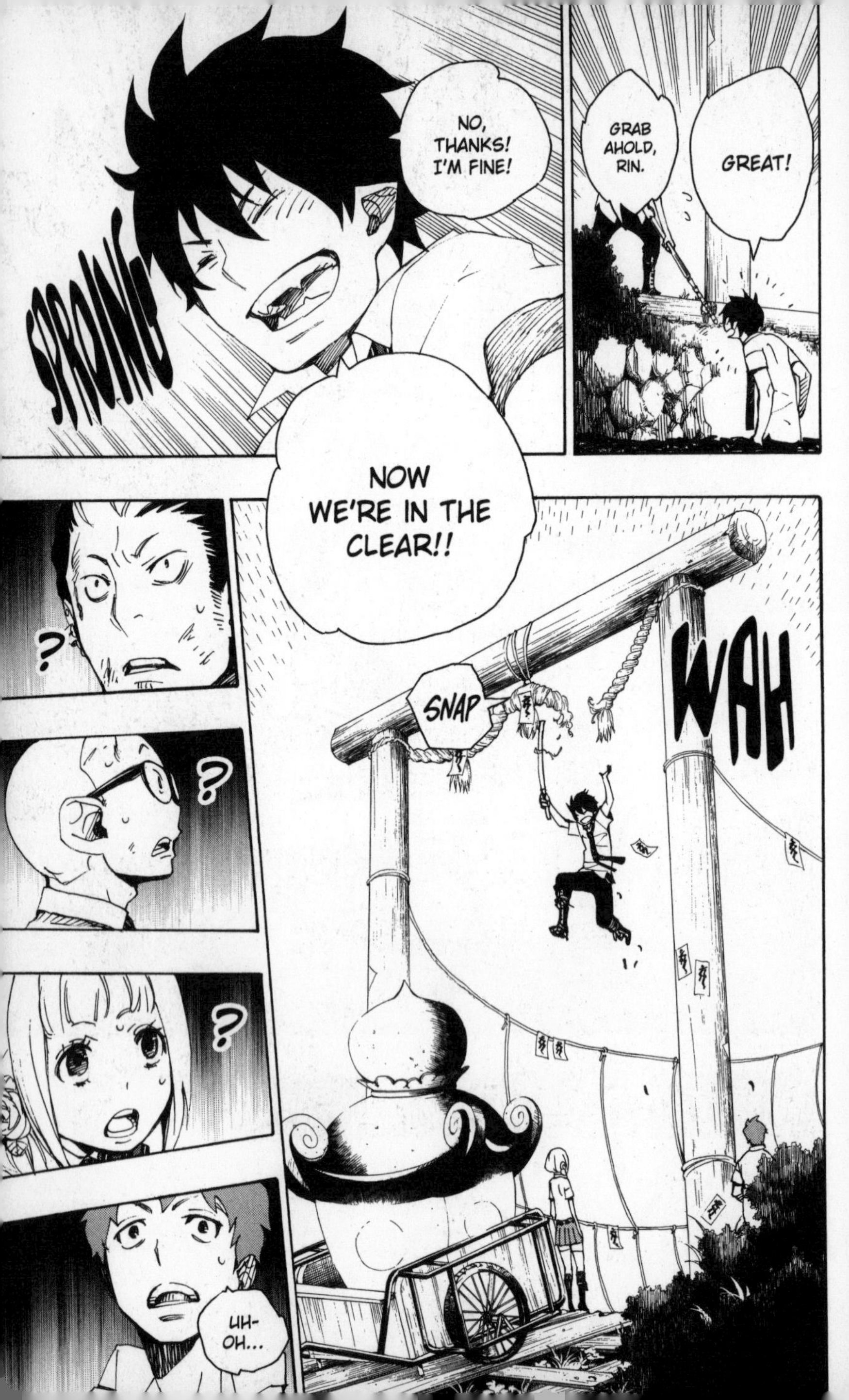
GREAT!
GRAB AHOLD, RIN.
NO, THANKS! I'M FINE!
SPROING
NOW WE'RE IN THE CLEAR!!
WAH
SNAP
?
?
?
UH-OH...

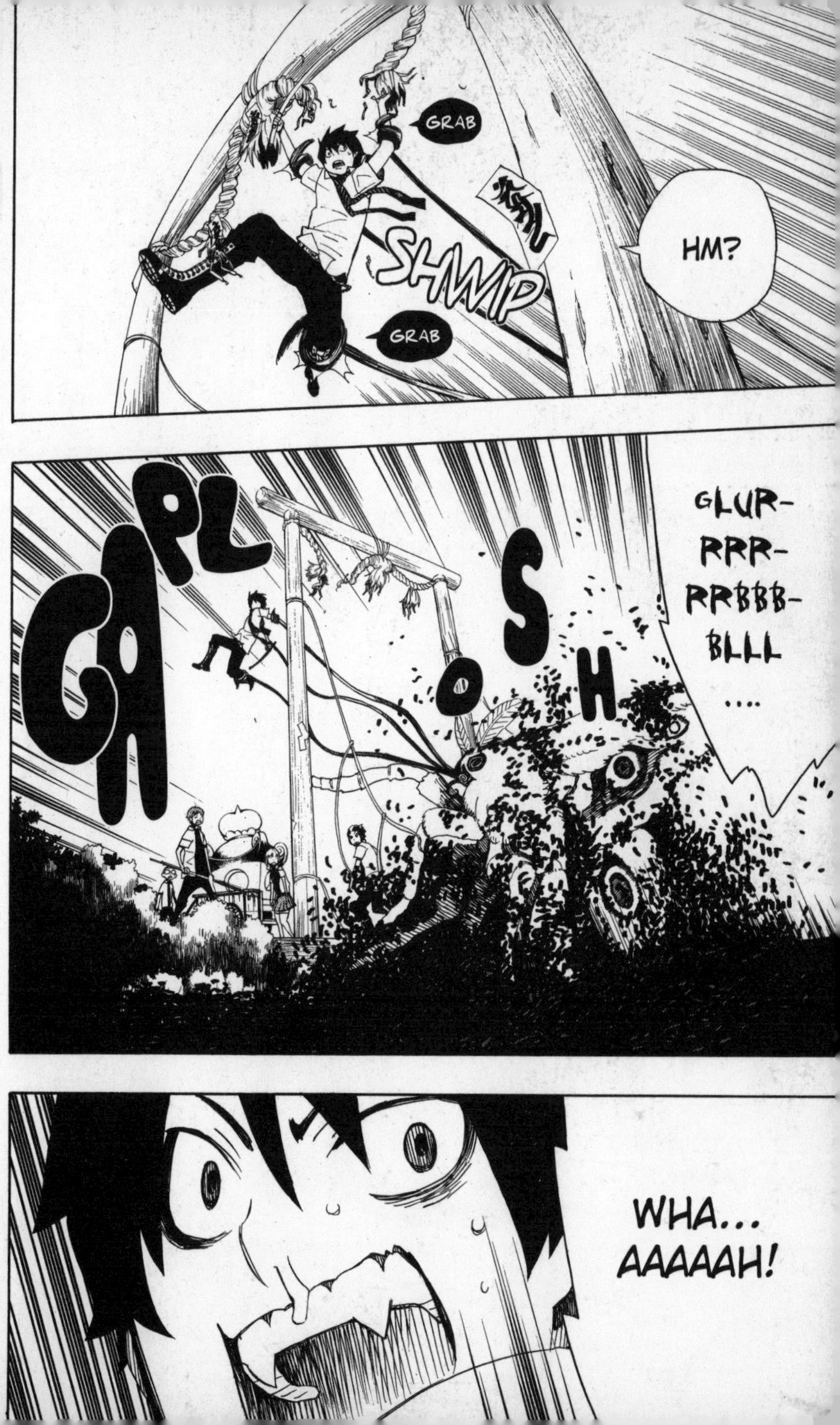
HM?
GRAB
SHWIP
GRAB
GLUR-RRR-RRBBB-BLLL....
GAPLOSH
WHA... AAAAAH!

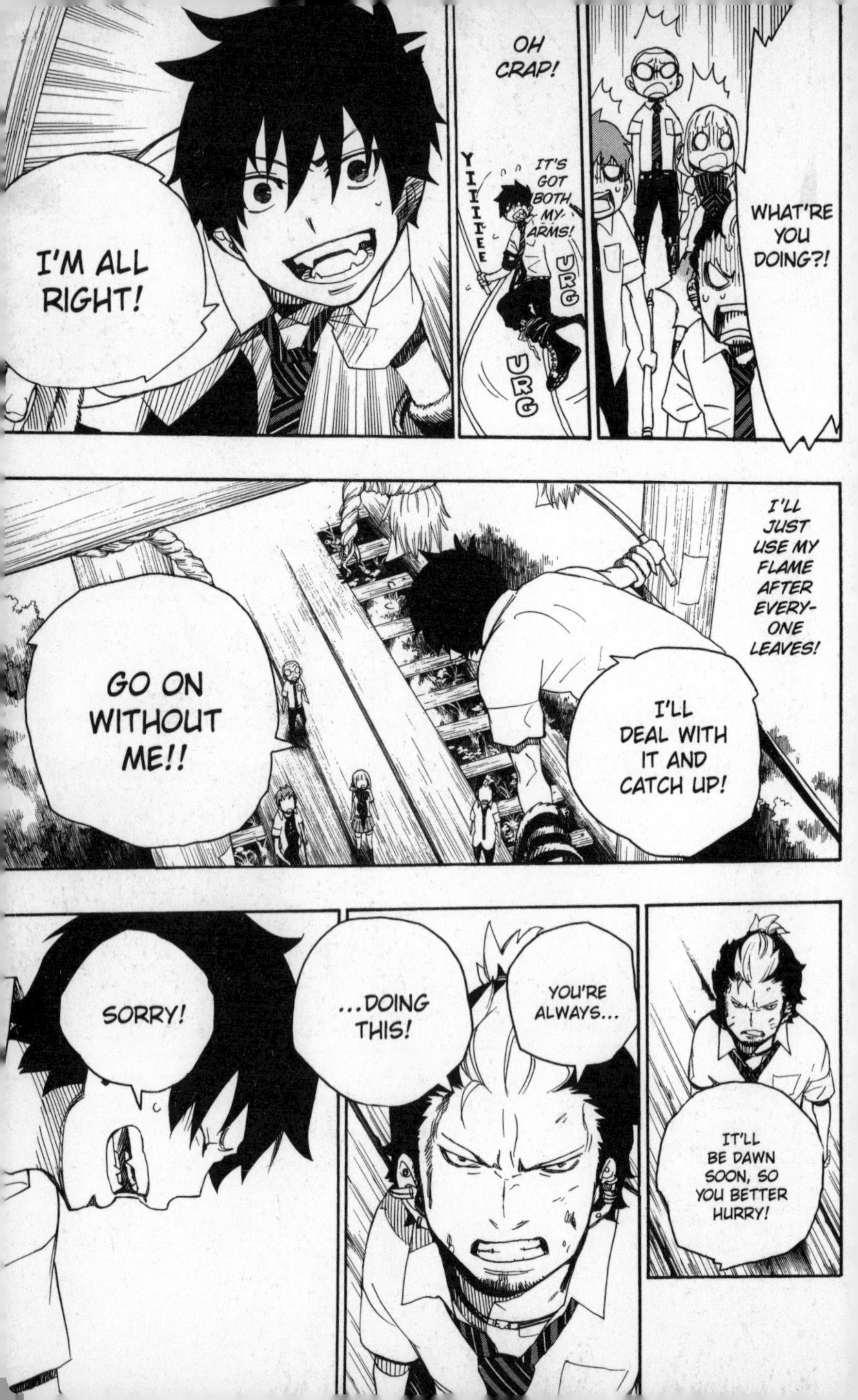
WHAT'RE YOU DOING?!
OH CRAP!
IT'S GOT BOTH MY ARMS!
YIIIIEE
URG
URG
I'M ALL RIGHT!
I'LL JUST USE MY FLAME AFTER EVERY-ONE LEAVES!
I'LL DEAL WITH IT AND CATCH UP!
GO ON WITHOUT ME!!
IT'LL BE DAWN SOON, SO YOU BETTER HURRY!
YOU'RE ALWAYS...
...DOING THIS!
SORRY!

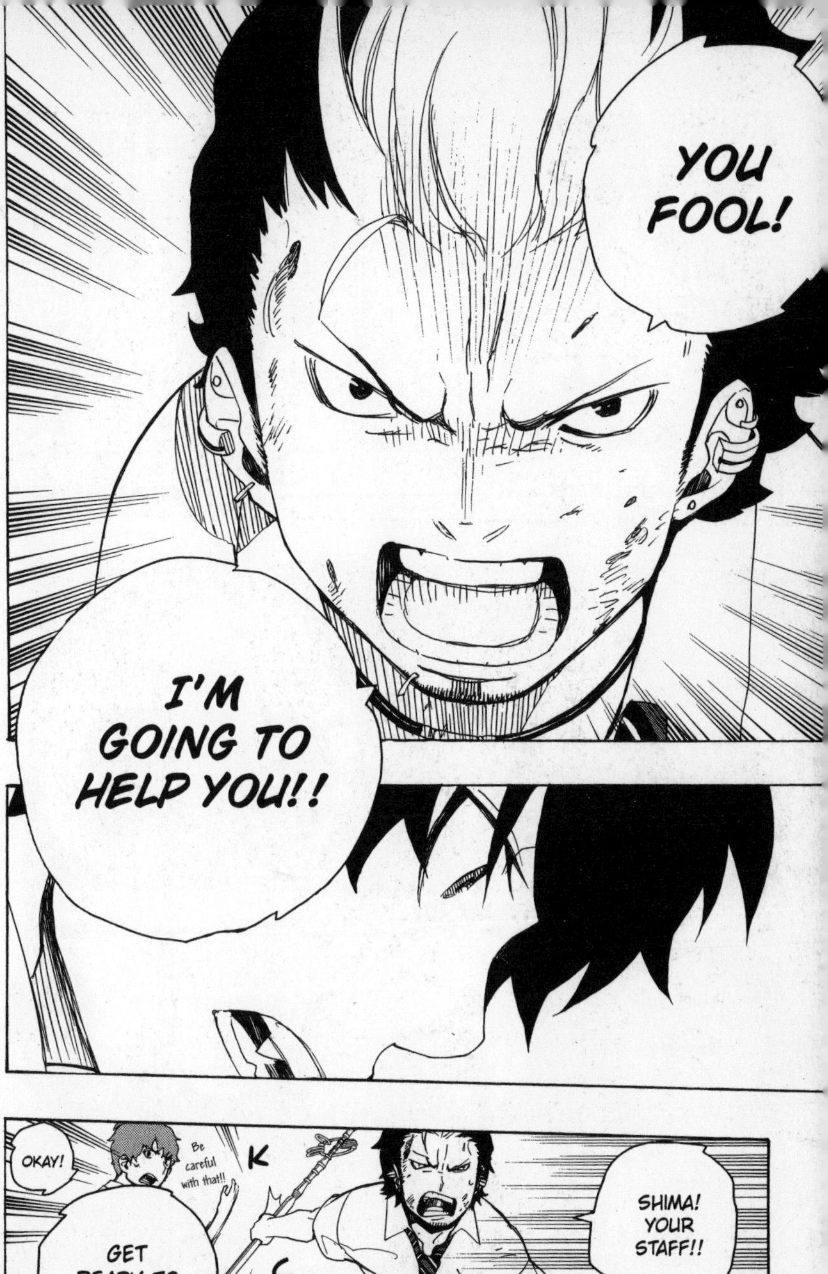
YOU FOOL!
I'M GOING TO HELP YOU!!
SHIMA! YOUR STAFF!!
K
CH
Be careful with that!!
OKAY!
GET READY TO RUN!!

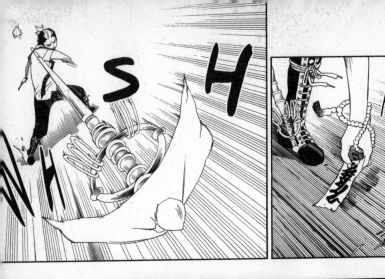

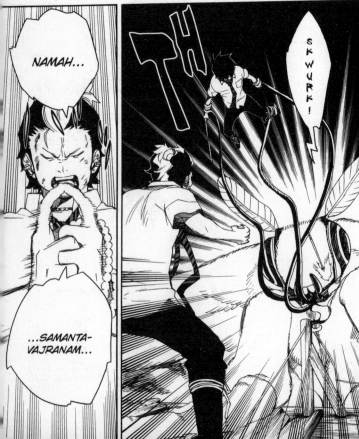

NAMAH...

...SAMANTA-
VAJRANAM...

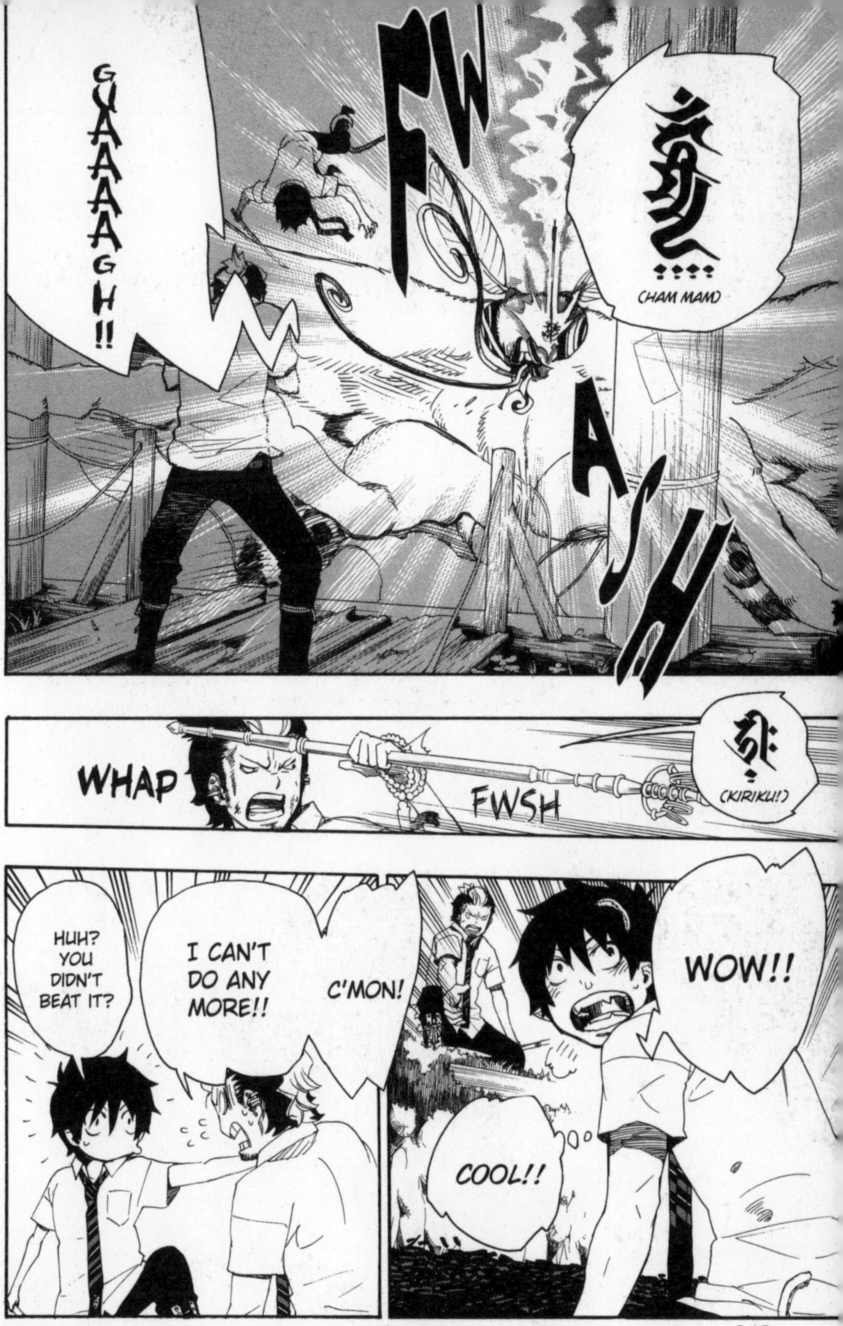
(HAM MAM)
FWASH
GUAAAAAGH!!
(KIRIKU!)
FWSH
WHAP
WOW!!
COOL!!
C'MON!
I CAN'T DO ANY MORE!!
HUH? YOU DIDN'T BEAT IT?

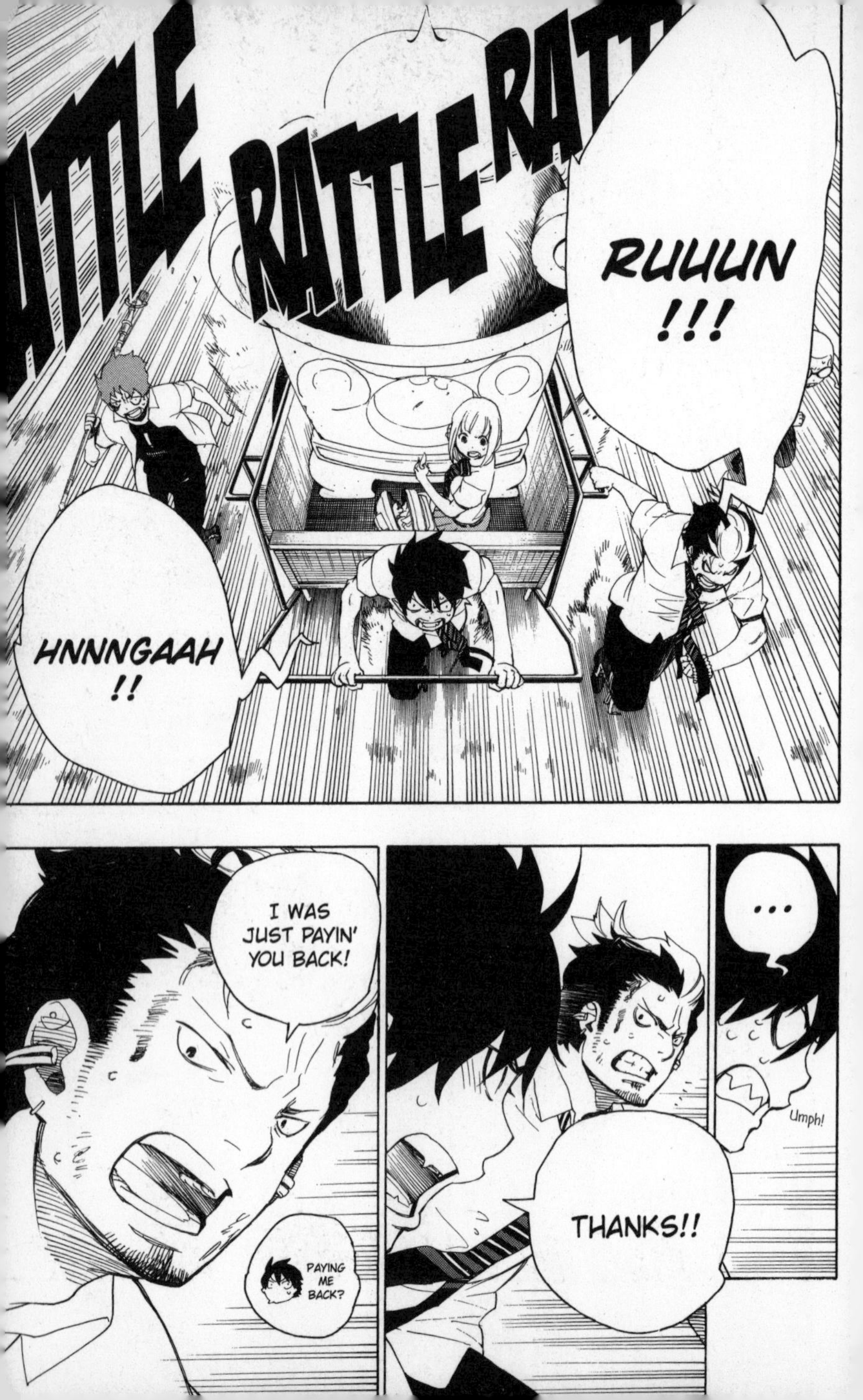
ATTLE RATTLE RATT
RUUUN !!!
HNNNGAAH !!
...
Umph!
THANKS!!
I WAS JUST PAYIN' YOU BACK!
PAYING ME BACK?

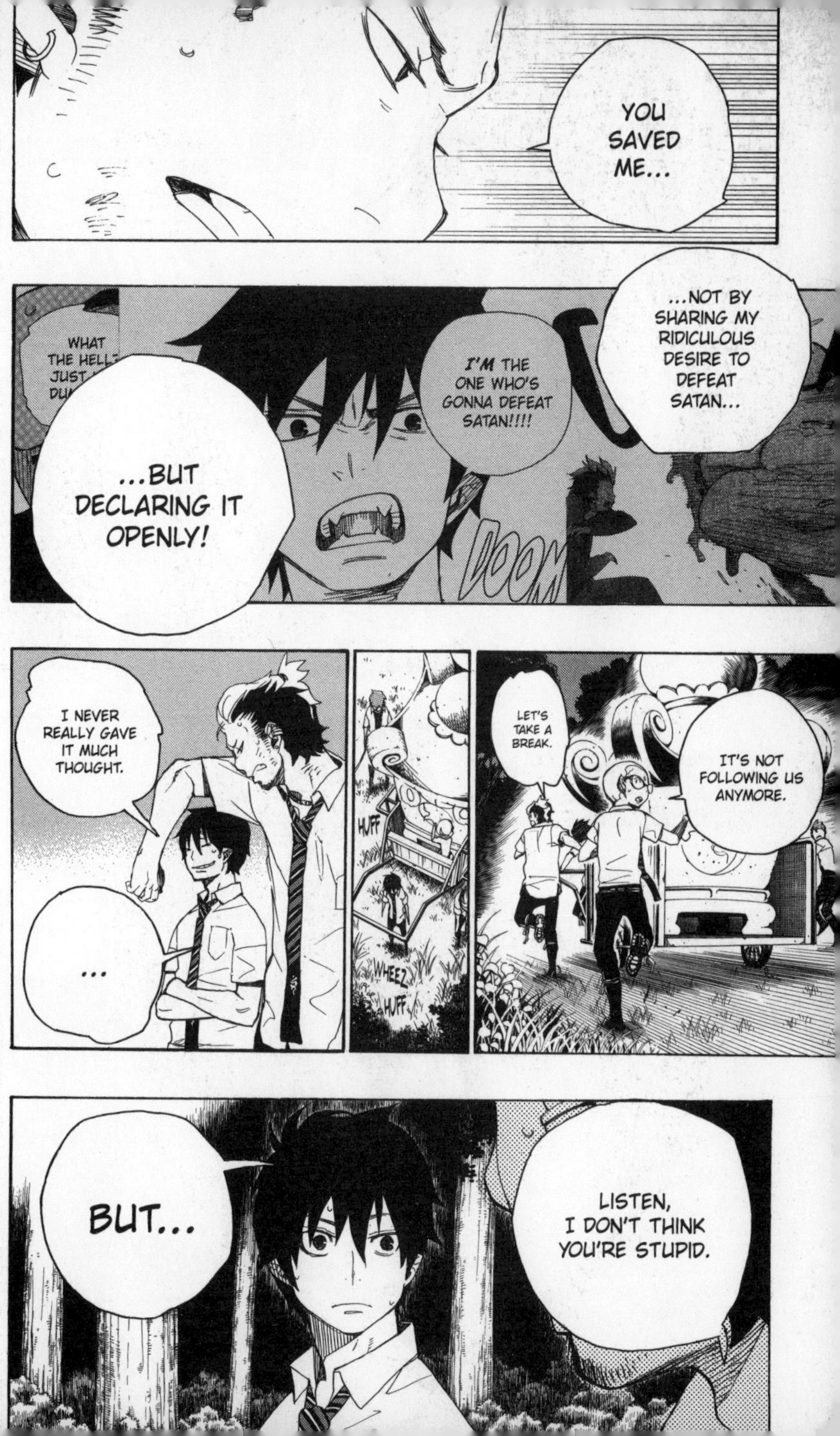
YOU SAVED ME...
...NOT BY SHARING MY RIDICULOUS DESIRE TO DEFEAT SATAN...
I'M THE ONE WHO'S GONNA DEFEAT SATAN!!!!
DOOM
...BUT DECLARING IT OPENLY!
WHAT THE HELL JUST
IT'S NOT FOLLOWING US ANYMORE.
LET'S TAKE A BREAK.
HUFF
WHEEZ
HUFF
I NEVER REALLY GAVE IT MUCH THOUGHT.
...
LISTEN, I DON'T THINK YOU'RE STUPID.
BUT...

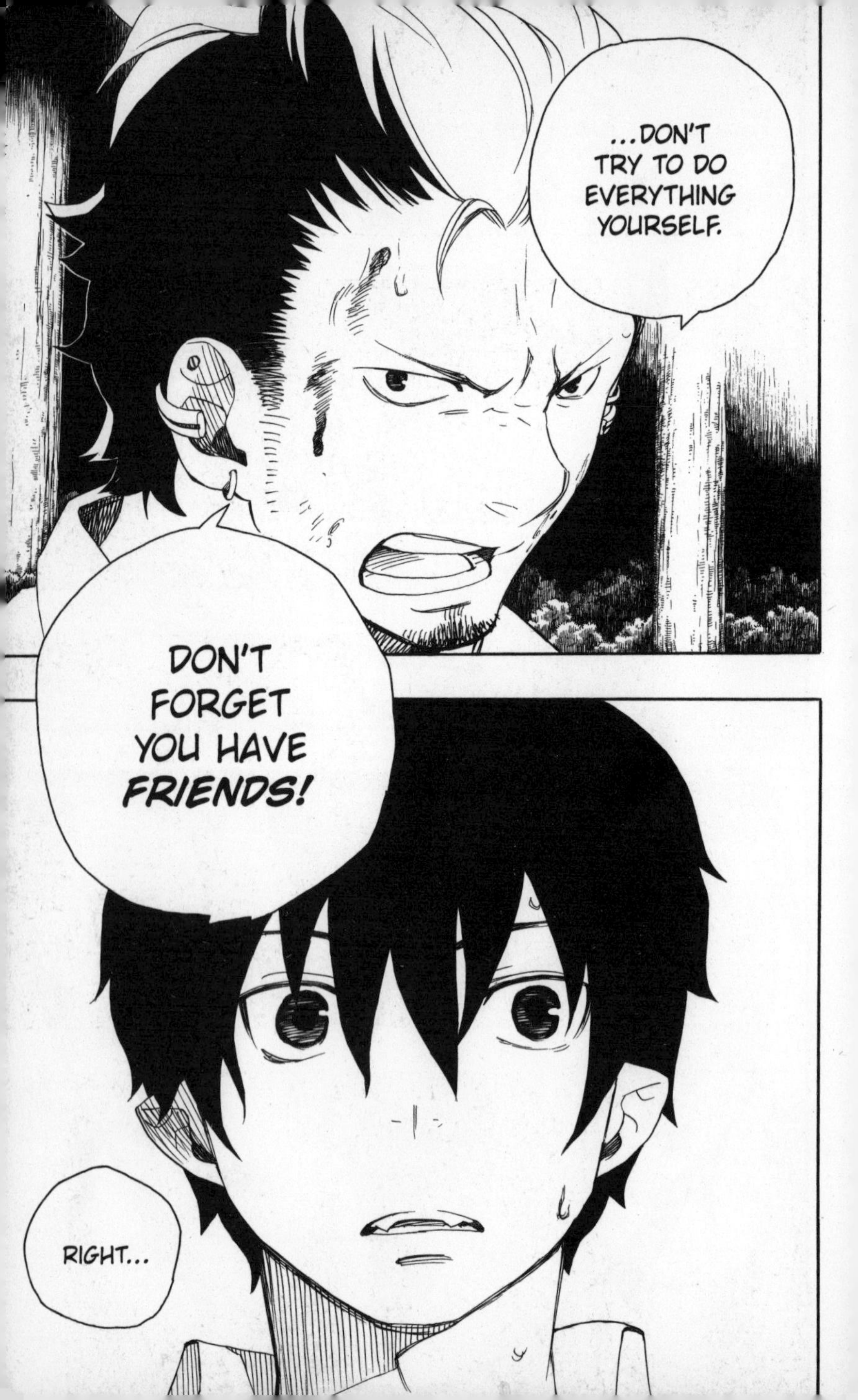
...DON'T TRY TO DO EVERYTHING YOURSELF.
DON'T FORGET YOU HAVE FRIENDS!
RIGHT...

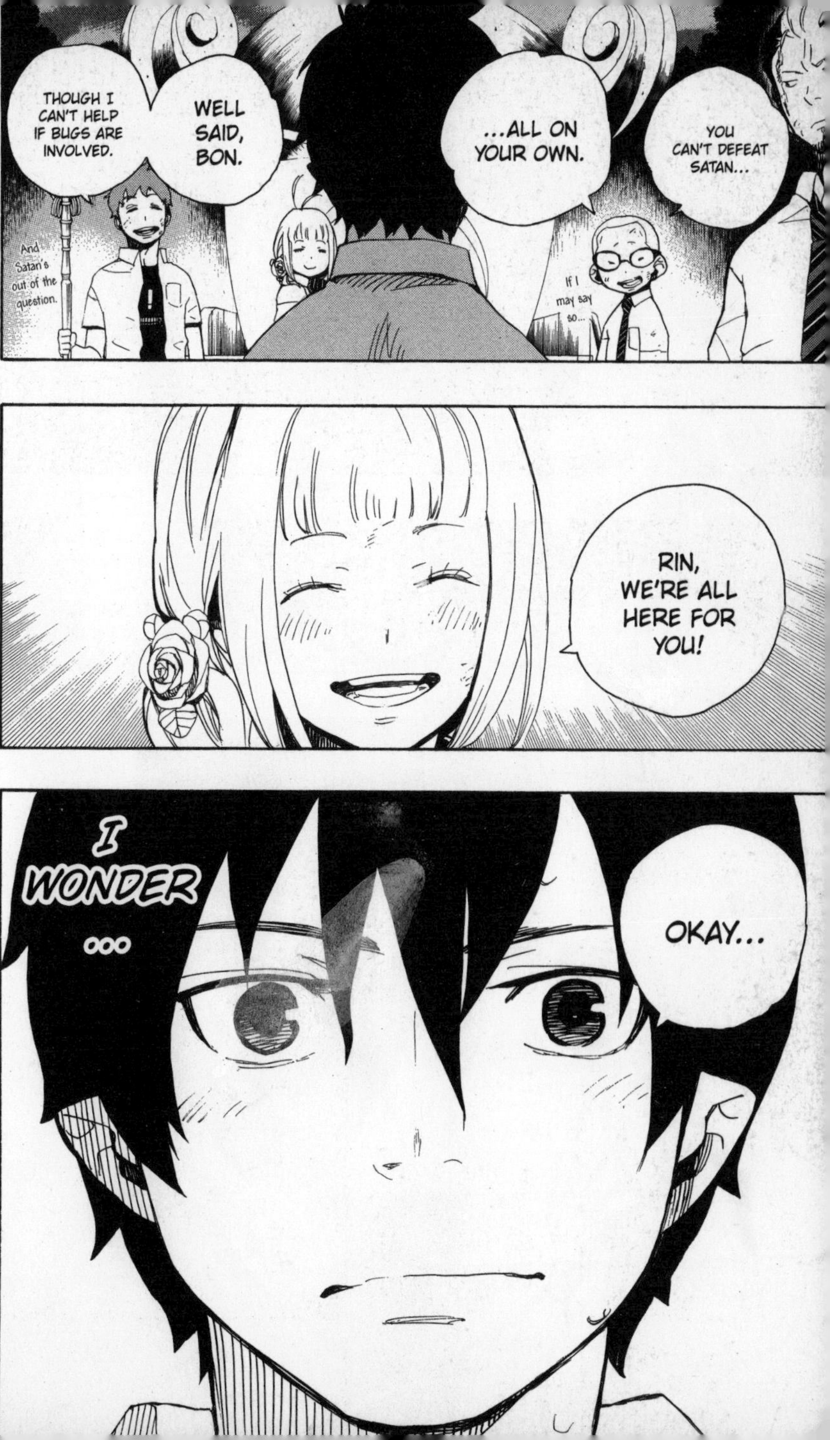
YOU CAN'T DEFEAT SATAN...
...ALL ON YOUR OWN.
If I may say so...
WELL SAID, BON.
THOUGH I CAN'T HELP IF BUGS ARE INVOLVED.
And Satan's out of the question.
RIN, WE'RE ALL HERE FOR YOU!
OKAY...
I WONDER...

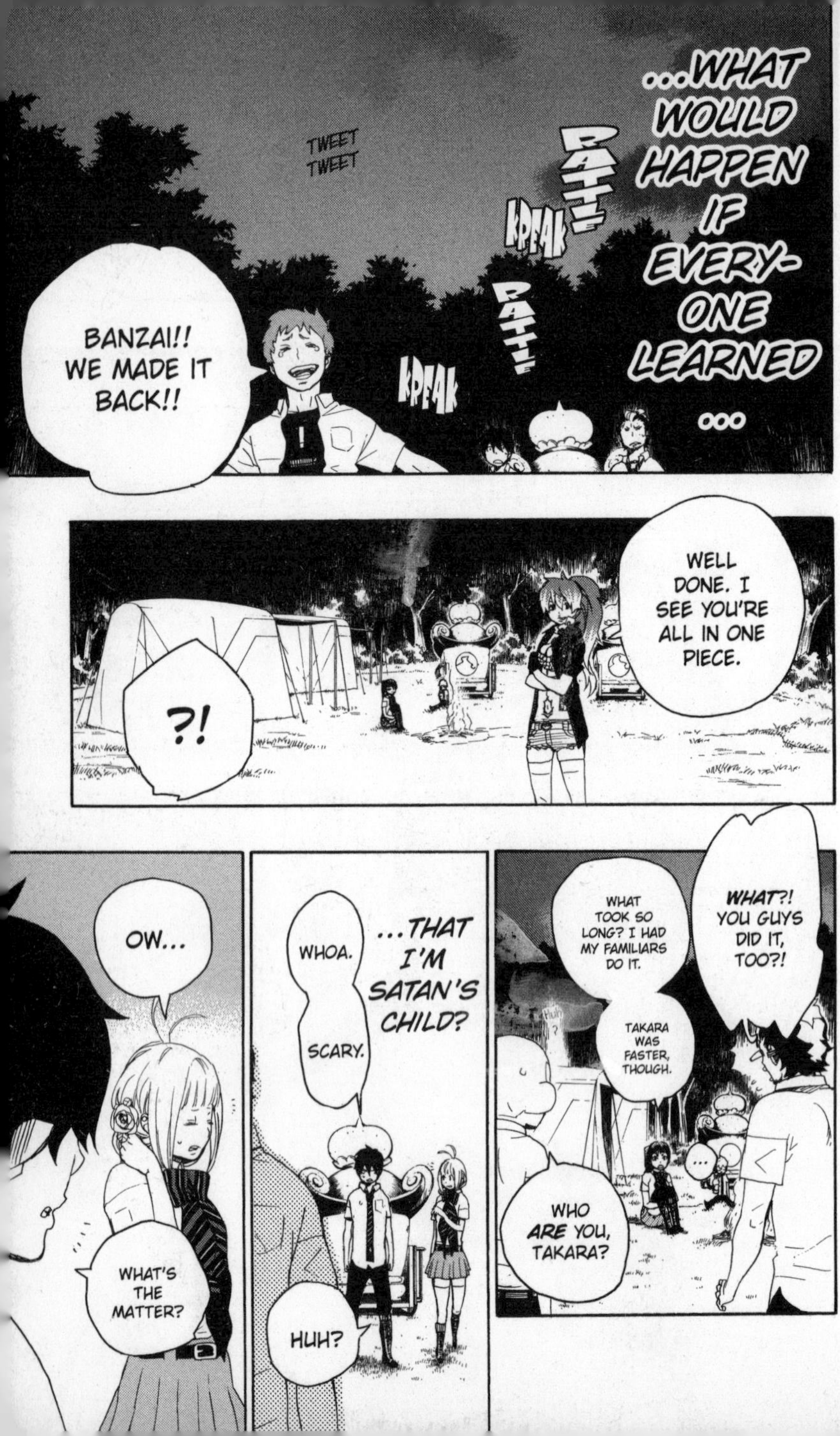
...WHAT WOULD HAPPEN IF EVERY-ONE LEARNED...
RATTLE
KREAK
TWEET TWEET
RATTLE
KREAK
BANZAI!! WE MADE IT BACK!!
WELL DONE. I SEE YOU'RE ALL IN ONE PIECE.
?!
WHAT?! YOU GUYS DID IT, TOO?!
WHAT TOOK SO LONG? I HAD MY FAMILIARS DO IT.
TAKARA WAS FASTER, THOUGH.
...
WHO *ARE* YOU, TAKARA?
...THAT I'M SATAN'S CHILD?
WHOA.
SCARY.
HUH?
OW...
WHAT'S THE MATTER?

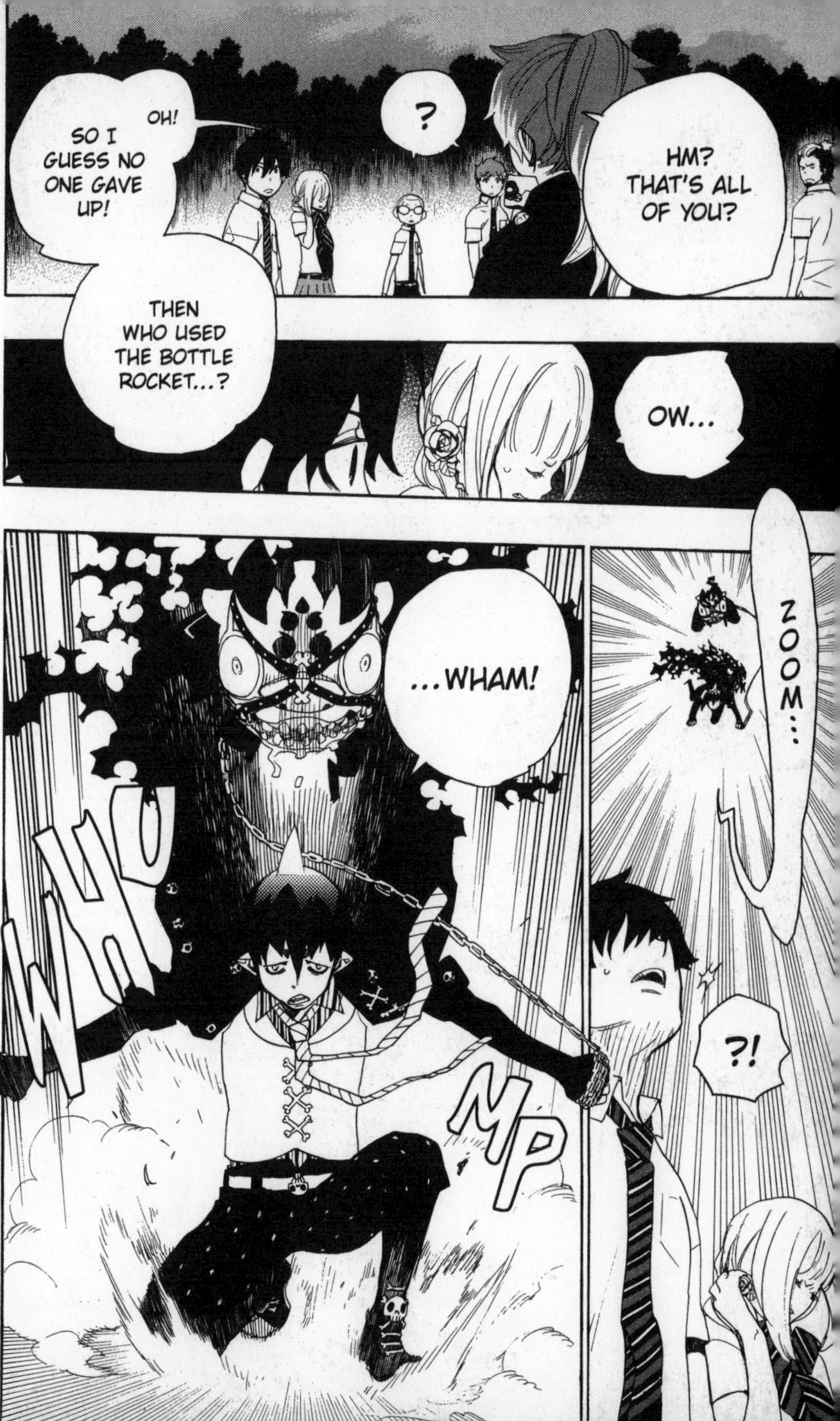
HM? THAT'S ALL OF YOU?
?
OH!
SO I GUESS NO ONE GAVE UP!
THEN WHO USED THE BOTTLE ROCKET...?
OW...
ZOOM...
?!
...WHAM!
WHUMP

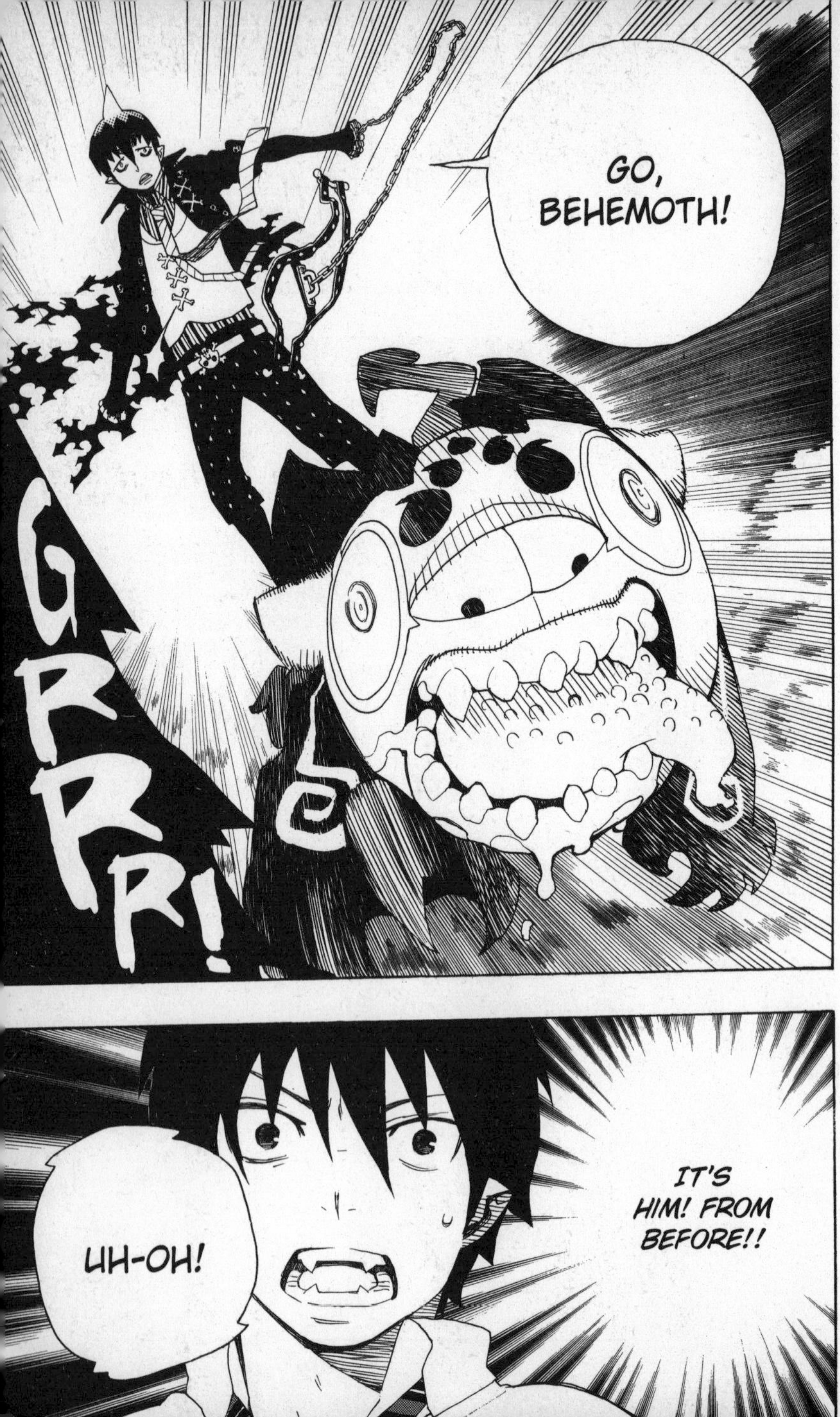
GO, BEHEMOTH!
GRRR!
IT'S HIM! FROM BEFORE!!
UH-OH!

Blue Exorcist Chapter 12 Light Trap

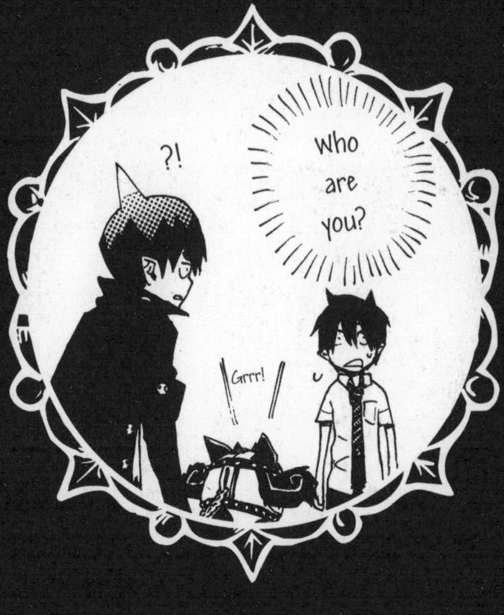
Who are you?
?!
Grrr!

Chapter 13: Something Kind

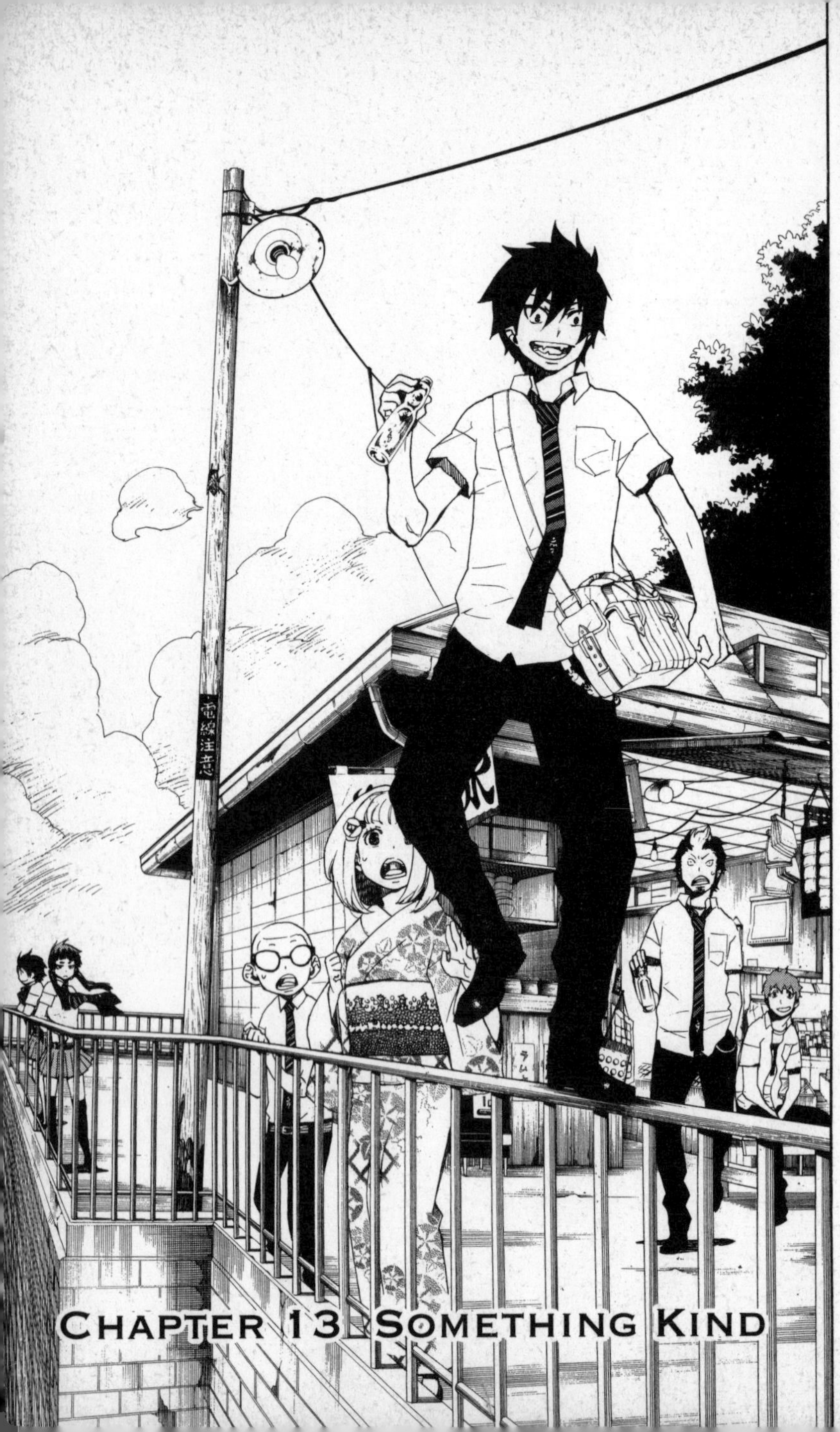
電線注意

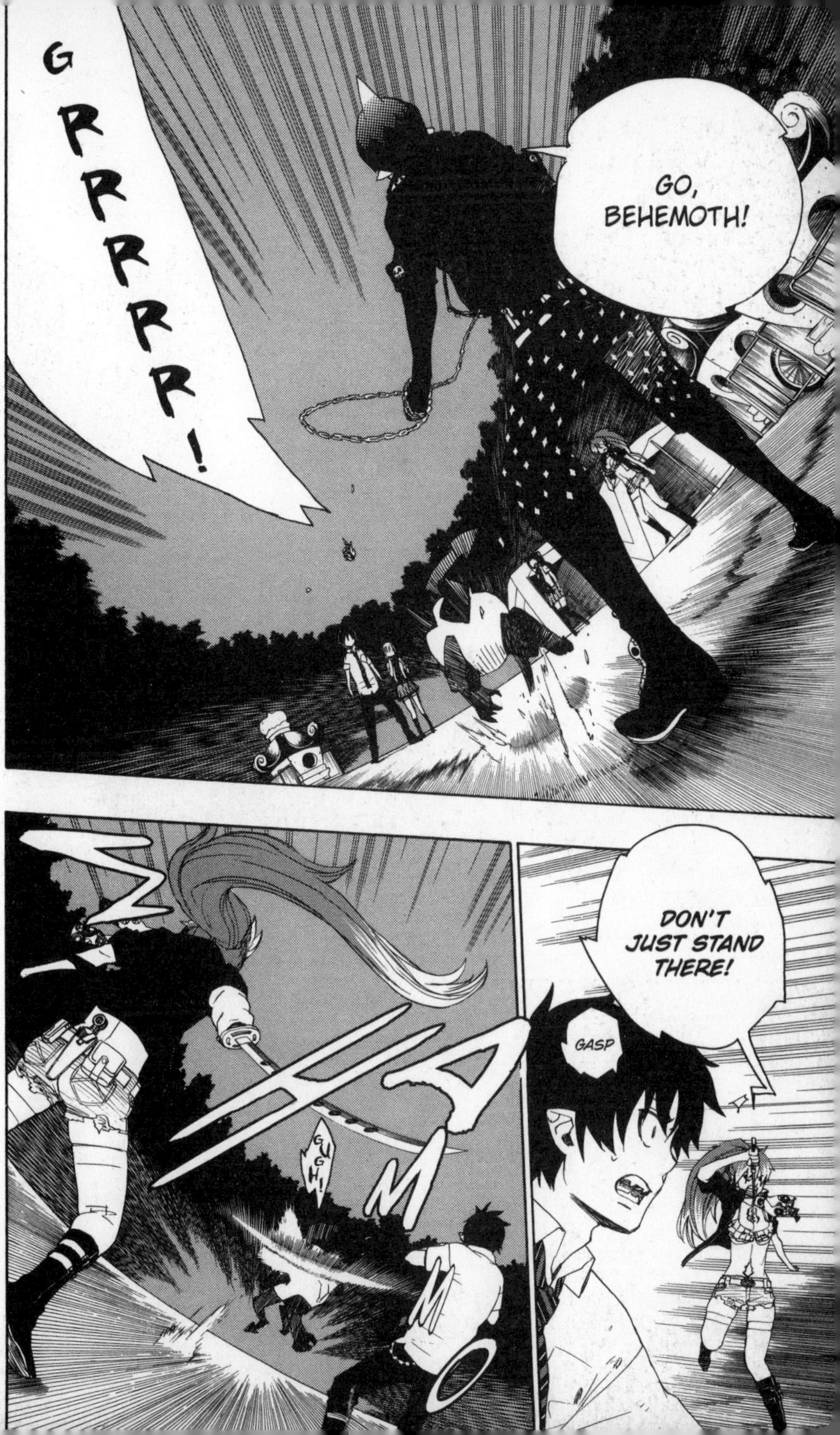
GO, BEHEMOTH!
GRRRRR!
DON'T JUST STAND THERE!
GASP
GUGH!

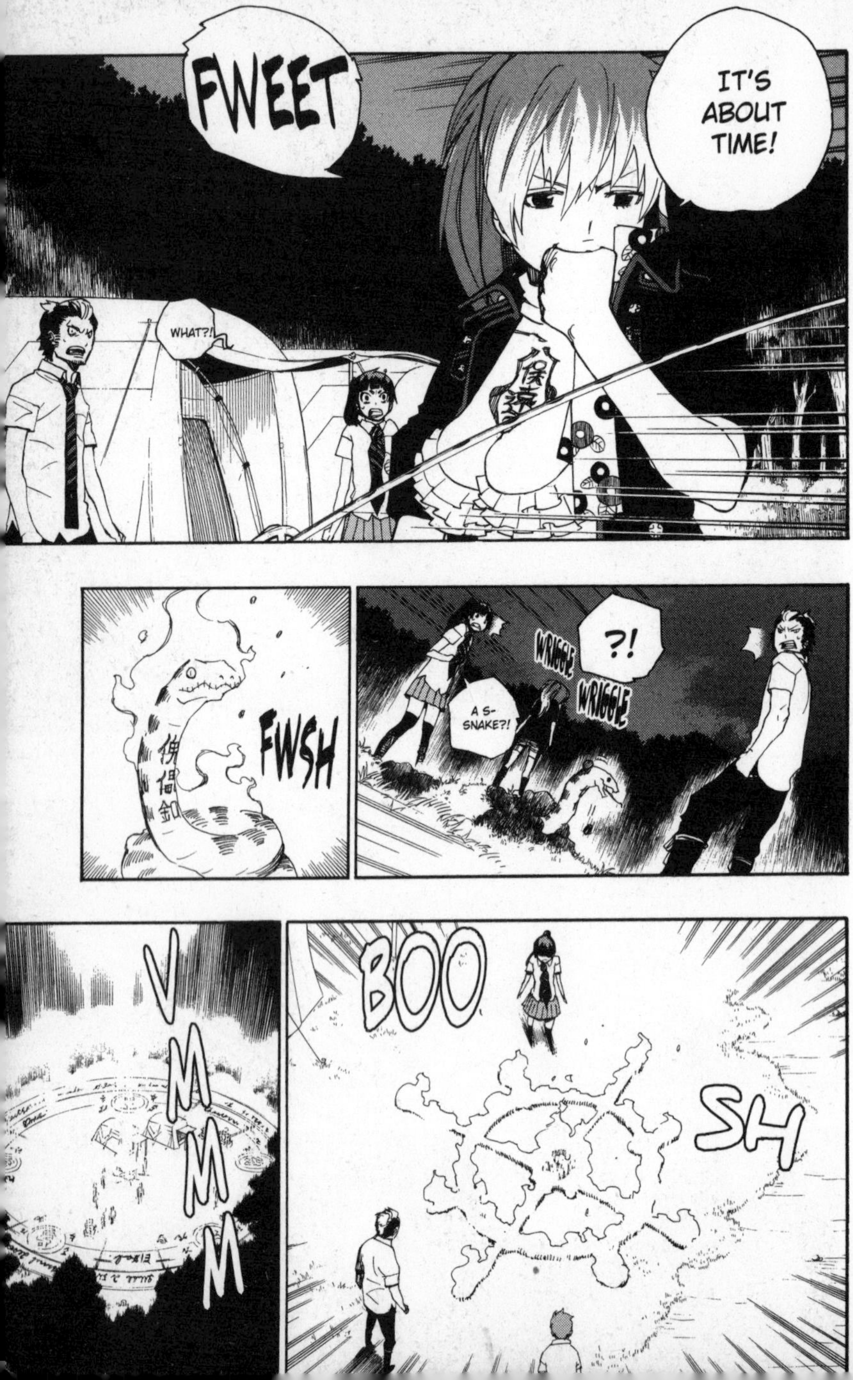
IT'S ABOUT TIME!
FWEET
WHAT?!
?!
WRIGGLE
WRIGGLE
A S-SNAKE?!
FWSH
BOO
SH
VMMMM

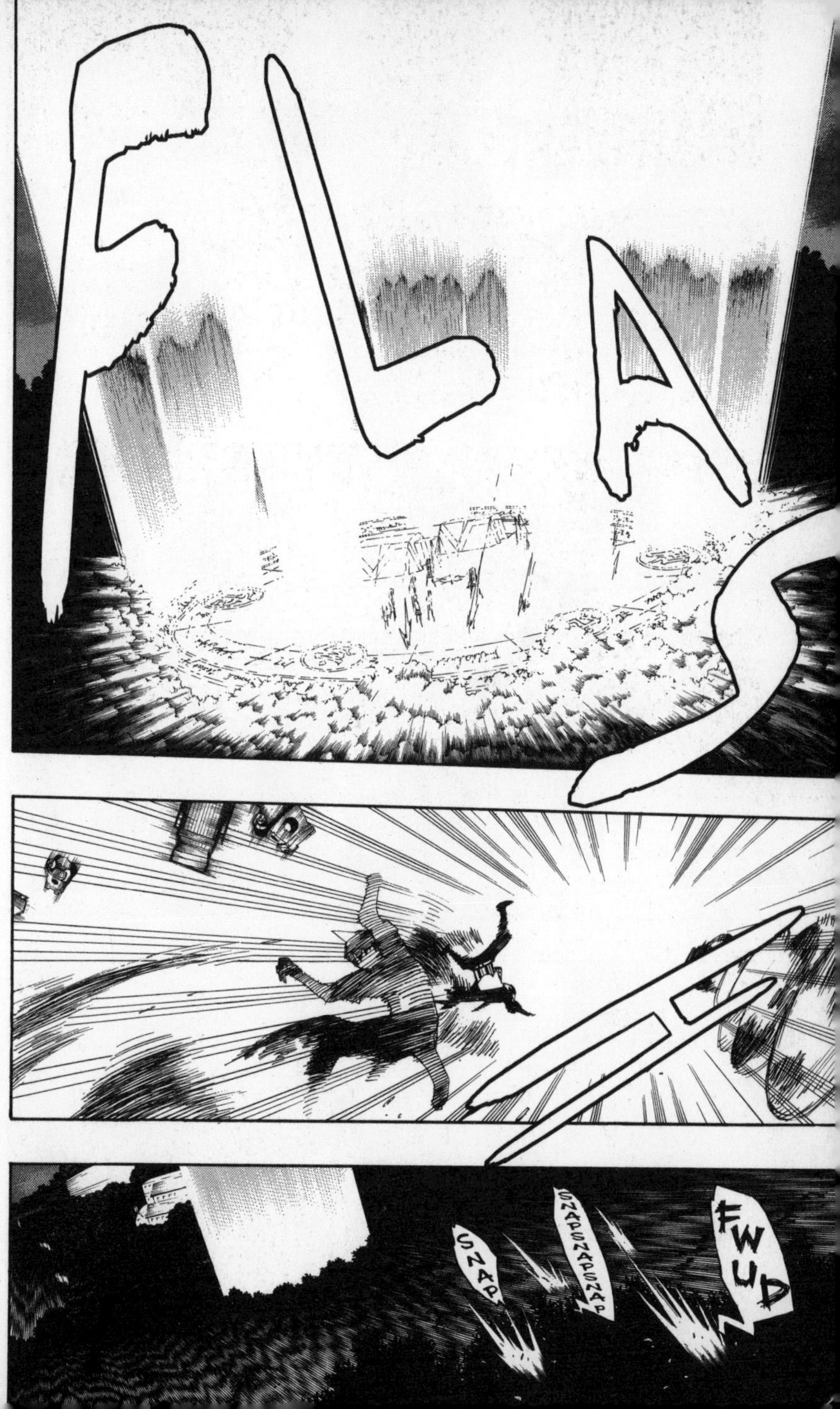
FLASH
FWUD
SNAPSNAPSNAP
SNAP

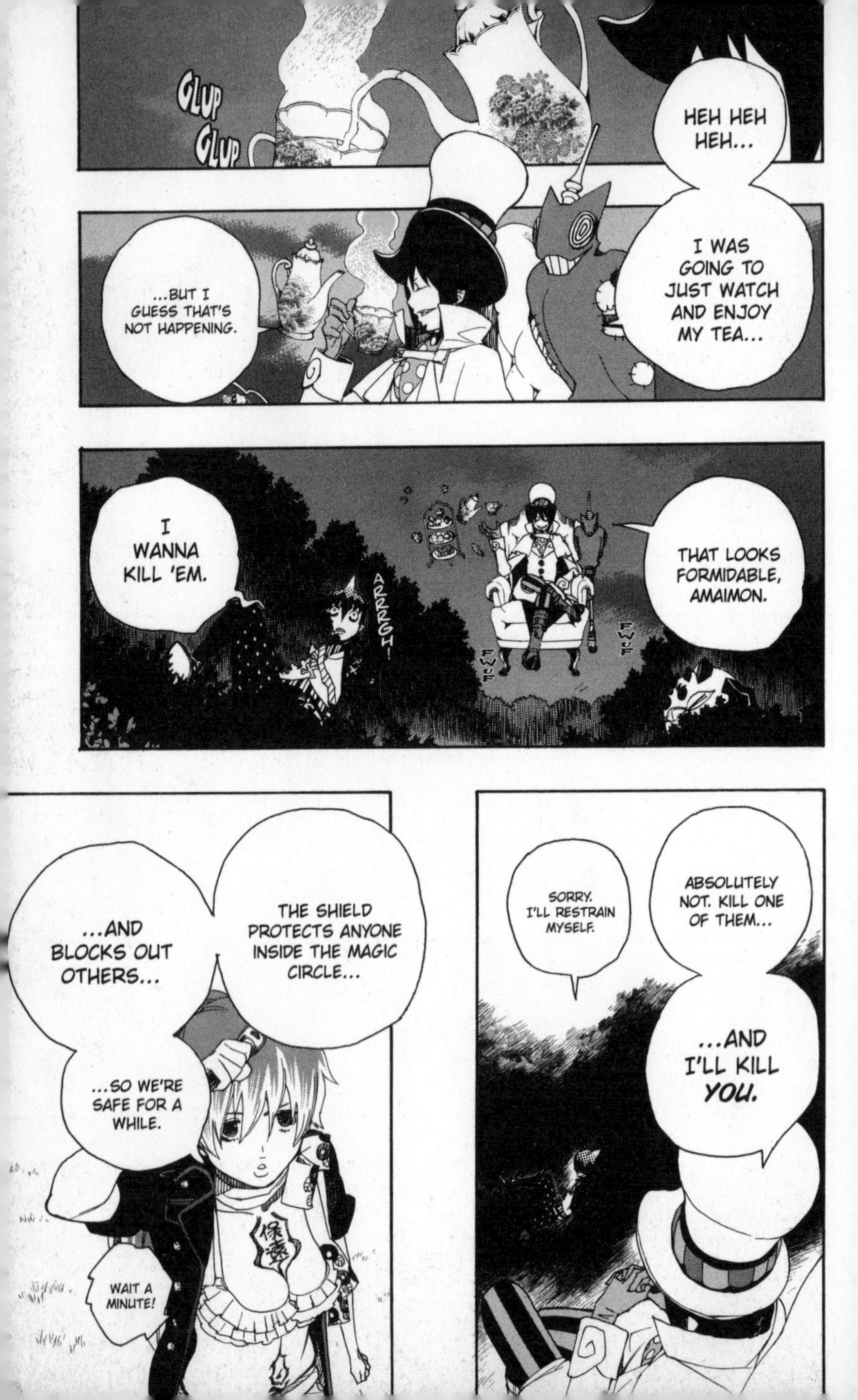
GLUP GLUP
HEH HEH HEH...
I WAS GOING TO JUST WATCH AND ENJOY MY TEA...
...BUT I GUESS THAT'S NOT HAPPENING.
THAT LOOKS FORMIDABLE, AMAIMON.
FWUF
FWUF
ARRRGH!
I WANNA KILL 'EM.
ABSOLUTELY NOT. KILL ONE OF THEM...
...AND I'LL KILL *YOU.*
SORRY. I'LL RESTRAIN MYSELF.
THE SHIELD PROTECTS ANYONE INSIDE THE MAGIC CIRCLE...
...AND BLOCKS OUT OTHERS...
...SO WE'RE SAFE FOR A WHILE.
WAIT A MINUTE!

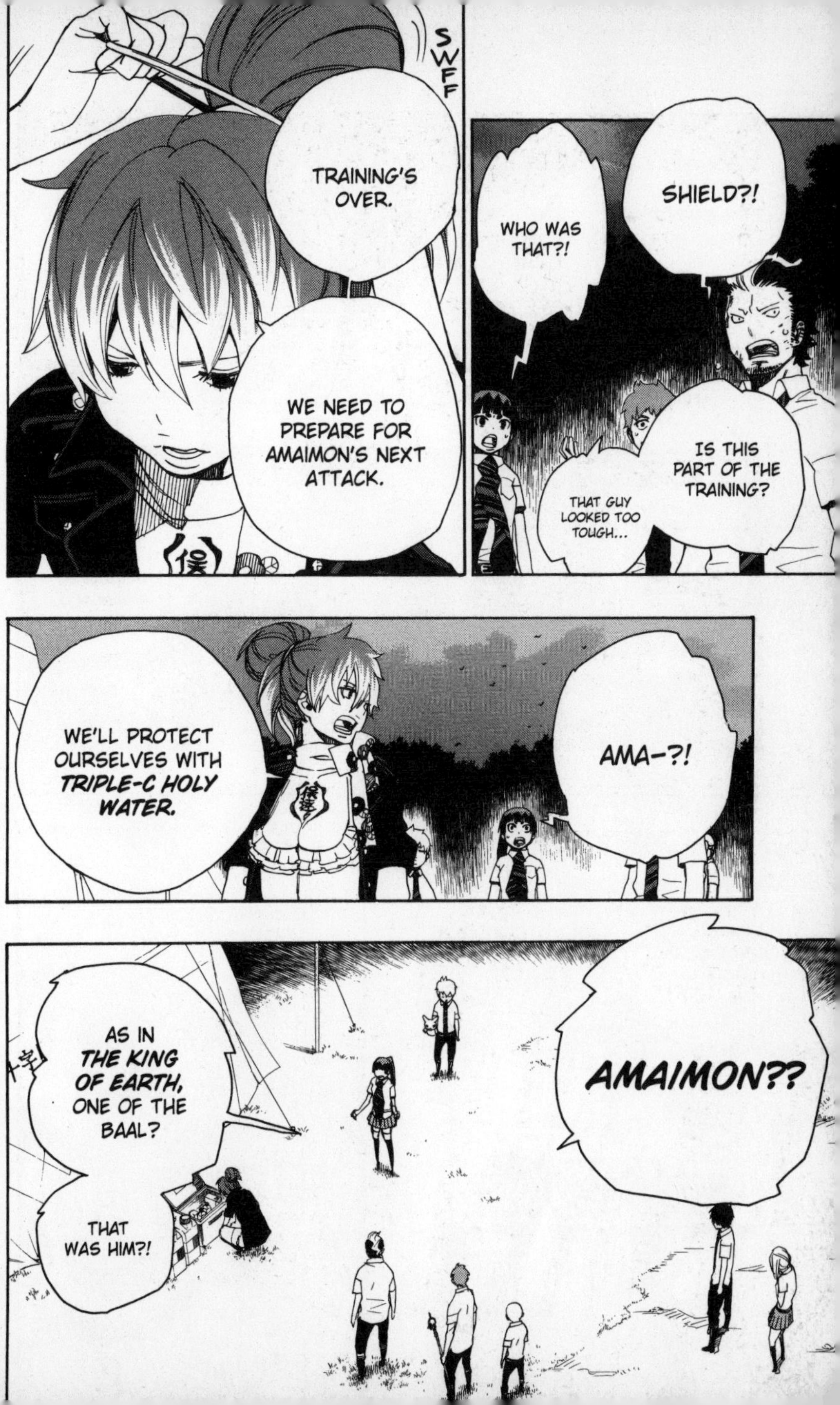
SHIELD?!
WHO WAS THAT?!
IS THIS PART OF THE TRAINING?
THAT GUY LOOKED TOO TOUGH...
SWFF
TRAINING'S OVER.
WE NEED TO PREPARE FOR AMAIMON'S NEXT ATTACK.
AMA-?!
WE'LL PROTECT OURSELVES WITH *TRIPLE-C HOLY WATER.*
AMAIMON??
AS IN *THE KING OF EARTH,* ONE OF THE BAAL?
THAT WAS HIM?!

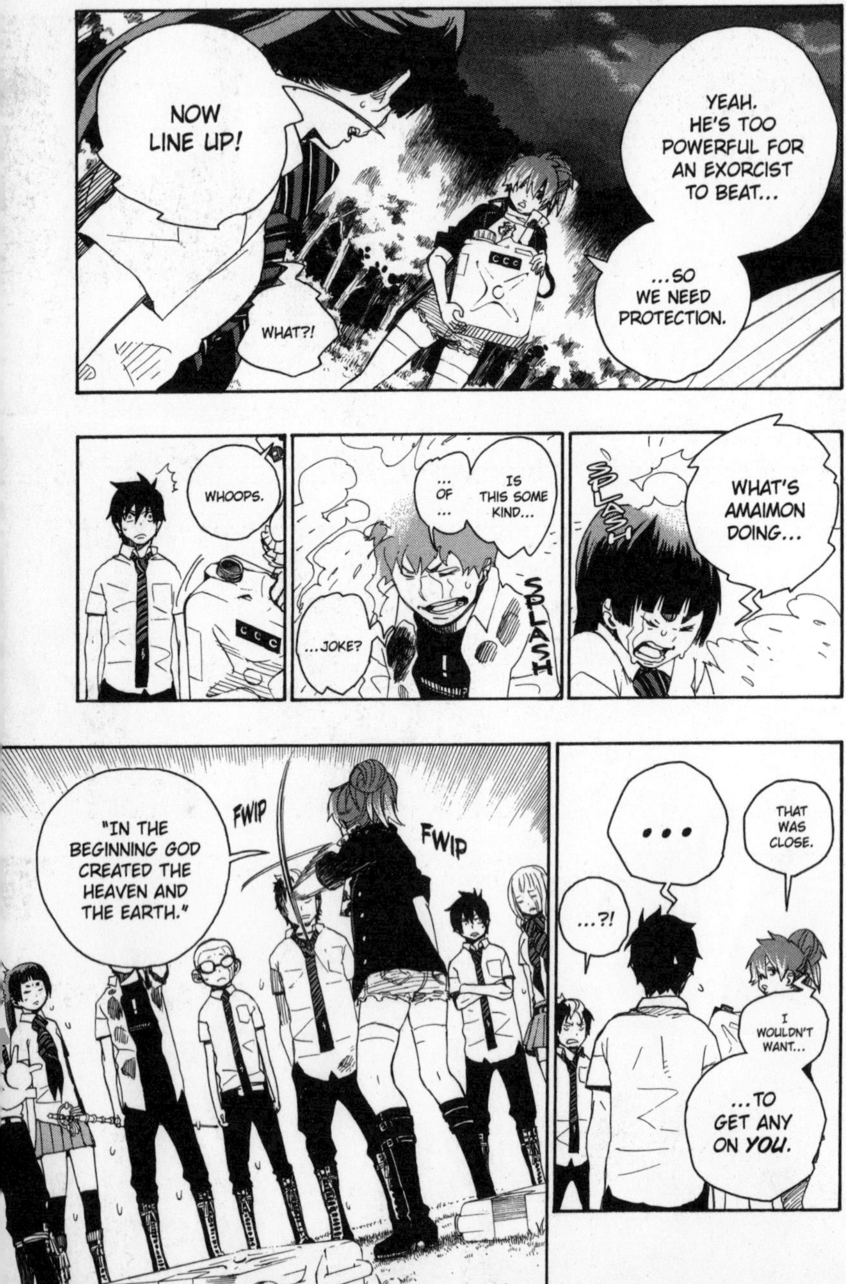
YEAH. HE'S TOO POWERFUL FOR AN EXORCIST TO BEAT...
...SO WE NEED PROTECTION.
NOW LINE UP!
WHAT?!
SPLASH
WHAT'S AMAIMON DOING...
IS THIS SOME KIND...
...OF...
SPLASH
...JOKE?
WHOOPS.
THAT WAS CLOSE.
...
...?!
I WOULDN'T WANT...
...TO GET ANY ON *YOU*.
FWIP
FWIP
"IN THE BEGINNING GOD CREATED THE HEAVEN AND THE EARTH."

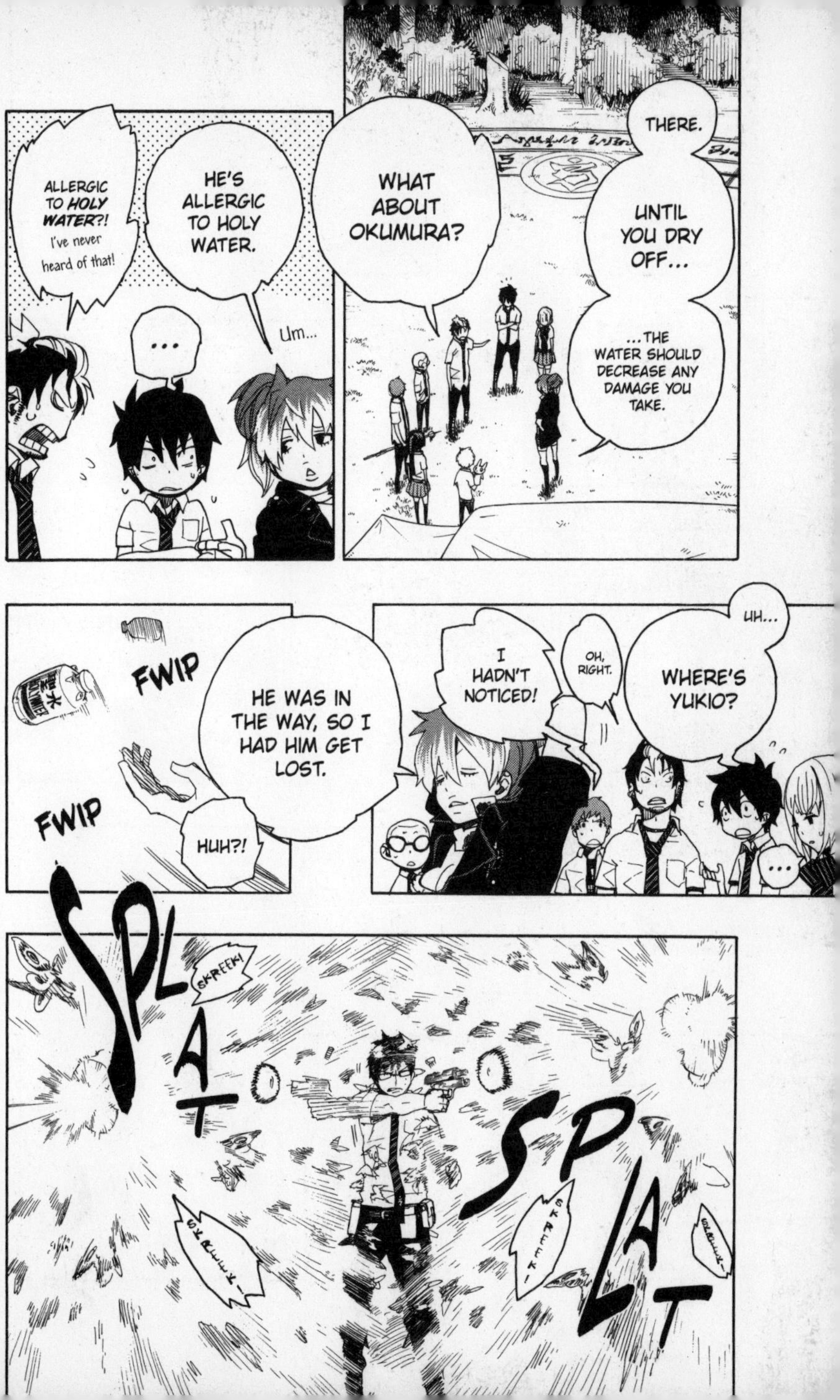

THERE.
UNTIL YOU DRY OFF...
...THE WATER SHOULD DECREASE ANY DAMAGE YOU TAKE.
WHAT ABOUT OKUMURA?
Um...
HE'S ALLERGIC TO HOLY WATER.
...
ALLERGIC TO *HOLY WATER*?! I've never heard of that!
UH...
WHERE'S YUKIO?
OH, RIGHT.
I HADN'T NOTICED!
...
HE WAS IN THE WAY, SO I HAD HIM GET LOST.
FWIP
HUH?!
FWIP
SPLAT
SKREEK!
SKRULLK!
SKREEK!
SPLAT

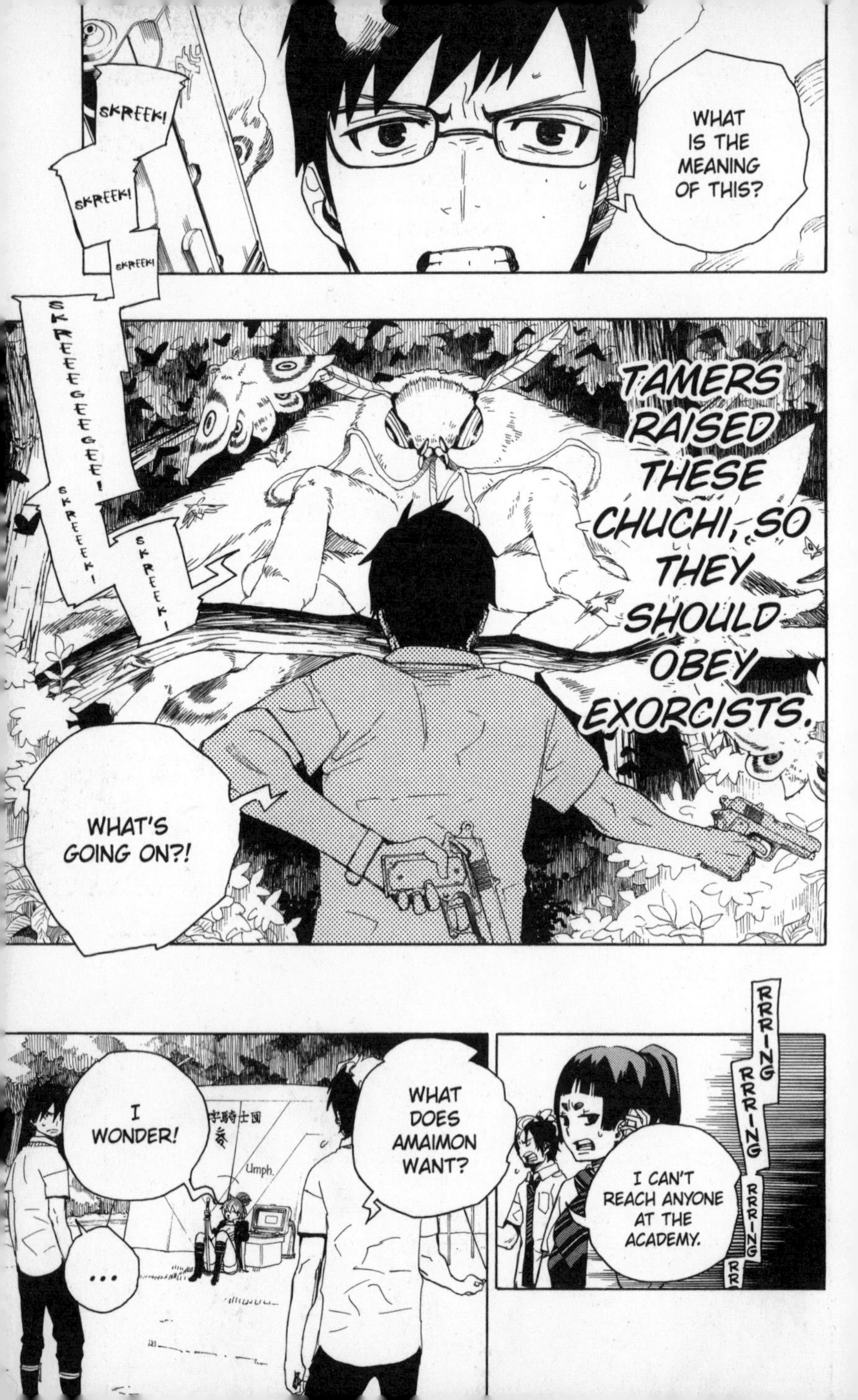
WHAT IS THE MEANING OF THIS?
SKREEK!
SKREEK!
SKREEK!
TAMERS RAISED THESE CHUCHI, SO THEY SHOULD OBEY EXORCISTS.
SKREEEGEEGEE!
SKREEEEK!
SKREEK!
WHAT'S GOING ON?!
RRRING RRRING RRRING RR
I CAN'T REACH ANYONE AT THE ACADEMY.
WHAT DOES AMAIMON WANT?
I WONDER!
Umph.
...

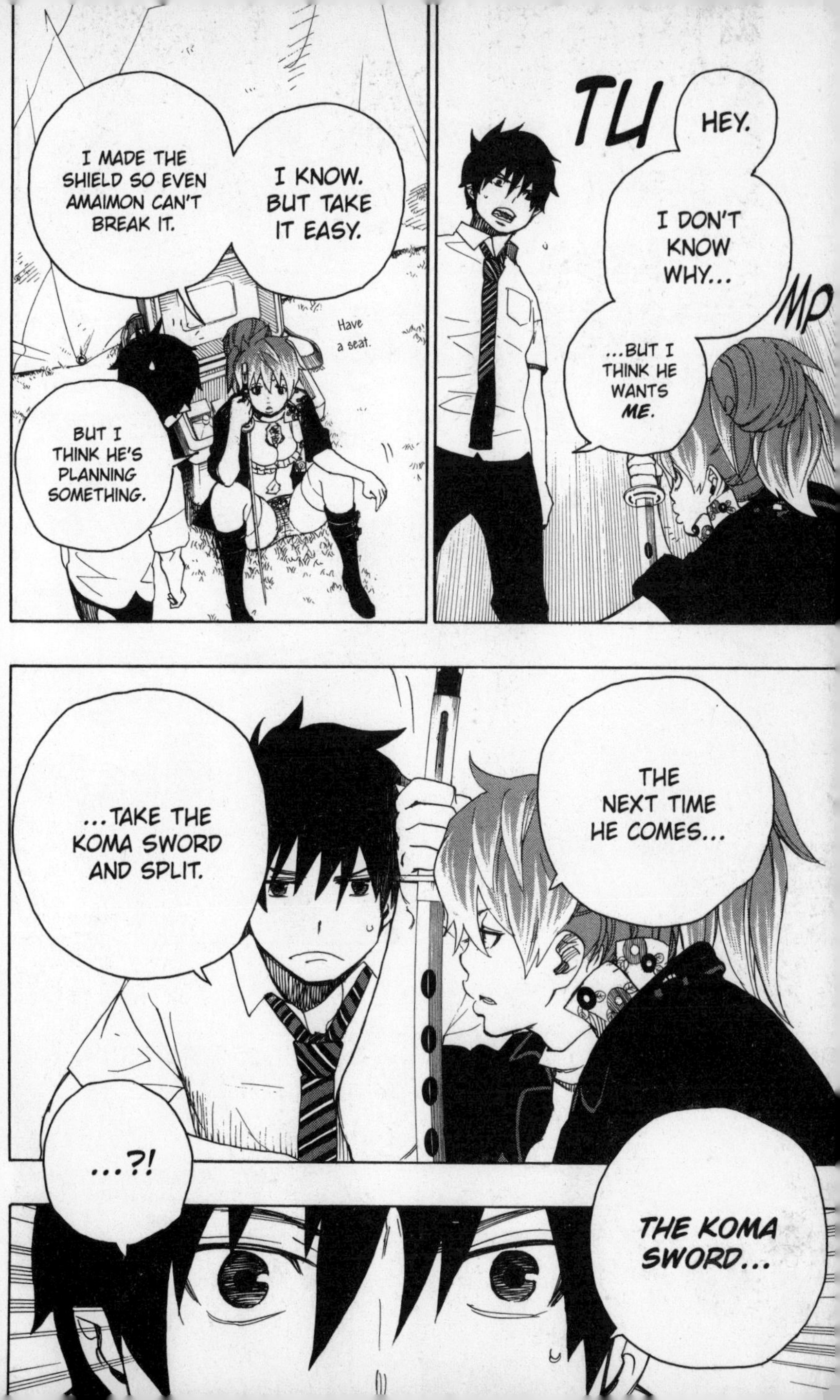
TU
MP
HEY.
I DON'T KNOW WHY...
...BUT I THINK HE WANTS *ME.*
I KNOW. BUT TAKE IT EASY.
I MADE THE SHIELD SO EVEN AMAIMON CAN'T BREAK IT.
Have a seat.
BUT I THINK HE'S PLANNING SOMETHING.
THE NEXT TIME HE COMES...
...TAKE THE KOMA SWORD AND SPLIT.
THE KOMA SWORD...
...?!

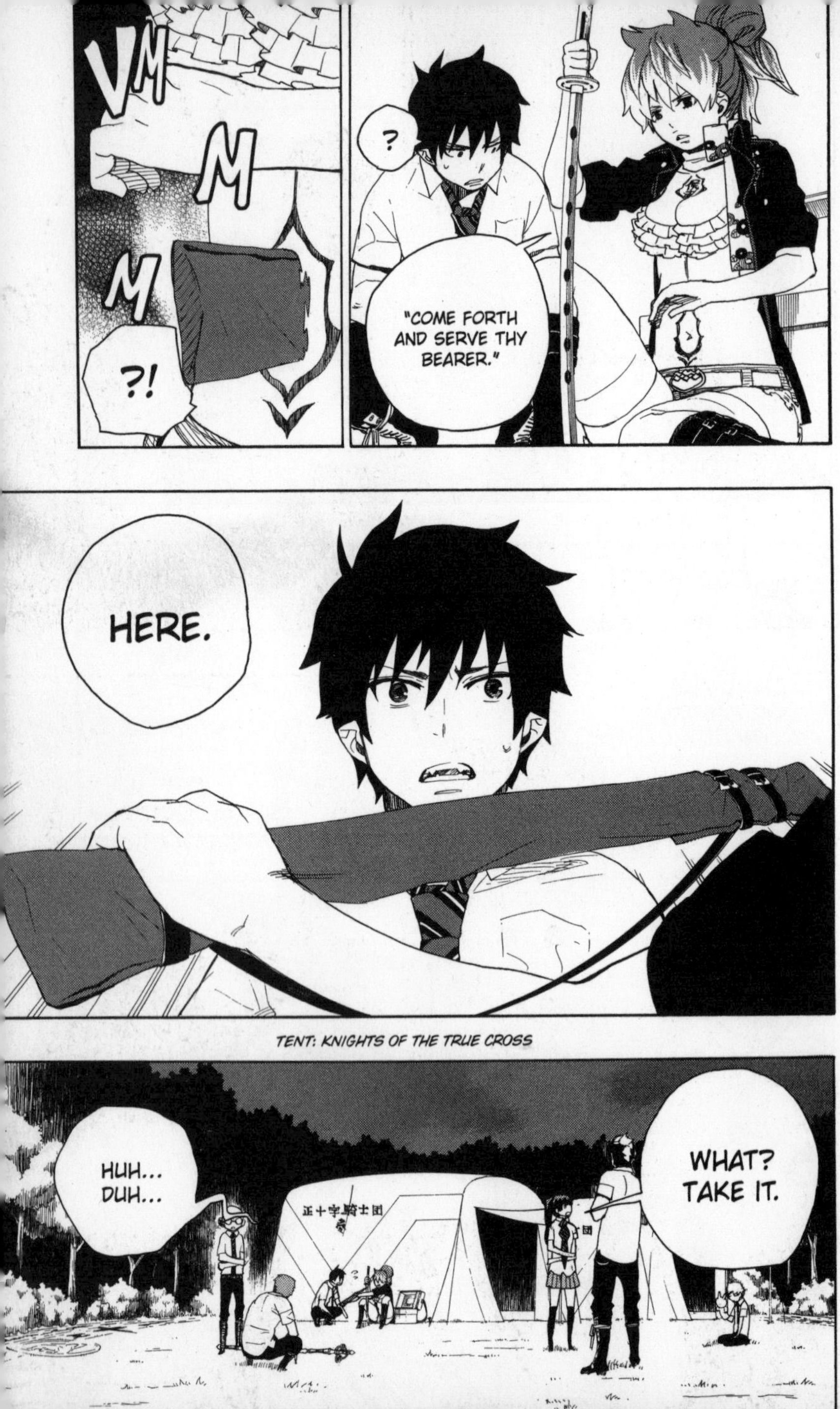
?
"COME FORTH AND SERVE THY BEARER."
VMMM
?!
HERE.
TENT: KNIGHTS OF THE TRUE CROSS
WHAT? TAKE IT.
HUH... DUH...

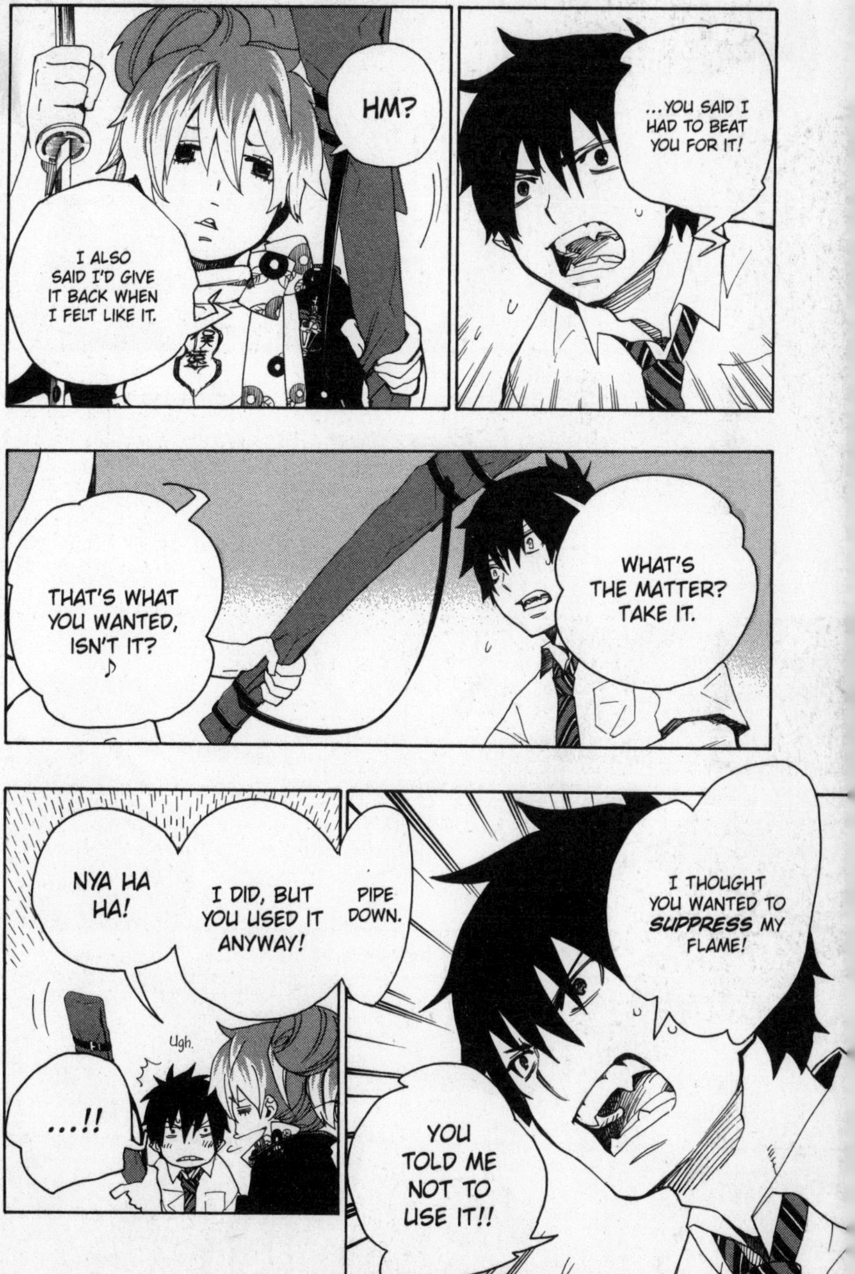
...YOU SAID I HAD TO BEAT YOU FOR IT!
HM?
I ALSO SAID I'D GIVE IT BACK WHEN I FELT LIKE IT.
WHAT'S THE MATTER? TAKE IT.
THAT'S WHAT YOU WANTED, ISN'T IT? ♪
I THOUGHT YOU WANTED TO *SUPPRESS* MY FLAME!
YOU TOLD ME NOT TO USE IT!!
PIPE DOWN.
I DID, BUT YOU USED IT ANYWAY!
NYA HA HA!
Ugh.
...!!

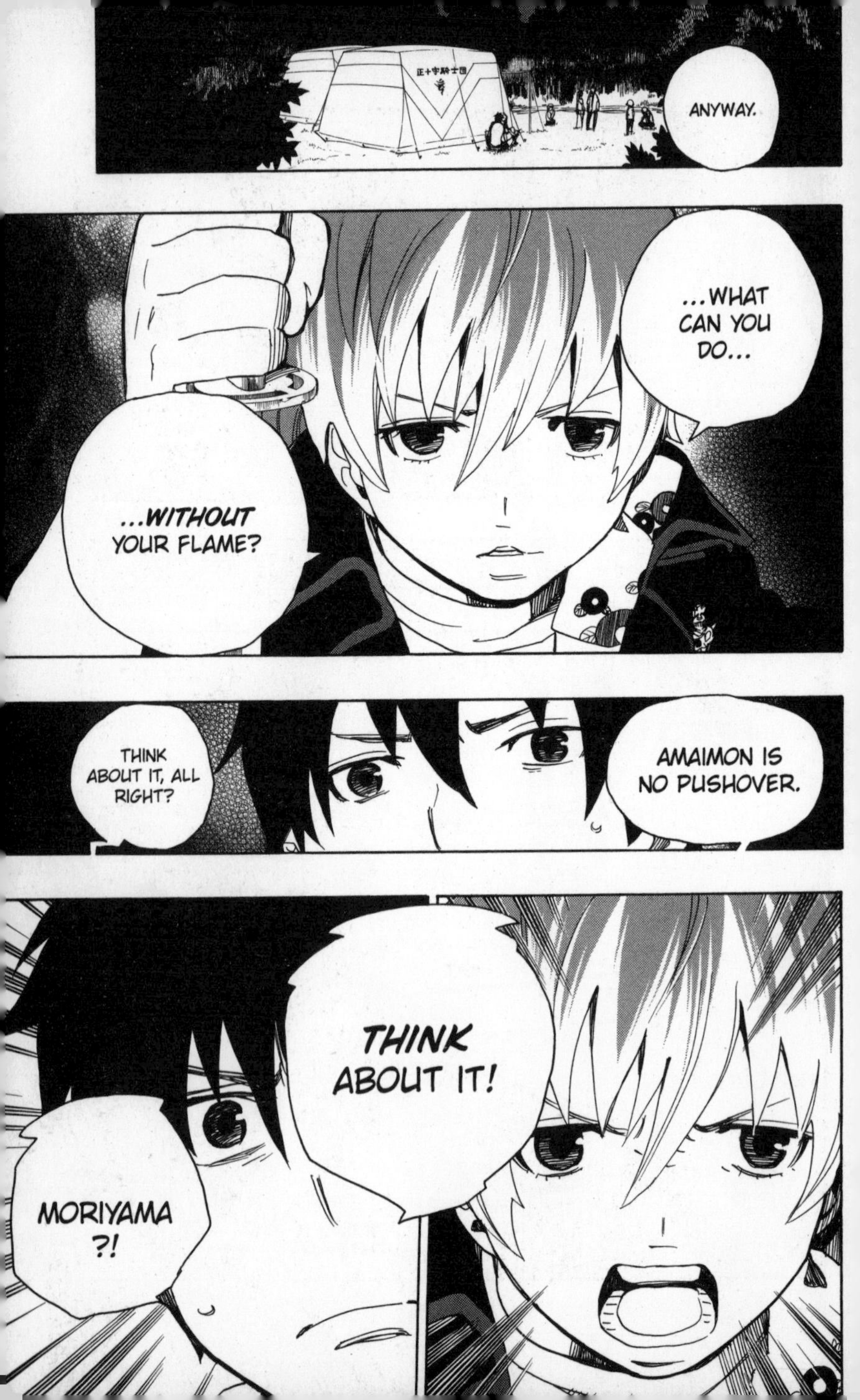
ANYWAY.
...WHAT CAN YOU DO...
...WITHOUT YOUR FLAME?
AMAIMON IS NO PUSHOVER.
THINK ABOUT IT, ALL RIGHT?
THINK ABOUT IT!
MORIYAMA?!

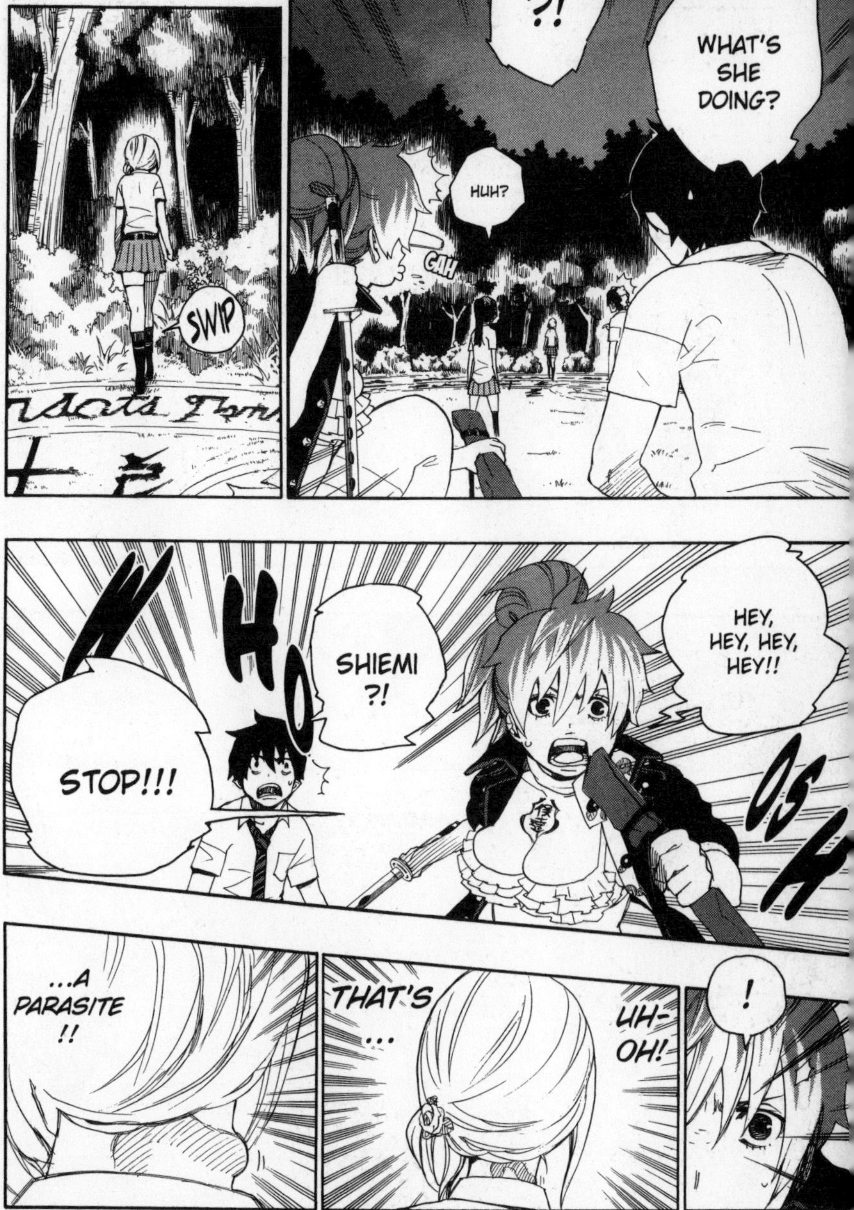
?!
WHAT'S SHE DOING?
HUH?
GAH
SWIP
HEY, HEY, HEY, HEY!!
WHOOSH
SHIEMI ?!
STOP!!!
!
UH-OH!
THAT'S ...
...A PARASITE !!

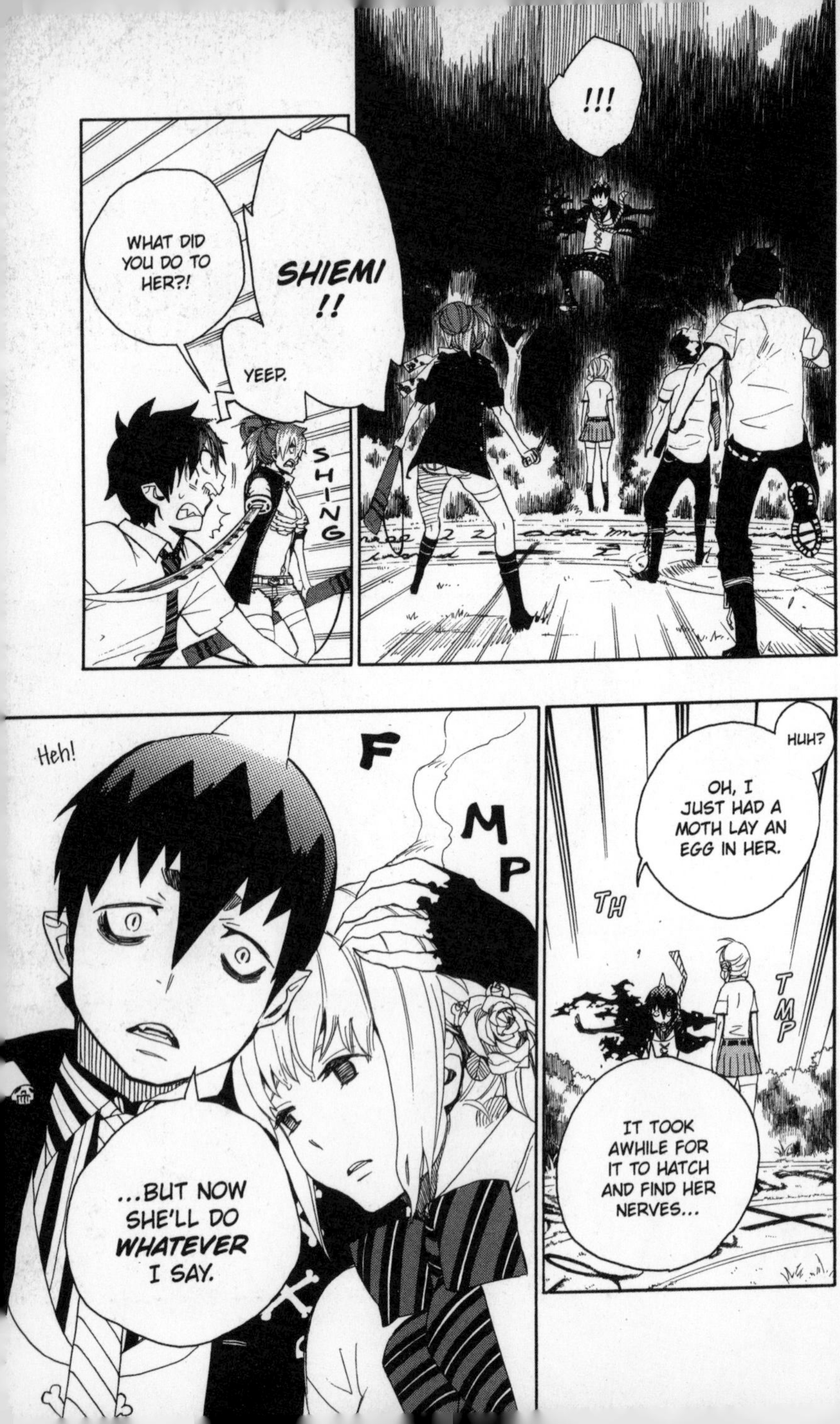
!!!
SHIEMI !!
WHAT DID YOU DO TO HER?!
YEEP.
SHING
HUH?
OH, I JUST HAD A MOTH LAY AN EGG IN HER.
TH
TMP
IT TOOK AWHILE FOR IT TO HATCH AND FIND HER NERVES...
FMP
Heh!
...BUT NOW SHE'LL DO WHATEVER I SAY.

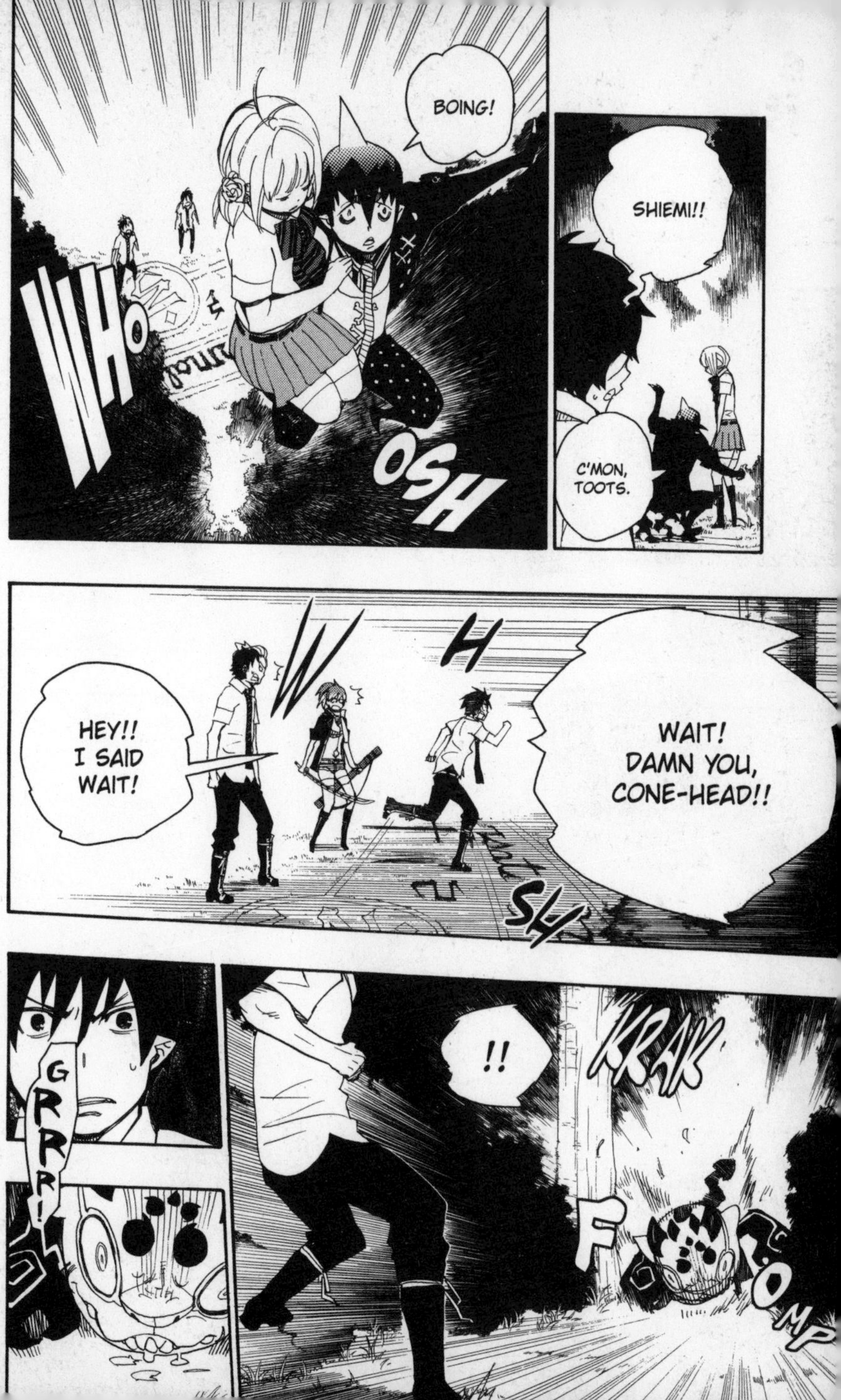
SHIEMI!!
C'MON, TOOTS.
BOING!
WHO
OSH
WAIT! DAMN YOU, CONE-HEAD!!
HEY!! I SAID WAIT!
KRAK
F
OMP
!!
GRRR!

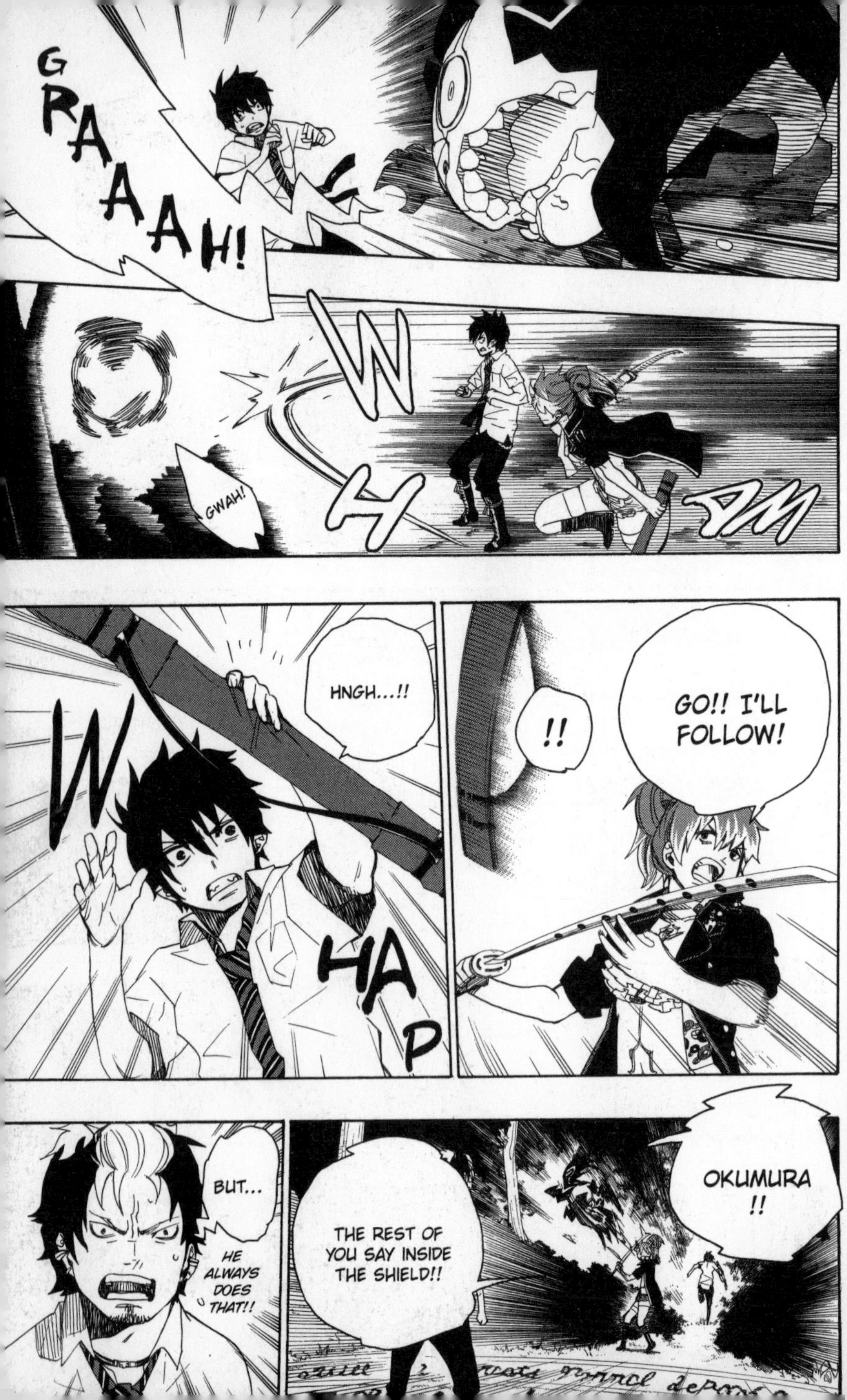
GRAAAAH!
WHAM
GWAH!
GO!! I'LL FOLLOW!
!!
HNGH...!!
WHAP
OKUMURA !!
THE REST OF YOU SAY INSIDE THE SHIELD!!
BUT...
HE ALWAYS DOES THAT!!

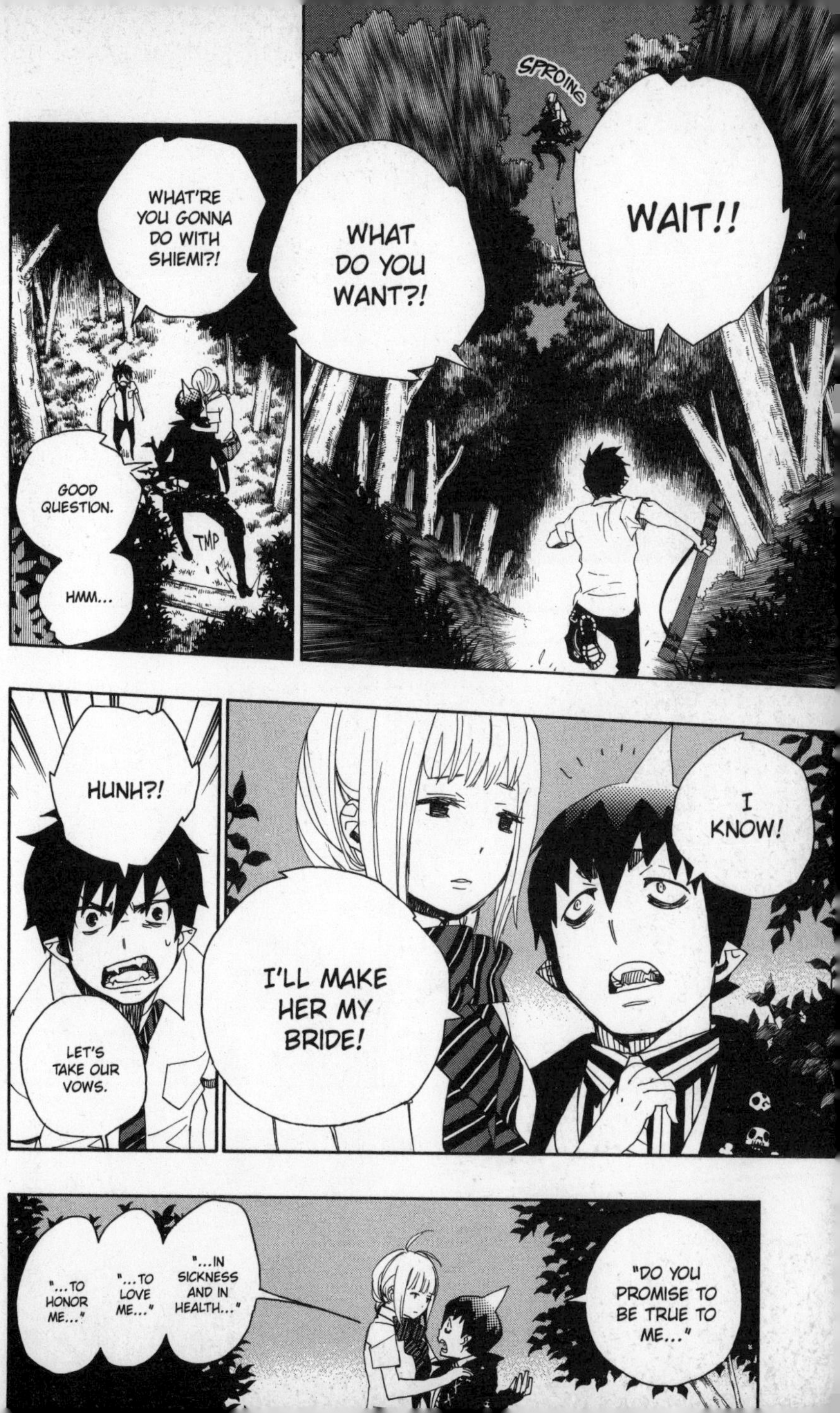
SPROING
WAIT!!
WHAT DO YOU WANT?!
WHAT'RE YOU GONNA DO WITH SHIEMI?!
GOOD QUESTION.
TMP
HMM...
I KNOW!
I'LL MAKE HER MY BRIDE!
HUNH?!
LET'S TAKE OUR VOWS.
"DO YOU PROMISE TO BE TRUE TO ME..."
"...IN SICKNESS AND IN HEALTH..."
"...TO LOVE ME..."
"...TO HONOR ME..."

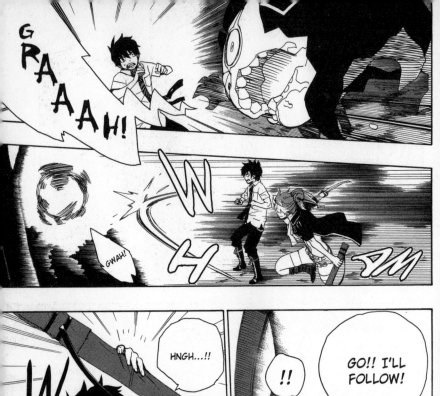

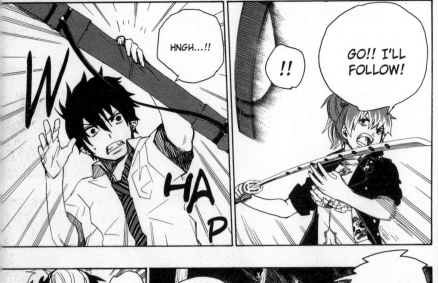

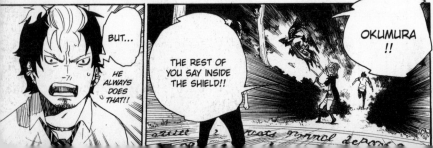

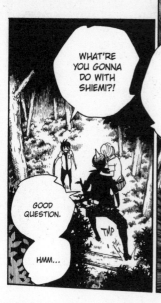

WHAT'RE YOU GONNA DO WITH SHIEMI?!

GOOD QUESTION.

HMM...

TMP

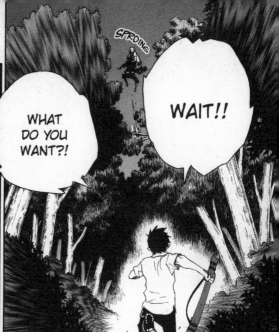

SPROING

WHAT DO YOU WANT?!

WAIT!!

HUNH?!

LET'S TAKE OUR VOWS.

I'LL MAKE HER MY BRIDE!

I KNOW!

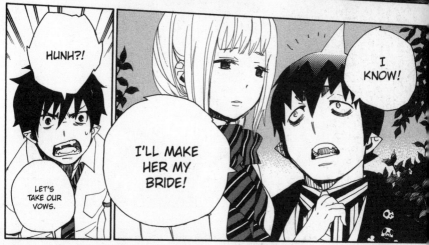

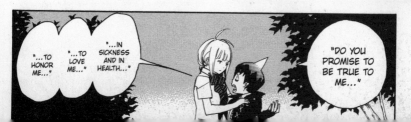

"...TO HONOR ME..."

"...TO LOVE ME..."

"...IN SICKNESS AND IN HEALTH..."

"DO YOU PROMISE TO BE TRUE TO ME..."

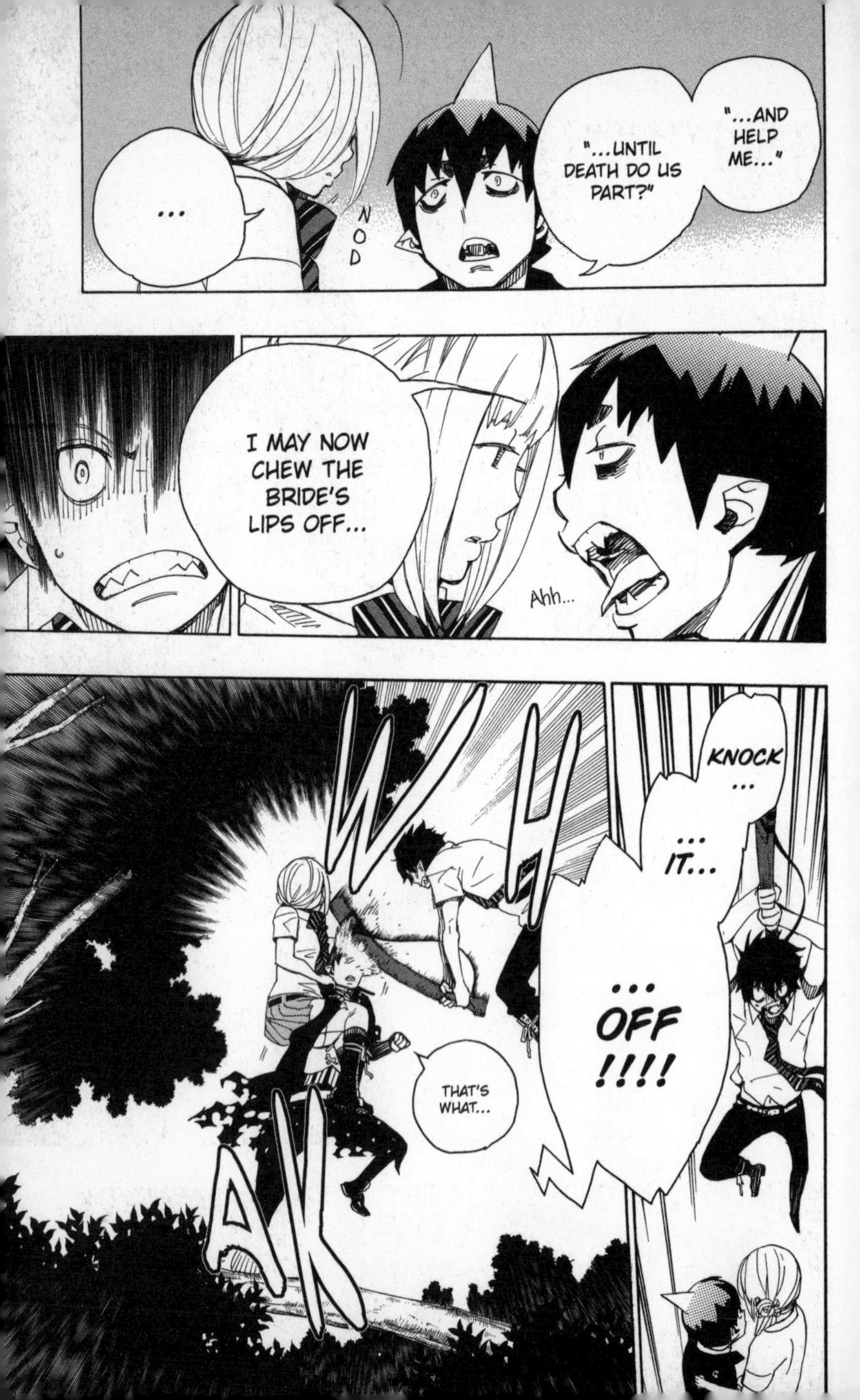
"...AND HELP ME..."
"...UNTIL DEATH DO US PART?"
NOD
...
I MAY NOW CHEW THE BRIDE'S LIPS OFF...
Ahh...
KNOCK ...
... IT...
... OFF !!!!
WHAK
THAT'S WHAT...

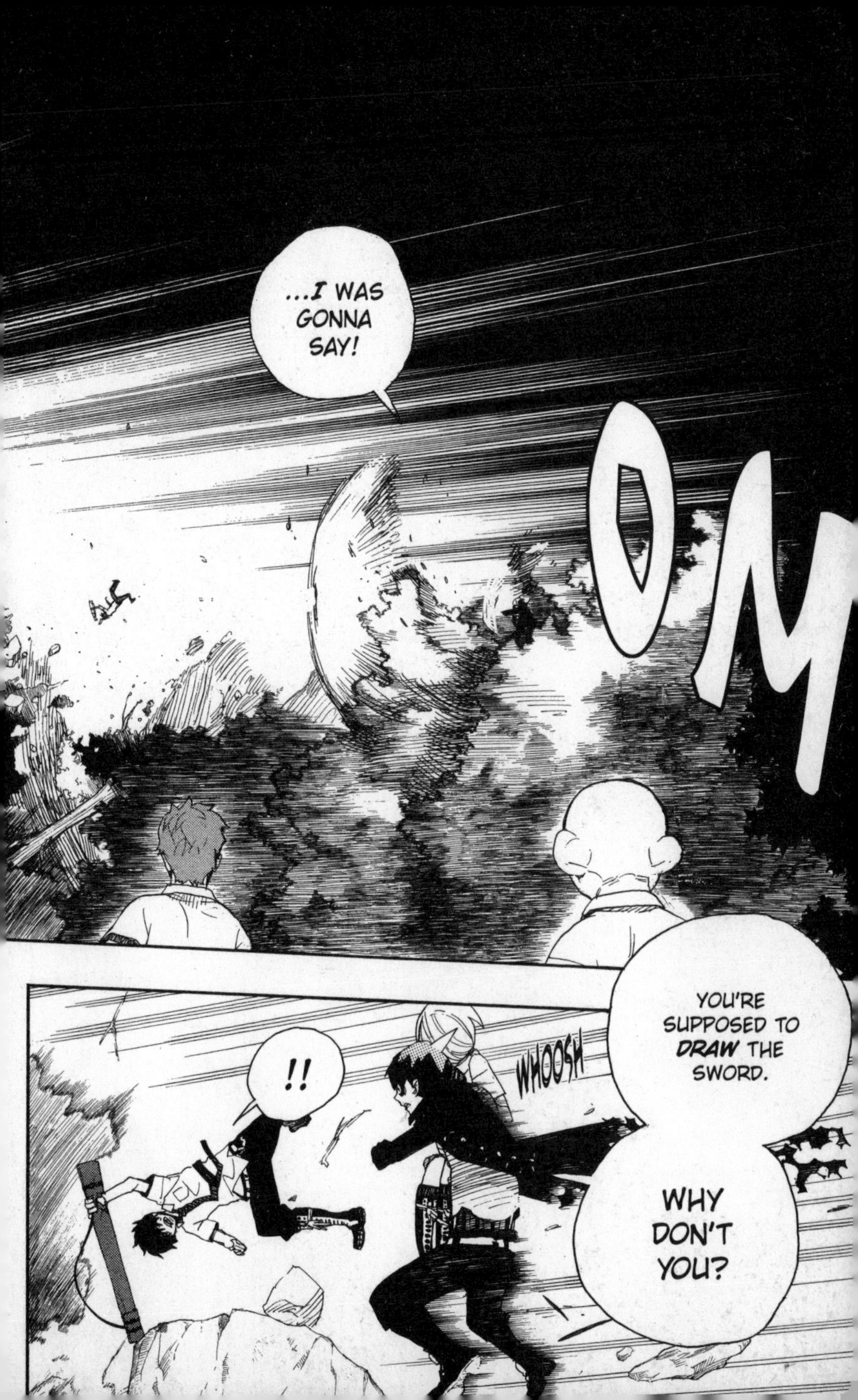
...I WAS GONNA SAY!
OM
YOU'RE SUPPOSED TO DRAW THE SWORD.
WHY DON'T YOU?
WHOOSH
!!

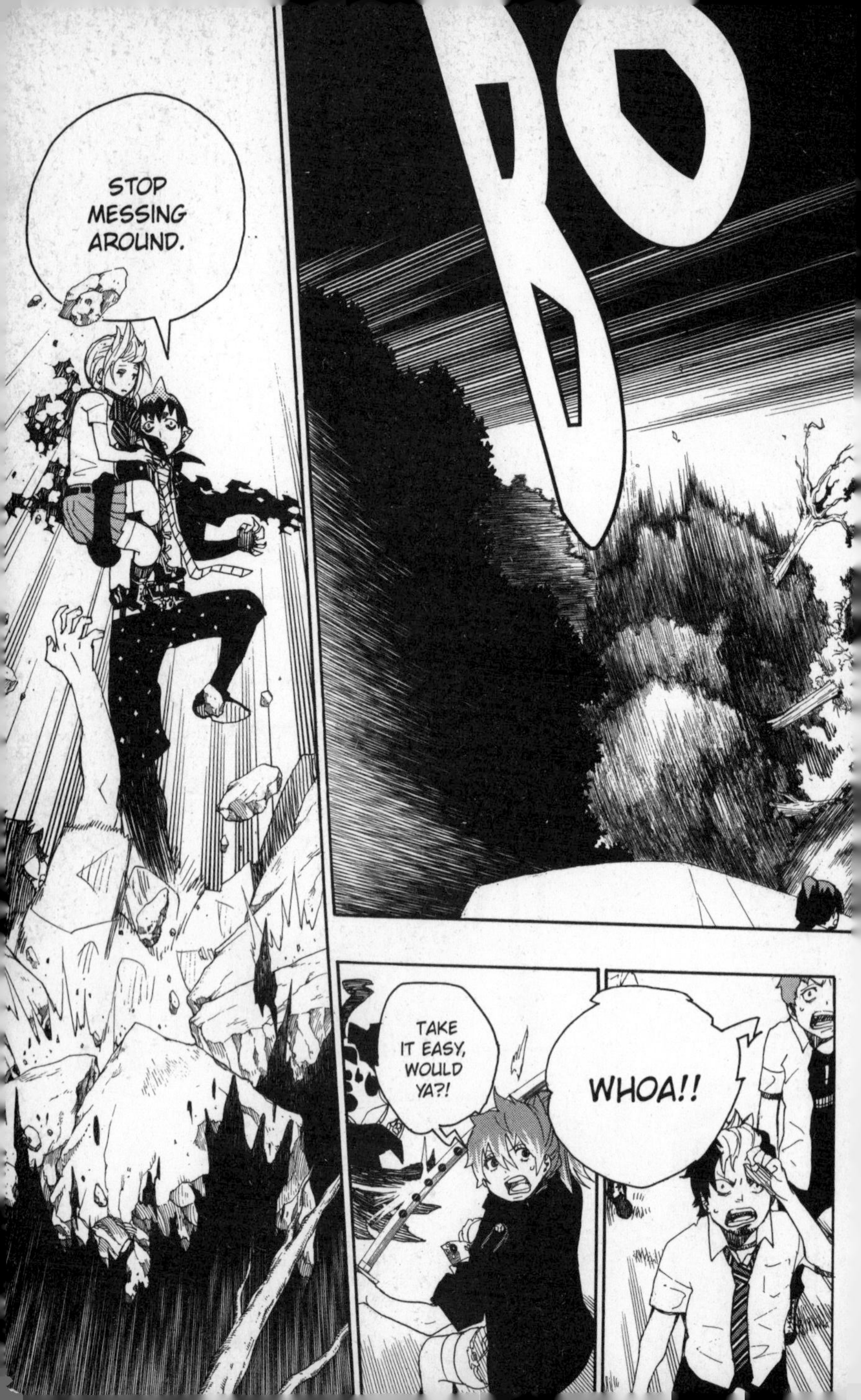
BO
WHOA!!
TAKE IT EASY, WOULD YA?!
STOP MESSING AROUND.

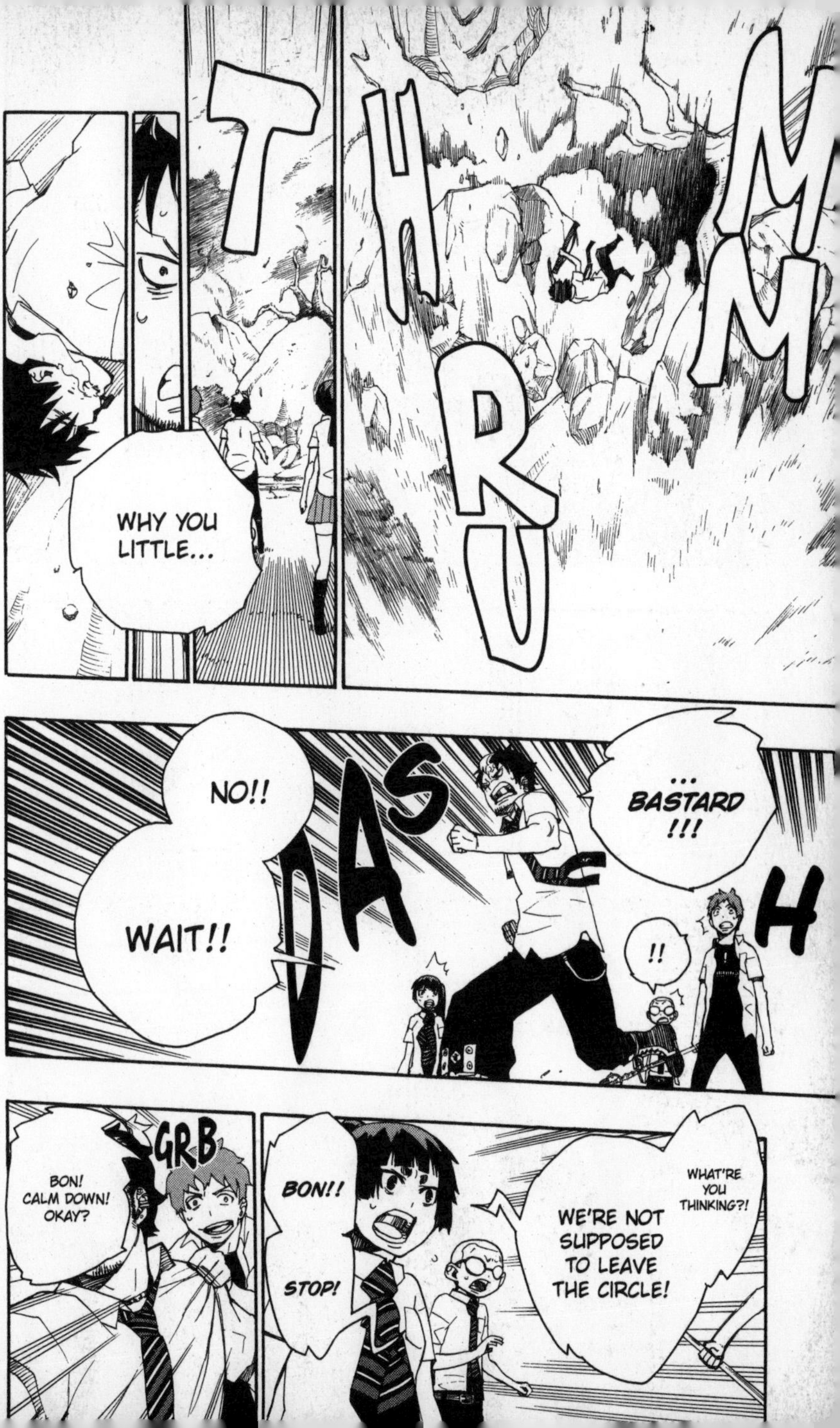
THRUMM
WHY YOU LITTLE...
...BASTARD!!!
DASH
!!
NO!!
WAIT!!
WHAT'RE YOU THINKING?!
WE'RE NOT SUPPOSED TO LEAVE THE CIRCLE!
BON!!
STOP!
GRB
BON! CALM DOWN! OKAY?

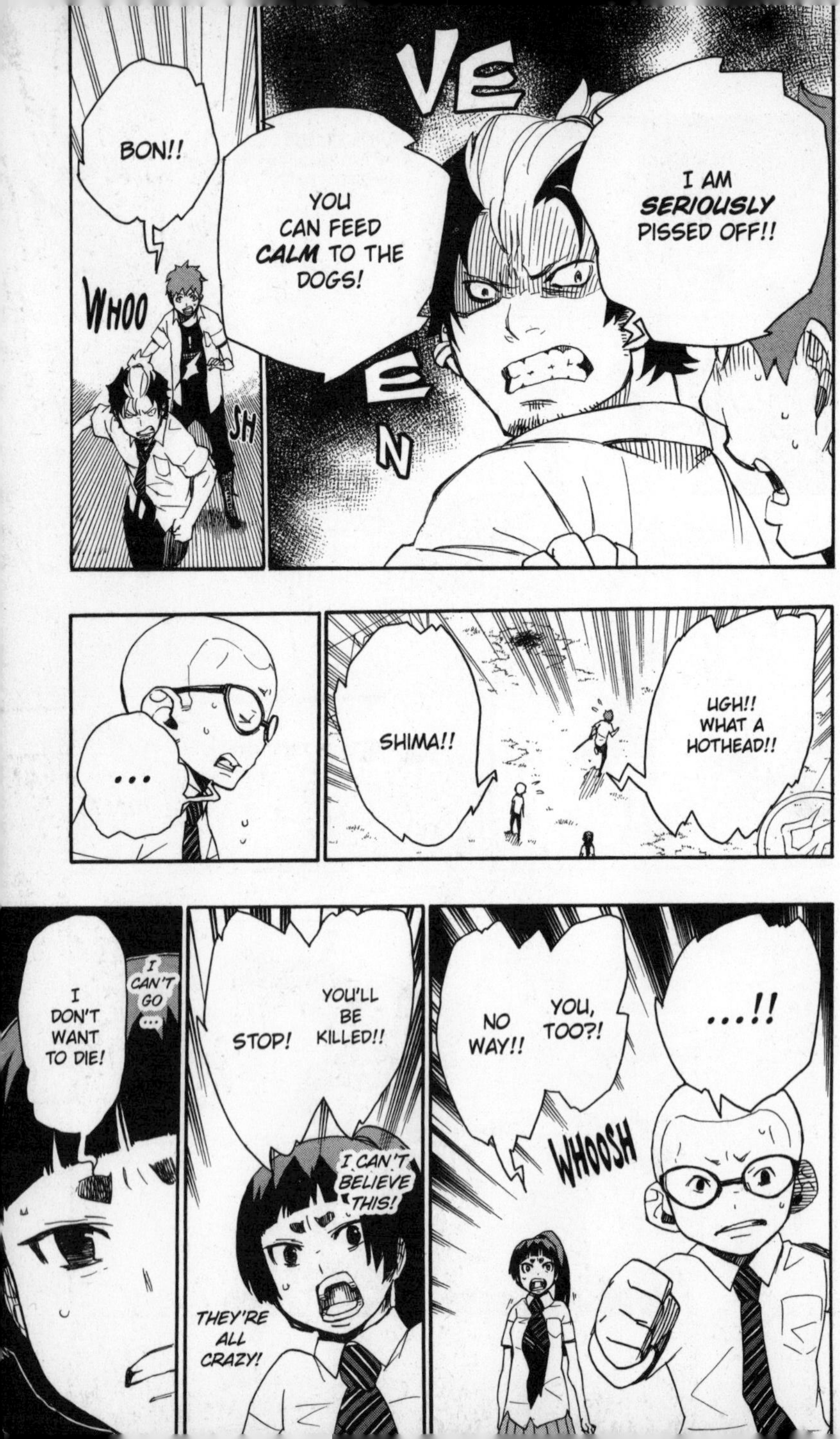
I AM SERIOUSLY PISSED OFF!!
VEEN
YOU CAN FEED CALM TO THE DOGS!
BON!!
WHOOSH
UGH!! WHAT A HOTHEAD!!
SHIMA!!
...
...!!
YOU, TOO?!
NO WAY!!
WHOOSH
YOU'LL BE KILLED!!
STOP!
I CAN'T BELIEVE THIS!
THEY'RE ALL CRAZY!
I CAN'T GO...
I DON'T WANT TO DIE!

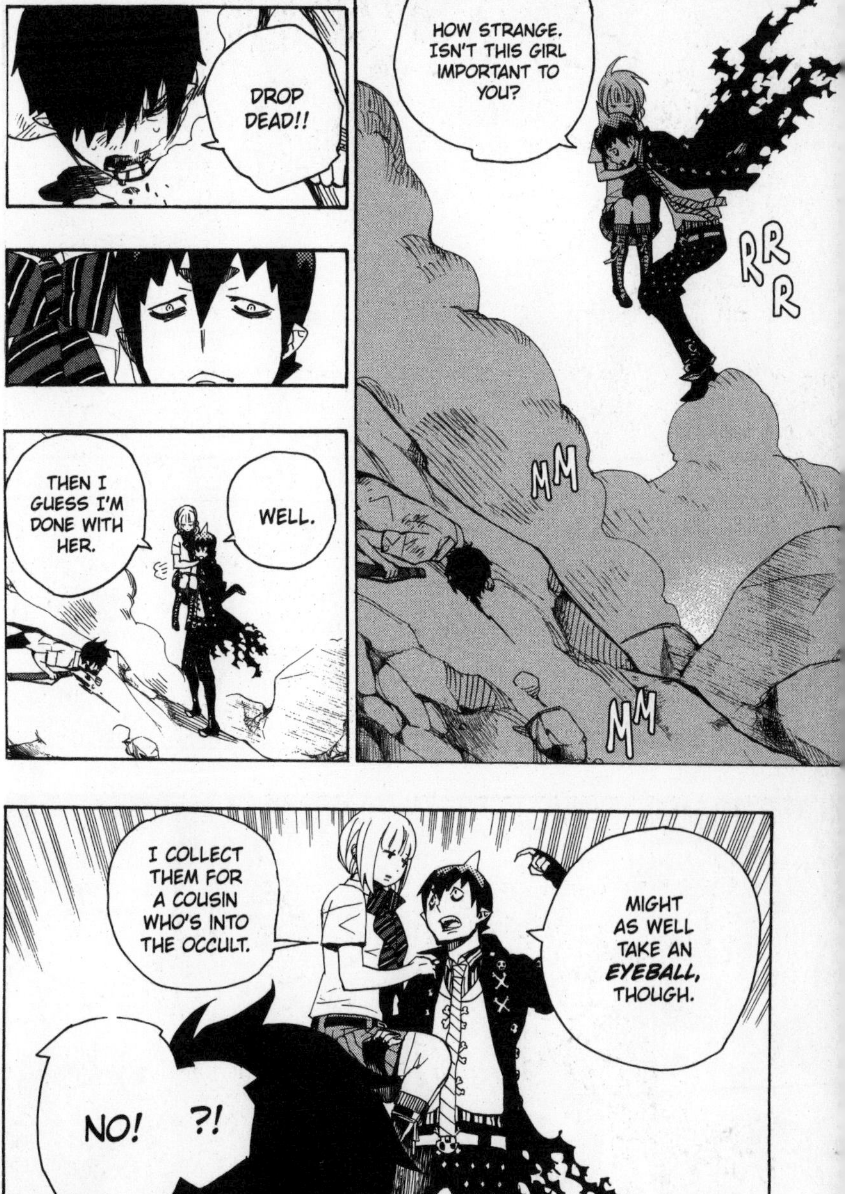
HOW STRANGE. ISN'T THIS GIRL IMPORTANT TO YOU?
RRR
MM
MM
DROP DEAD!!
WELL.
THEN I GUESS I'M DONE WITH HER.
MIGHT AS WELL TAKE AN *EYEBALL,* THOUGH.
I COLLECT THEM FOR A COUSIN WHO'S INTO THE OCCULT.
?!
NO!

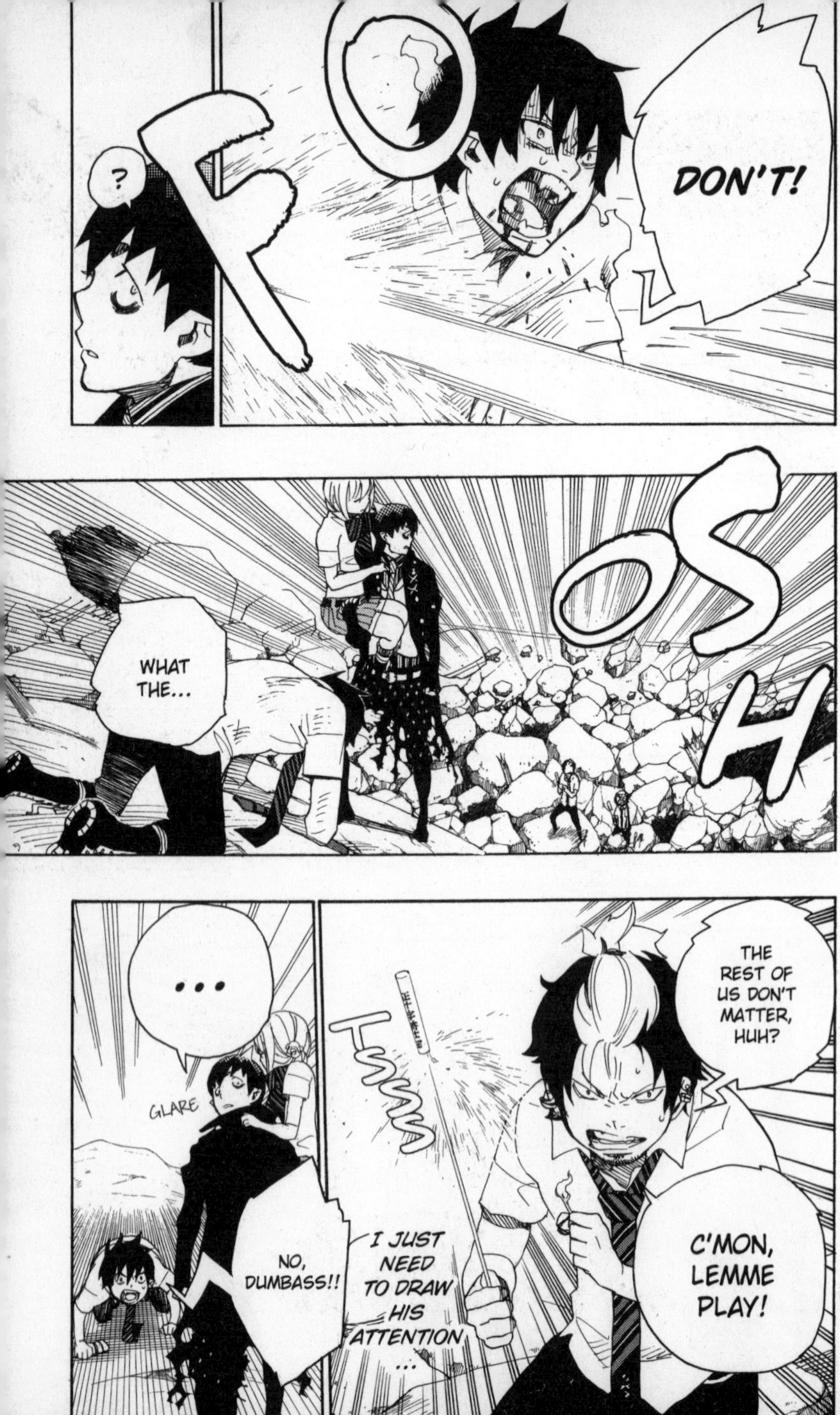
DON'T!
?
WHAT THE...
THE REST OF US DON'T MATTER, HUH?
C'MON, LEMME PLAY!
TSSS
I JUST NEED TO DRAW HIS ATTENTION...
...
GLARE
NO, DUMBASS!!

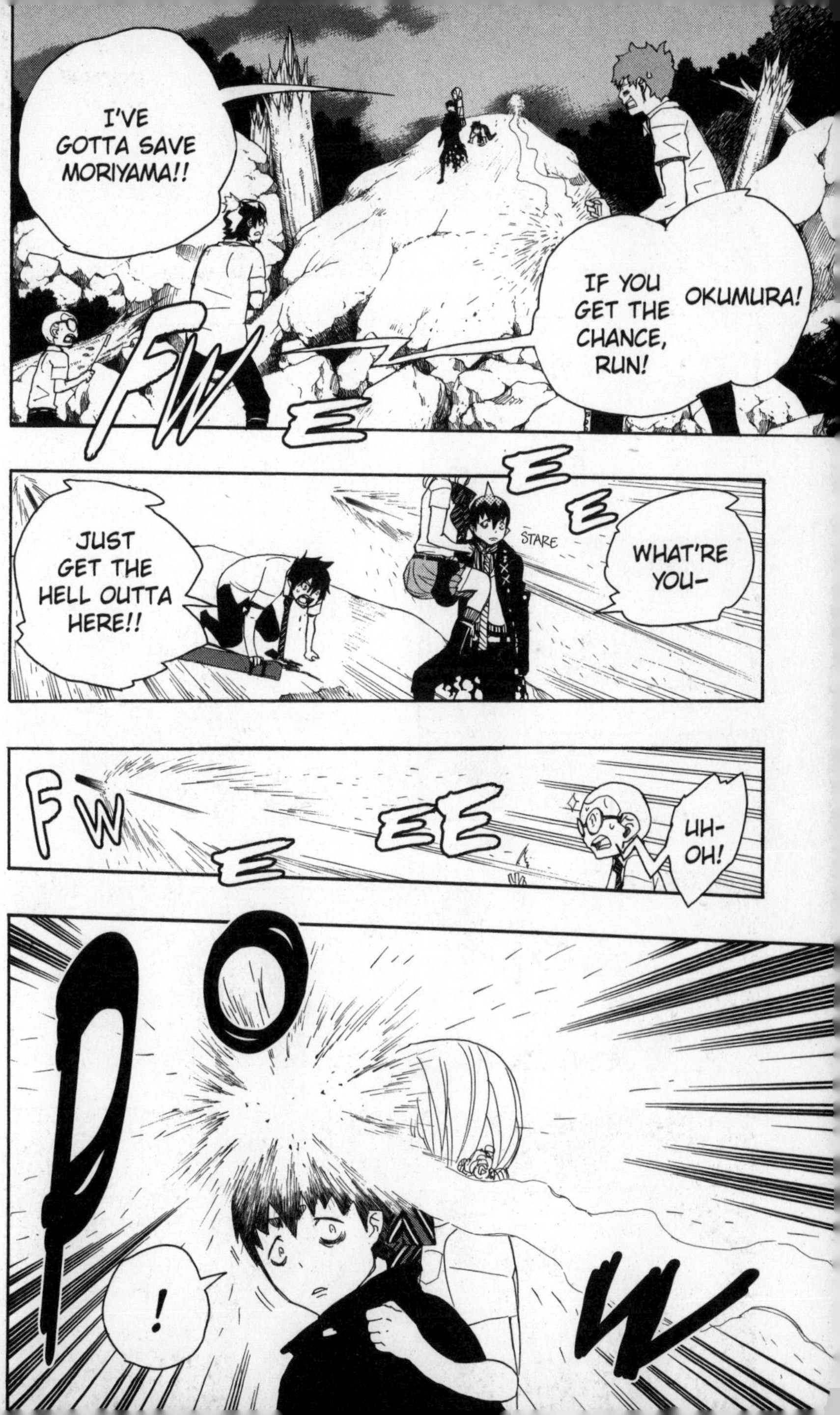
OKUMURA!
IF YOU GET THE CHANCE, RUN!
I'VE GOTTA SAVE MORIYAMA!!
FWE
EE
STARE
WHAT'RE YOU-
JUST GET THE HELL OUTTA HERE!!
UH-OH!
FWEEE
POW
!

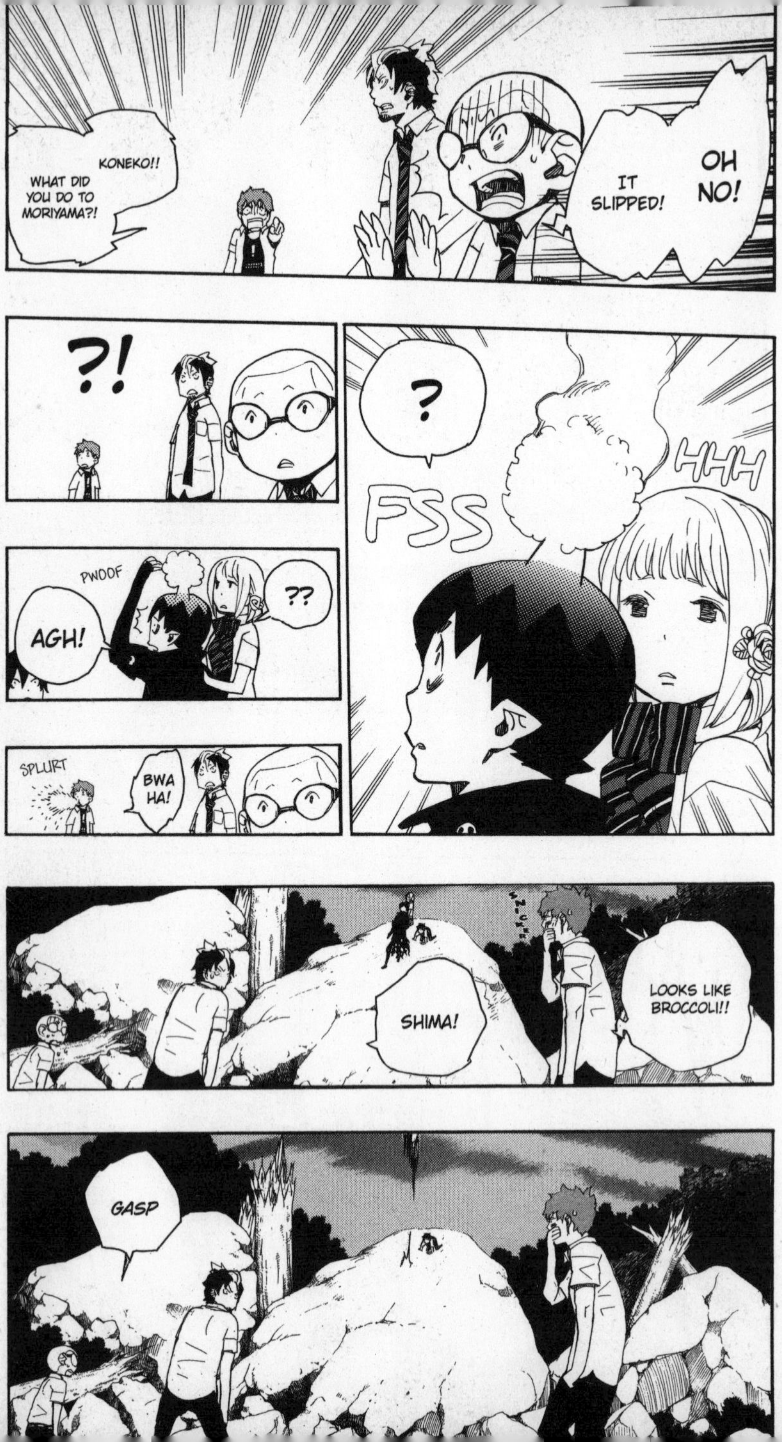
OH NO!
IT SLIPPED!
KONEKO!!
WHAT DID YOU DO TO MORIYAMA?!
HHH
?
FSS
?!
??
PWOOF
AGH!
BWA HA!
SPLURT
LOOKS LIKE BROCCOLI!!
SNICKER
SHIMA!
GASP

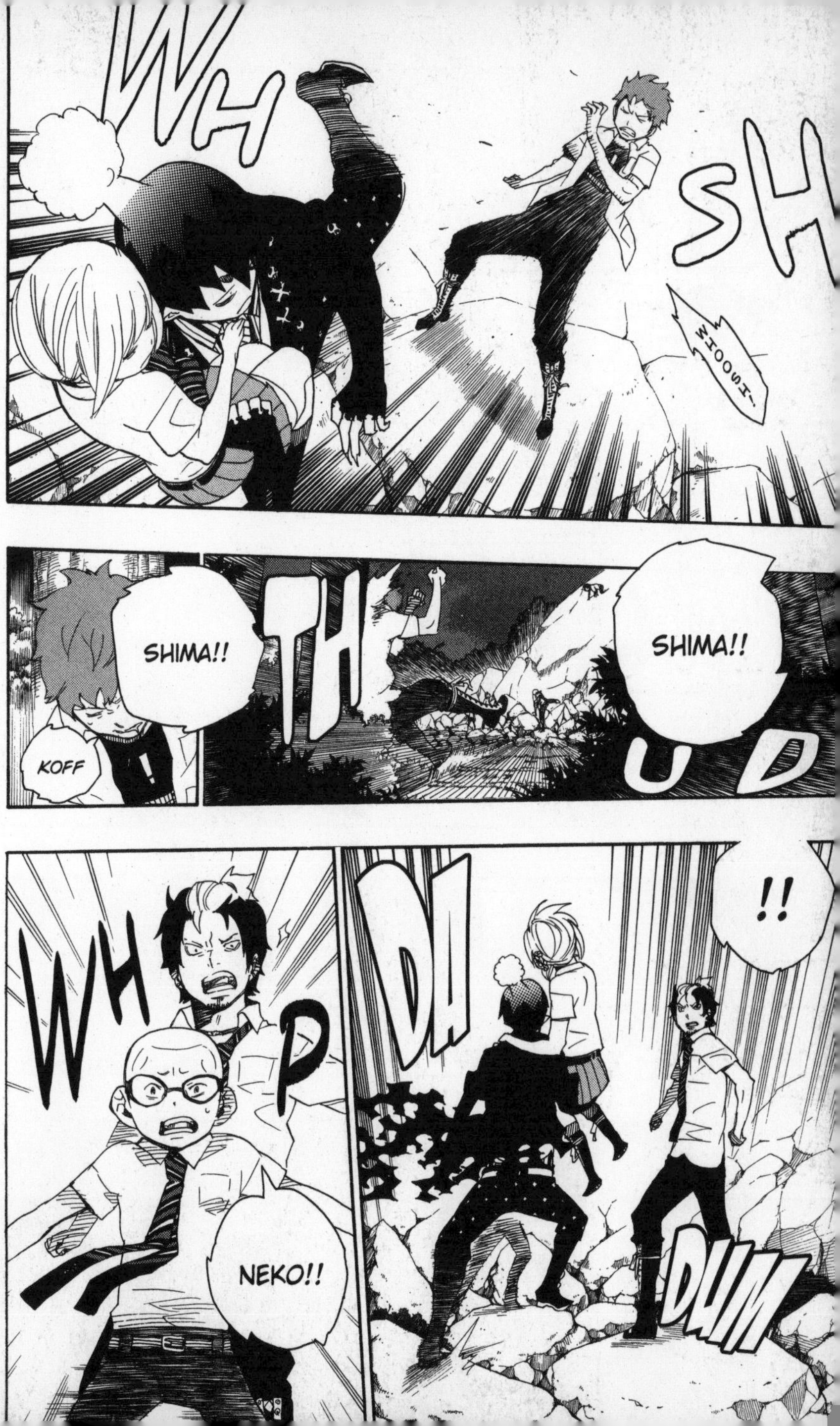
SH
WHOOSH!
WH
SHIMA!!
TH
UD
SHIMA!!
KOFF
!!
DA
DUN
WH
P
NEKO!!

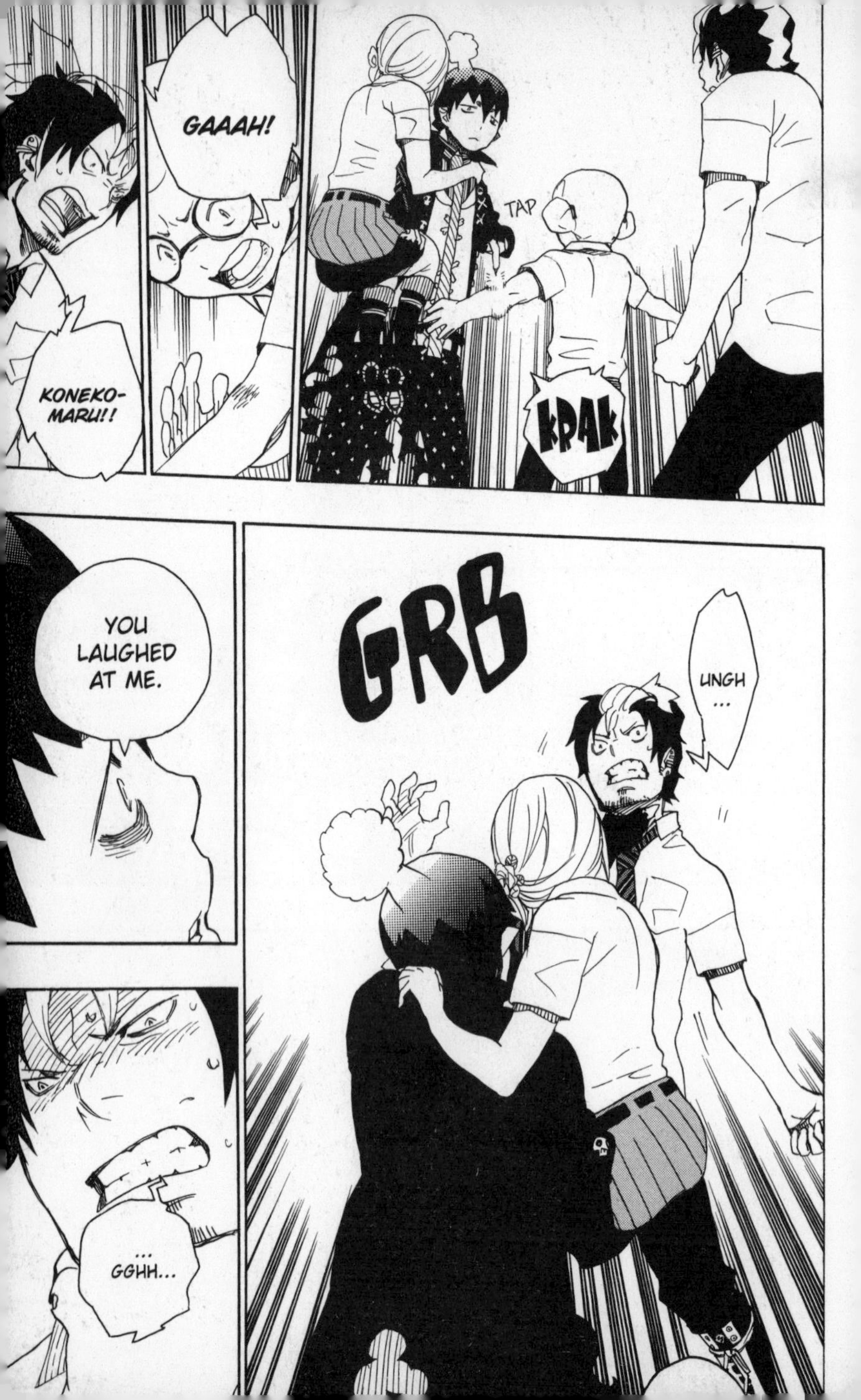
TAP
KRAK
GAAAH!
KONEKO-MARU!!
GRB
UNGH …
YOU LAUGHED AT ME.
… GGHH…

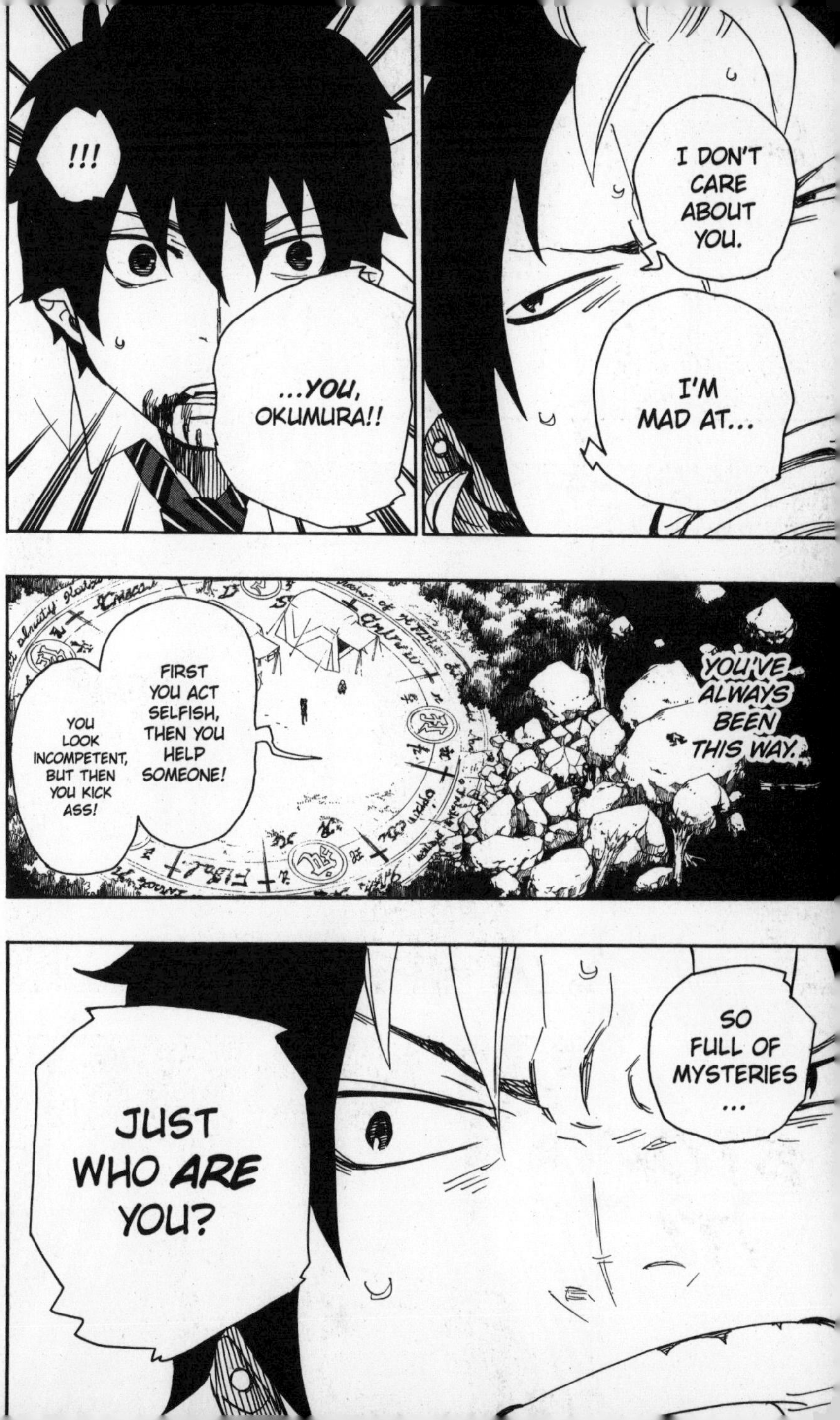
I DON'T CARE ABOUT YOU.
I'M MAD AT...
...YOU, OKUMURA!!
!!!
YOU'VE ALWAYS BEEN THIS WAY.
FIRST YOU ACT SELFISH, THEN YOU HELP SOMEONE!
YOU LOOK INCOMPETENT, BUT THEN YOU KICK ASS!
SO FULL OF MYSTERIES...
JUST WHO ARE YOU?

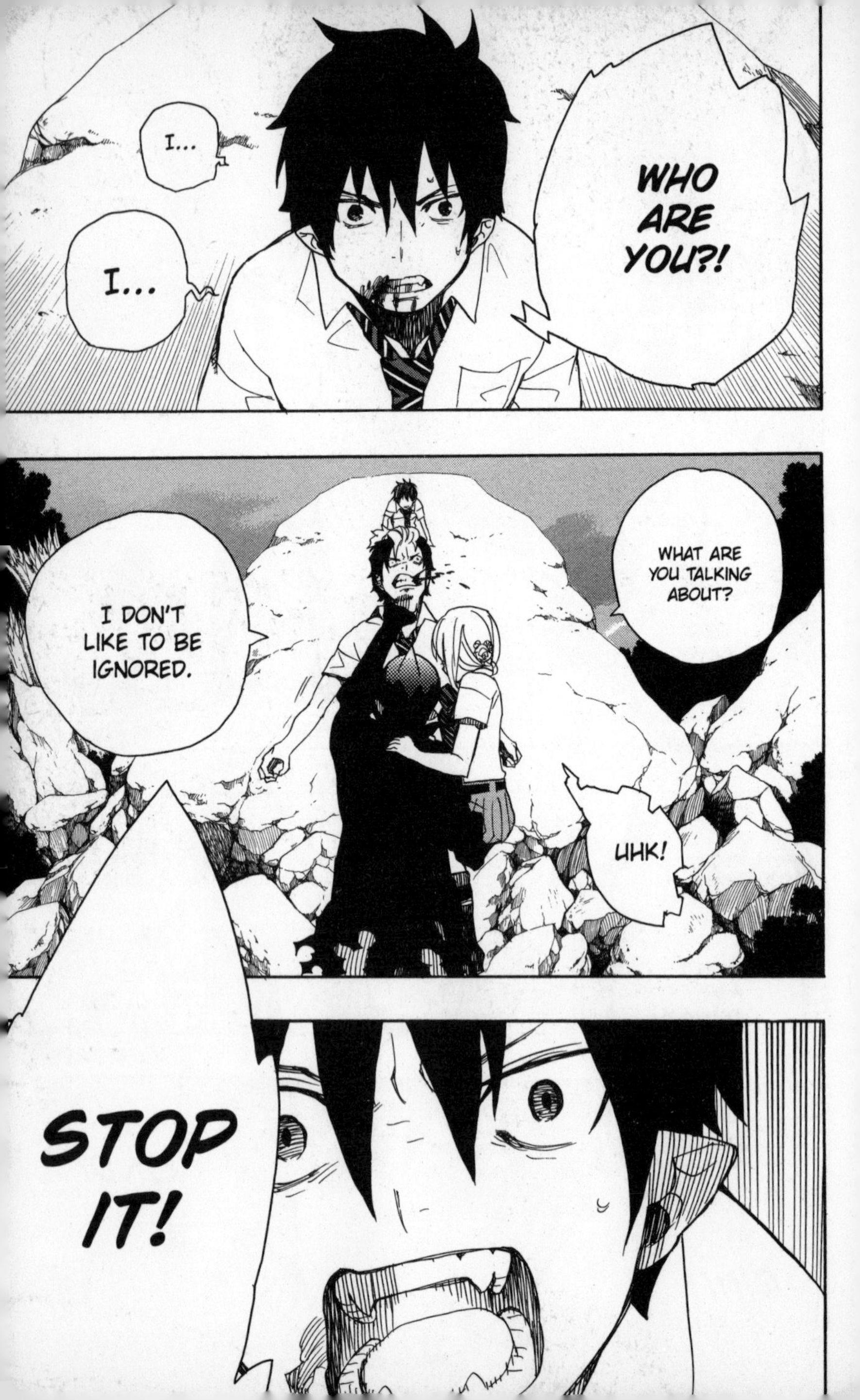
WHO ARE YOU?!
I...
I...
WHAT ARE YOU TALKING ABOUT?
I DON'T LIKE TO BE IGNORED.
UHK!
STOP IT!

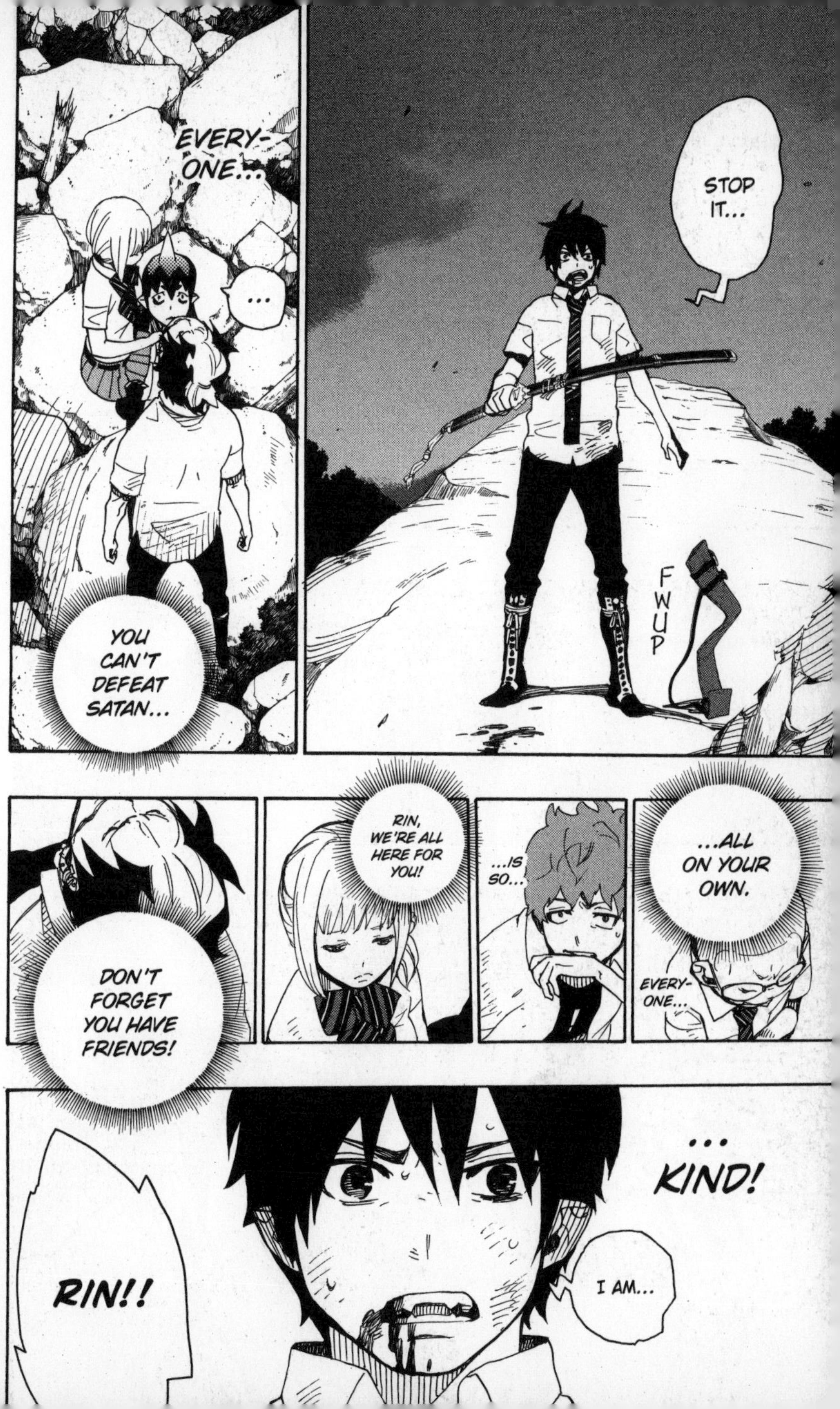
STOP IT...
FWUP
EVERY-ONE...
...
YOU CAN'T DEFEAT SATAN...
...ALL ON YOUR OWN.
EVERY-ONE...
...IS SO...
RIN, WE'RE ALL HERE FOR YOU!
DON'T FORGET YOU HAVE FRIENDS!
... KIND!
I AM...
RIN!!

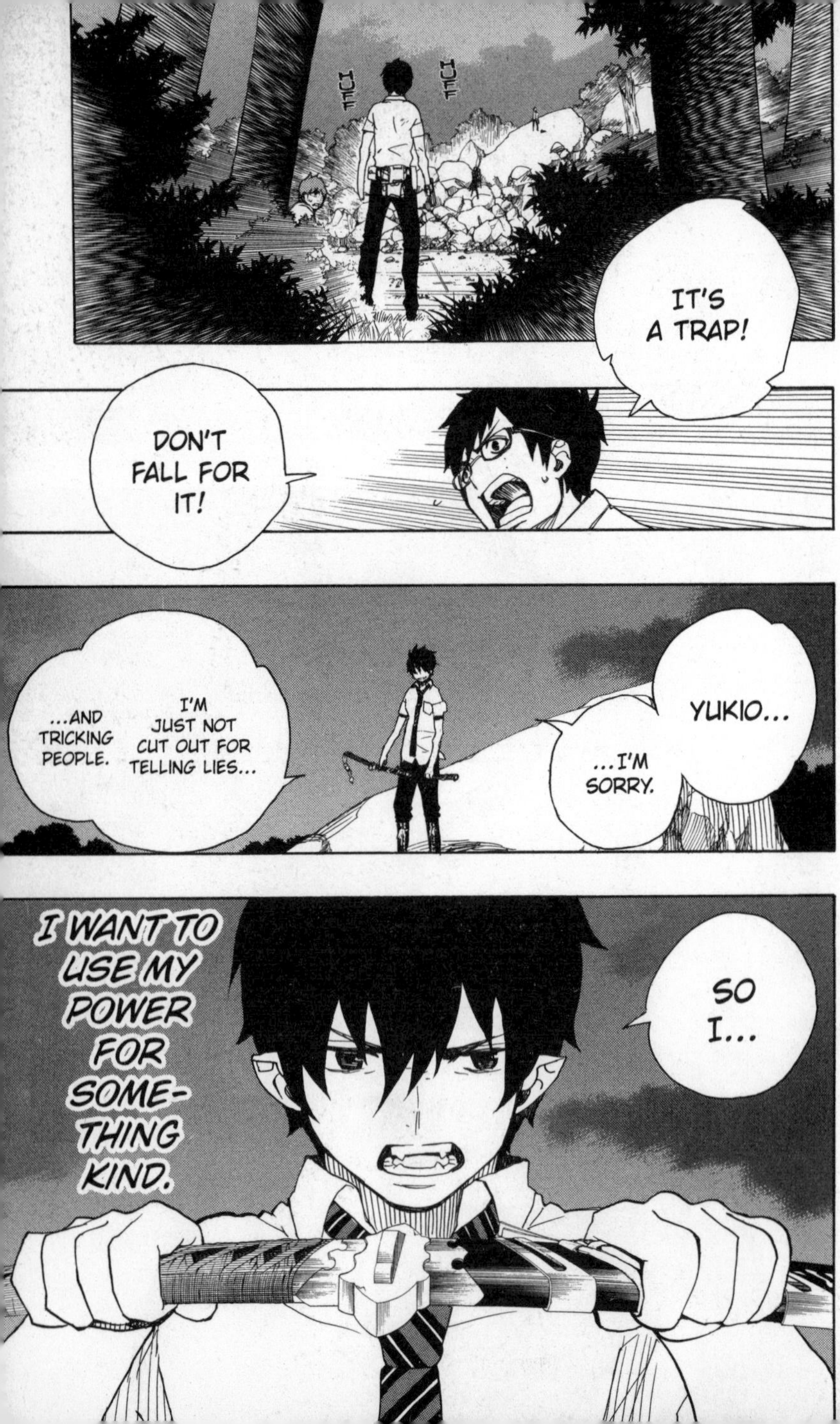
HUFF
HUFF
IT'S A TRAP!
DON'T FALL FOR IT!
YUKIO...
...I'M SORRY.
I'M JUST NOT CUT OUT FOR TELLING LIES...
...AND TRICKING PEOPLE.
SO I...
I WANT TO USE MY POWER FOR SOME-THING KIND.

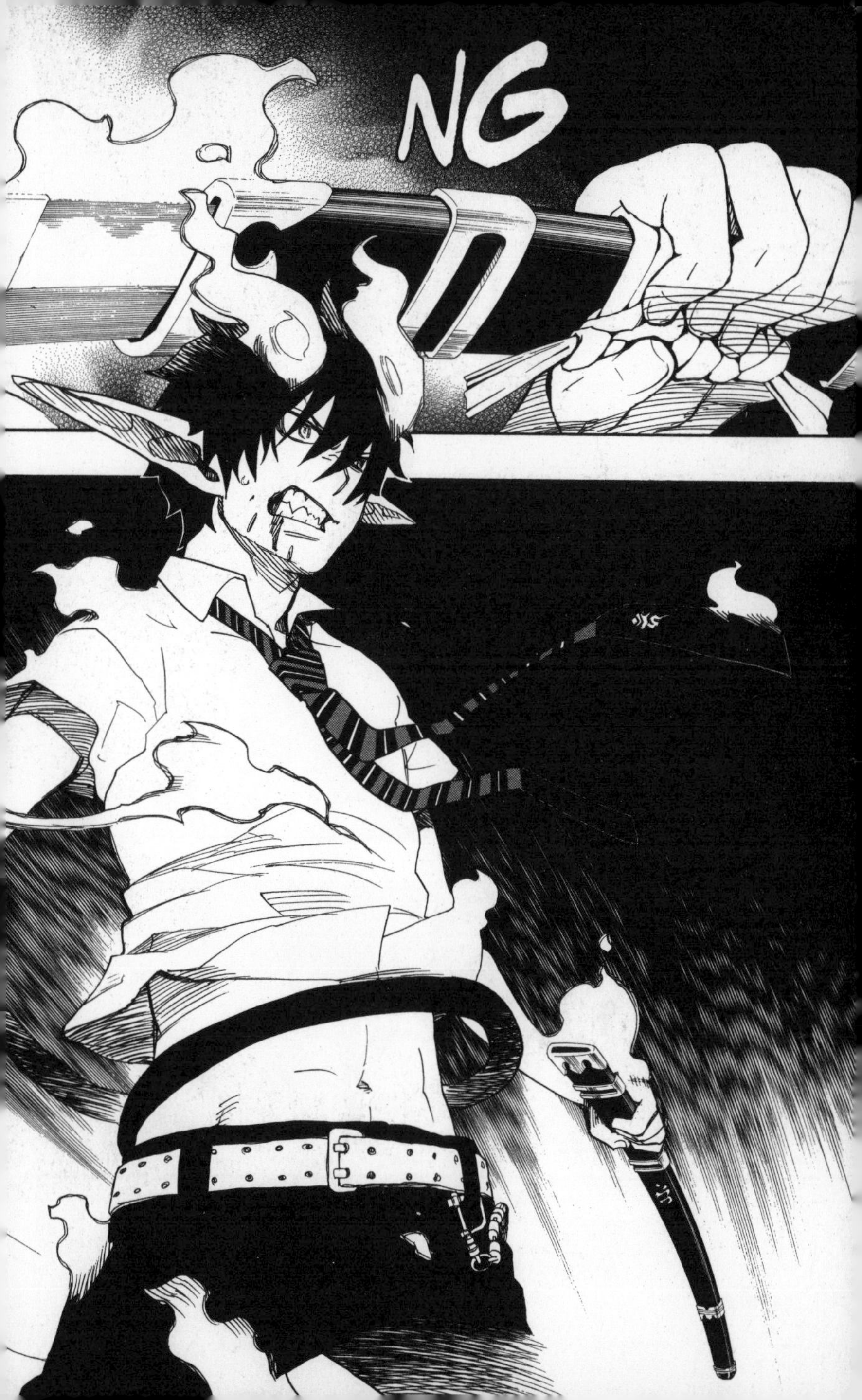
NG

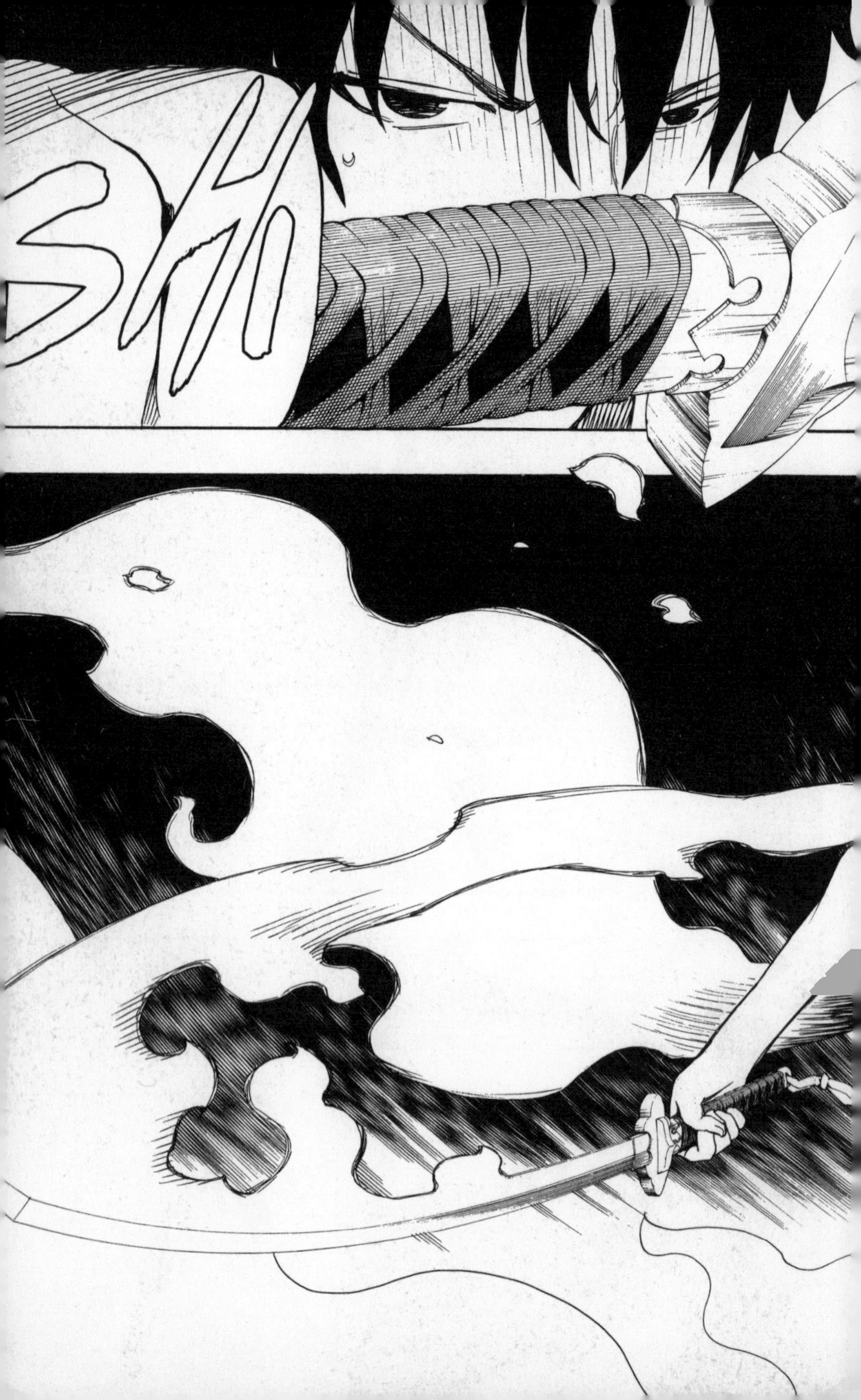
SHA

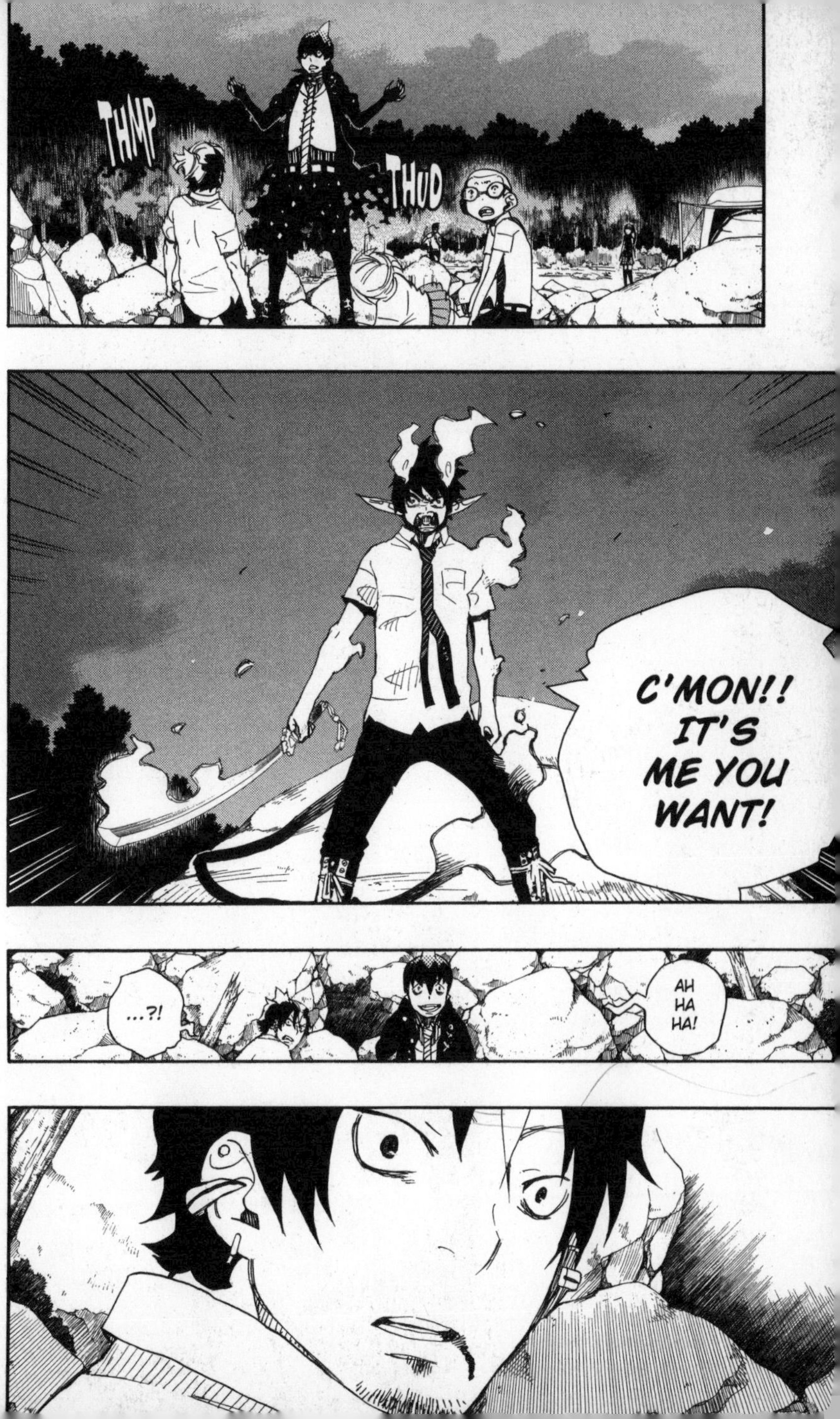
THUD
THMP
C'MON!! IT'S ME YOU WANT!
AH HA HA!
...?!

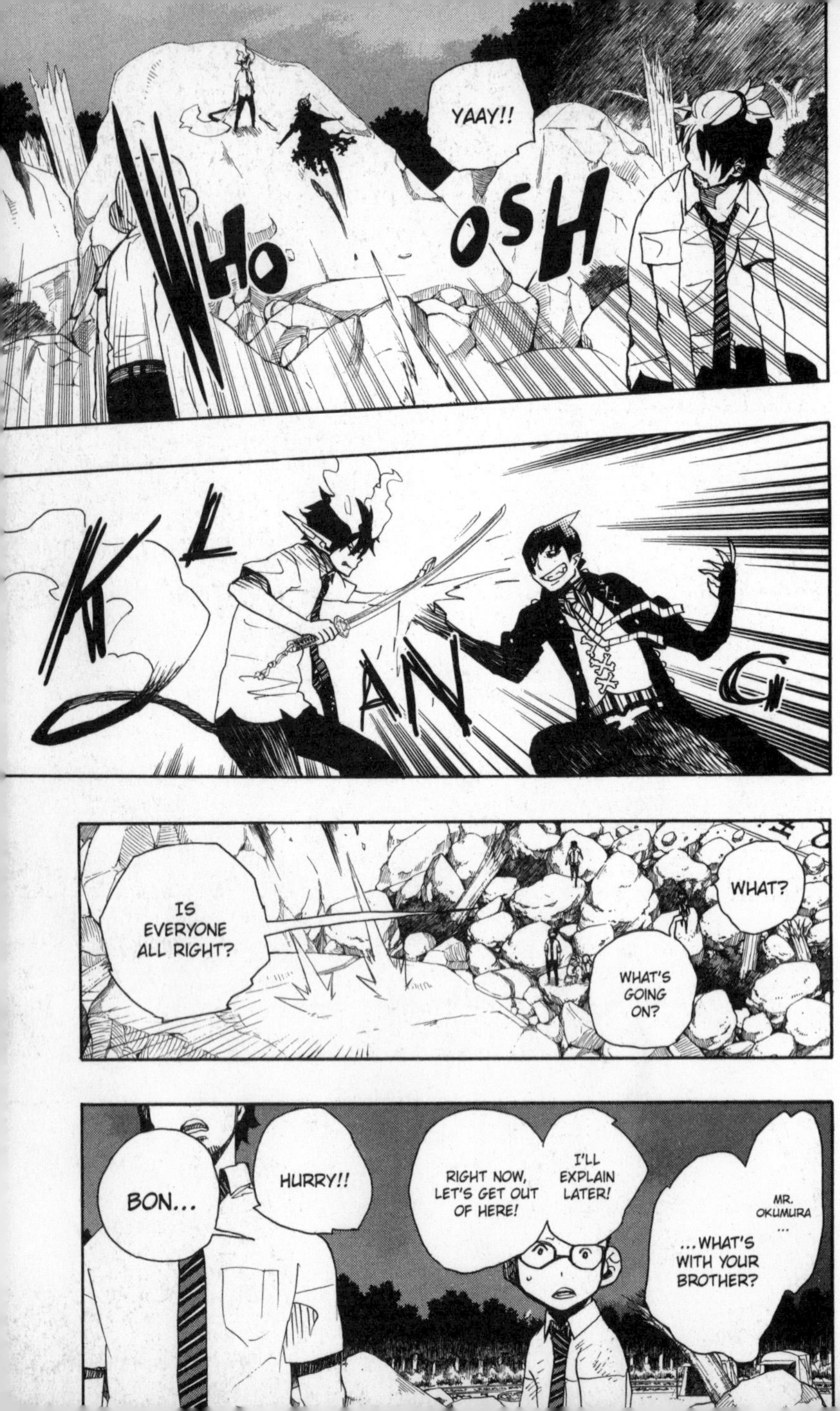
YAAY!!
WHOOSH
KLANG
WHAT?
WHAT'S GOING ON?
IS EVERYONE ALL RIGHT?
MR. OKUMURA...
...WHAT'S WITH YOUR BROTHER?
I'LL EXPLAIN LATER!
RIGHT NOW, LET'S GET OUT OF HERE!
HURRY!!
BON...

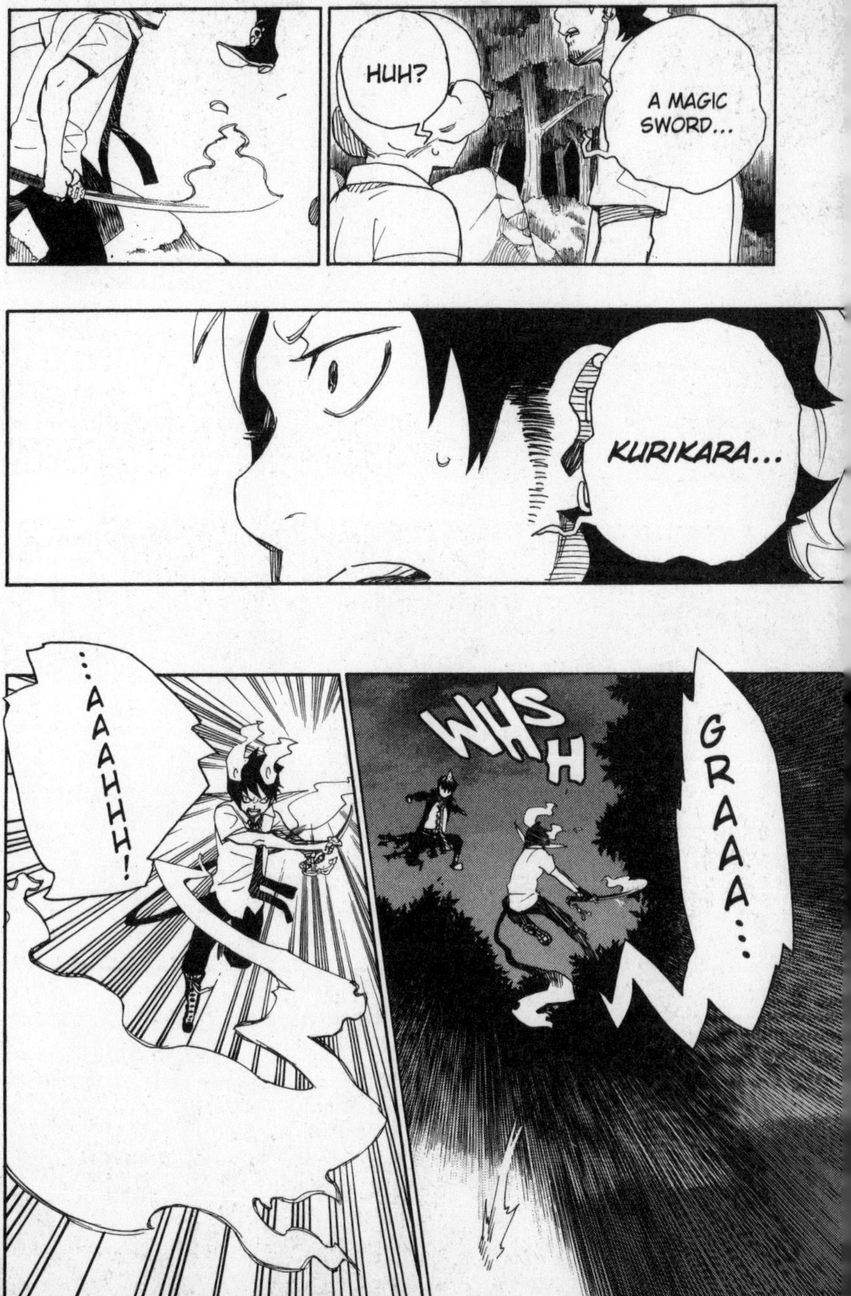
A MAGIC SWORD...
HUH?
KURIKARA...
GRAAA...
WHSH
...AAAHHH!

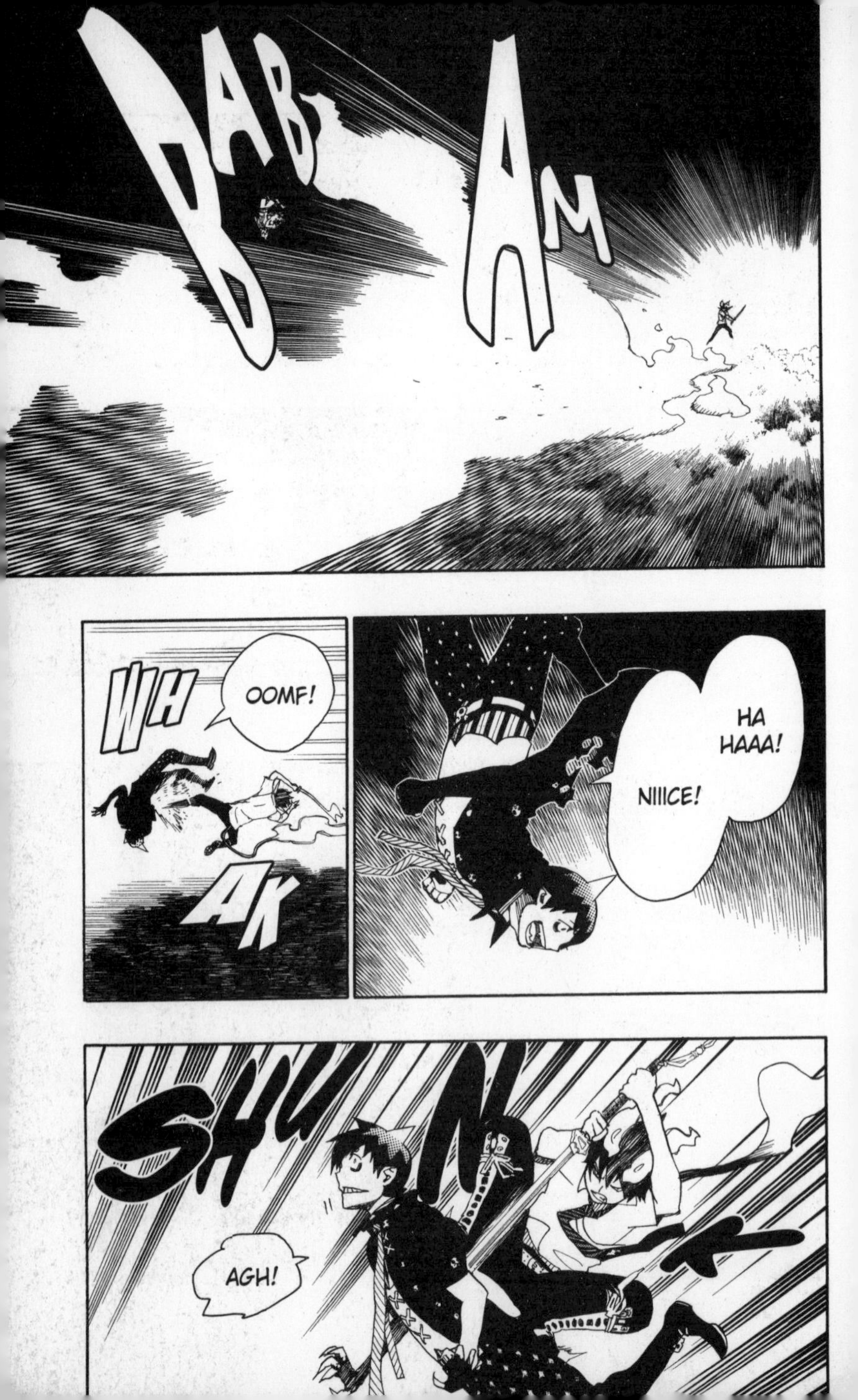
BABAM
HA HAAA!
NIIICE!
OOMF!
WHAK
SHUNK
AGH!

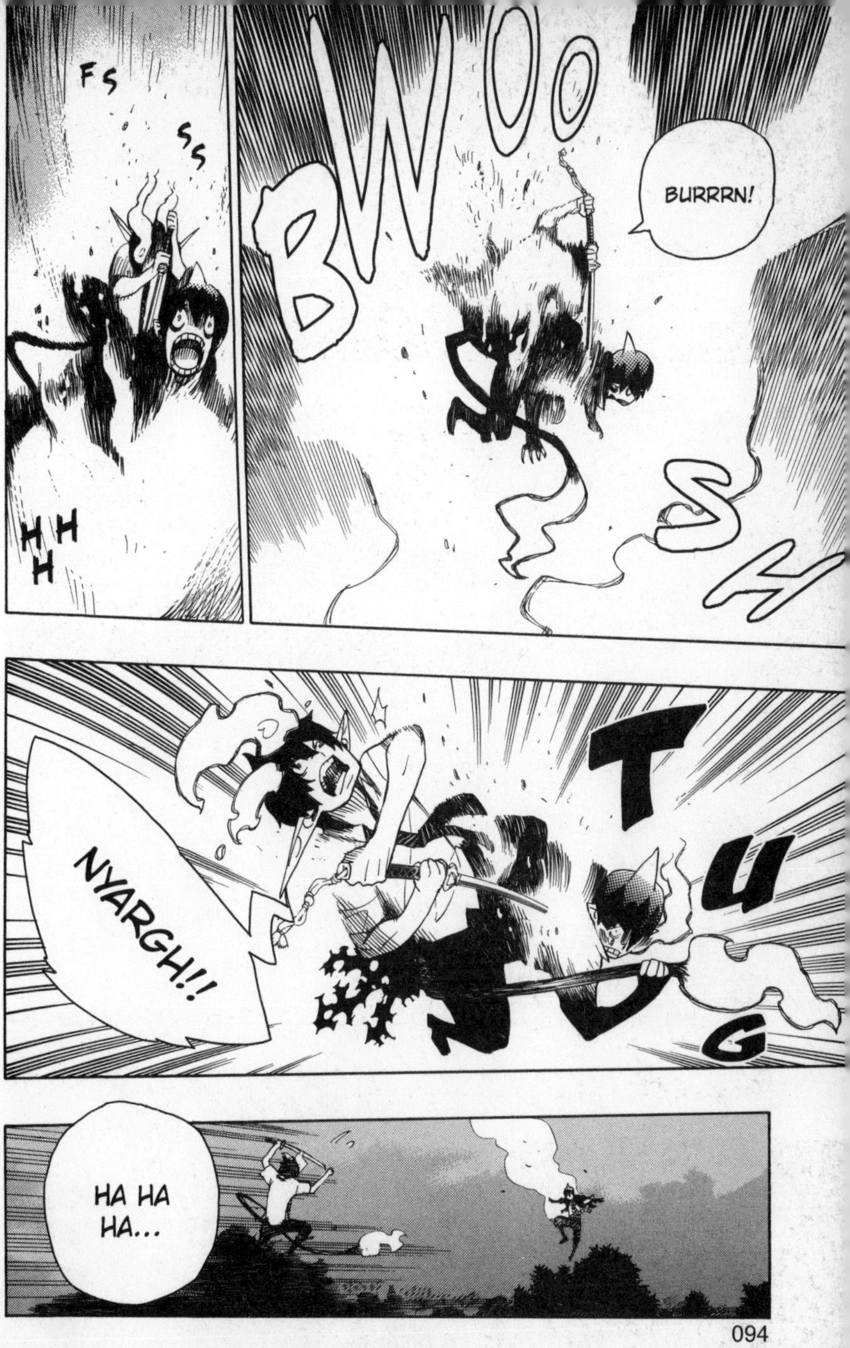
BWOO
BURRRN!
SH
FSSS
HHH
TUG
NYARGH!!
HA HA HA...

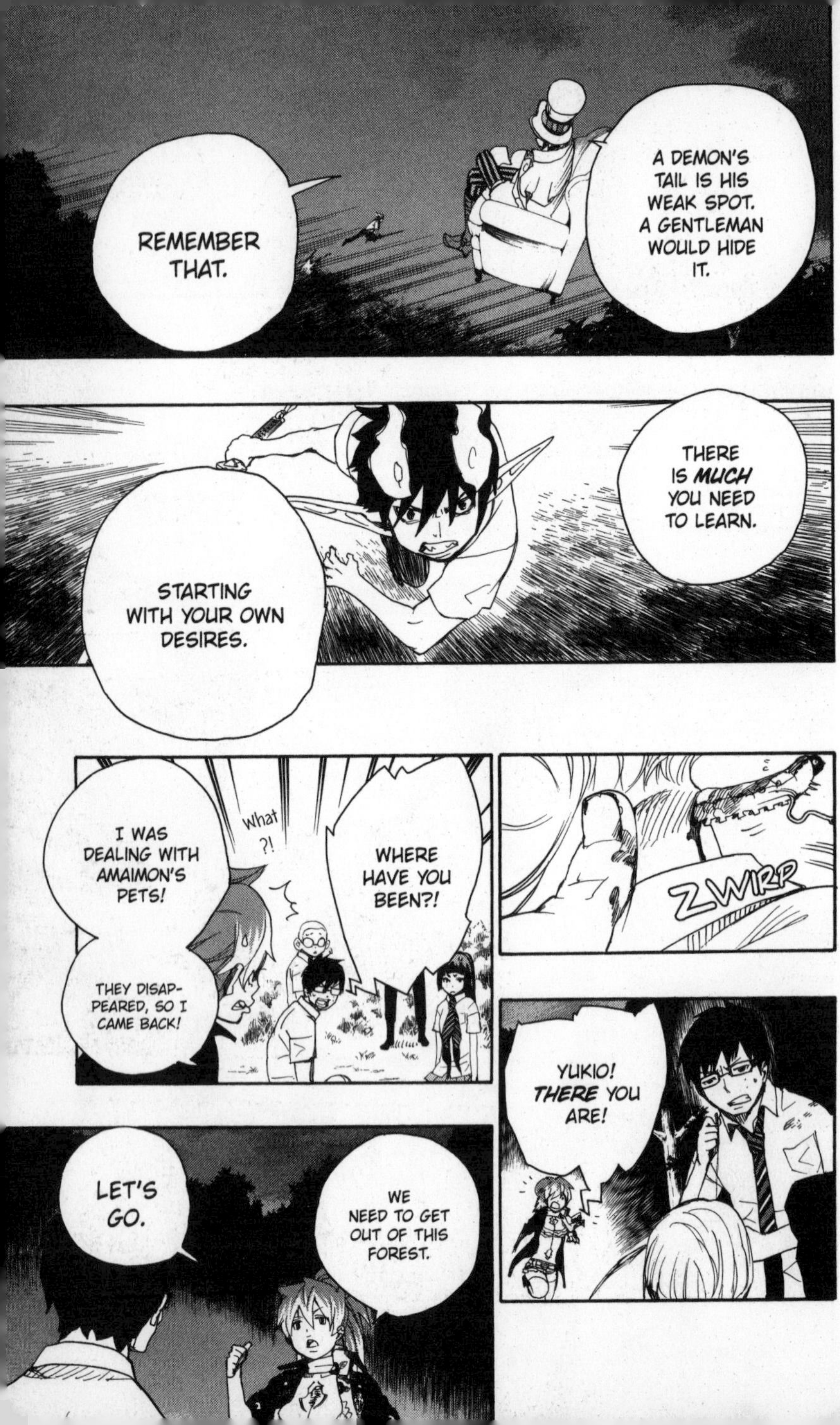
A DEMON'S TAIL IS HIS WEAK SPOT. A GENTLEMAN WOULD HIDE IT.
REMEMBER THAT.
THERE IS MUCH YOU NEED TO LEARN.
STARTING WITH YOUR OWN DESIRES.
ZWIRP
WHERE HAVE YOU BEEN?!
What ?!
I WAS DEALING WITH AMAIMON'S PETS!
THEY DISAP-PEARED, SO I CAME BACK!
YUKIO! THERE YOU ARE!
WE NEED TO GET OUT OF THIS FOREST.
LET'S GO.

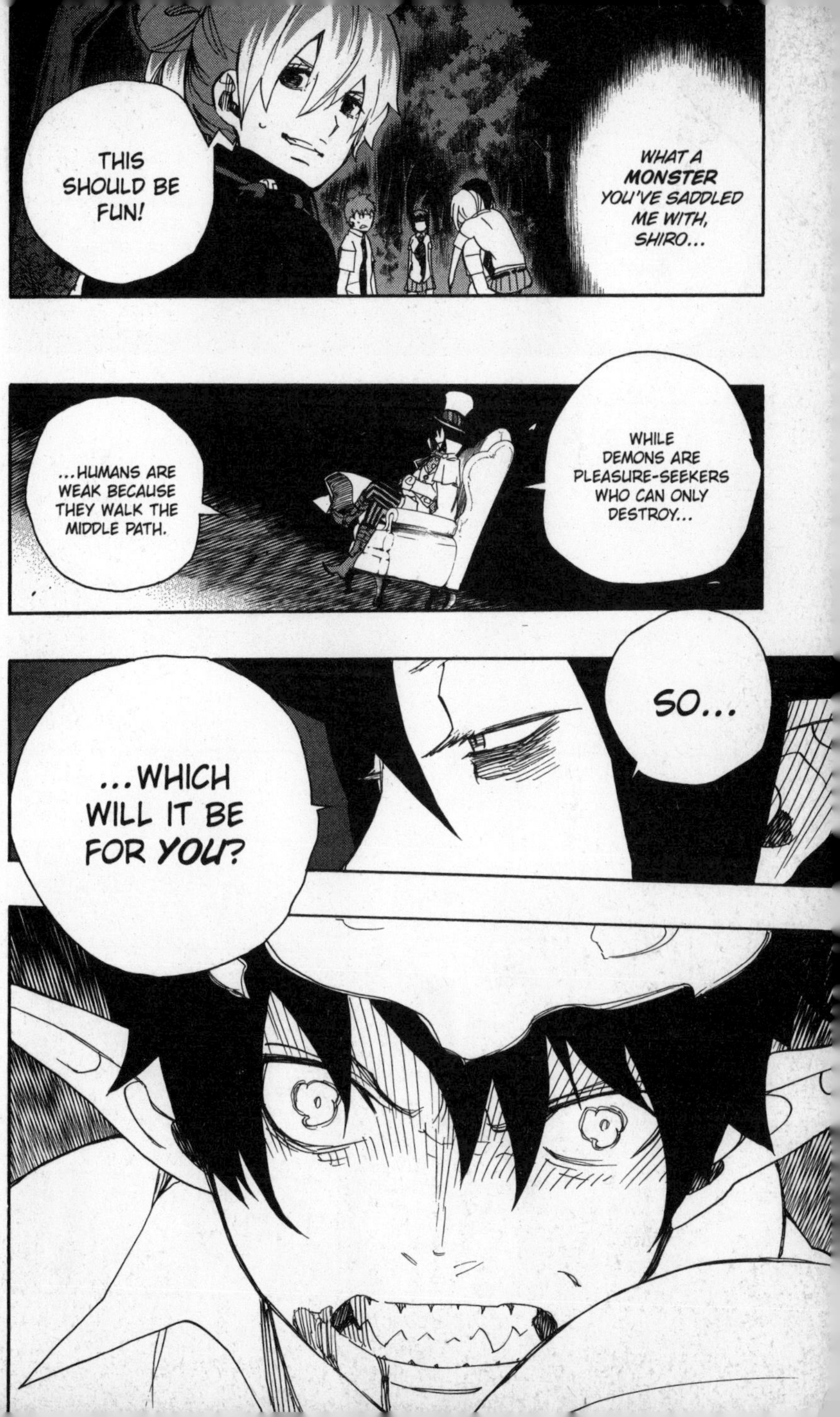
WHAT A MONSTER YOU'VE SADDLED ME WITH, SHIRO...
THIS SHOULD BE FUN!
WHILE DEMONS ARE PLEASURE-SEEKERS WHO CAN ONLY DESTROY...
...HUMANS ARE WEAK BECAUSE THEY WALK THE MIDDLE PATH.
SO...
...WHICH WILL IT BE FOR YOU?

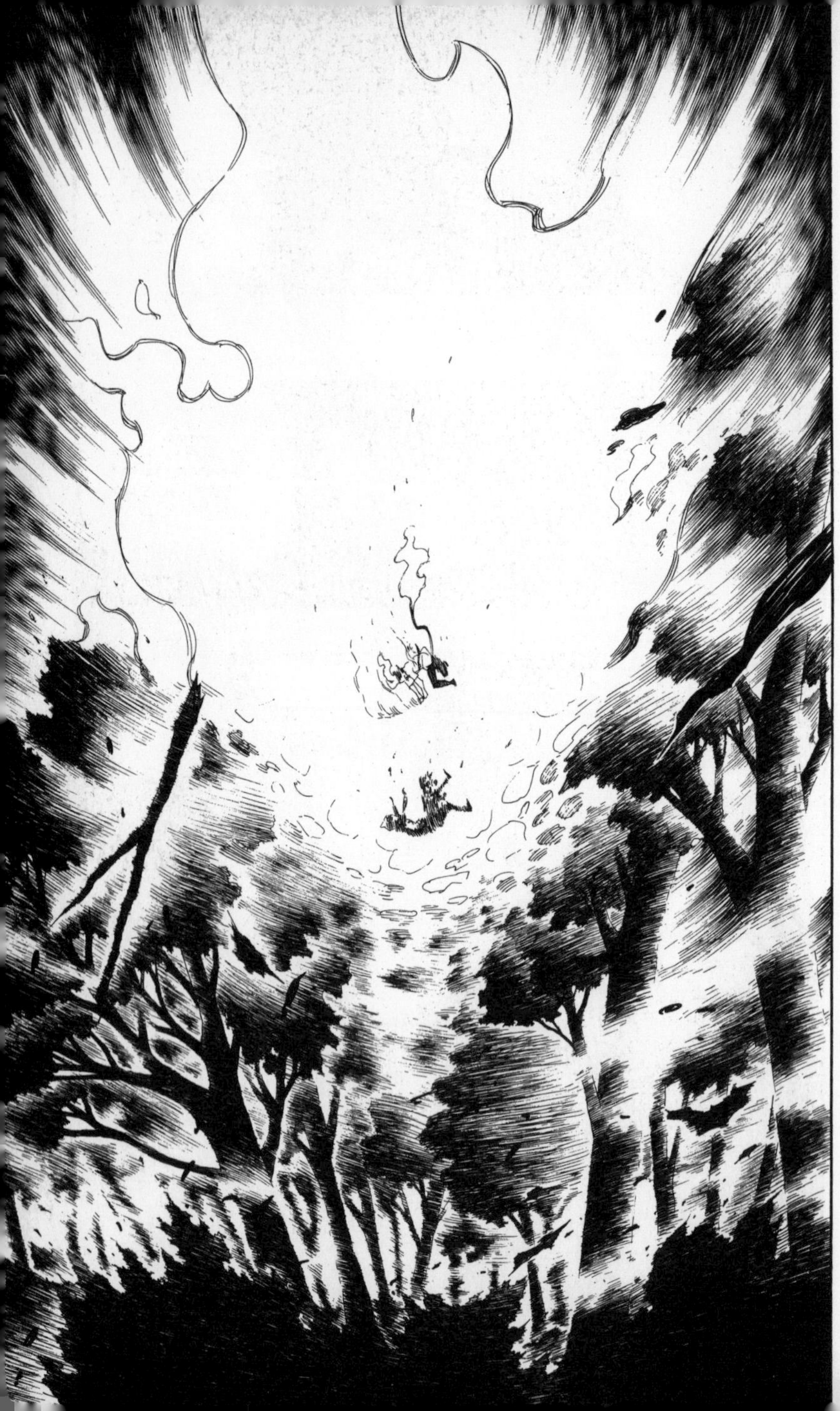

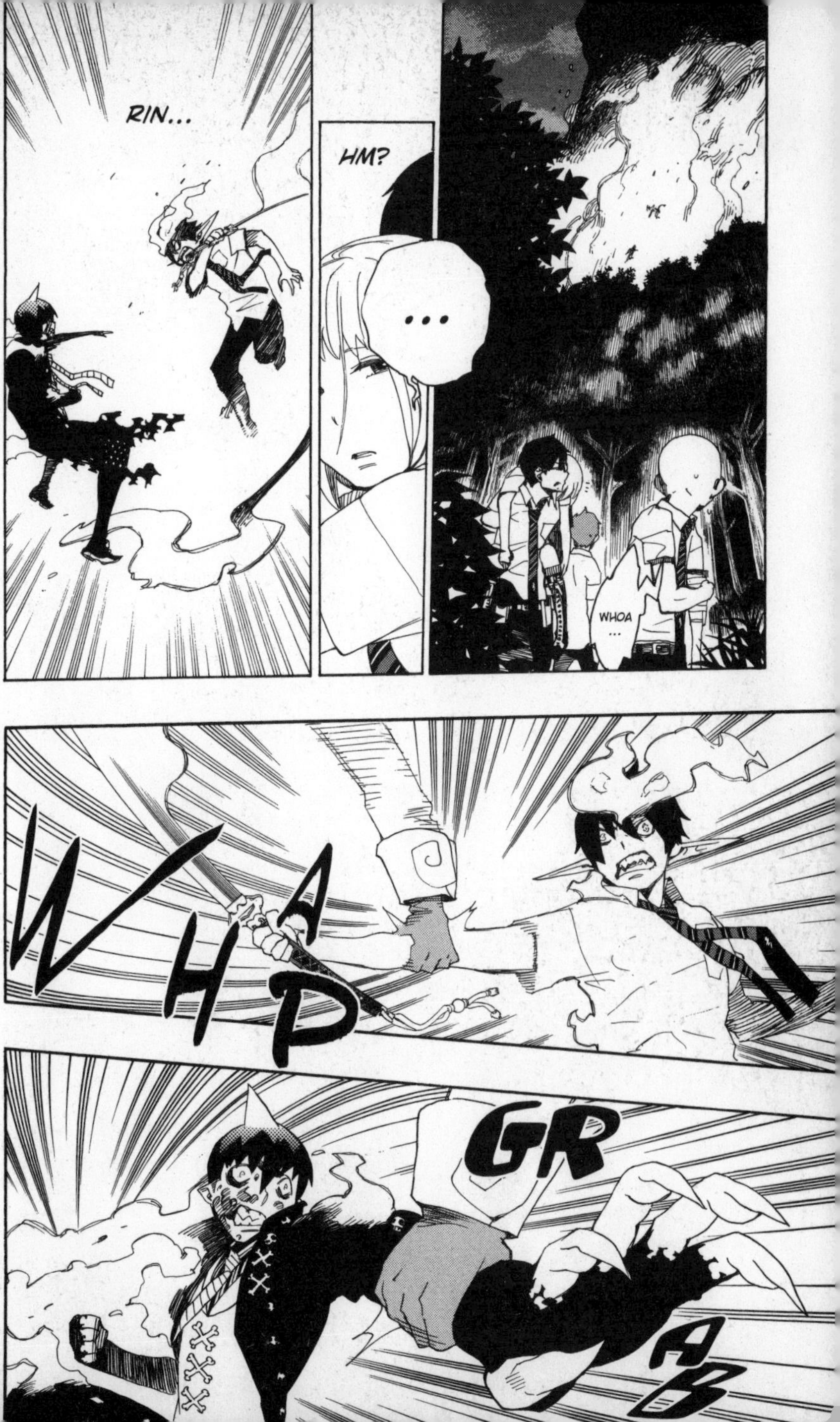
WHOA ...
HM?
...
RIN...
WHAP
GRAB

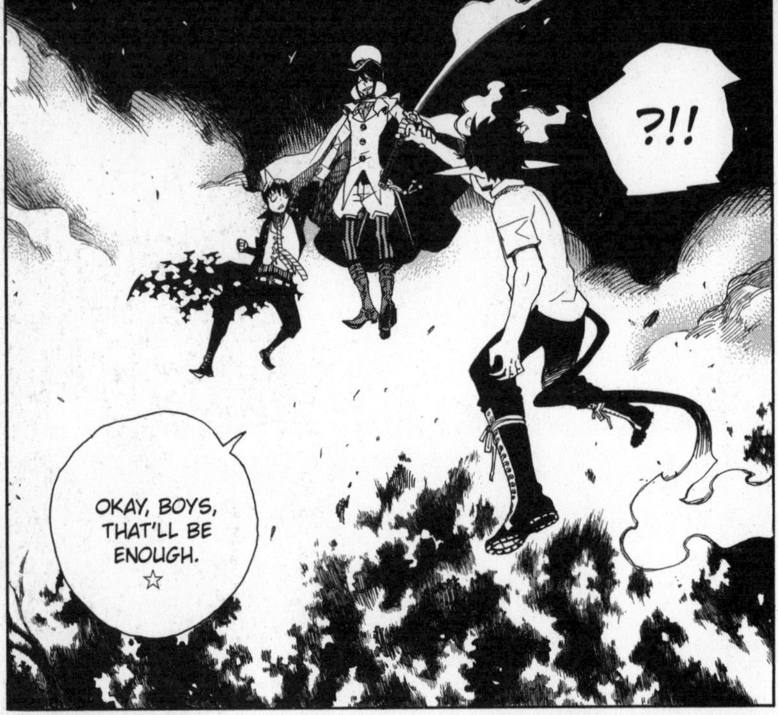
?!!
OKAY, BOYS, THAT'LL BE ENOUGH. ☆

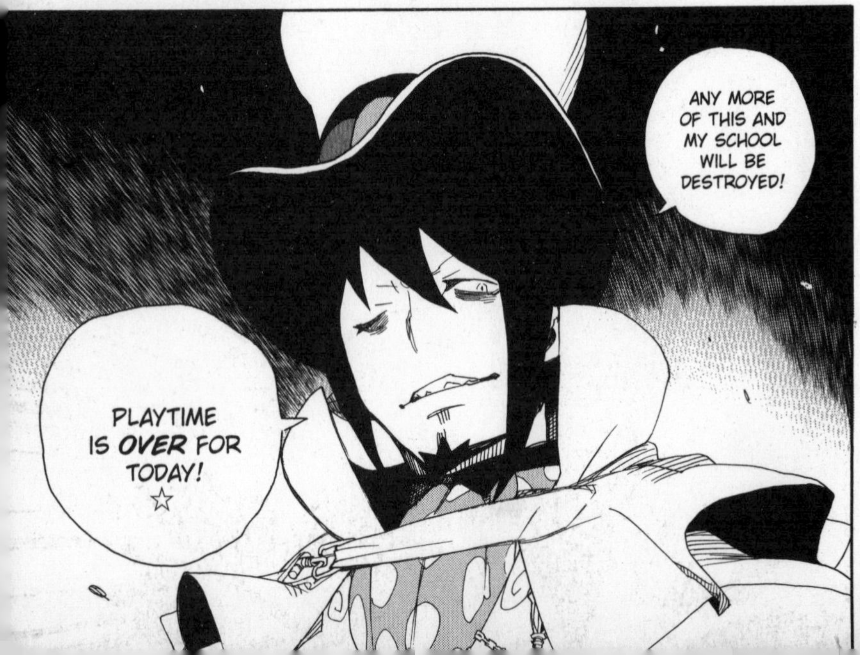
ANY MORE OF THIS AND MY SCHOOL WILL BE DESTROYED!
PLAYTIME IS *OVER* FOR TODAY! ☆

Blue Exorcist Chapter 13 Something Kind

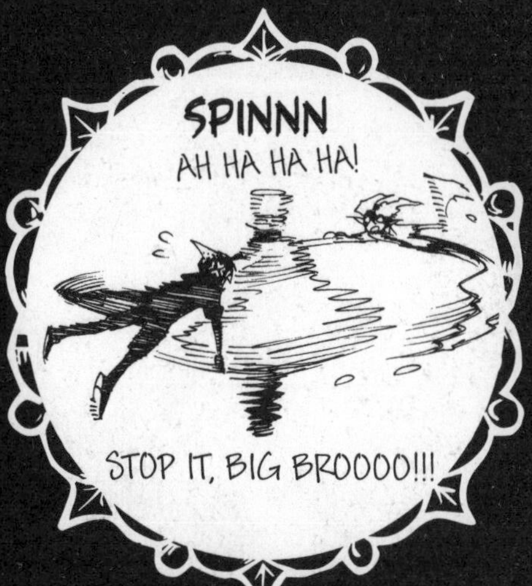
SPINNN
AH HA HA HA!
STOP IT, BIG BROOOO!!!

Chapter 14
The Wager

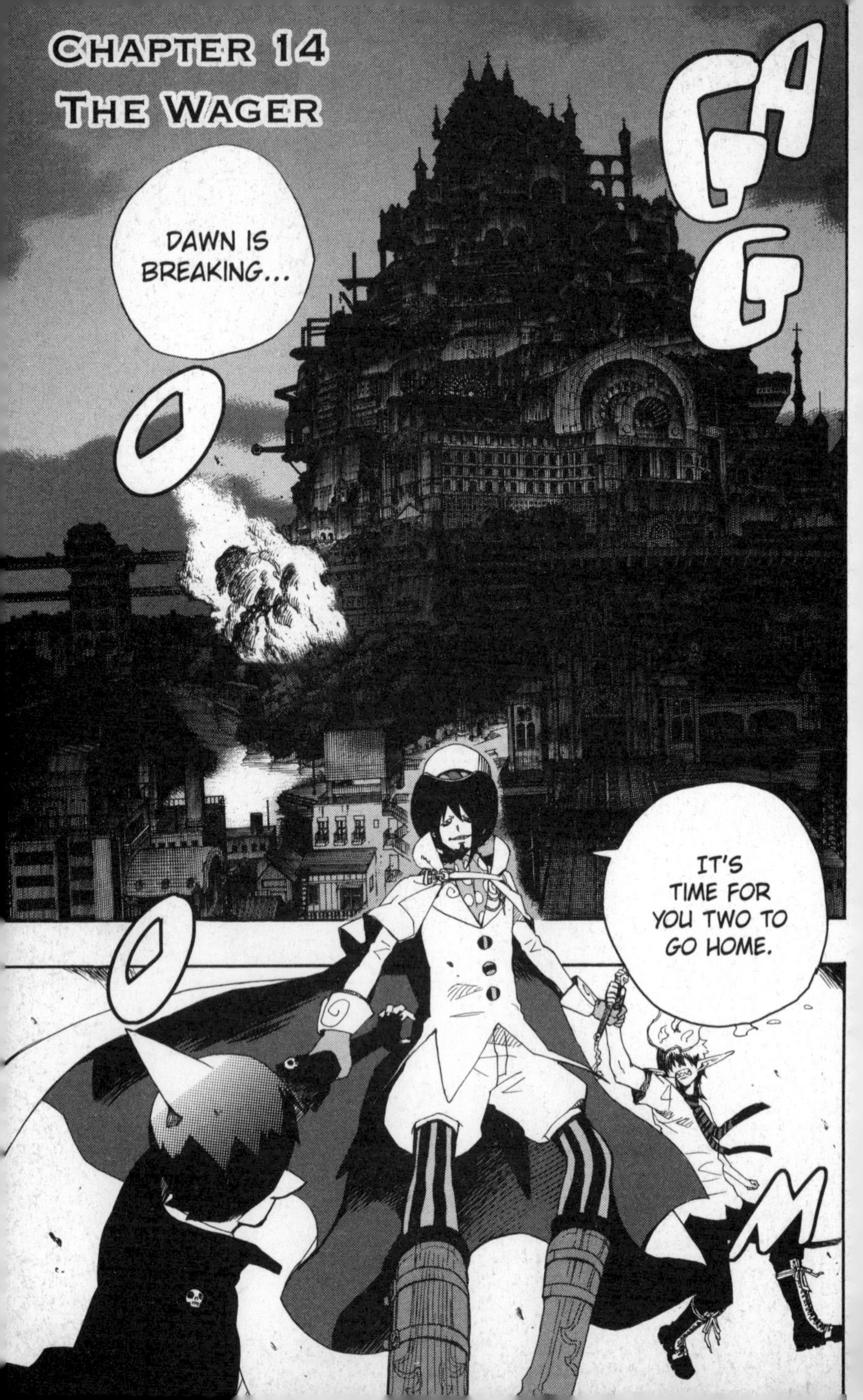
GAGOOM
DAWN IS BREAKING...
IT'S TIME FOR YOU TWO TO GO HOME.

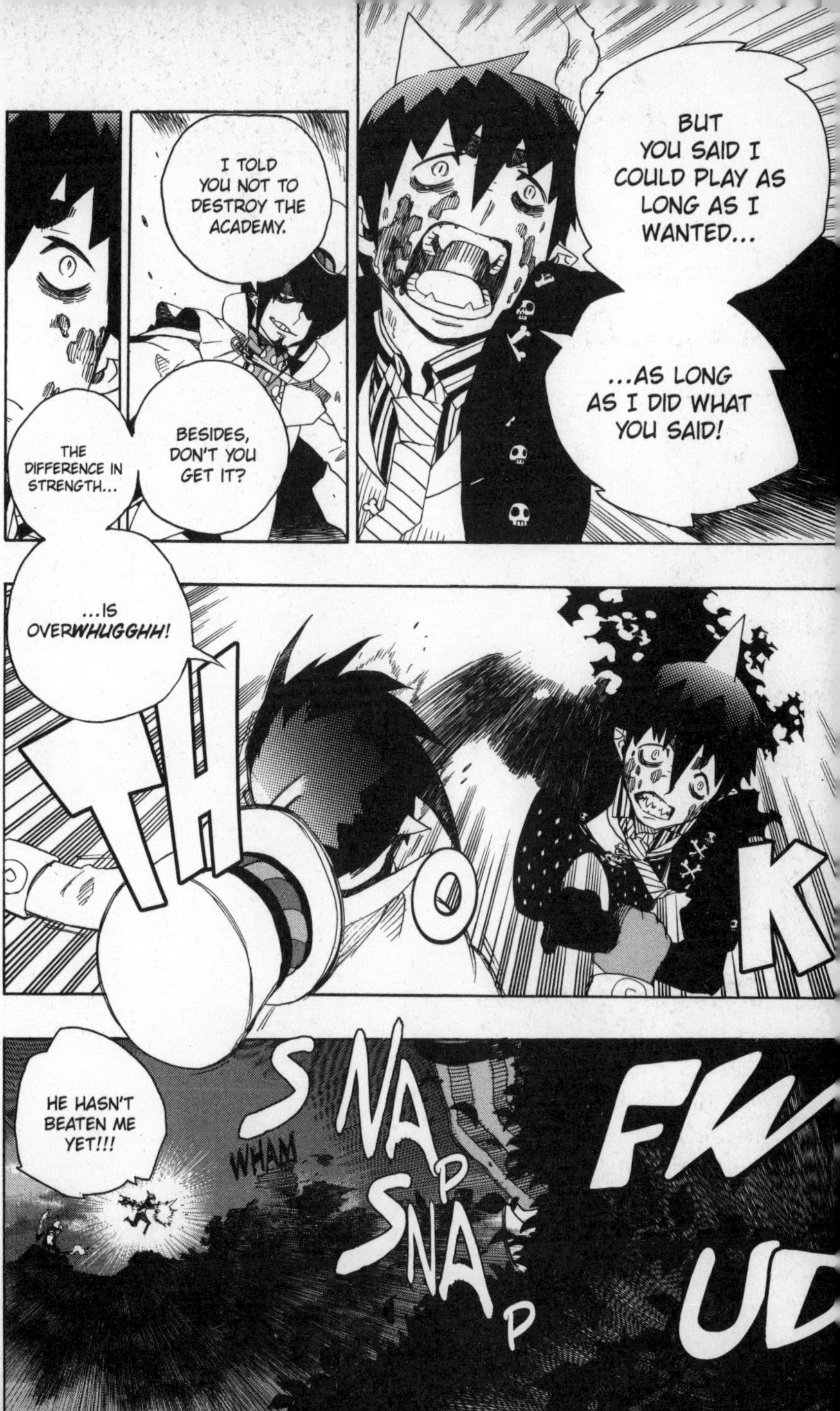
BUT YOU SAID I COULD PLAY AS LONG AS I WANTED...
...AS LONG AS I DID WHAT YOU SAID!
I TOLD YOU NOT TO DESTROY THE ACADEMY.
BESIDES, DON'T YOU GET IT?
THE DIFFERENCE IN STRENGTH...
...IS OVERWHUGGHH!
THOOK
FWUD
SNAP SNAP
WHAM
HE HASN'T BEATEN ME YET!!!

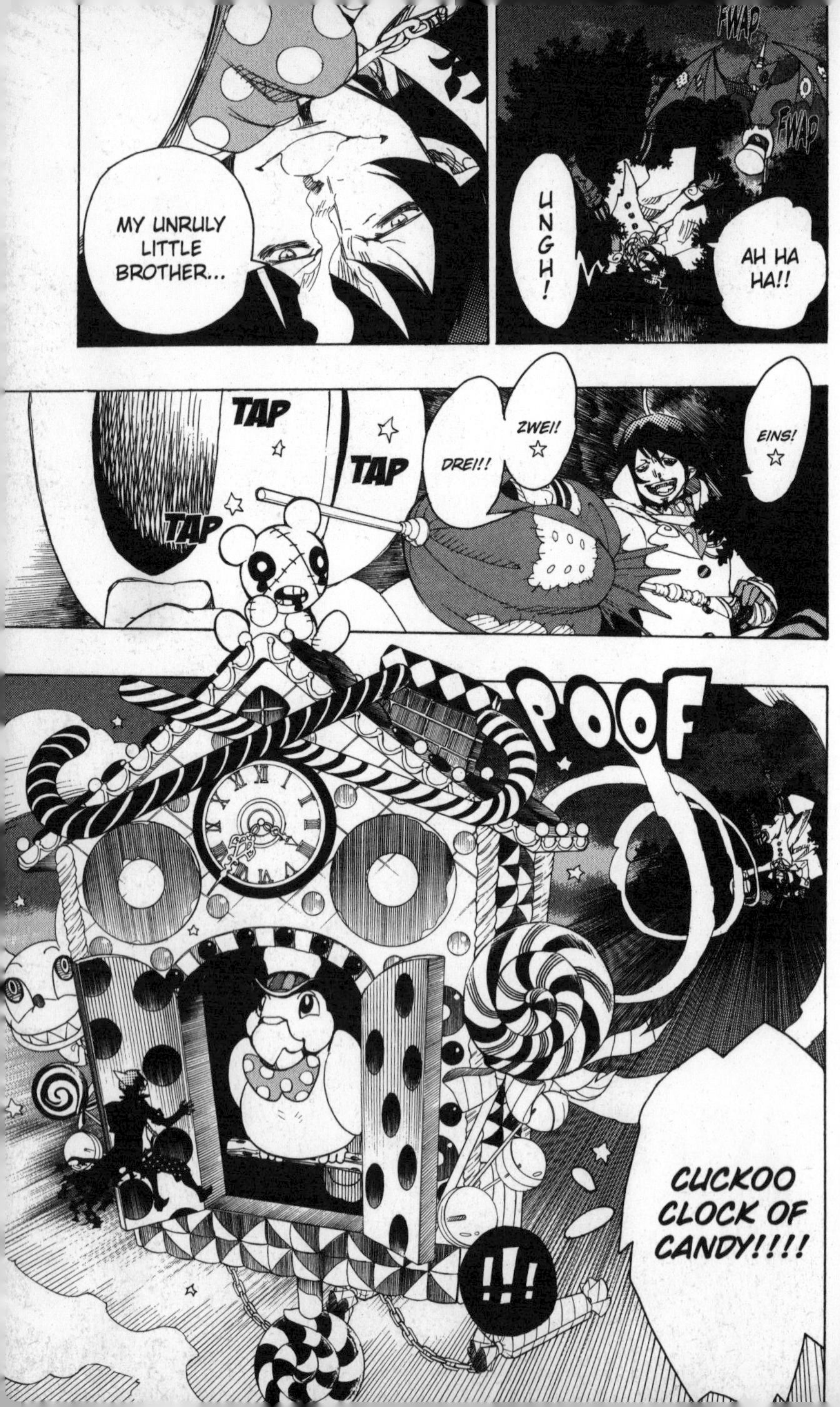
FWAP
FWAP
AH HA HA!!
UNGH!
MY UNRULY LITTLE BROTHER...
EINS!
ZWEI!
DREI!!
TAP
TAP
TAP
POOF
CUCKOO CLOCK OF CANDY!!!!
!!!

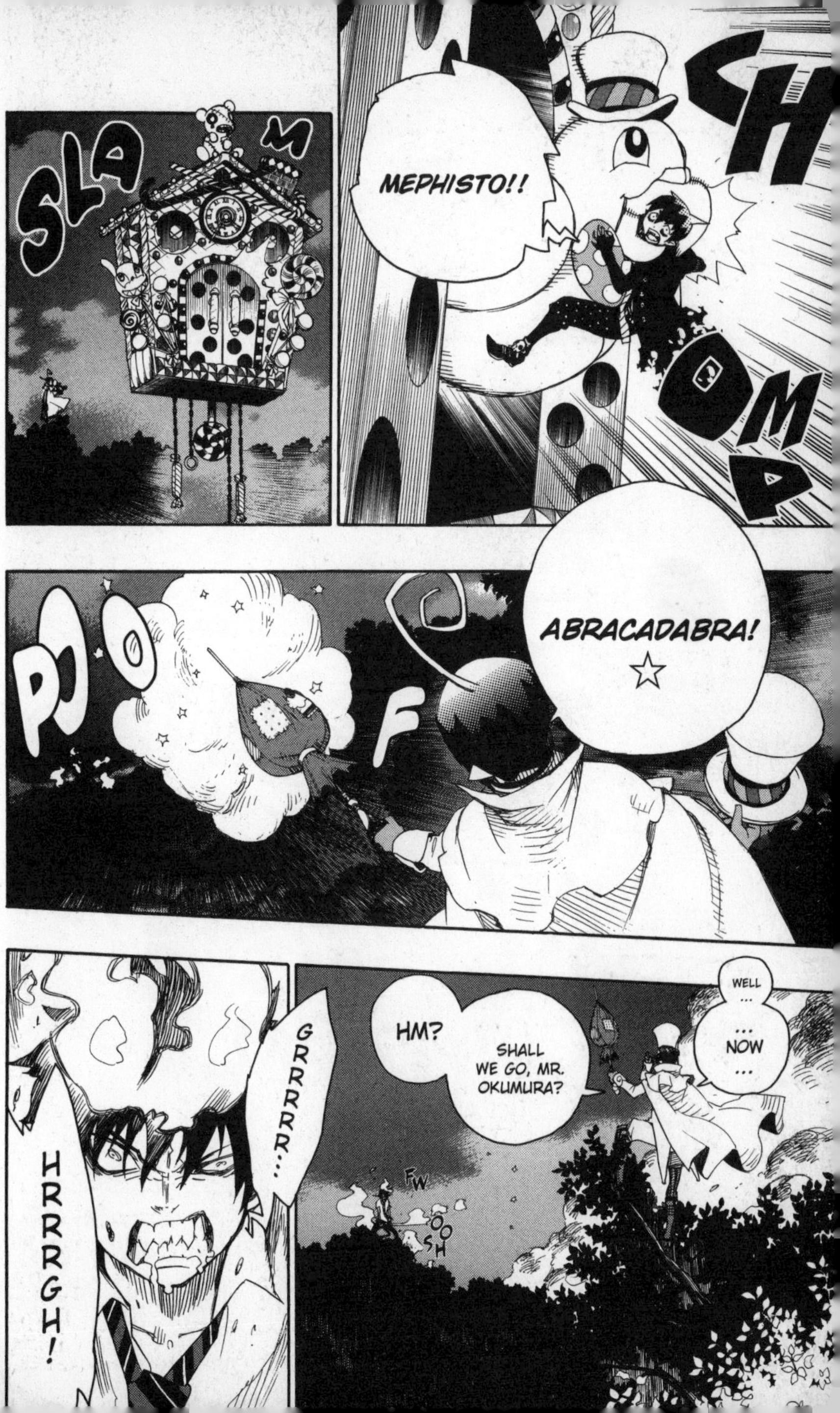
CHOMP
MEPHISTO!!
SLAM
ABRACADABRA! ☆
POOF
WELL... ...NOW...
HM?
SHALL WE GO, MR. OKUMURA?
FWOOSH
GRRRRRR...
HRRRGH!

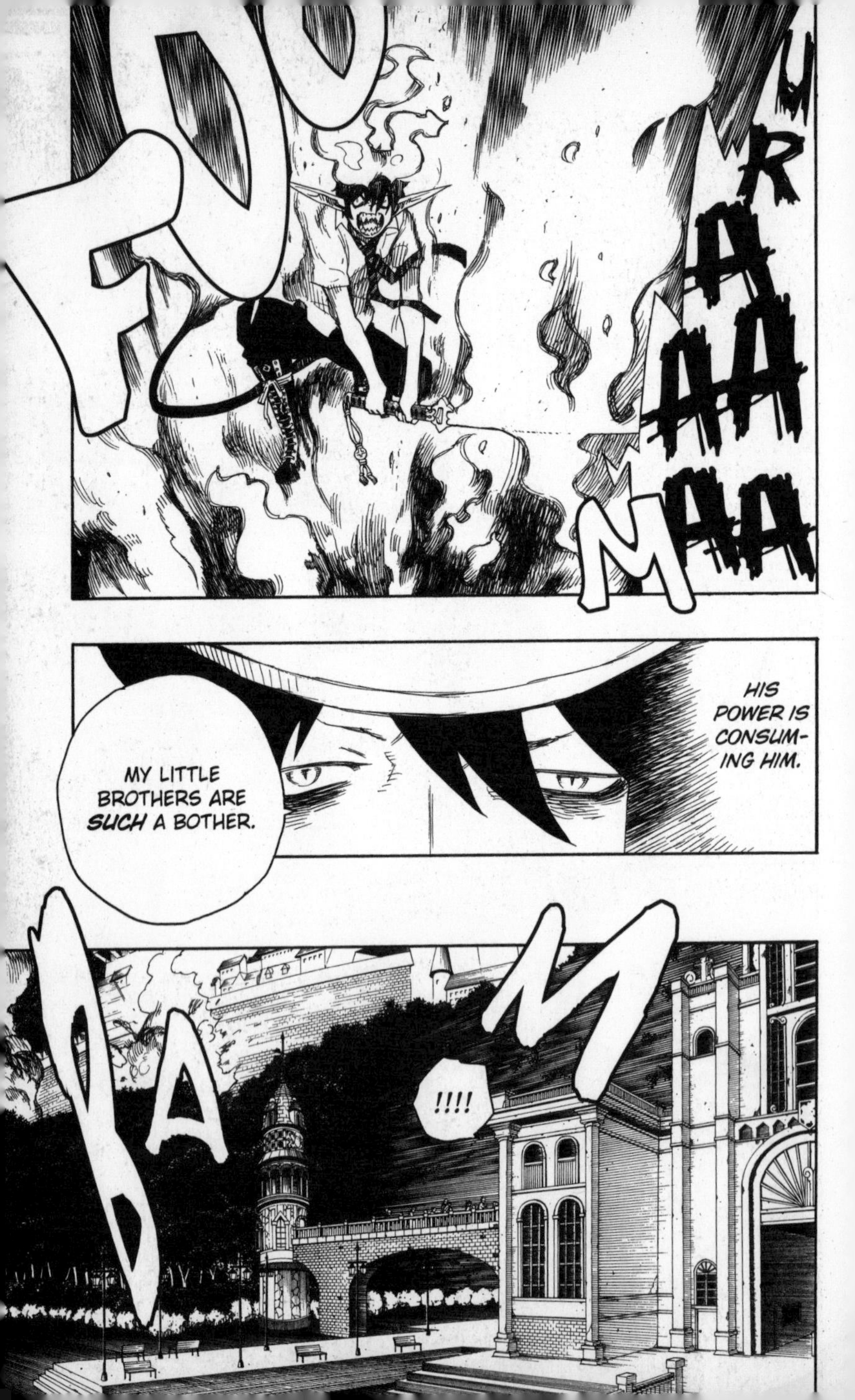
HIS POWER IS CONSUMING HIM.
MY LITTLE BROTHERS ARE *SUCH* A BOTHER.
BAM
!!!!

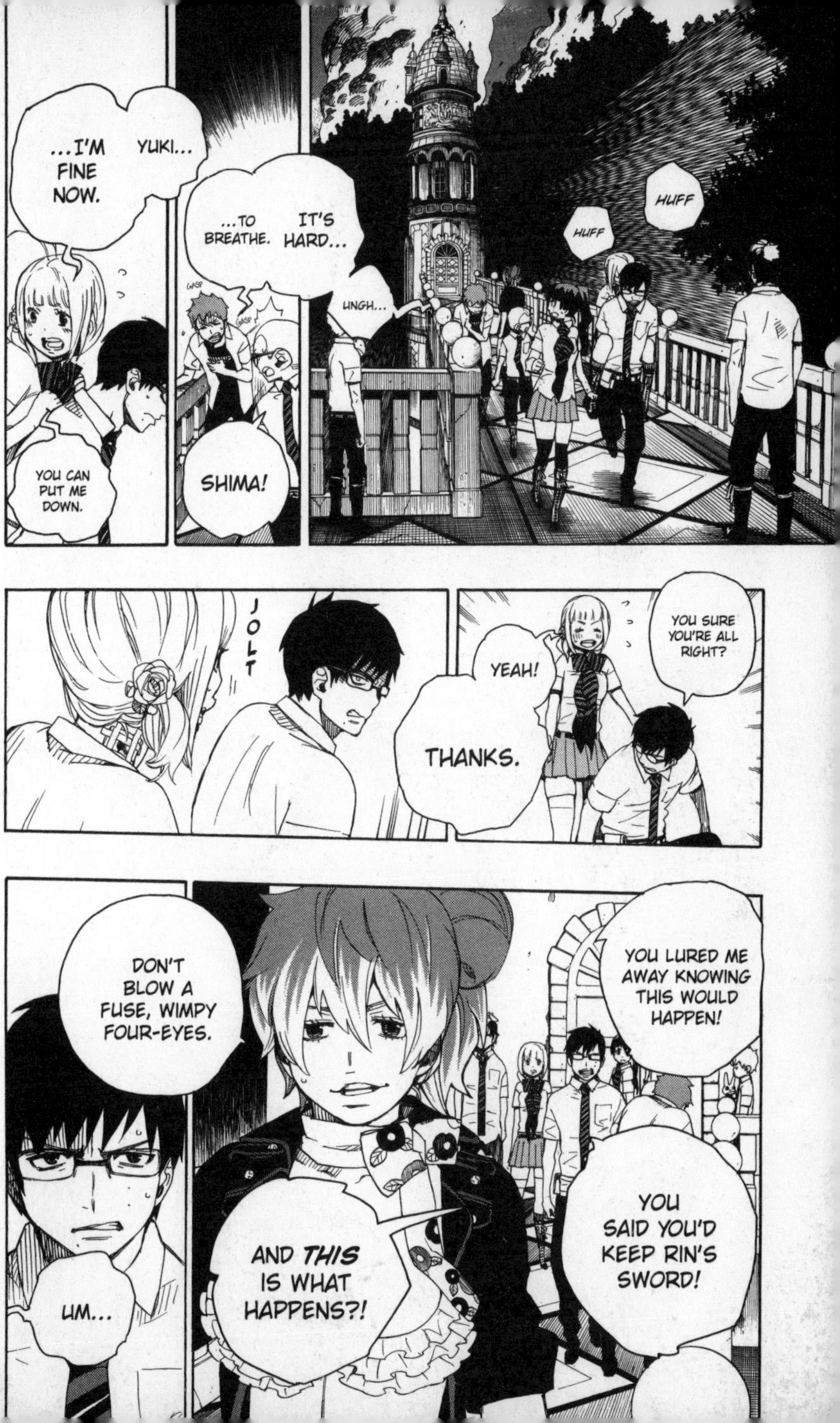
HUFF
HUFF
UNGH...
IT'S HARD...
...TO BREATHE.
GASP
GASP
SHIMA!
YUKI...
...I'M FINE NOW.
YOU CAN PUT ME DOWN.
YOU SURE YOU'RE ALL RIGHT?
YEAH!
THANKS.
JOLT
YOU LURED ME AWAY KNOWING THIS WOULD HAPPEN!
YOU SAID YOU'D KEEP RIN'S SWORD!
AND *THIS* IS WHAT HAPPENS?!
DON'T BLOW A FUSE, WIMPY FOUR-EYES.
UM...

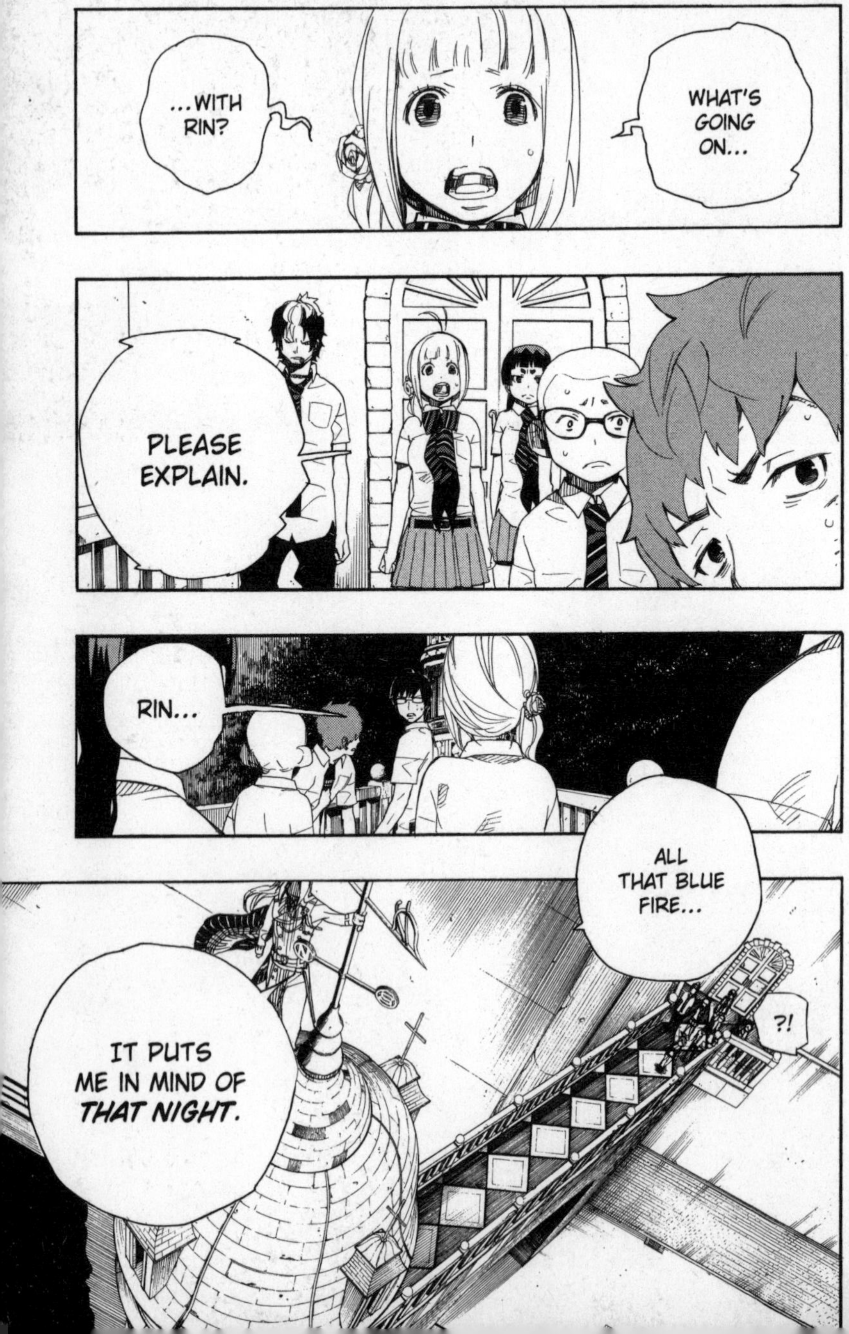
WHAT'S GOING ON...
...WITH RIN?
PLEASE EXPLAIN.
RIN...
ALL THAT BLUE FIRE...
?!
IT PUTS ME IN MIND OF *THAT NIGHT*.

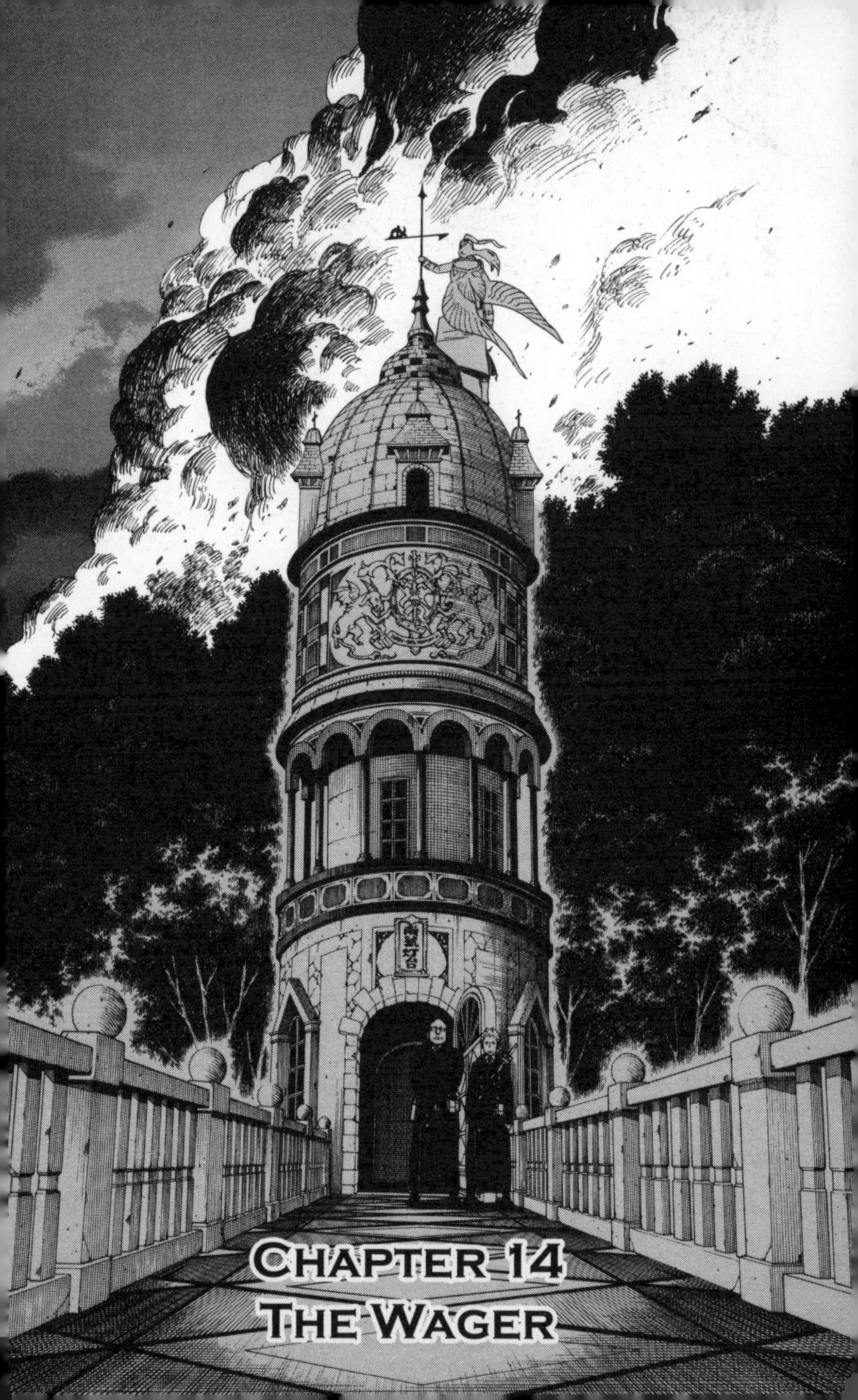
CHAPTER 14
THE WAGER

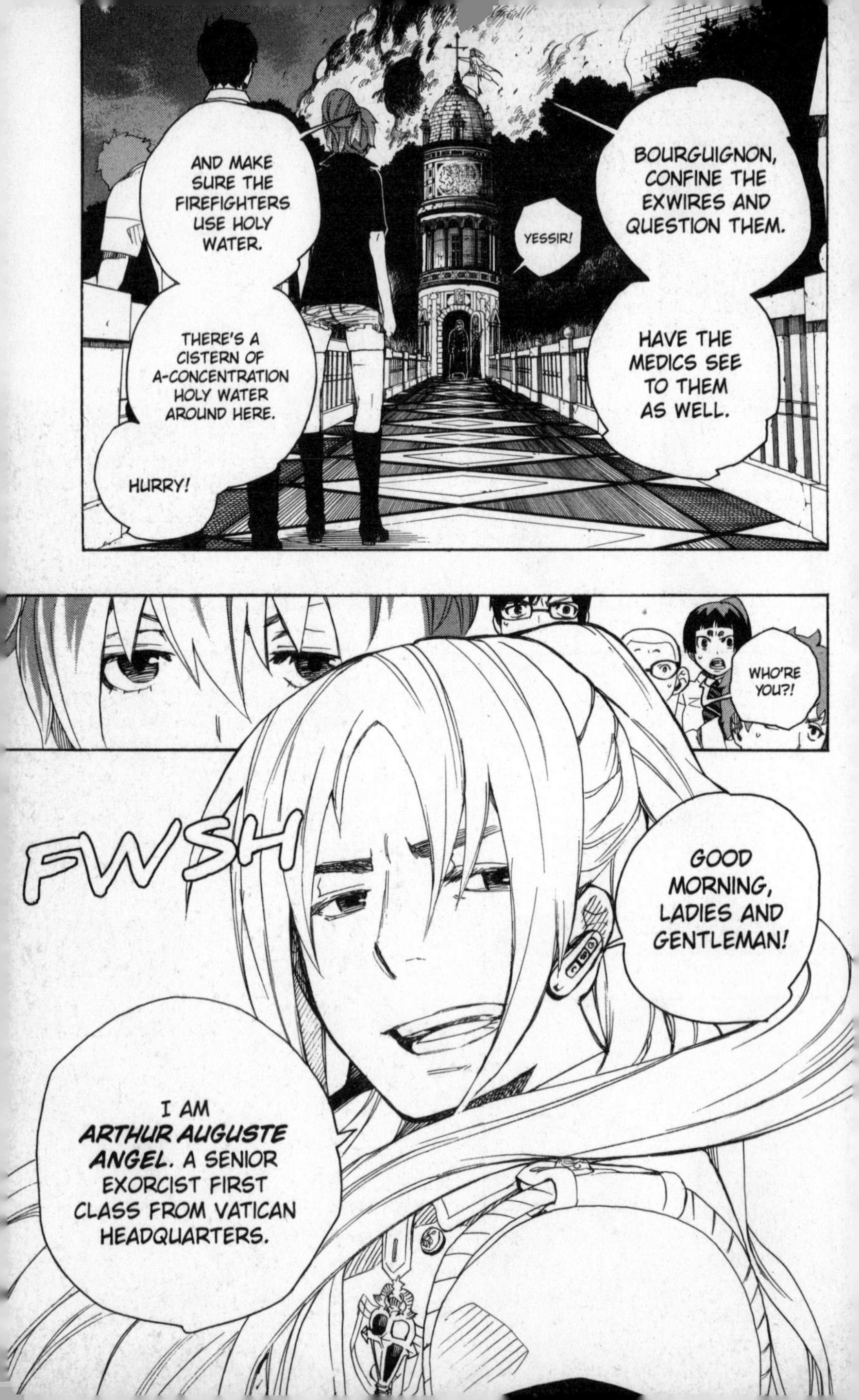
BOURGUIGNON, CONFINE THE EXWIRES AND QUESTION THEM.
HAVE THE MEDICS SEE TO THEM AS WELL.
YESSIR!
AND MAKE SURE THE FIREFIGHTERS USE HOLY WATER.
THERE'S A CISTERN OF A-CONCENTRATION HOLY WATER AROUND HERE.
HURRY!
WHO'RE YOU?!
GOOD MORNING, LADIES AND GENTLEMAN!
FWSH
I AM **ARTHUR AUGUSTE ANGEL**. A SENIOR EXORCIST FIRST CLASS FROM VATICAN HEADQUARTERS.

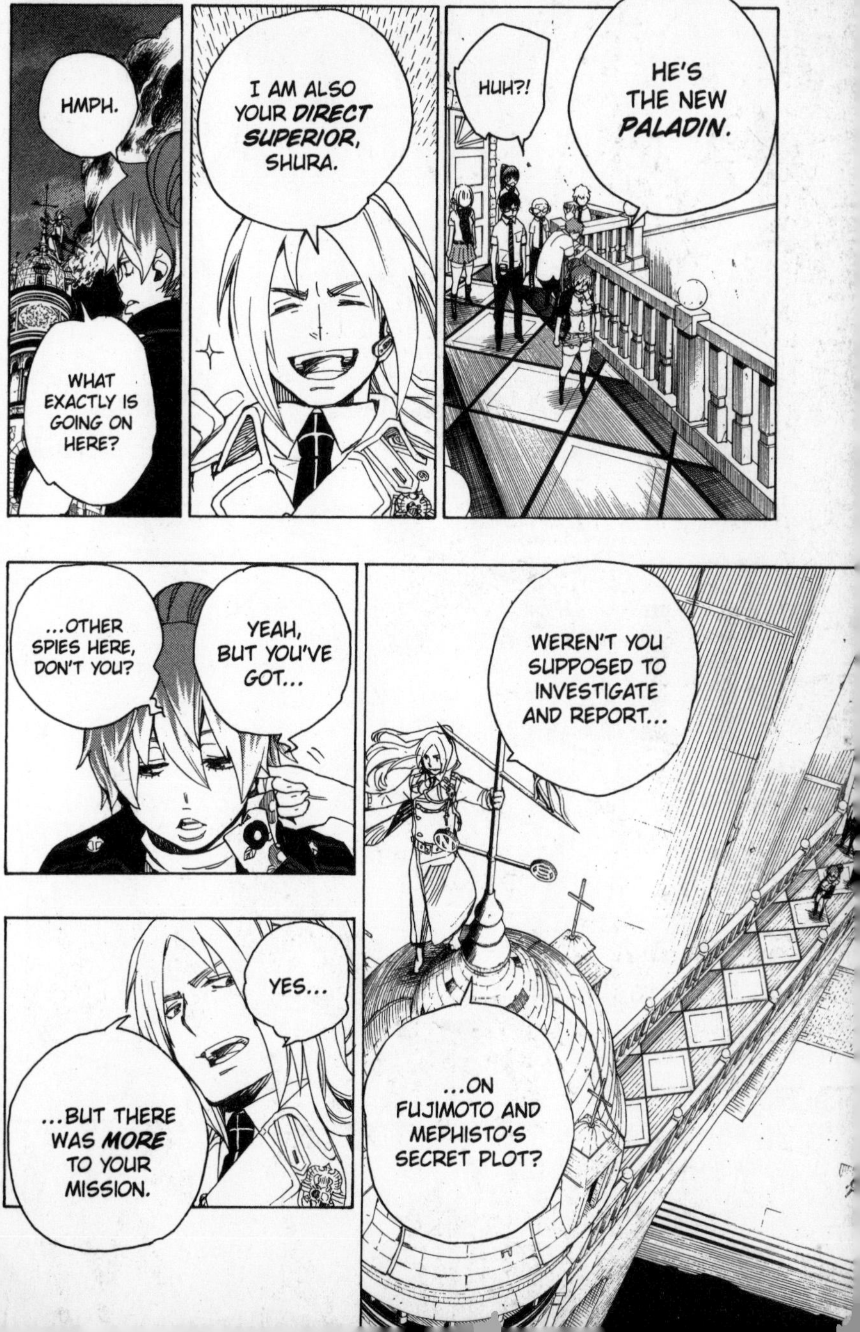
HE'S THE NEW PALADIN.
HUH?!
I AM ALSO YOUR DIRECT SUPERIOR, SHURA.
HMPH.
WHAT EXACTLY IS GOING ON HERE?
WEREN'T YOU SUPPOSED TO INVESTIGATE AND REPORT...
...ON FUJIMOTO AND MEPHISTO'S SECRET PLOT?
YEAH, BUT YOU'VE GOT...
...OTHER SPIES HERE, DON'T YOU?
YES...
...BUT THERE WAS MORE TO YOUR MISSION.

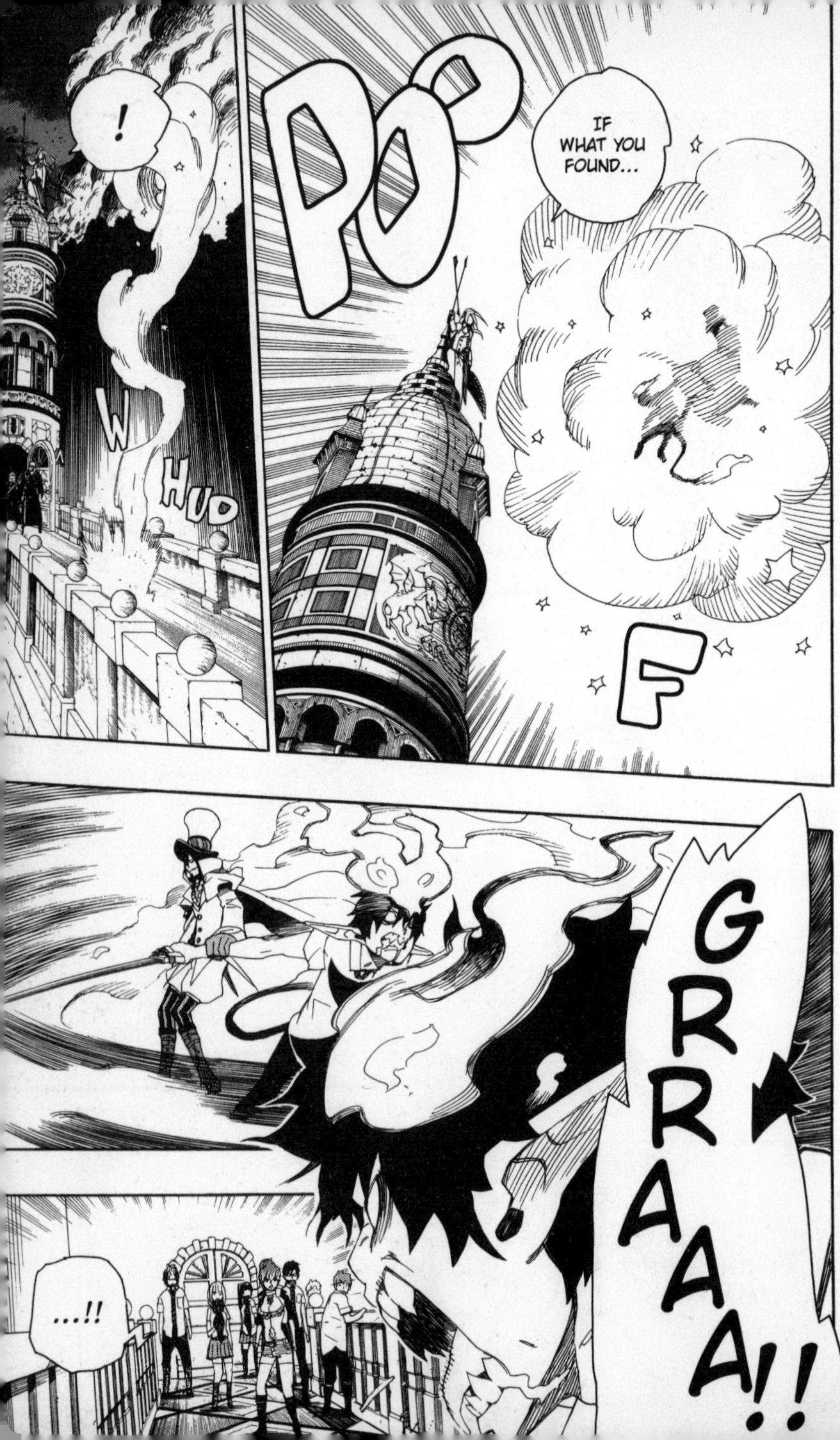

POOF
IF WHAT YOU FOUND...
!
WHUD
GRRAAA!!
...!!

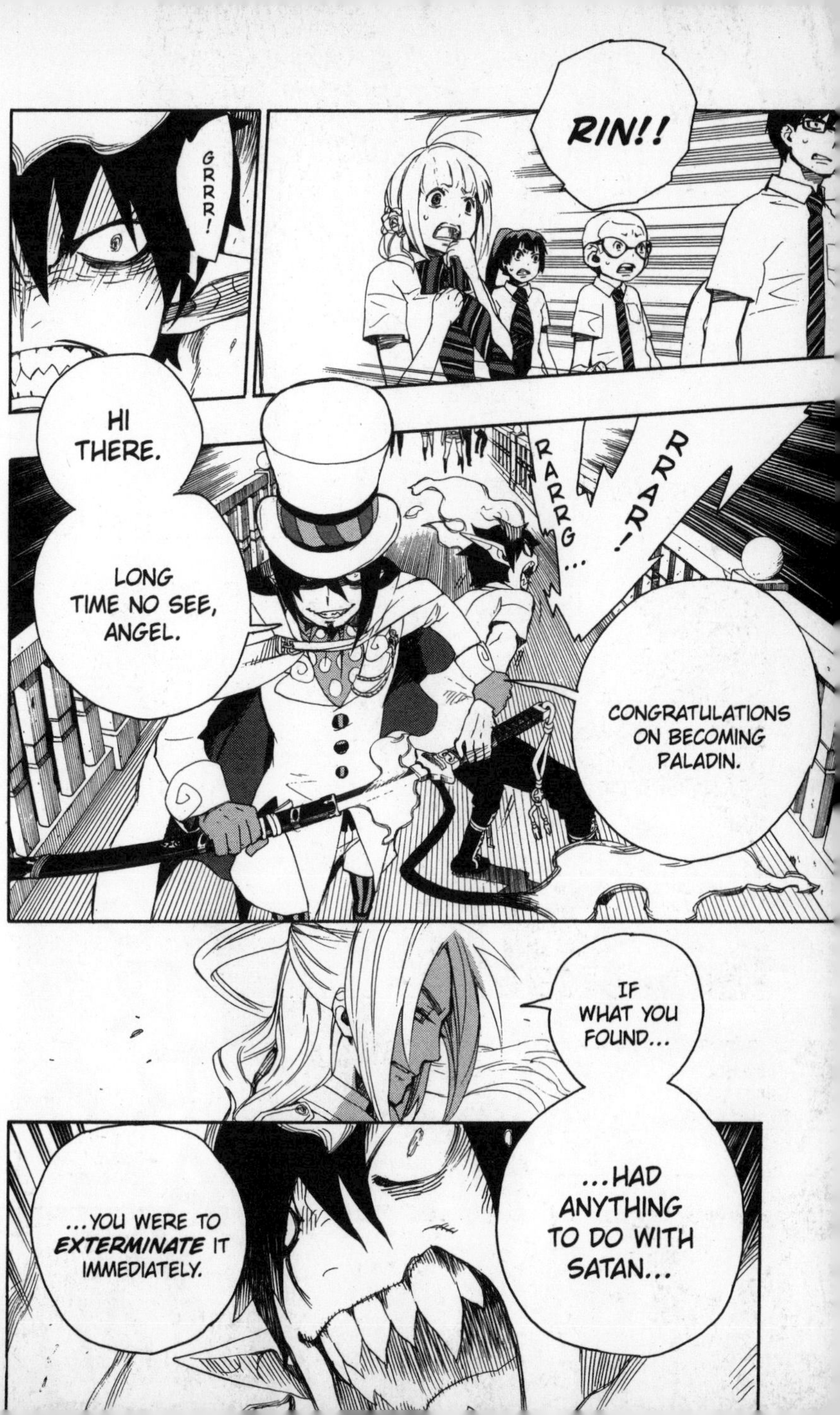
RIN!!
GRRR!
RRAR!
RARRG...
HI THERE.
LONG TIME NO SEE, ANGEL.
CONGRATULATIONS ON BECOMING PALADIN.
IF WHAT YOU FOUND...
...HAD ANYTHING TO DO WITH SATAN...
...YOU WERE TO *EXTERMINATE* IT IMMEDIATELY.

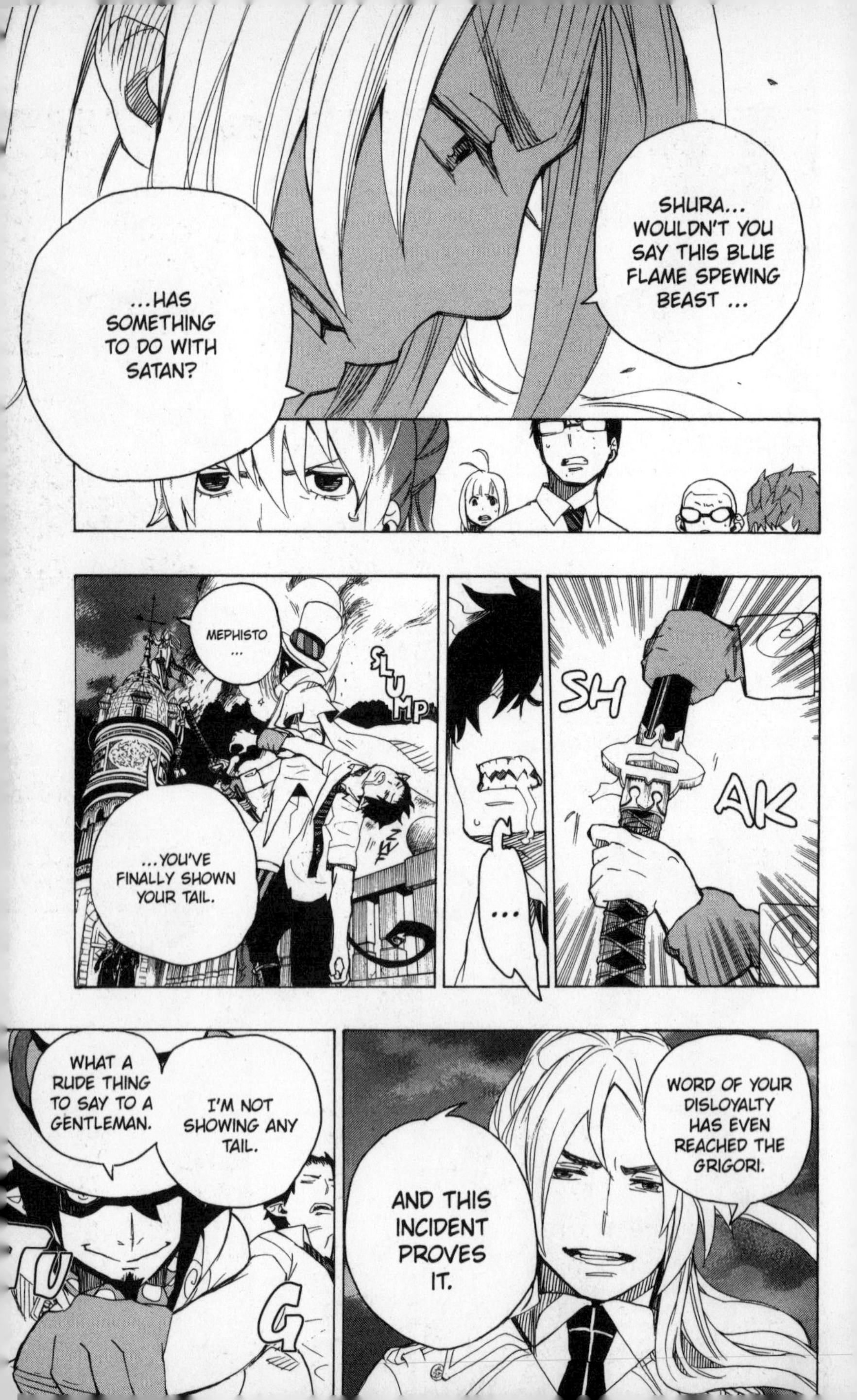
SHURA... WOULDN'T YOU SAY THIS BLUE FLAME SPEWING BEAST ...
...HAS SOMETHING TO DO WITH SATAN?
SHAK
...
MEPHISTO ...
SLUMP
...YOU'VE FINALLY SHOWN YOUR TAIL.
WORD OF YOUR DISLOYALTY HAS EVEN REACHED THE GRIGORI.
AND THIS INCIDENT PROVES IT.
I'M NOT SHOWING ANY TAIL.
WHAT A RUDE THING TO SAY TO A GENTLEMAN.
UG

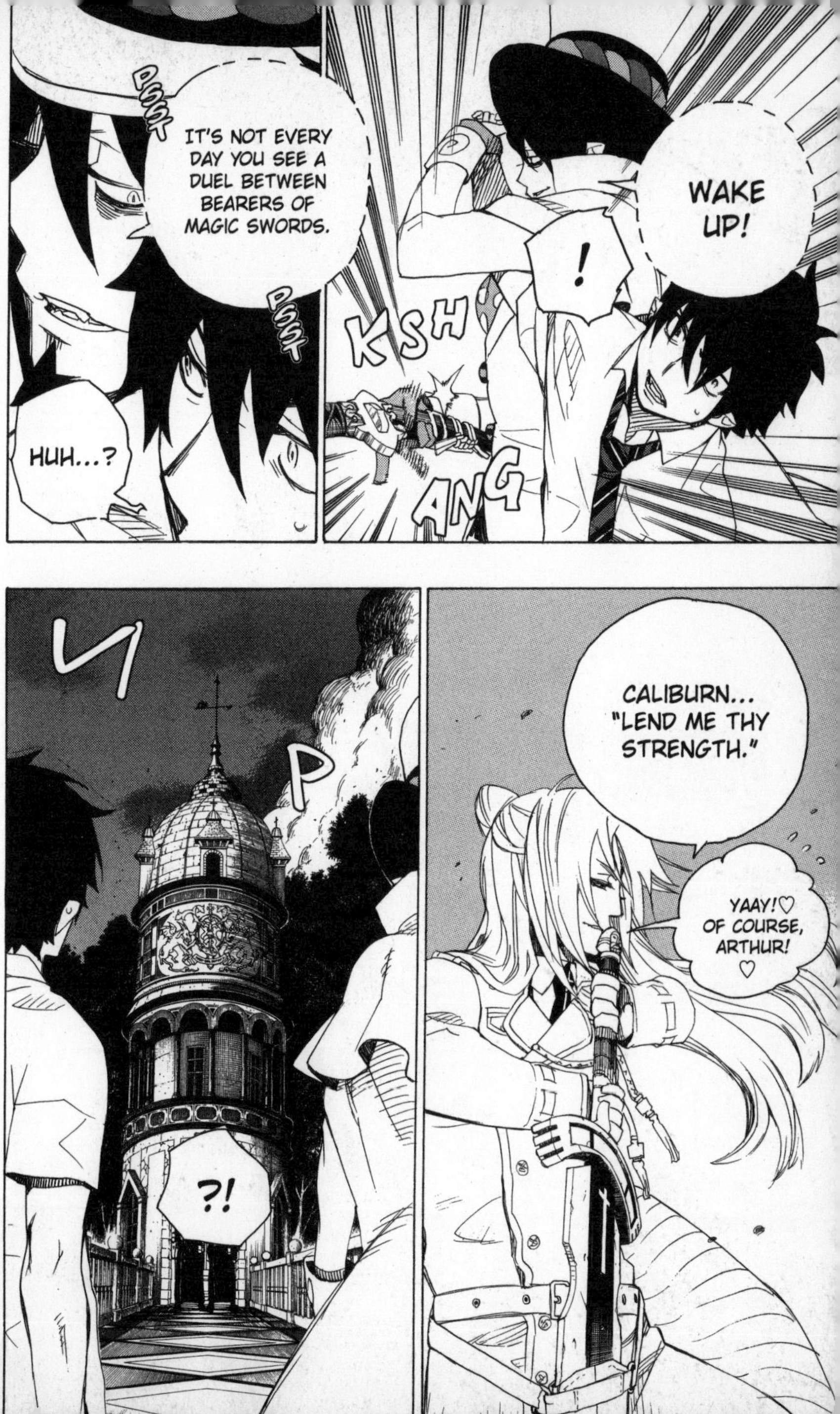
WAKE UP!
!
KSH
ANG
PSST
IT'S NOT EVERY DAY YOU SEE A DUEL BETWEEN BEARERS OF MAGIC SWORDS.
PSST
HUH...?
CALIBURN... "LEND ME THY STRENGTH."
YAAY!♡ OF COURSE, ARTHUR! ♡
U
P
?!

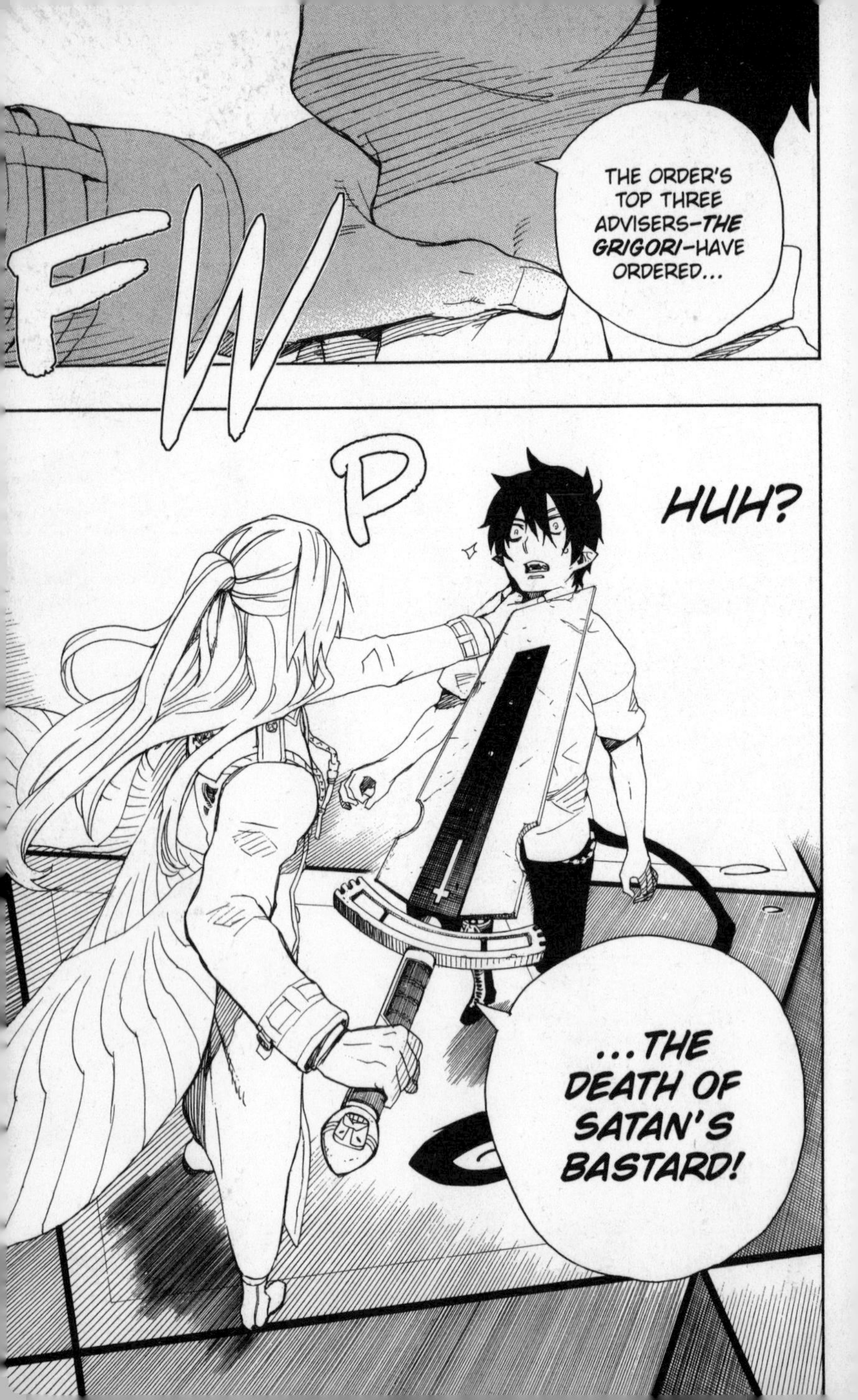
THE ORDER'S TOP THREE ADVISERS—THE GRIGORI—HAVE ORDERED...
FWP
HUH?
...THE DEATH OF SATAN'S BASTARD!

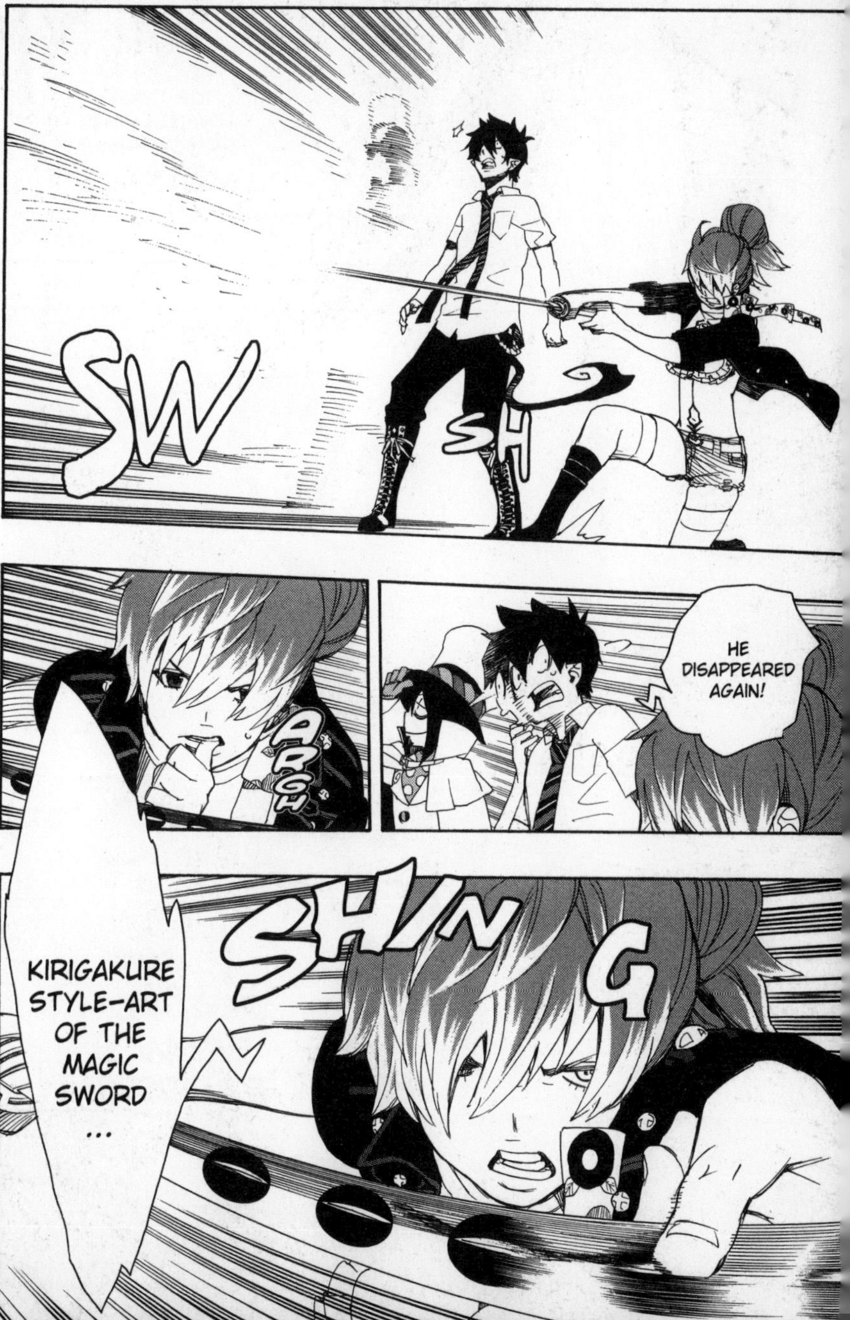
SW
SH
HE DISAPPEARED AGAIN!
ARGH
SHING
KIRIGAKURE STYLE-ART OF THE MAGIC SWORD ...

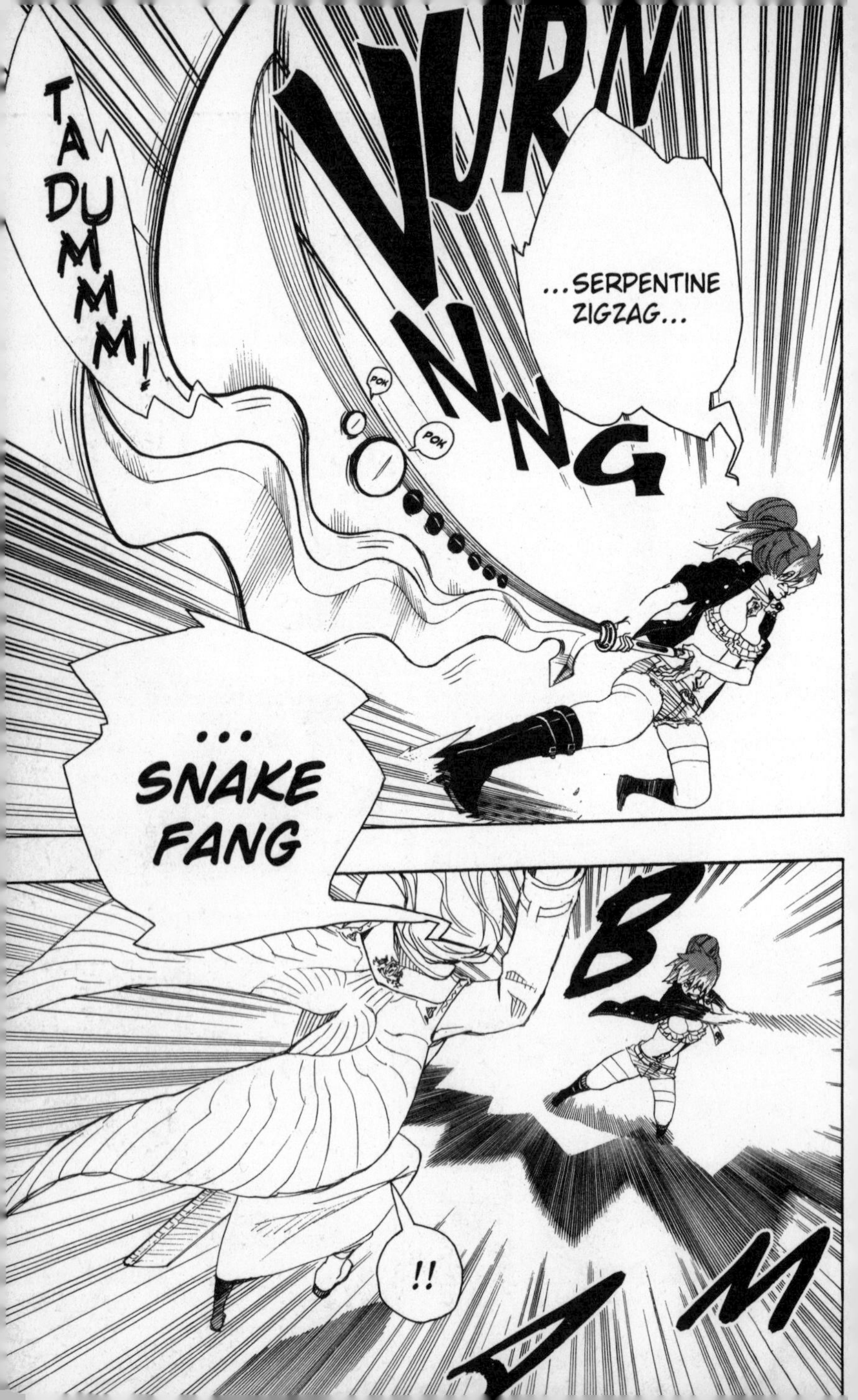
...SERPENTINE ZIGZAG...
VURNNNG
POK
POK
TADUMMM!
...SNAKE FANG
BAM
!!

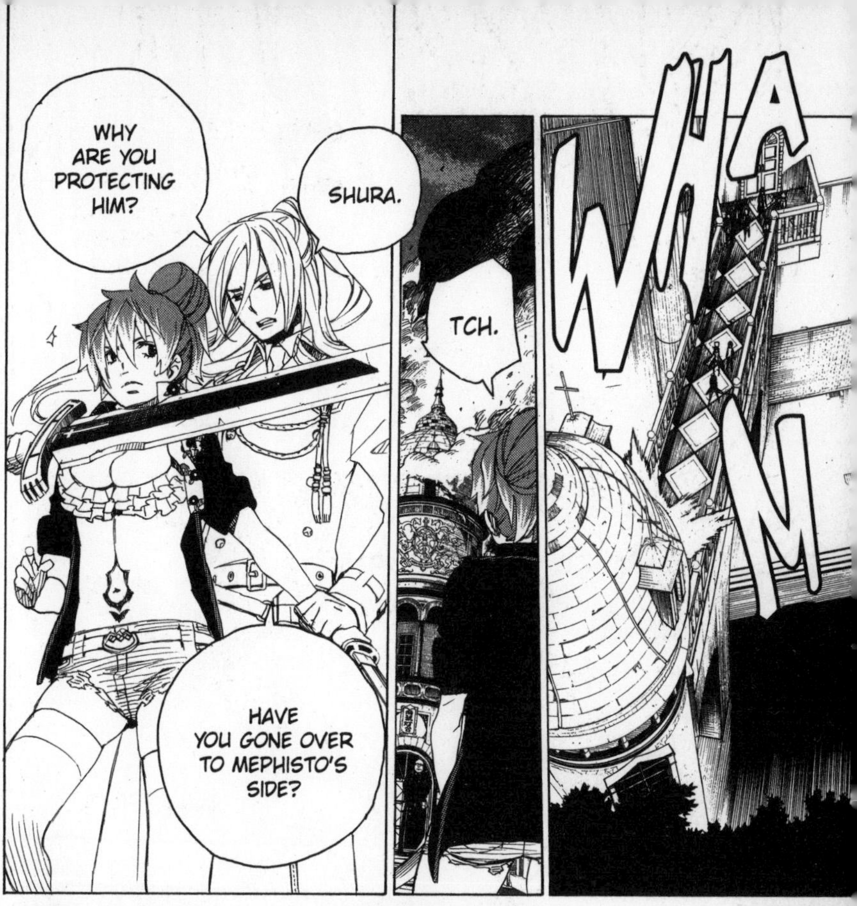
WHAM
TCH.
SHURA.
WHY ARE YOU PROTECTING HIM?
HAVE YOU GONE OVER TO MEPHISTO'S SIDE?

TOWER: SOUTH LIGHTHOUSE

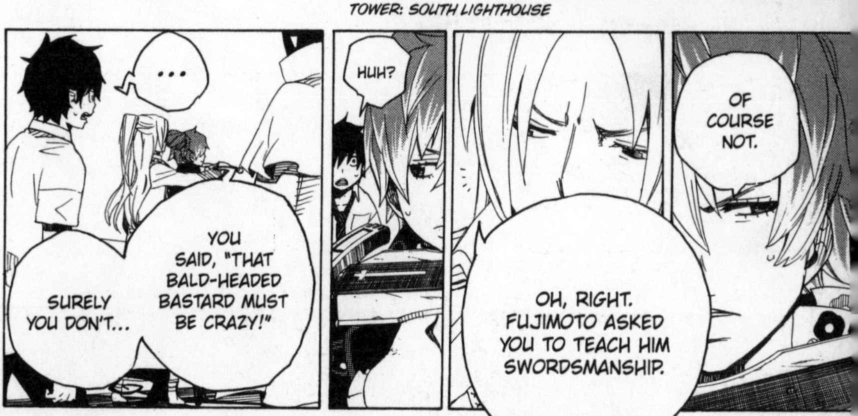
OF COURSE NOT.
OH, RIGHT. FUJIMOTO ASKED YOU TO TEACH HIM SWORDSMANSHIP.
HUH?
...
YOU SAID, "THAT BALD-HEADED BASTARD MUST BE CRAZY!"
SURELY YOU DON'T...

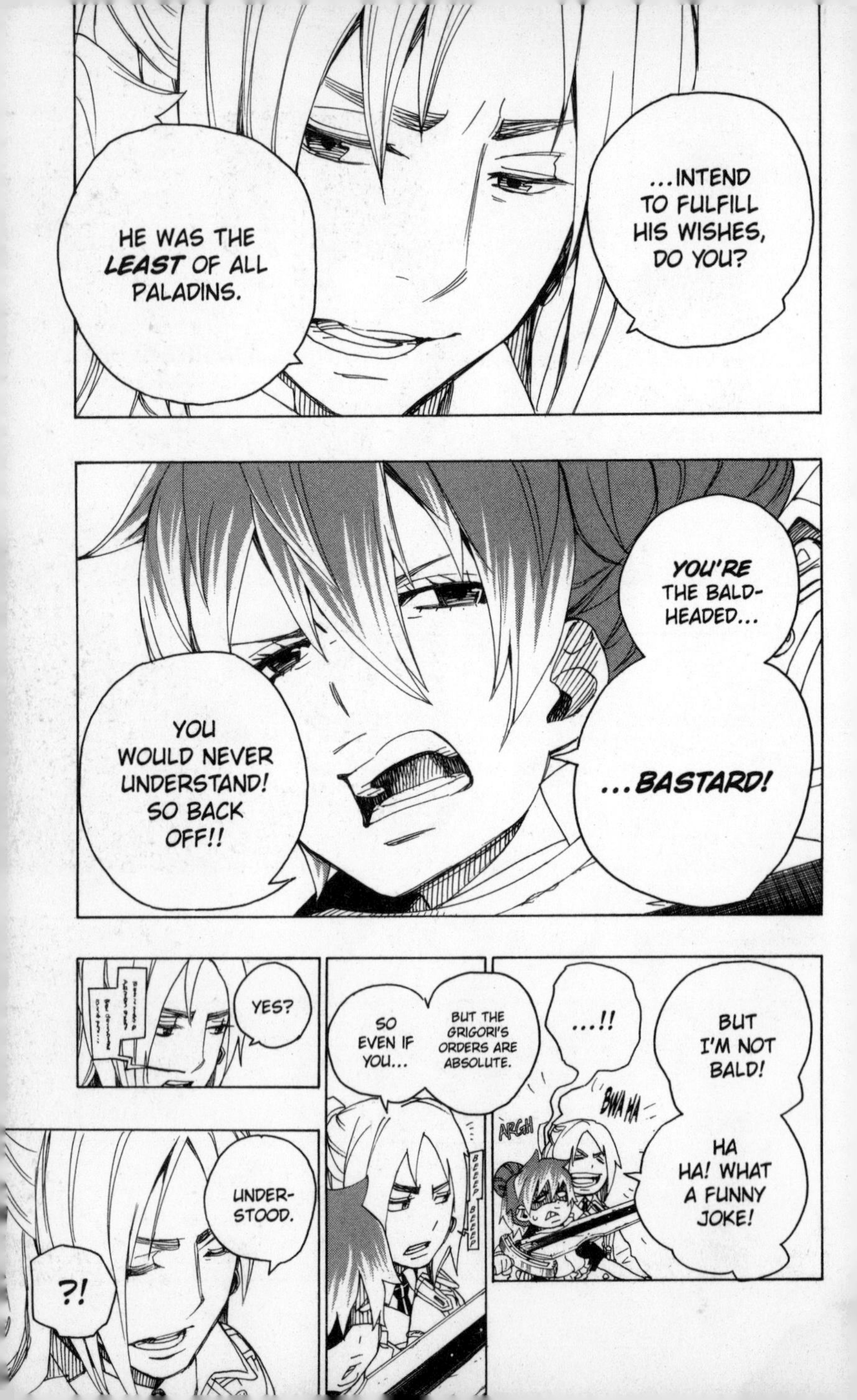
...INTEND TO FULFILL HIS WISHES, DO YOU?
HE WAS THE *LEAST* OF ALL PALADINS.
YOU'RE THE BALD-HEADED...
...*BASTARD!*
YOU WOULD NEVER UNDERSTAND! SO BACK OFF!!
...!!
BUT I'M NOT BALD!
BWA HA
HA HA! WHAT A FUNNY JOKE!
ARGH
BUT THE GRIGORI'S ORDERS ARE ABSOLUTE.
SO EVEN IF YOU...
BEEEP BEEEP
YES?
UNDER-STOOD.
?!

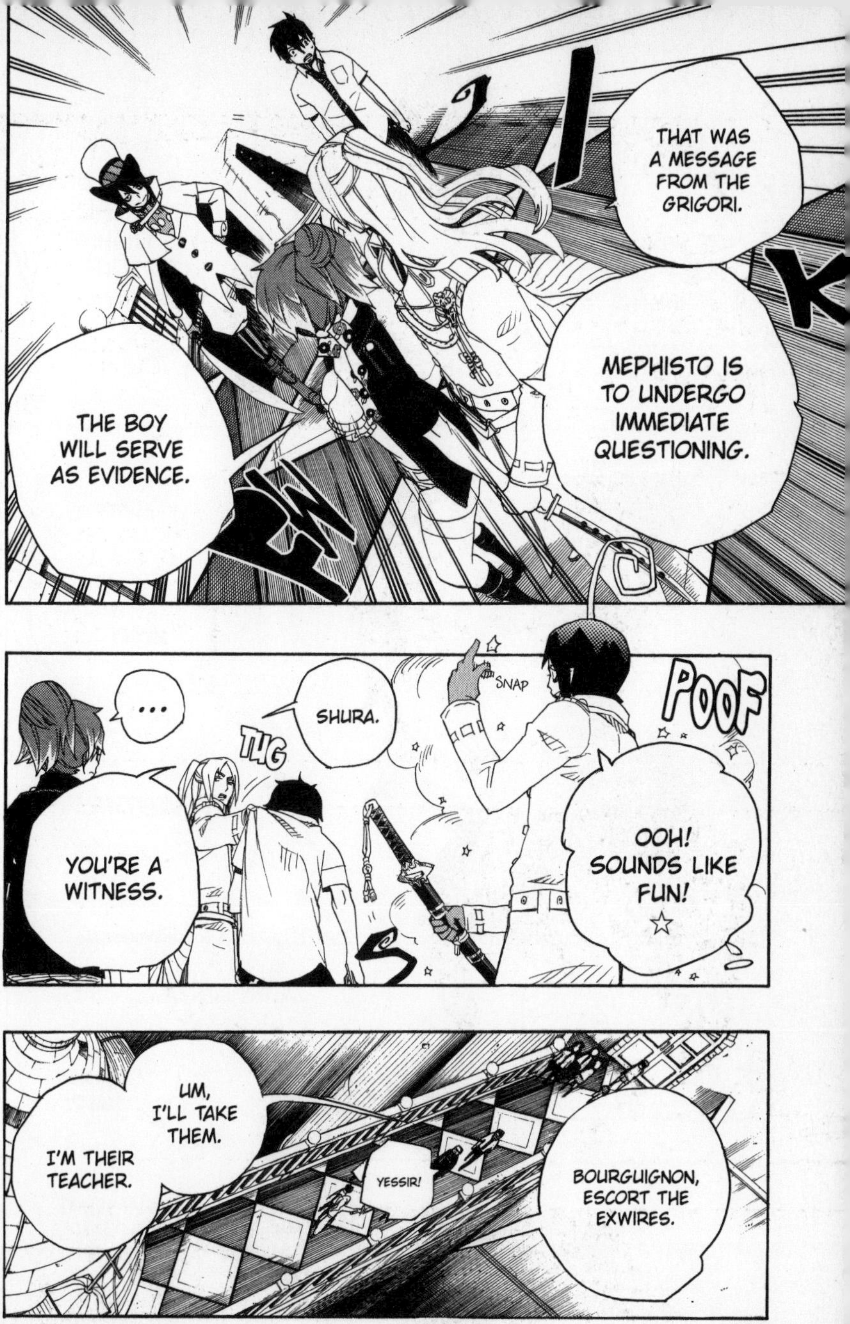
THAT WAS A MESSAGE FROM THE GRIGORI.
MEPHISTO IS TO UNDERGO IMMEDIATE QUESTIONING.
THE BOY WILL SERVE AS EVIDENCE.
POOF
SNAP
OOH! SOUNDS LIKE FUN! ☆
SHURA.
THG
...
YOU'RE A WITNESS.
BOURGUIGNON, ESCORT THE EXWIRES.
YESSIR!
UM, I'LL TAKE THEM.
I'M THEIR TEACHER.

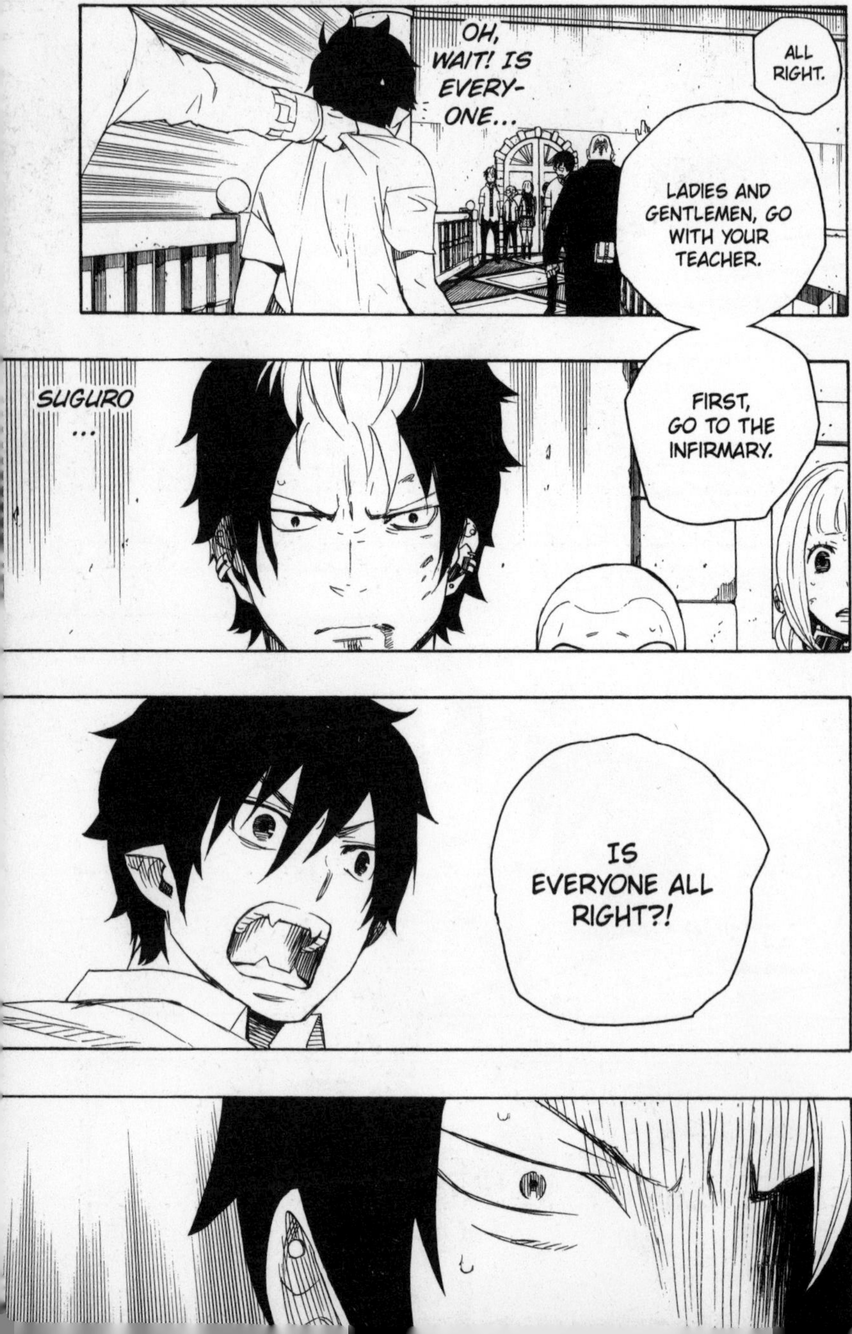
ALL RIGHT.
LADIES AND GENTLEMEN, GO WITH YOUR TEACHER.
FIRST, GO TO THE INFIRMARY.
OH, WAIT! IS EVERY-ONE...
SUGURO ...
IS EVERYONE ALL RIGHT?!

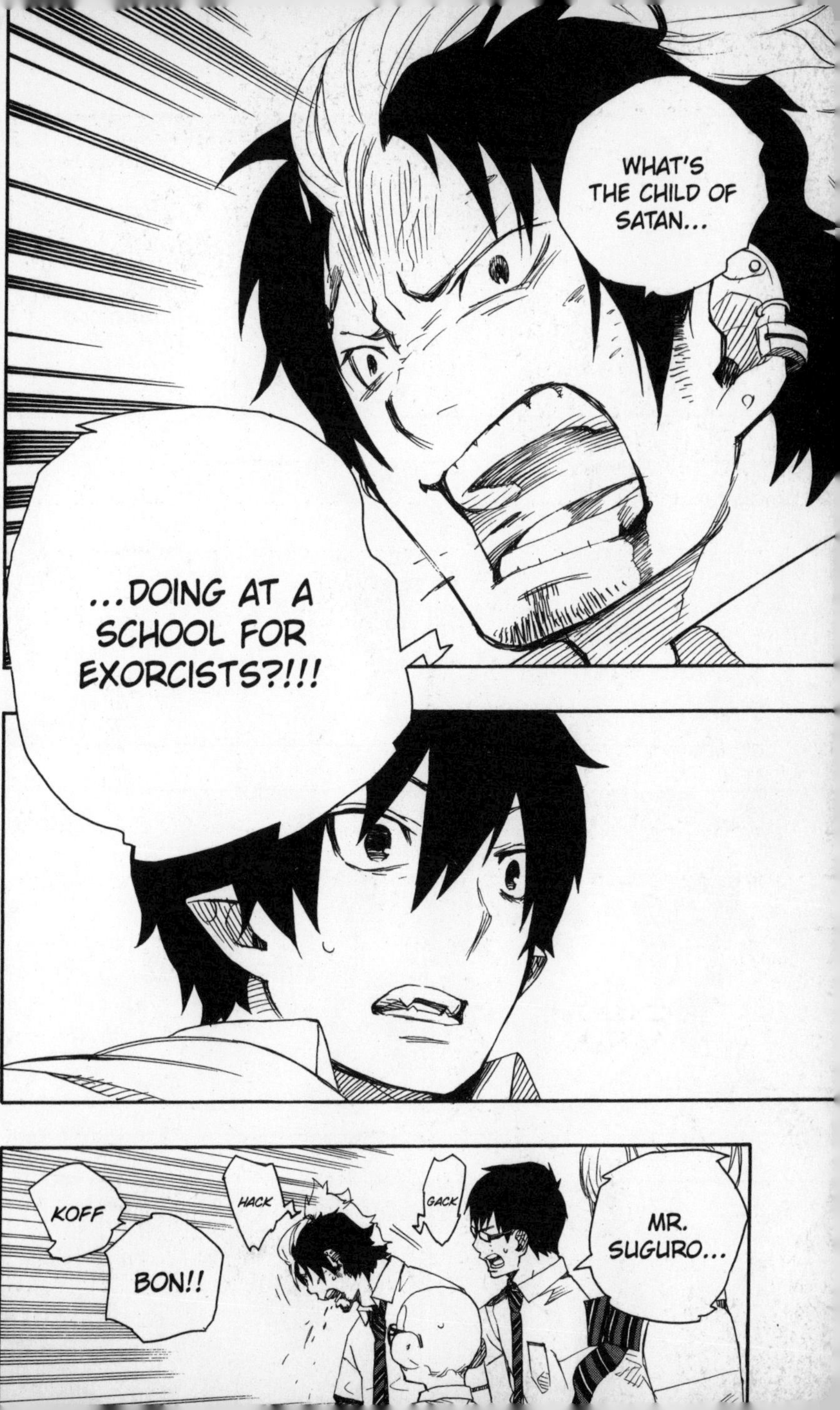
WHAT'S THE CHILD OF SATAN...
...DOING AT A SCHOOL FOR EXORCISTS?!!!
MR. SUGURO...
GACK
HACK
KOFF
BON!!

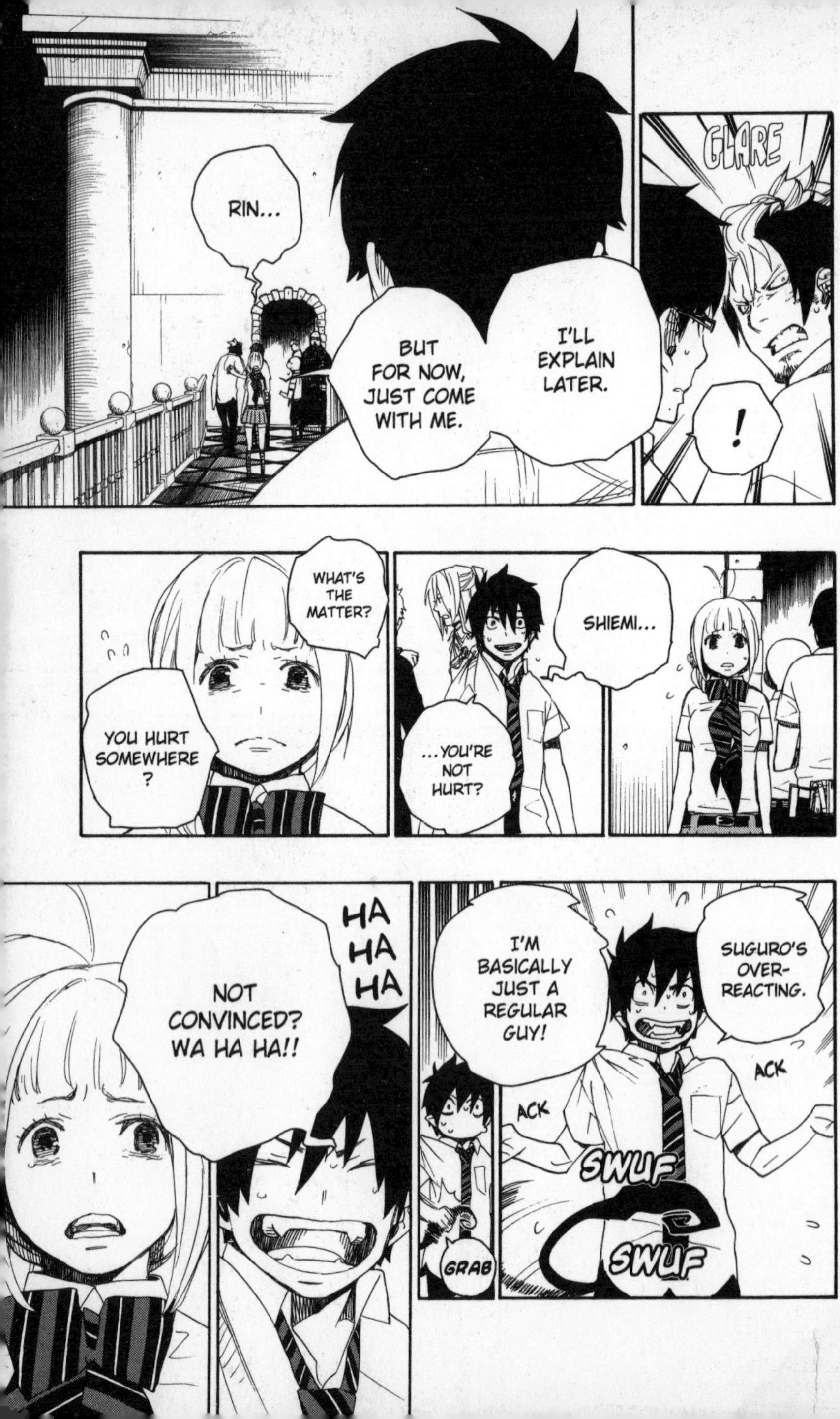
GLARE
!
RIN...
I'LL EXPLAIN LATER.
BUT FOR NOW, JUST COME WITH ME.
SHIEMI...
...YOU'RE NOT HURT?
WHAT'S THE MATTER?
YOU HURT SOMEWHERE?
SUGURO'S OVER-REACTING.
I'M BASICALLY JUST A REGULAR GUY!
ACK
ACK
SWUF
SWUF
GRAB
HA HA HA
NOT CONVINCED? WA HA HA!!

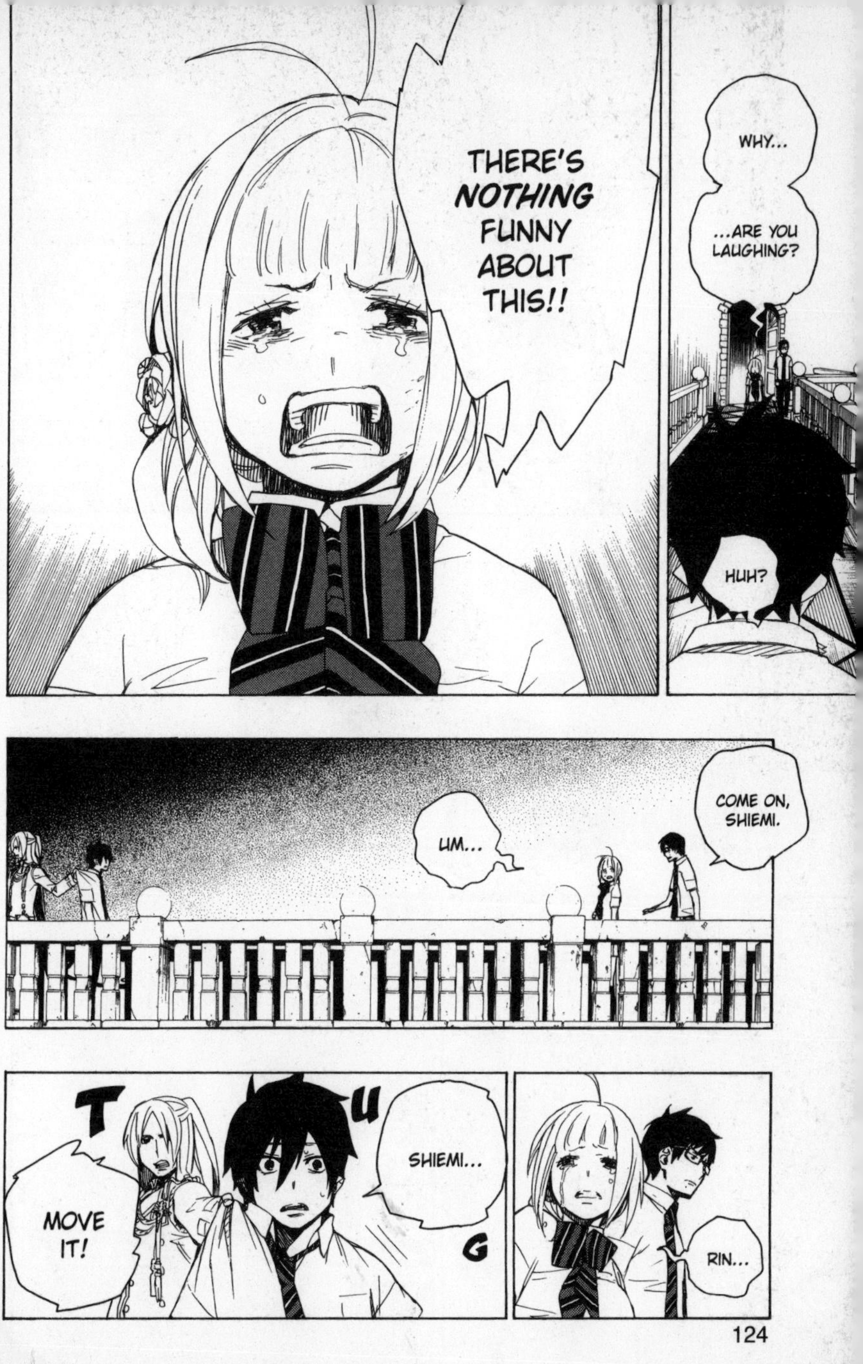
WHY...
...ARE YOU LAUGHING?
HUH?
THERE'S *NOTHING* FUNNY ABOUT THIS!!
COME ON, SHIEMI.
UM...
RIN...
SHIEMI...
TUG
MOVE IT!

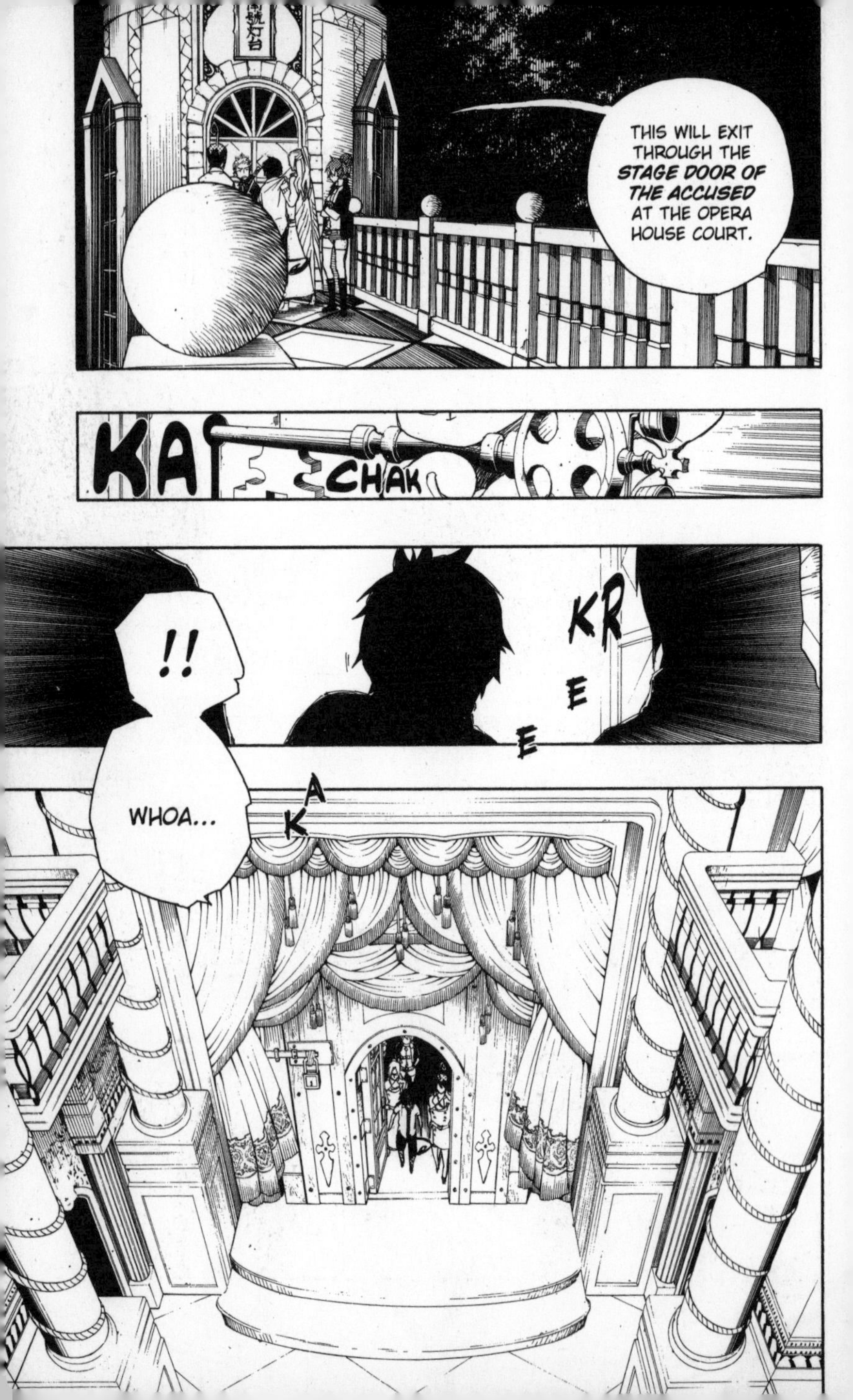
THIS WILL EXIT THROUGH THE ***STAGE DOOR OF THE ACCUSED*** AT THE OPERA HOUSE COURT.
KA
CHAK
!!
KREE
WHOA...
KA

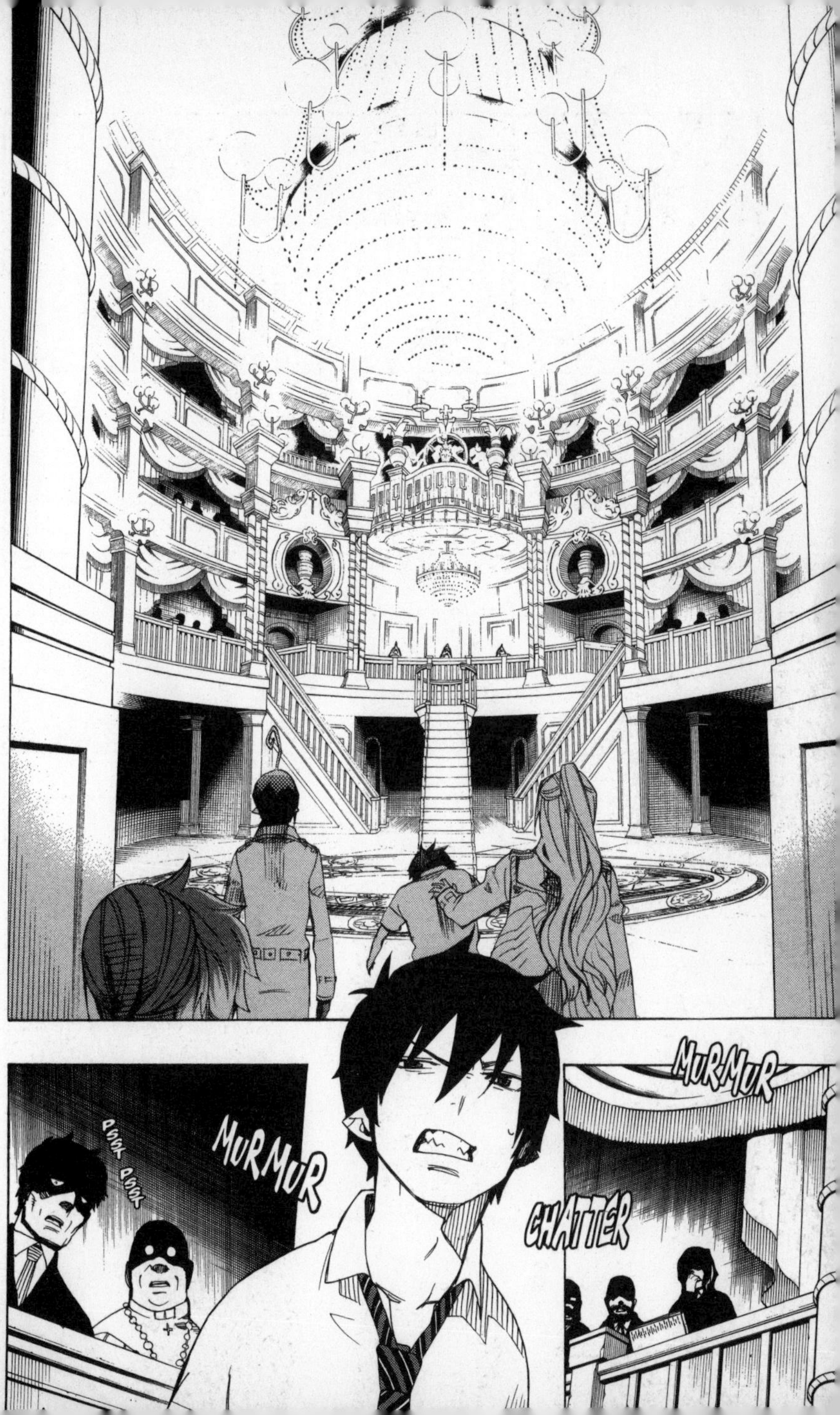
MURMUR
CHATTER
MURMUR
PSST PSST

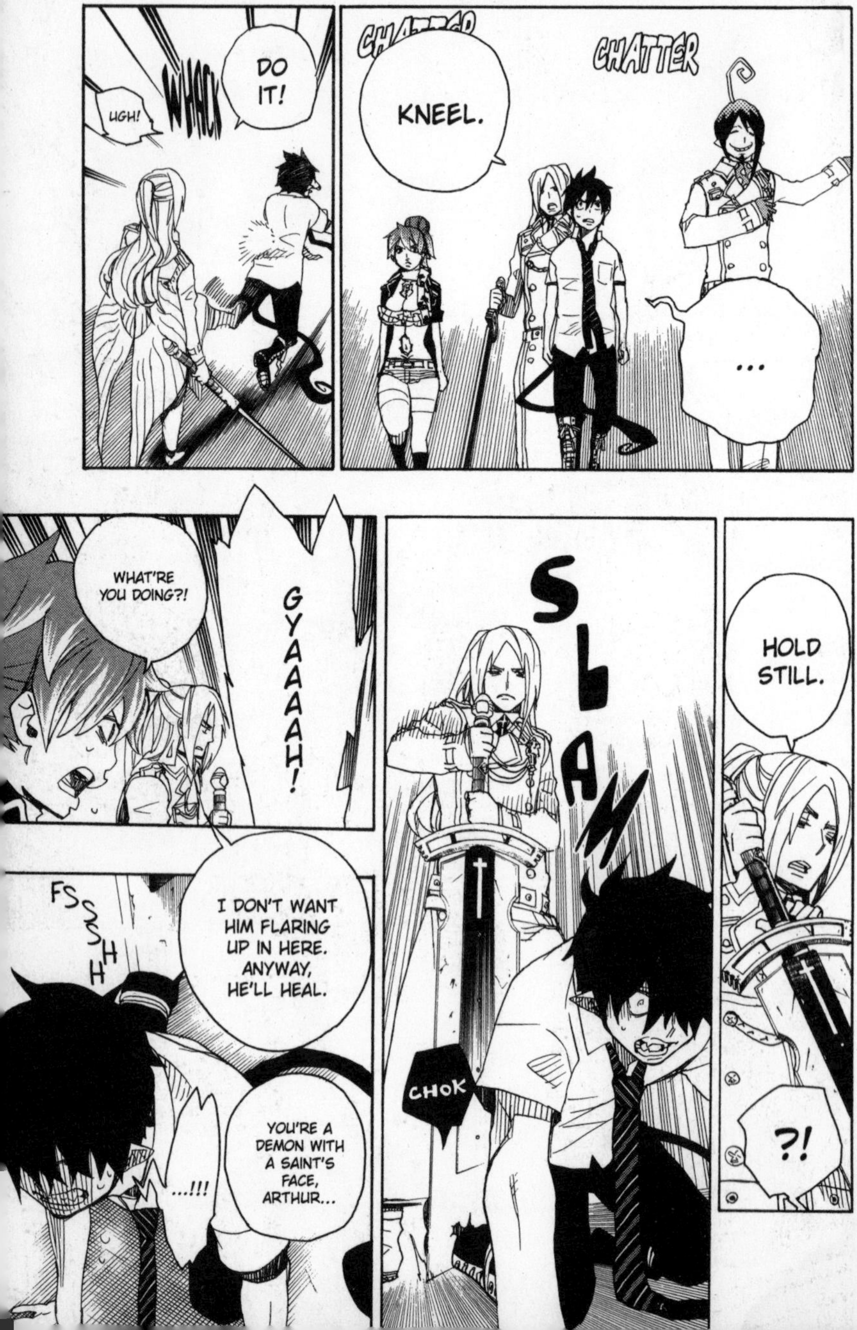
CHATTER
KNEEL.
...
DO IT!
WHACK
UGH!
HOLD STILL.
?!
SLAM
CHOK
GYAAAAAH!
WHAT'RE YOU DOING?!
I DON'T WANT HIM FLARING UP IN HERE. ANYWAY, HE'LL HEAL.
FSSHH
YOU'RE A DEMON WITH A SAINT'S FACE, ARTHUR...
...!!!

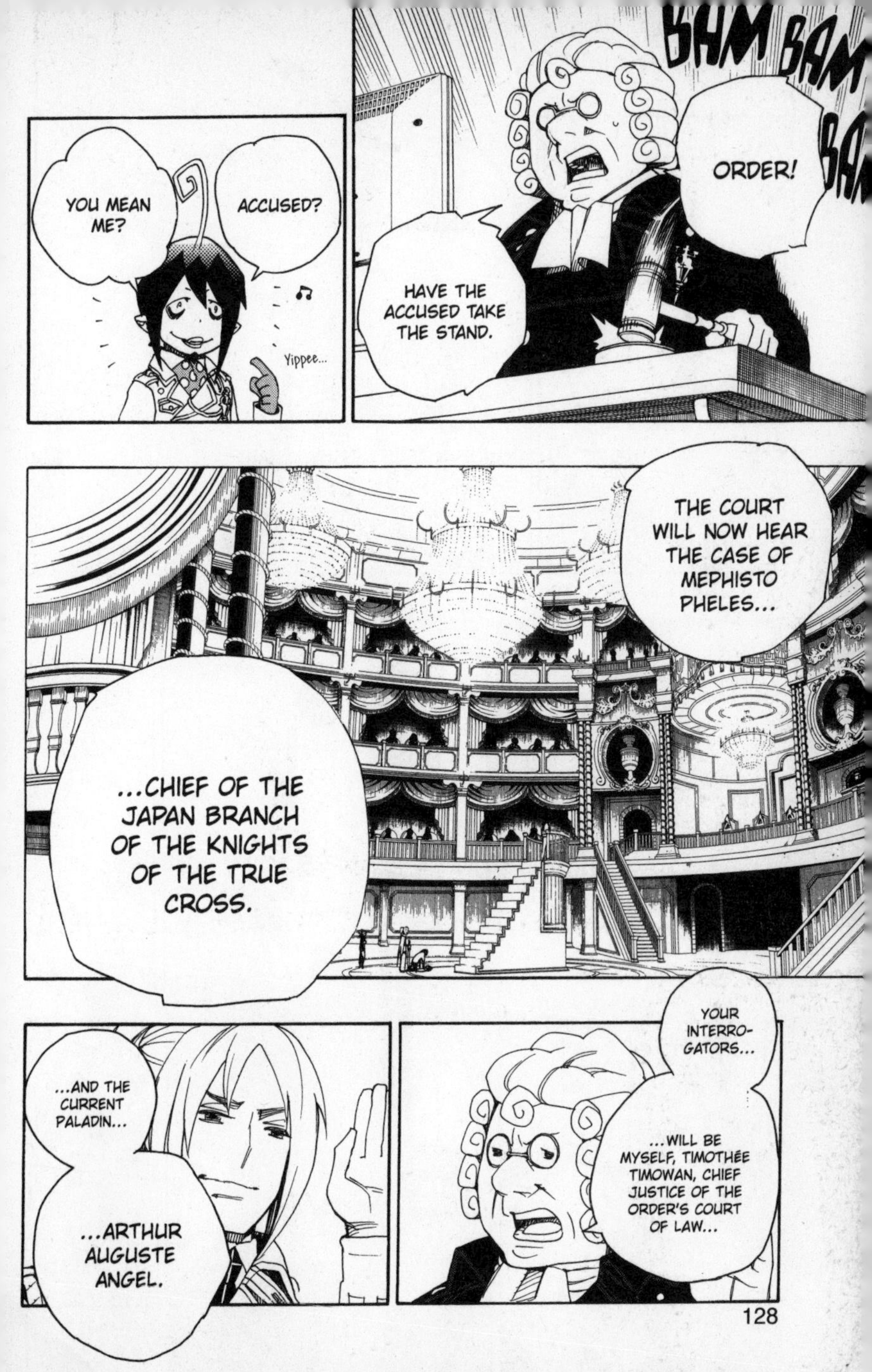
BAM BAM BAM
ORDER!
HAVE THE ACCUSED TAKE THE STAND.
ACCUSED?
YOU MEAN ME?
Yippee...
THE COURT WILL NOW HEAR THE CASE OF MEPHISTO PHELES...
...CHIEF OF THE JAPAN BRANCH OF THE KNIGHTS OF THE TRUE CROSS.
YOUR INTERROGATORS...
...WILL BE MYSELF, TIMOTHÉE TIMOWAN, CHIEF JUSTICE OF THE ORDER'S COURT OF LAW...
...AND THE CURRENT PALADIN...
...ARTHUR AUGUSTE ANGEL.

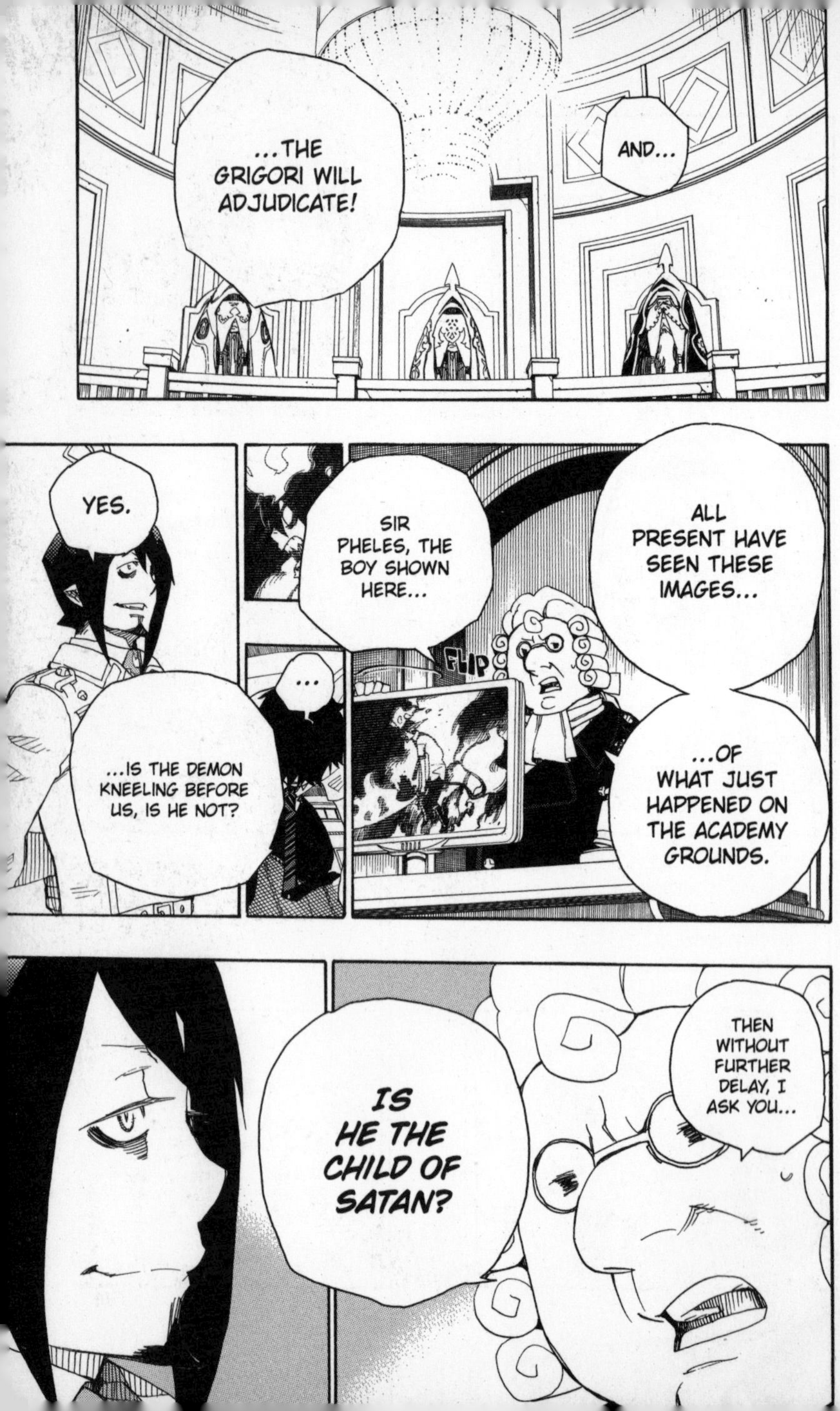
AND...
...THE GRIGORI WILL ADJUDICATE!
ALL PRESENT HAVE SEEN THESE IMAGES...
...OF WHAT JUST HAPPENED ON THE ACADEMY GROUNDS.
FLIP
SIR PHELES, THE BOY SHOWN HERE...
...
...IS THE DEMON KNEELING BEFORE US, IS HE NOT?
YES.
THEN WITHOUT FURTHER DELAY, I ASK YOU...
IS HE THE CHILD OF SATAN?

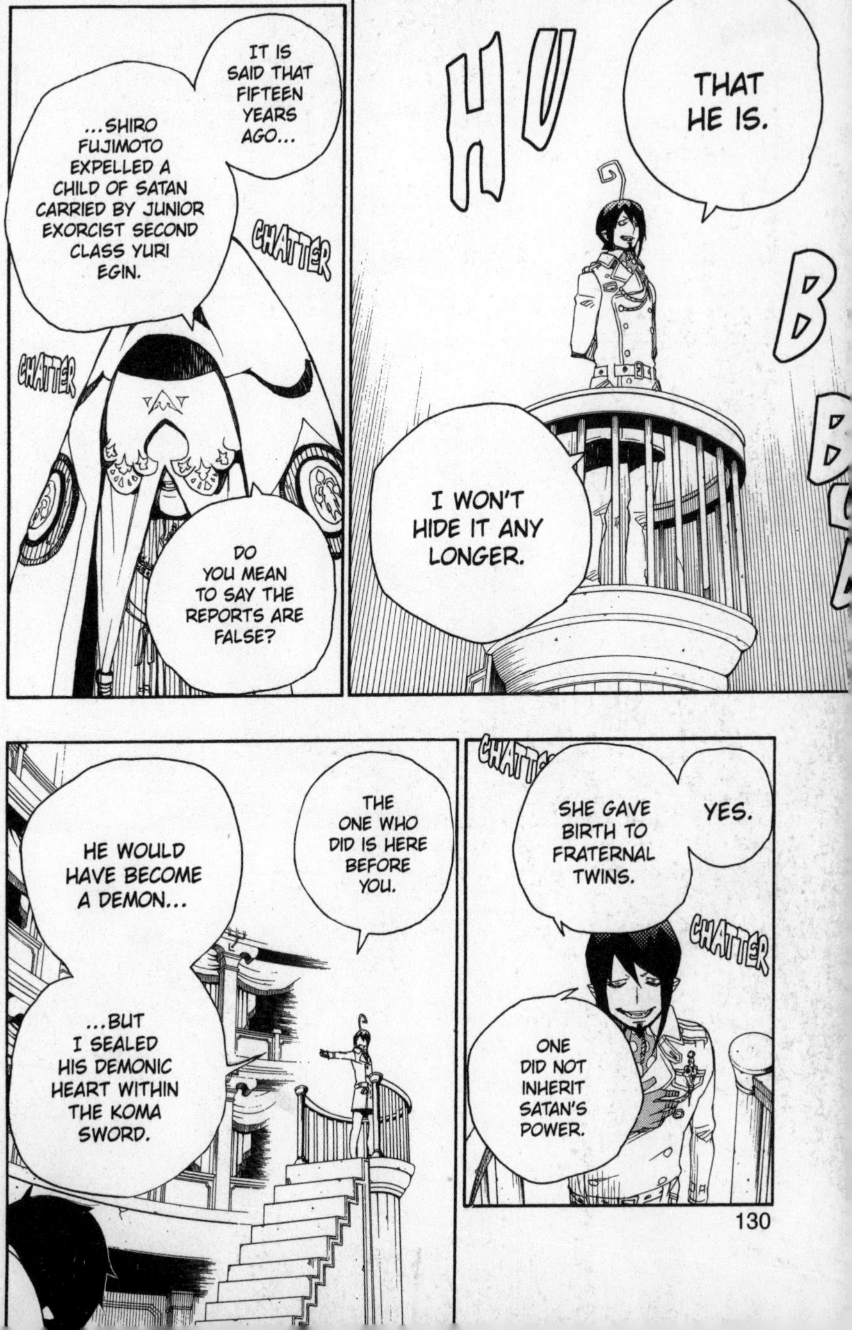
THAT HE IS.
HU
B
I WON'T HIDE IT ANY LONGER.
IT IS SAID THAT FIFTEEN YEARS AGO...
...SHIRO FUJIMOTO EXPELLED A CHILD OF SATAN CARRIED BY JUNIOR EXORCIST SECOND CLASS YURI EGIN.
CHATTER
CHATTER
DO YOU MEAN TO SAY THE REPORTS ARE FALSE?
YES.
SHE GAVE BIRTH TO FRATERNAL TWINS.
CHATTER
ONE DID NOT INHERIT SATAN'S POWER.
THE ONE WHO DID IS HERE BEFORE YOU.
HE WOULD HAVE BECOME A DEMON...
...BUT I SEALED HIS DEMONIC HEART WITHIN THE KOMA SWORD.

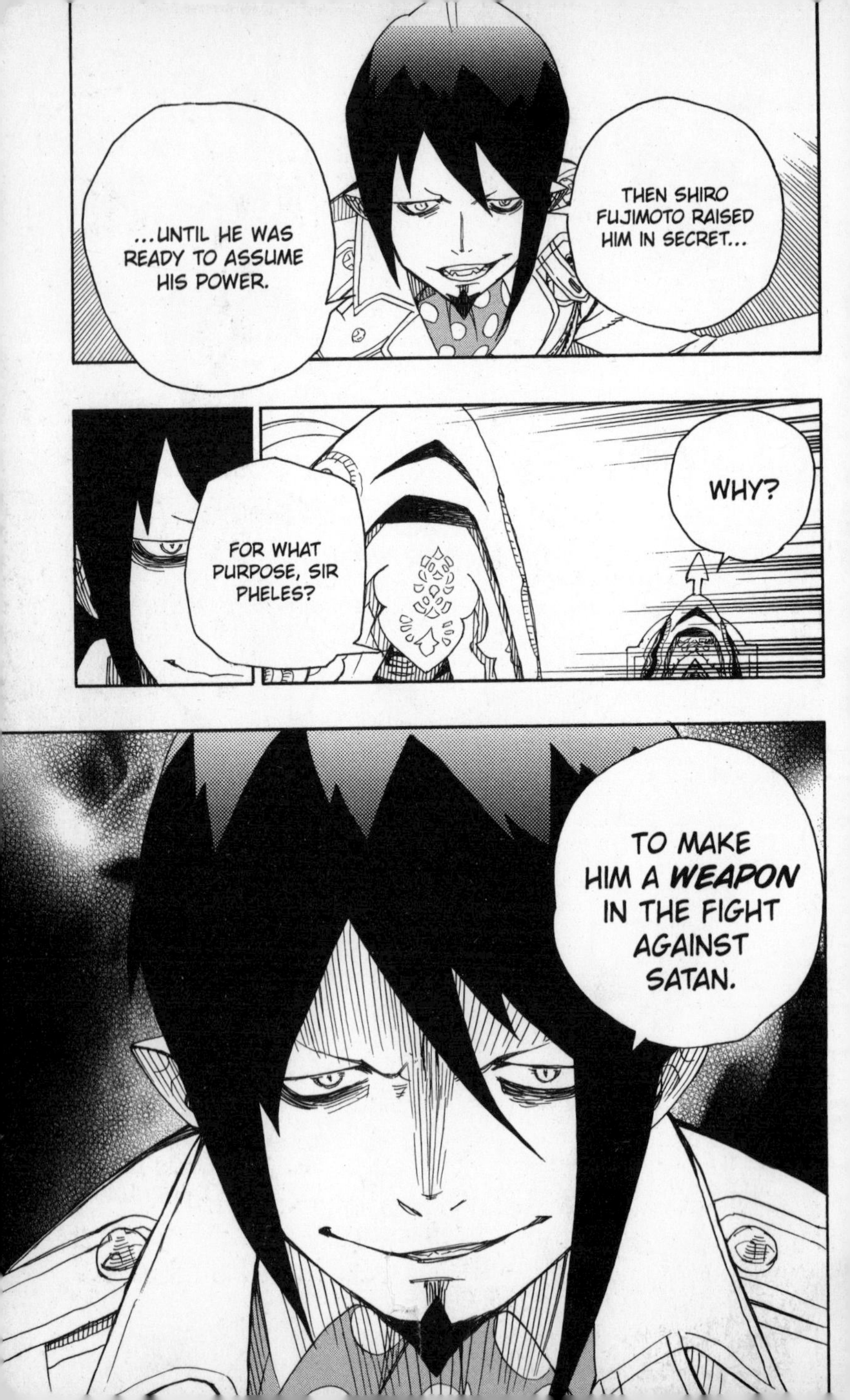
THEN SHIRO FUJIMOTO RAISED HIM IN SECRET...
...UNTIL HE WAS READY TO ASSUME HIS POWER.
WHY?
FOR WHAT PURPOSE, SIR PHELES?
TO MAKE HIM A *WEAPON* IN THE FIGHT AGAINST SATAN.

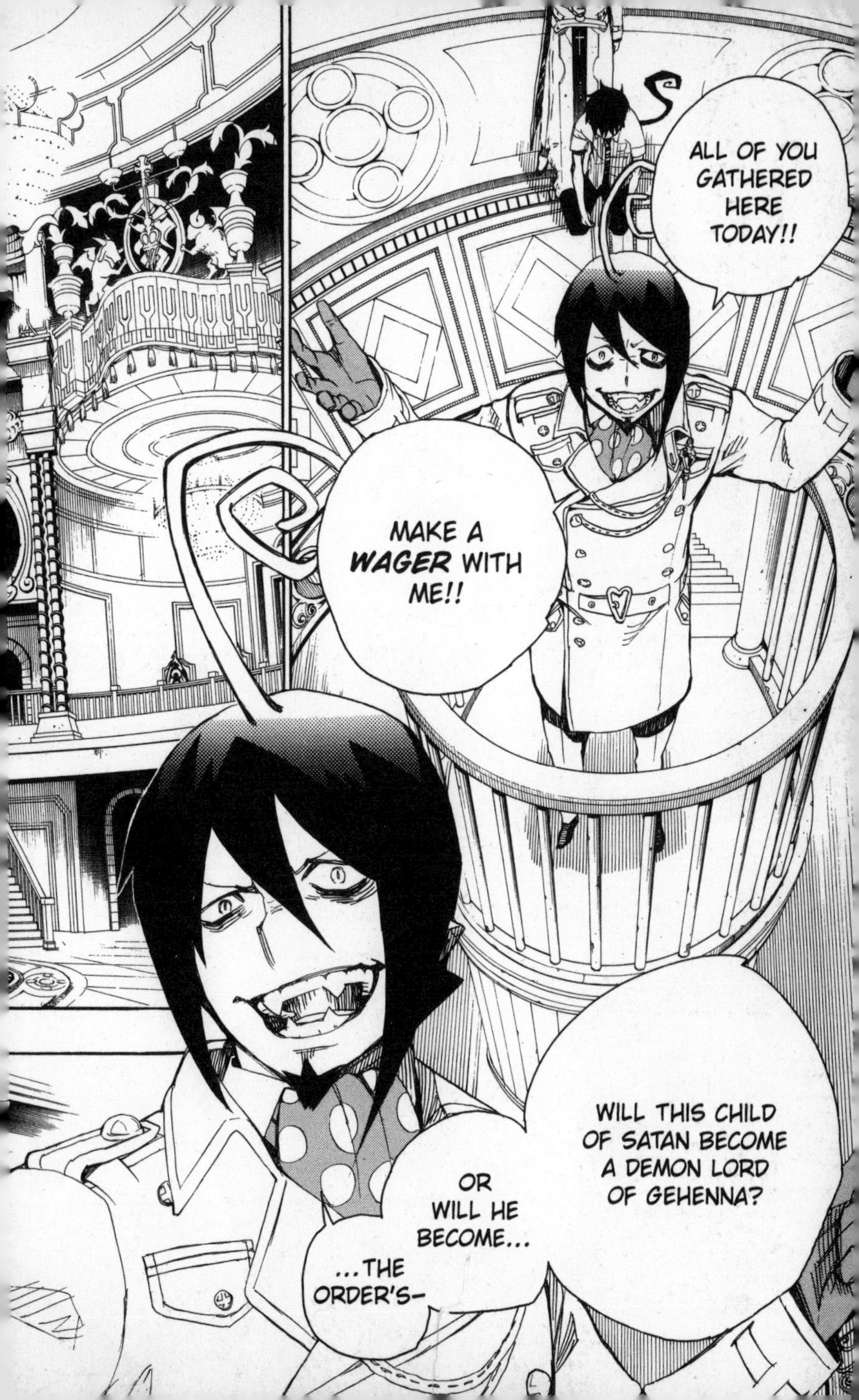
ALL OF YOU GATHERED HERE TODAY!!
MAKE A *WAGER* WITH ME!!
WILL THIS CHILD OF SATAN BECOME A DEMON LORD OF GEHENNA?
OR WILL HE BECOME...
...THE ORDER'S-

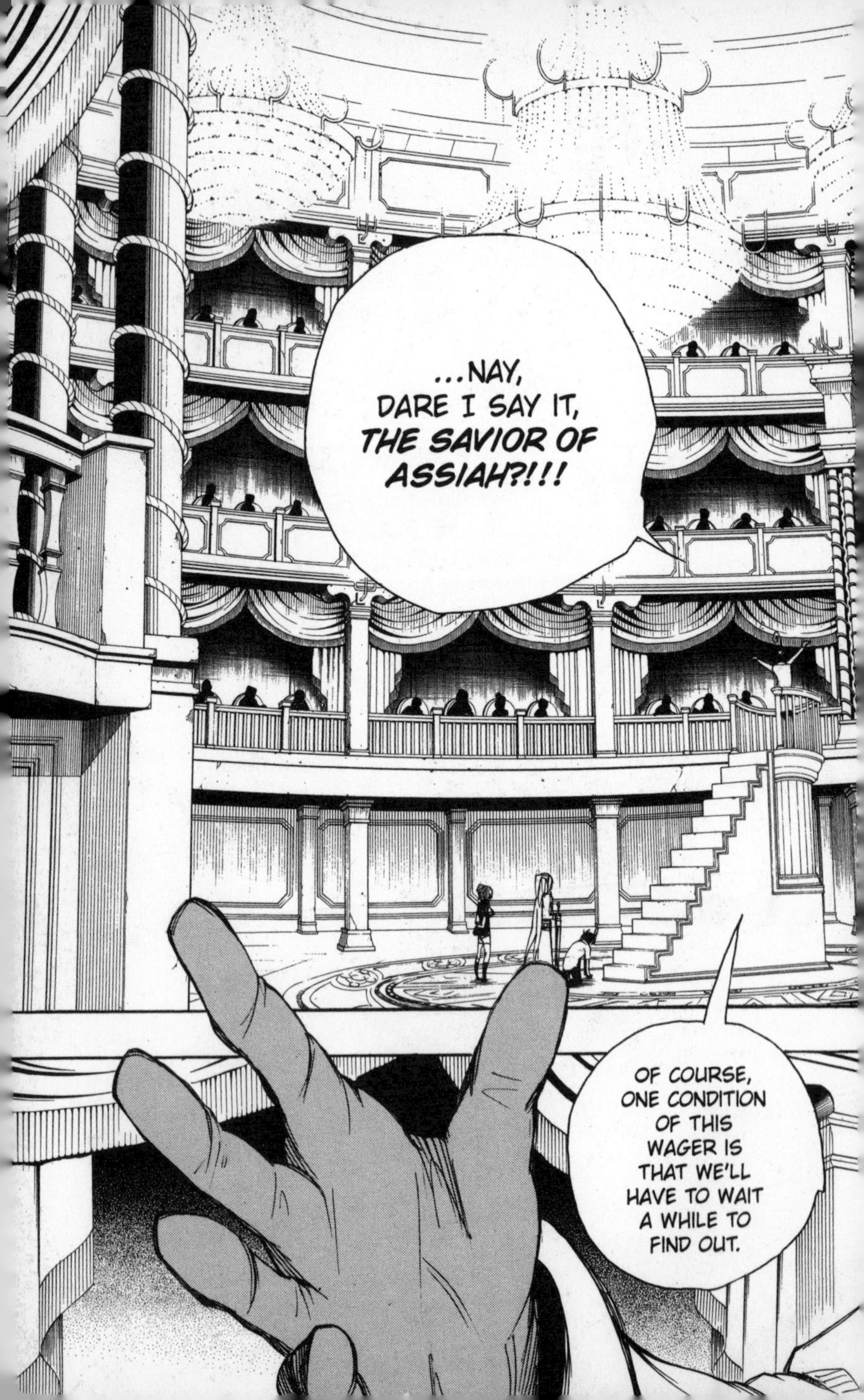
...NAY, DARE I SAY IT, THE SAVIOR OF ASSIAH?!!!
OF COURSE, ONE CONDITION OF THIS WAGER IS THAT WE'LL HAVE TO WAIT A WHILE TO FIND OUT.

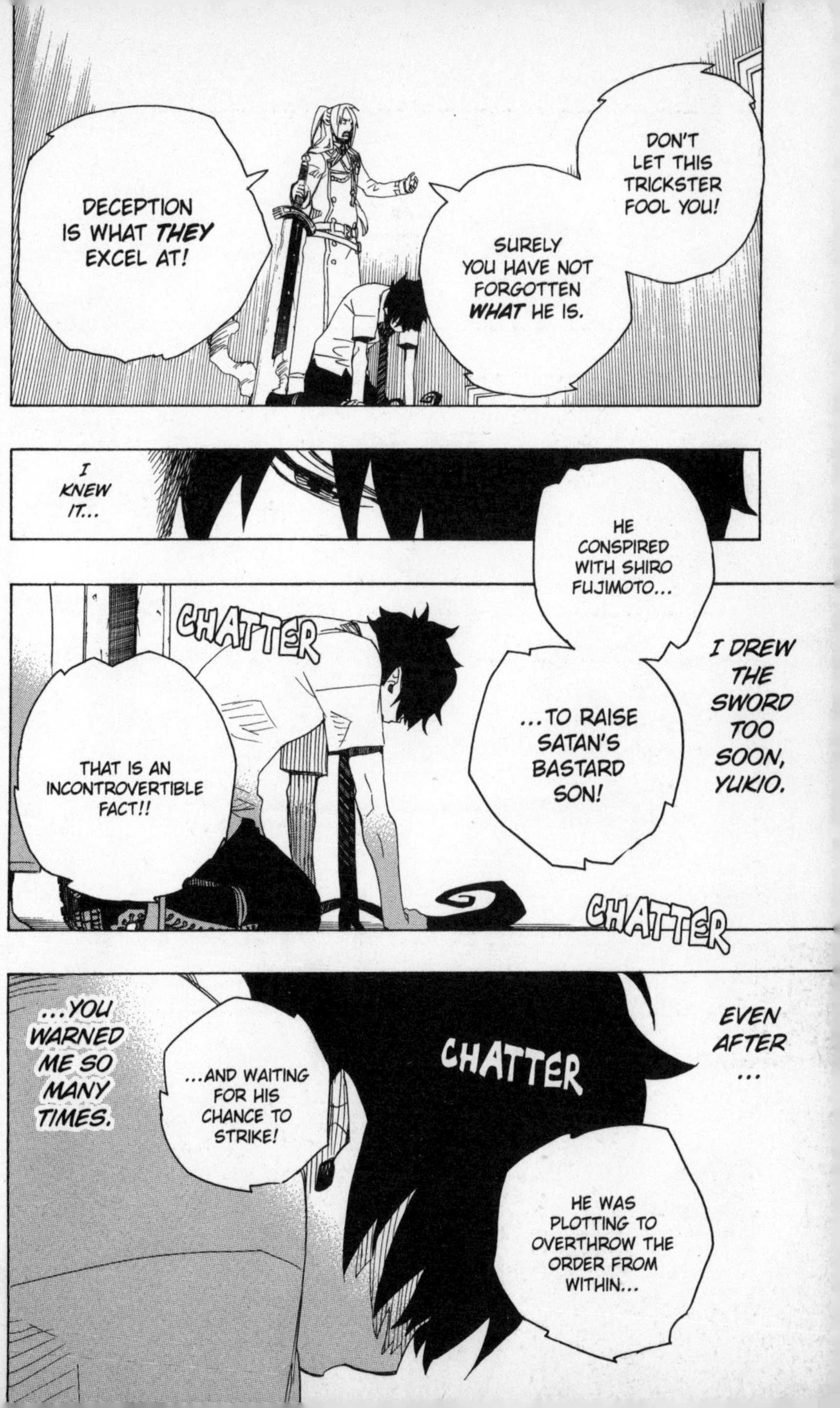

DON'T LET THIS TRICKSTER FOOL YOU!
SURELY YOU HAVE NOT FORGOTTEN *WHAT* HE IS.
DECEPTION IS WHAT *THEY* EXCEL AT!
HE CONSPIRED WITH SHIRO FUJIMOTO...
I KNEW IT...
I DREW THE SWORD TOO SOON, YUKIO.
...TO RAISE SATAN'S BASTARD SON!
CHATTER
CHATTER
THAT IS AN INCONTROVERTIBLE FACT!!
EVEN AFTER...
HE WAS PLOTTING TO OVERTHROW THE ORDER FROM WITHIN...
CHATTER
...AND WAITING FOR HIS CHANCE TO STRIKE!
...YOU WARNED ME SO MANY TIMES.

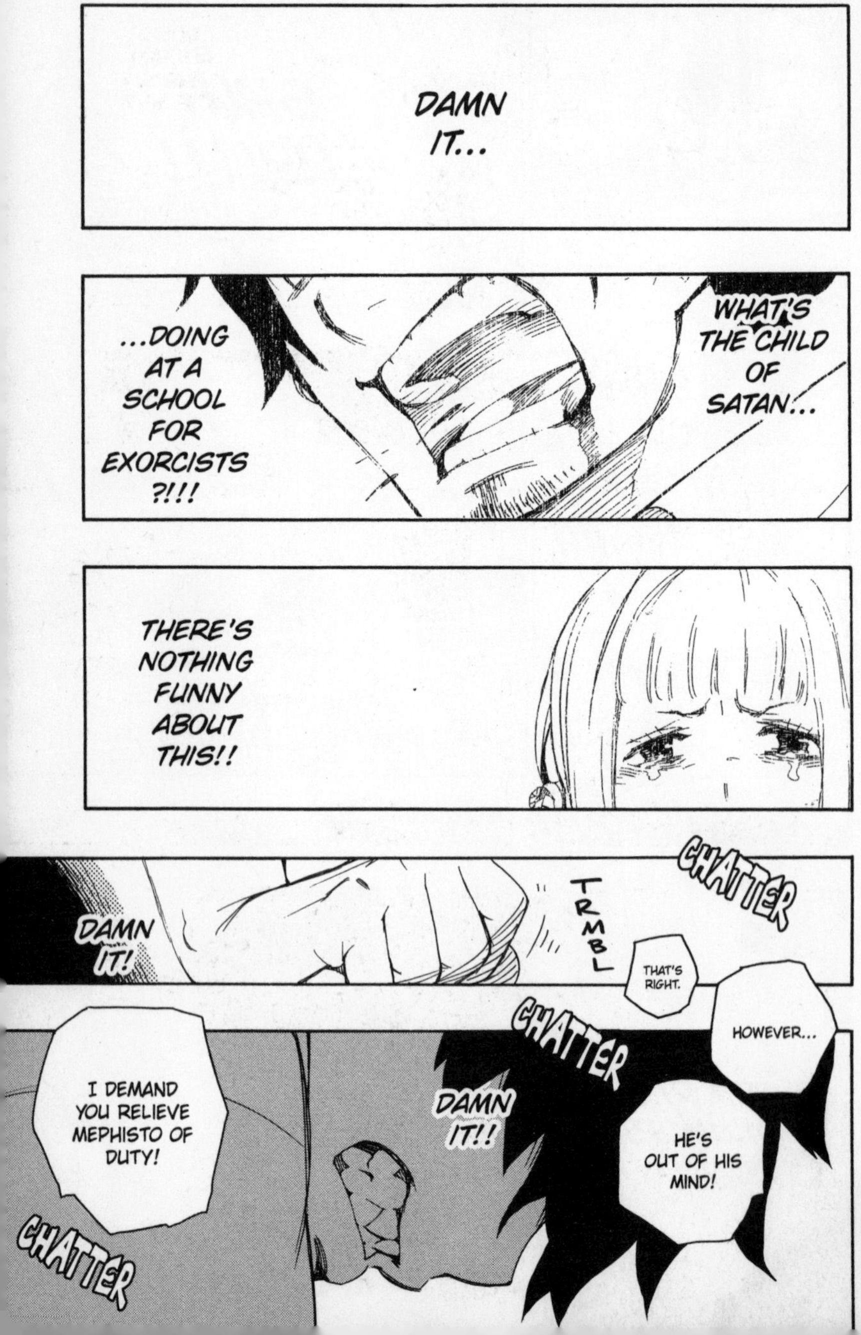
DAMN IT...
WHAT'S THE CHILD OF SATAN...
...DOING AT A SCHOOL FOR EXORCISTS?!!!
THERE'S NOTHING FUNNY ABOUT THIS!!
CHATTER
TRMBL
DAMN IT!
THAT'S RIGHT.
HOWEVER...
CHATTER
HE'S OUT OF HIS MIND!
DAMN IT!!
I DEMAND YOU RELIEVE MEPHISTO OF DUTY!
CHATTER

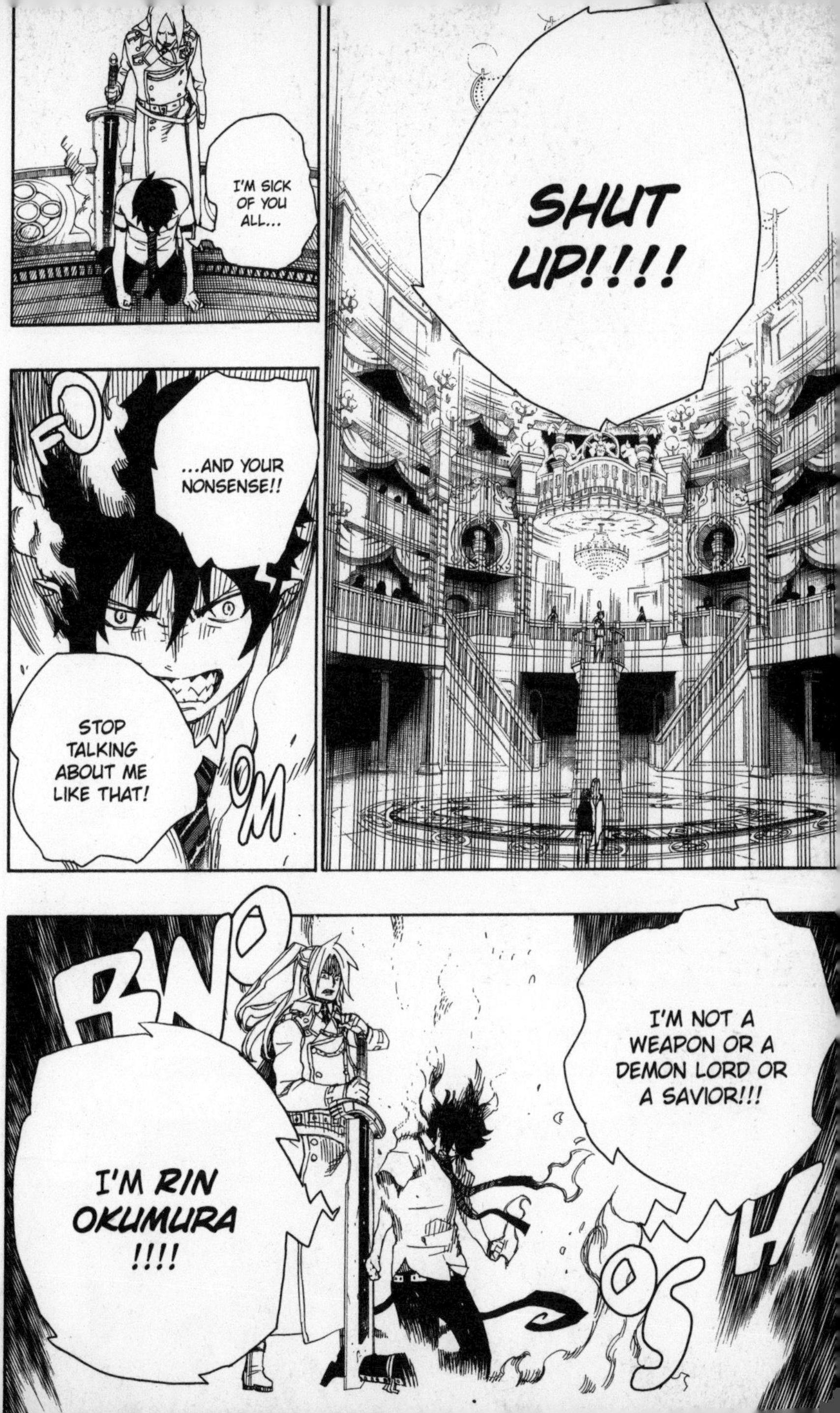
SHUT UP!!!!
I'M SICK OF YOU ALL...
...AND YOUR NONSENSE!!
STOP TALKING ABOUT ME LIKE THAT!
I'M NOT A WEAPON OR A DEMON LORD OR A SAVIOR!!!
I'M *RIN OKUMURA* !!!!

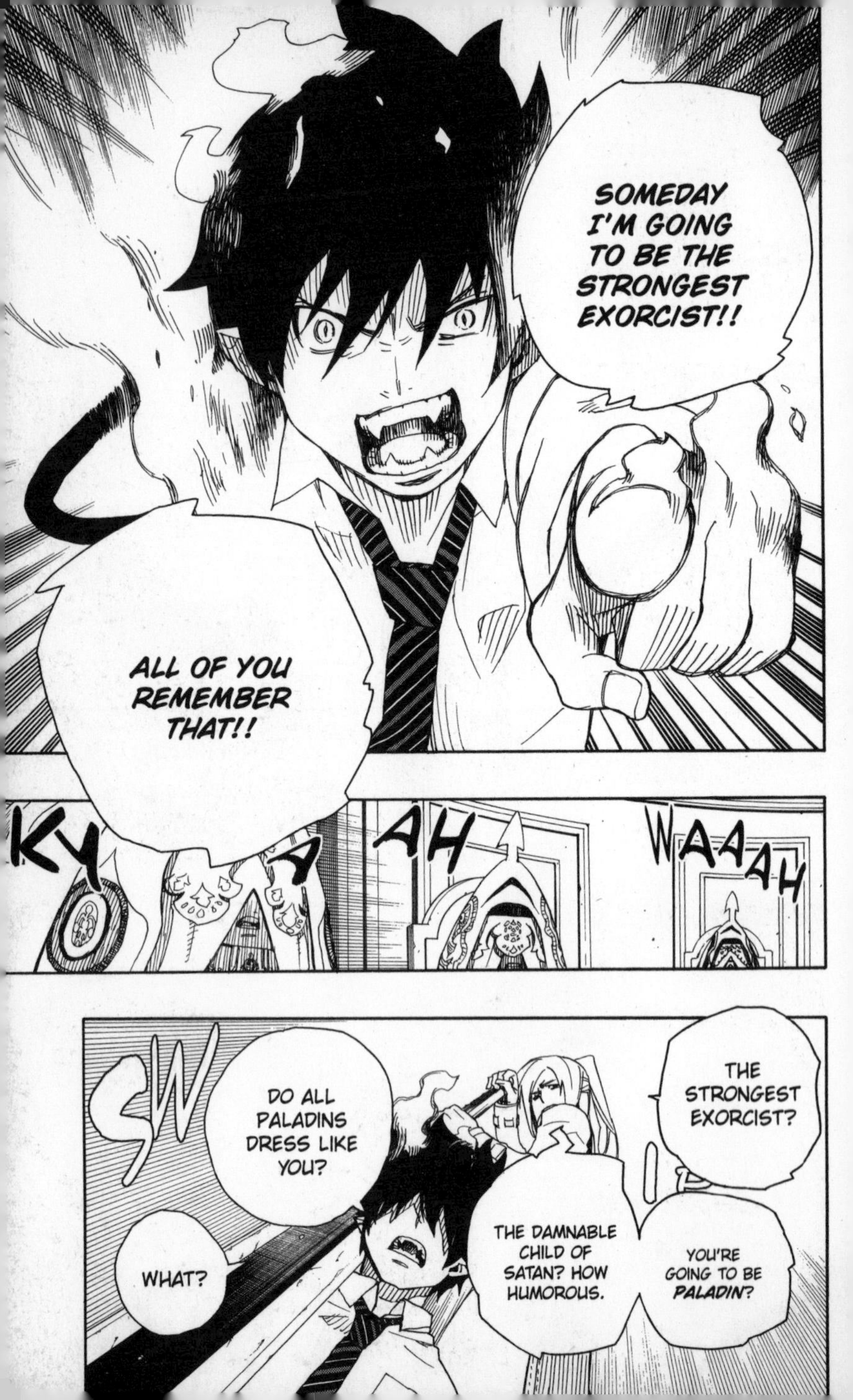
SOMEDAY I'M GOING TO BE THE STRONGEST EXORCIST!!
ALL OF YOU REMEMBER THAT!!
WAAAAH
KYAAH
THE STRONGEST EXORCIST?
YOU'RE GOING TO BE *PALADIN*?
THE DAMNABLE CHILD OF SATAN? HOW HUMOROUS.
DO ALL PALADINS DRESS LIKE YOU?
SW
WHAT?

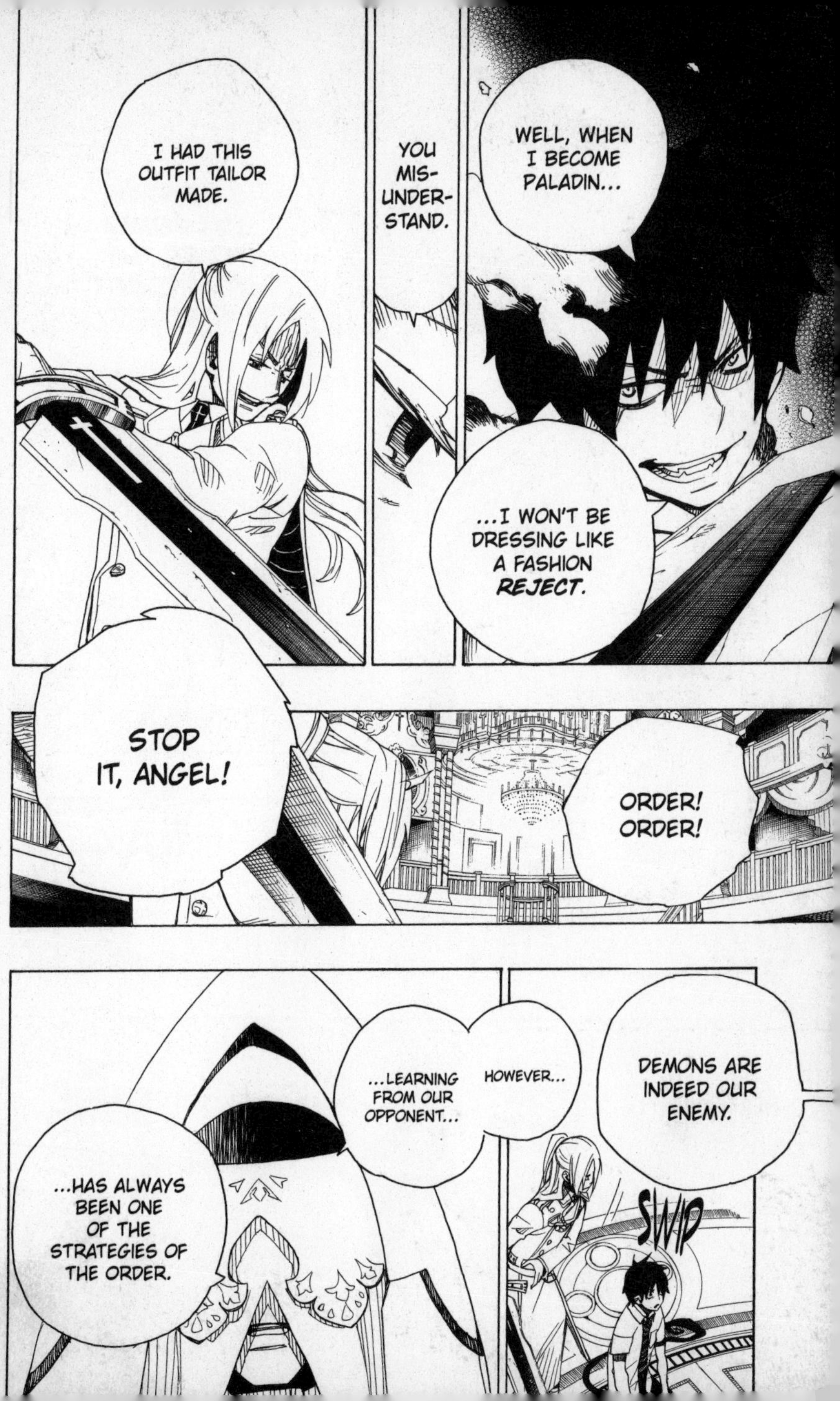
WELL, WHEN I BECOME PALADIN...
...I WON'T BE DRESSING LIKE A FASHION *REJECT*.
YOU MIS-UNDER-STAND.
I HAD THIS OUTFIT TAILOR MADE.
ORDER! ORDER!
STOP IT, ANGEL!
DEMONS ARE INDEED OUR ENEMY.
SWIP
HOWEVER...
...LEARNING FROM OUR OPPONENT...
...HAS ALWAYS BEEN ONE OF THE STRATEGIES OF THE ORDER.

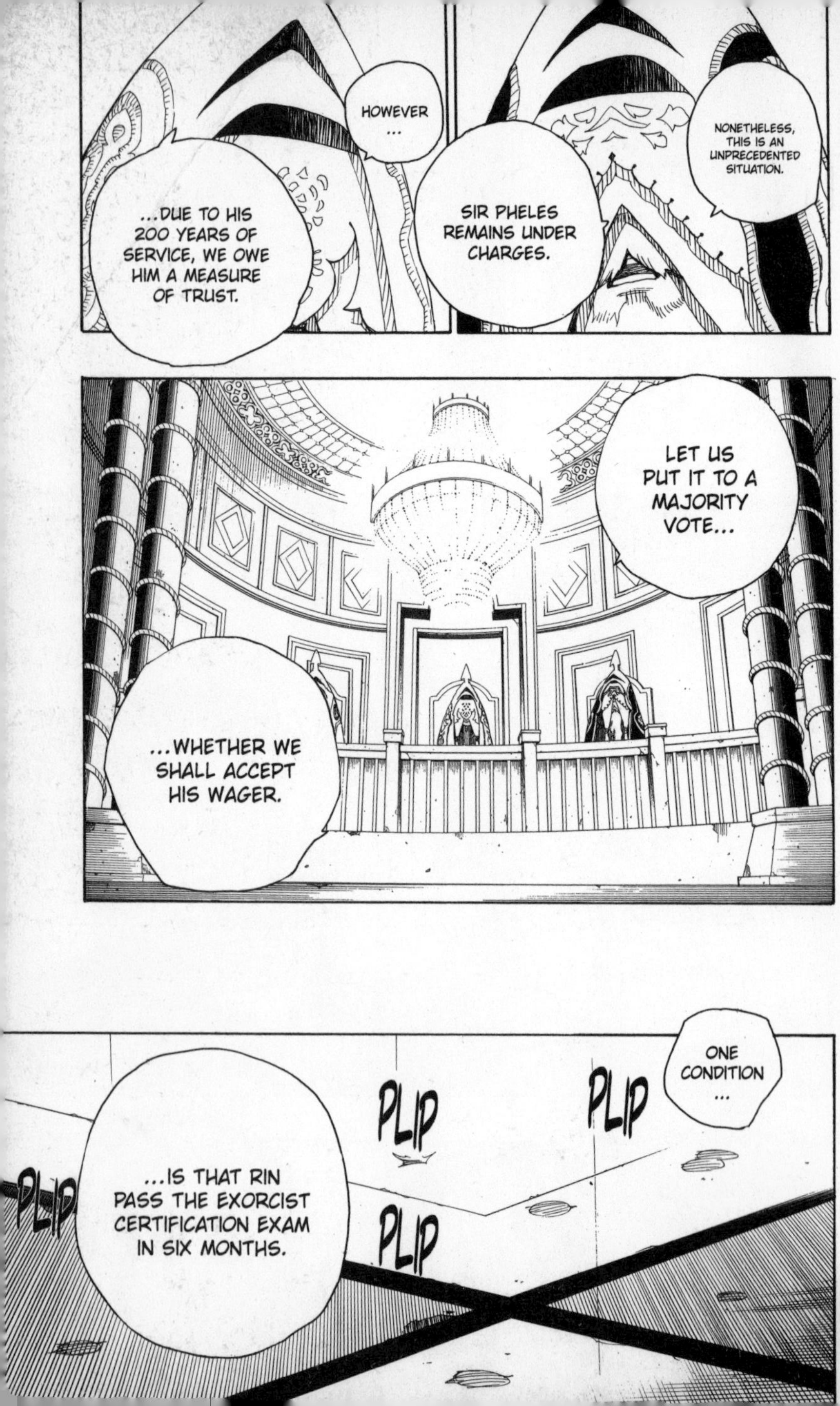
NONETHELESS, THIS IS AN UNPRECEDENTED SITUATION.
SIR PHELES REMAINS UNDER CHARGES.
HOWEVER...
...DUE TO HIS 200 YEARS OF SERVICE, WE OWE HIM A MEASURE OF TRUST.
LET US PUT IT TO A MAJORITY VOTE...
...WHETHER WE SHALL ACCEPT HIS WAGER.
ONE CONDITION...
PLIP
PLIP
PLIP
PLIP
...IS THAT RIN PASS THE EXORCIST CERTIFICATION EXAM IN SIX MONTHS.

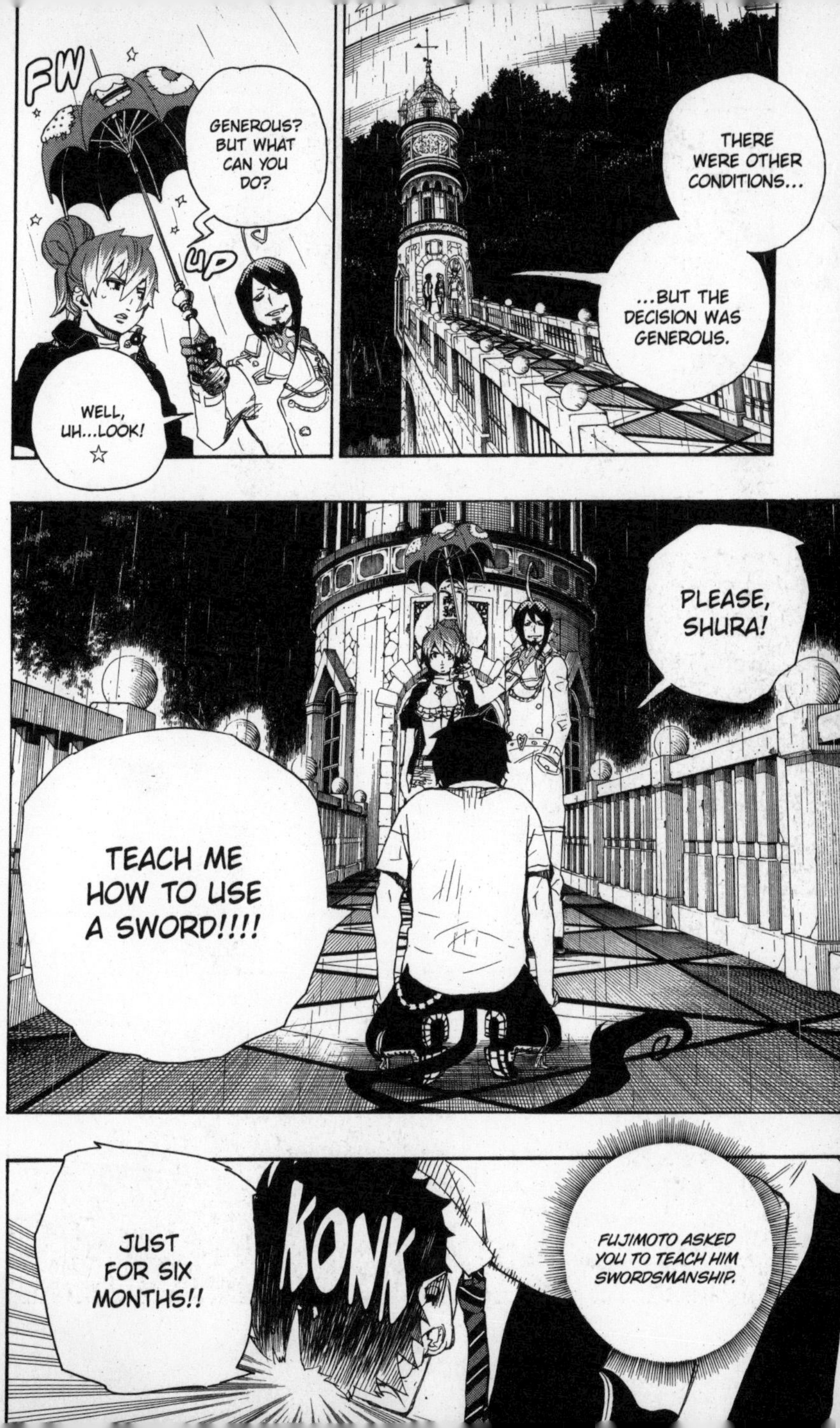
THERE WERE OTHER CONDITIONS...
...BUT THE DECISION WAS GENEROUS.
FW
GENEROUS? BUT WHAT CAN YOU DO?
UP
WELL, UH...LOOK! ☆
PLEASE, SHURA!
TEACH ME HOW TO USE A SWORD!!!!
FUJIMOTO ASKED YOU TO TEACH HIM SWORDSMANSHIP.
KONK
JUST FOR SIX MONTHS!!

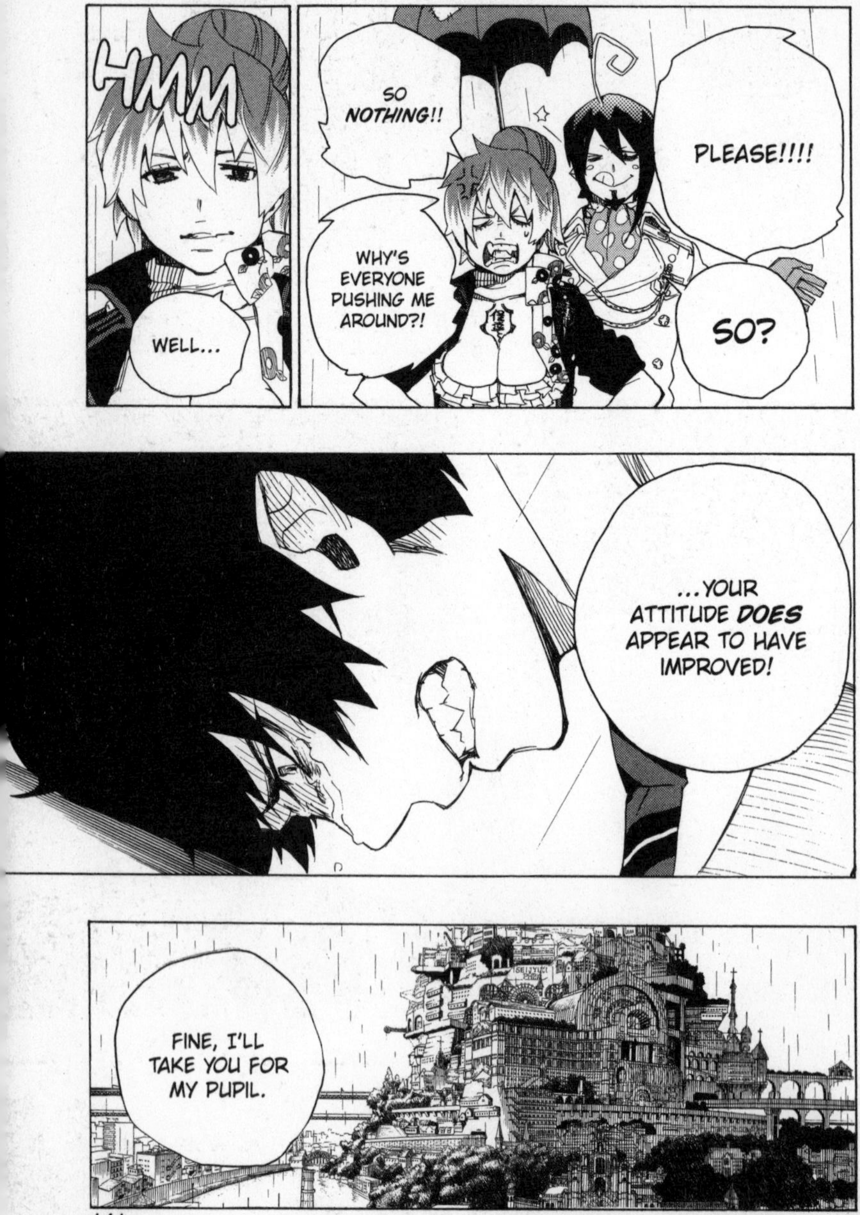
PLEASE!!!!
SO?
SO NOTHING!!
WHY'S EVERYONE PUSHING ME AROUND?!
HMM
WELL...
...YOUR ATTITUDE DOES APPEAR TO HAVE IMPROVED!
FINE, I'LL TAKE YOU FOR MY PUPIL.

Blue Exorcist Chapter Fourteen The Wager

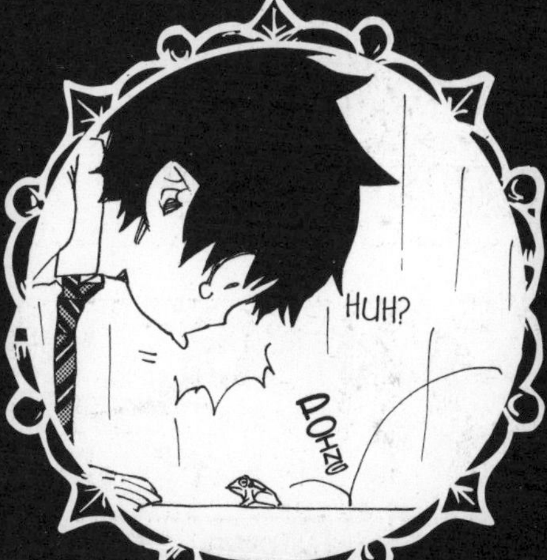
HUH?

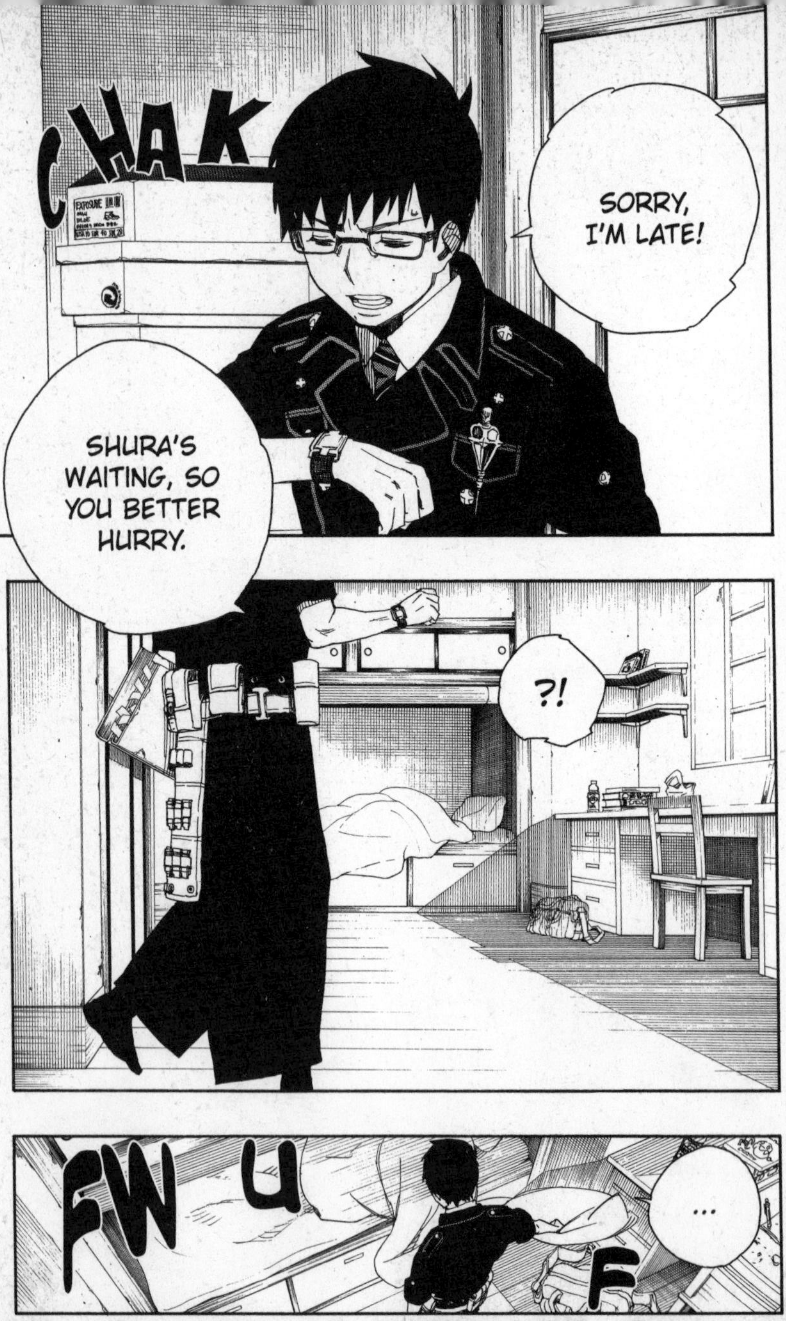
SORRY, I'M LATE!
CHAK
SHURA'S WAITING, SO YOU BETTER HURRY.
?!
...
FWUF

CHAPTER 15 EVERY LAST ONE

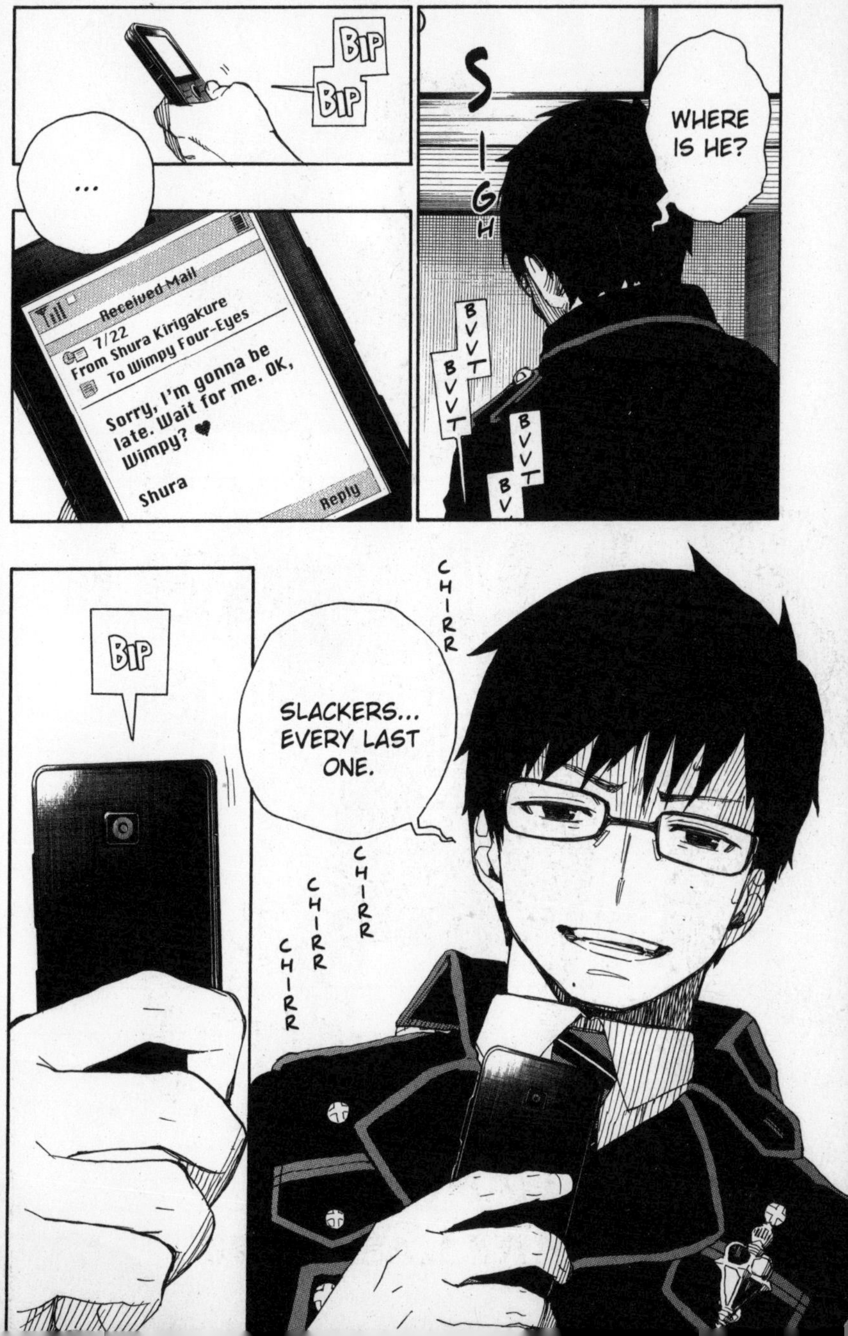
SIGH
WHERE IS HE?
BVVT
BVVT
BVVT
BV
BIP
BIP
...
Received Mail
7/22
From Shura Kirigakure
To Wimpy Four-Eyes
Sorry, I'm gonna be late. Wait for me. OK, Wimpy? ♥
Shura
Reply
CHIRR
SLACKERS... EVERY LAST ONE.
CHIRR
CHIRR
CHIRR
BIP

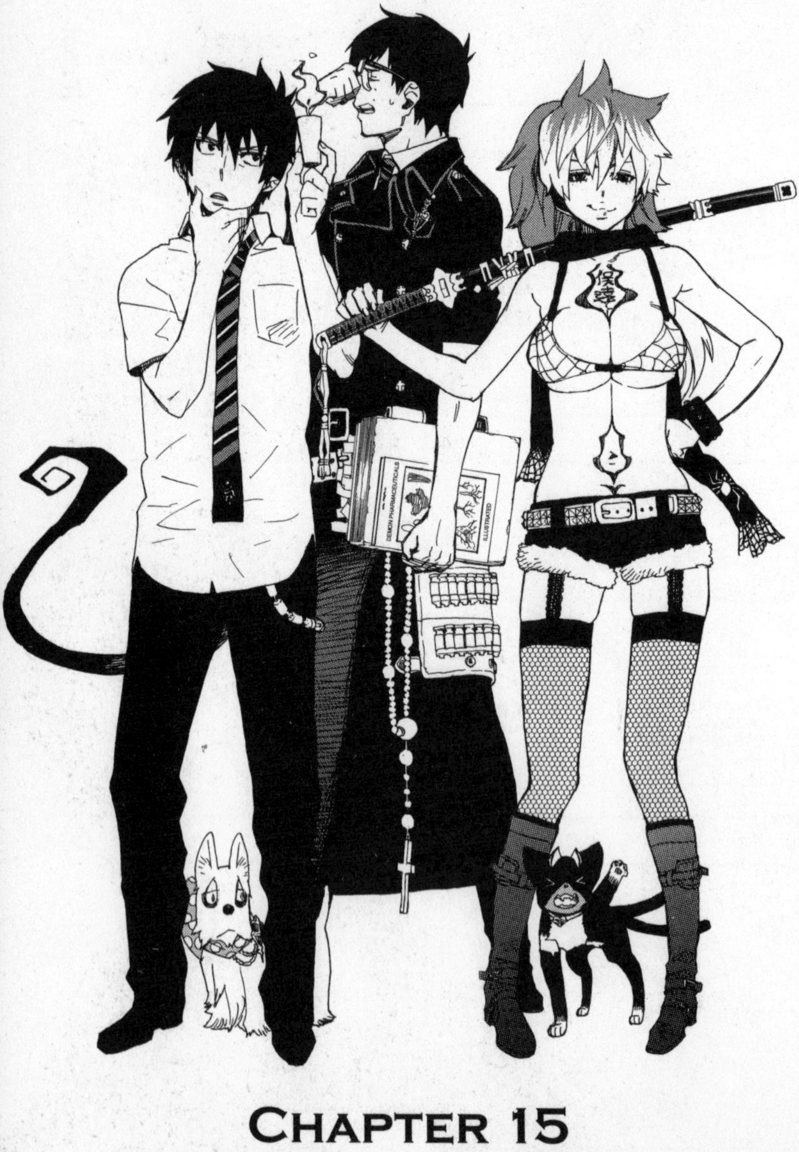
DEMON PHARMACEUTICALS
ILLUSTRATED

CHAPTER 15
EVERY LAST ONE

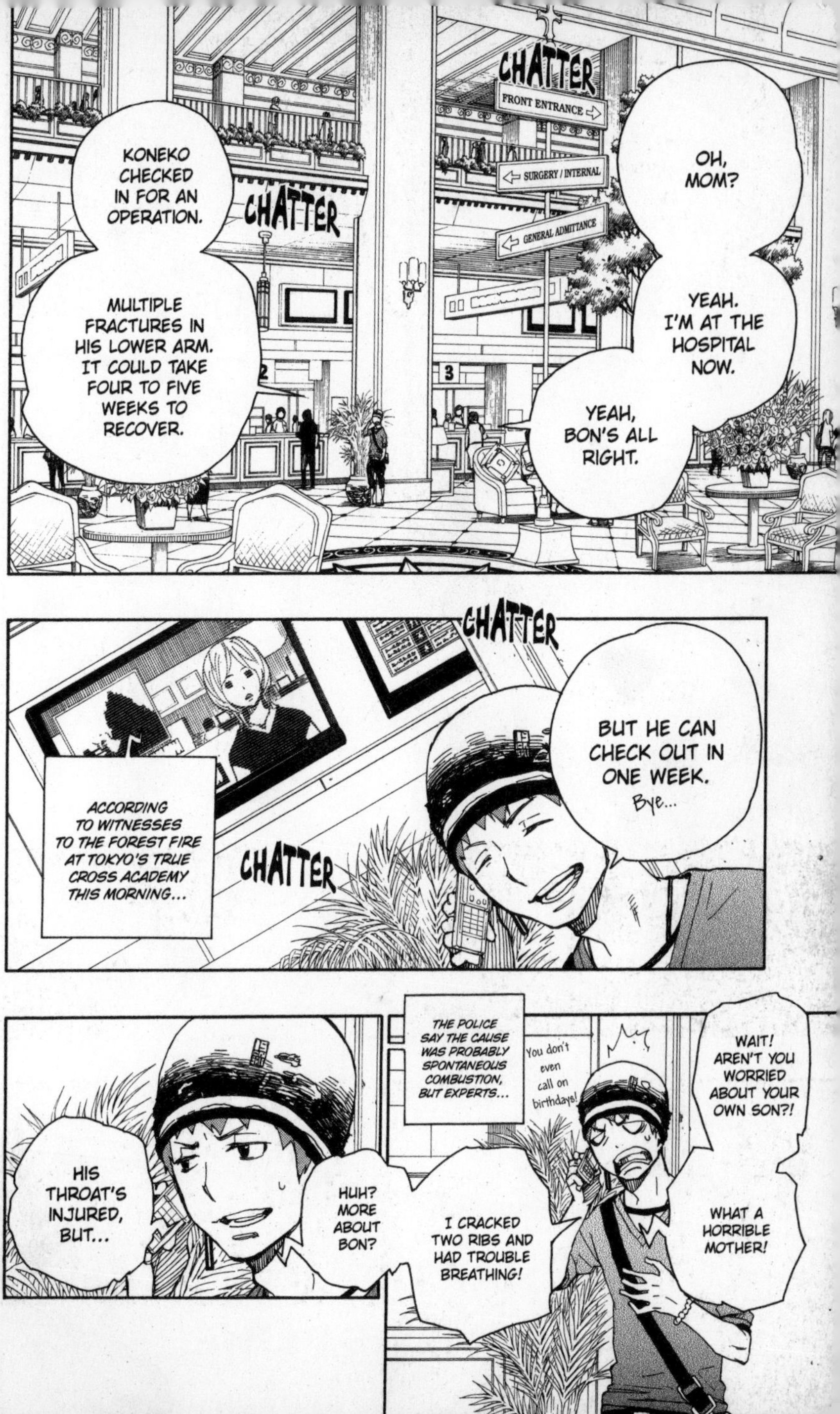
CHATTER
FRONT ENTRANCE
SURGERY / INTERNAL
GENERAL ADMITTANCE
OH, MOM?
YEAH. I'M AT THE HOSPITAL NOW.
YEAH, BON'S ALL RIGHT.
CHATTER
KONEKO CHECKED IN FOR AN OPERATION.
MULTIPLE FRACTURES IN HIS LOWER ARM. IT COULD TAKE FOUR TO FIVE WEEKS TO RECOVER.
CHATTER
BUT HE CAN CHECK OUT IN ONE WEEK.
Bye...
ACCORDING TO WITNESSES TO THE FOREST FIRE AT TOKYO'S TRUE CROSS ACADEMY THIS MORNING...
CHATTER
WAIT! AREN'T YOU WORRIED ABOUT YOUR OWN SON?!
THE POLICE SAY THE CAUSE WAS PROBABLY SPONTANEOUS COMBUSTION, BUT EXPERTS...
You don't even call on birthdays!
WHAT A HORRIBLE MOTHER!
I CRACKED TWO RIBS AND HAD TROUBLE BREATHING!
HUH? MORE ABOUT BON?
HIS THROAT'S INJURED, BUT...

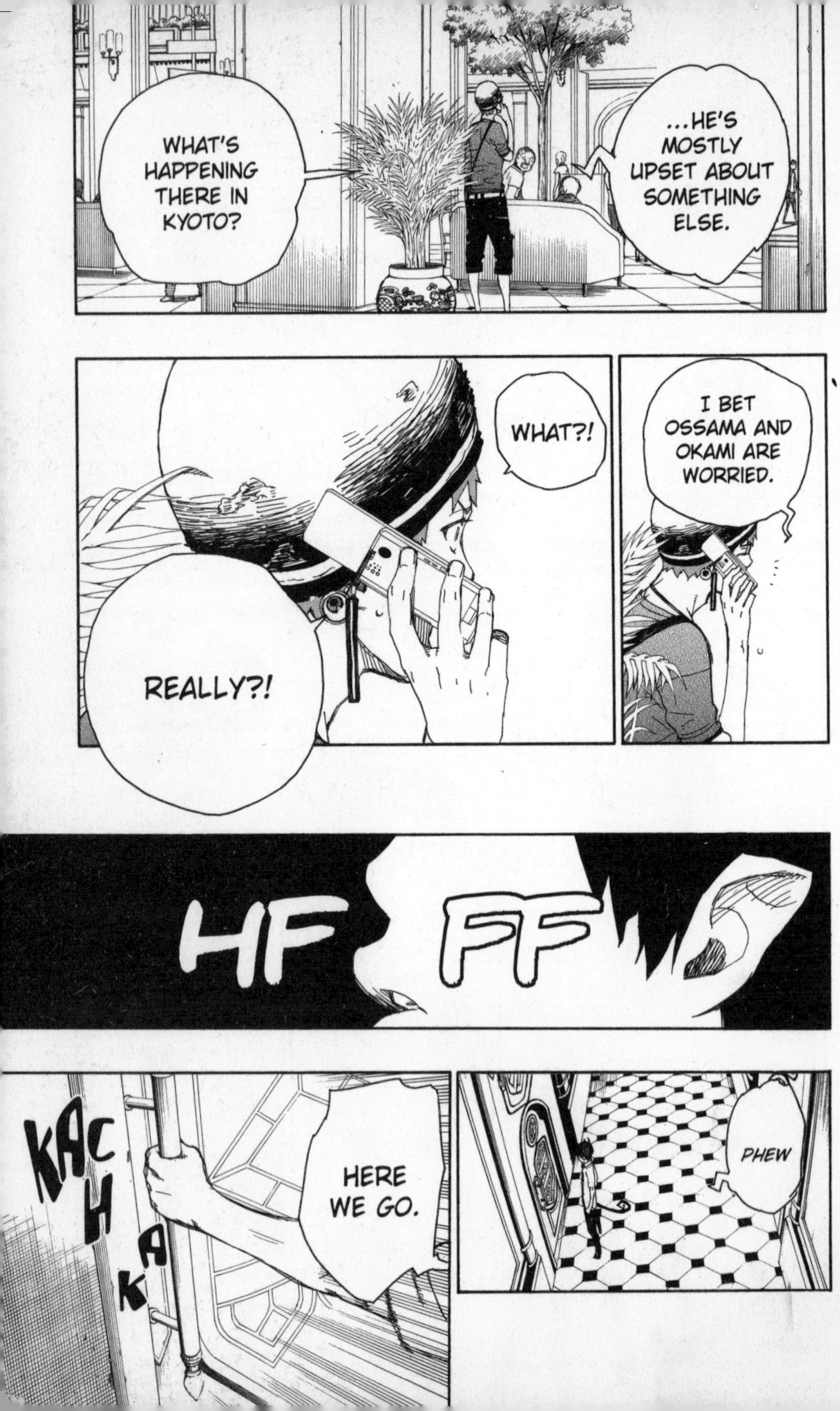
...HE'S MOSTLY UPSET ABOUT SOMETHING ELSE.
WHAT'S HAPPENING THERE IN KYOTO?
I BET OSSAMA AND OKAMI ARE WORRIED.
WHAT?!
REALLY?!
HF FF
PHEW
HERE WE GO.
KACHAKA

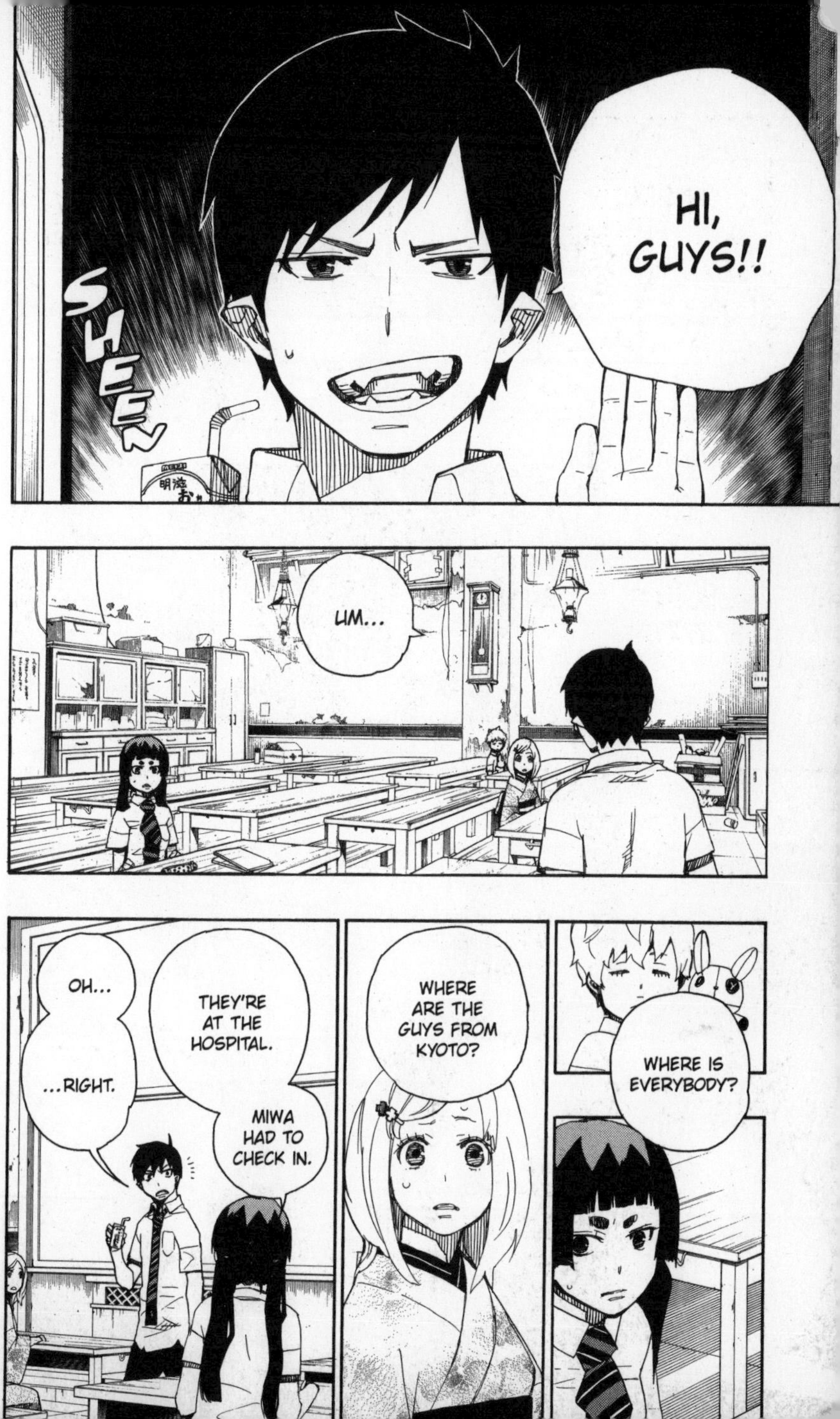
HI, GUYS!!
SHEEN
UM...
WHERE IS EVERYBODY?
WHERE ARE THE GUYS FROM KYOTO?
THEY'RE AT THE HOSPITAL.
MIWA HAD TO CHECK IN.
OH...
...RIGHT.

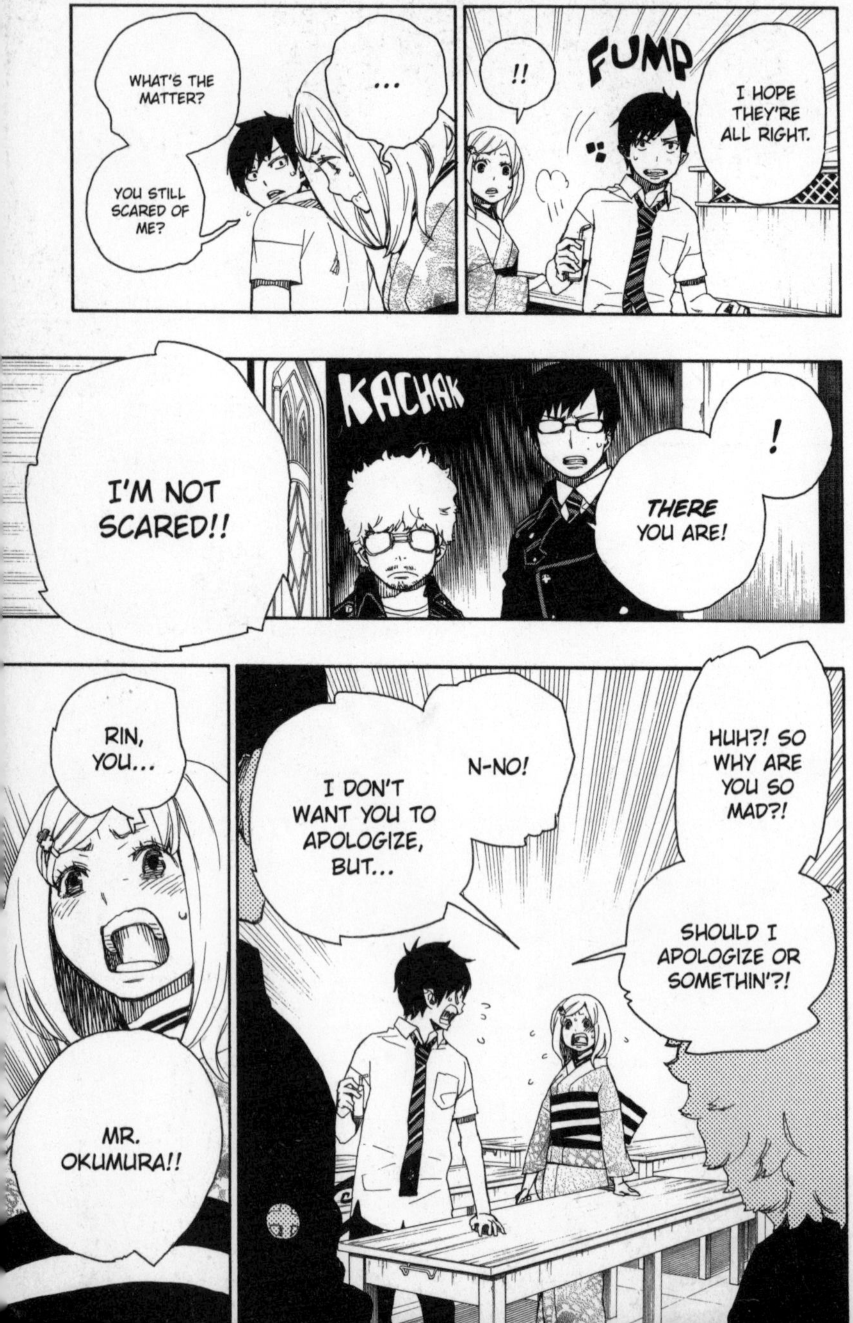
I HOPE THEY'RE ALL RIGHT.
FUMP
!!
...
WHAT'S THE MATTER?
YOU STILL SCARED OF ME?
!
THERE YOU ARE!
KACHAK
I'M NOT SCARED!!
HUH?! SO WHY ARE YOU SO MAD?!
SHOULD I APOLOGIZE OR SOMETHIN'?!
N-NO!
I DON'T WANT YOU TO APOLOGIZE, BUT...
RIN, YOU...
MR. OKUMURA!!

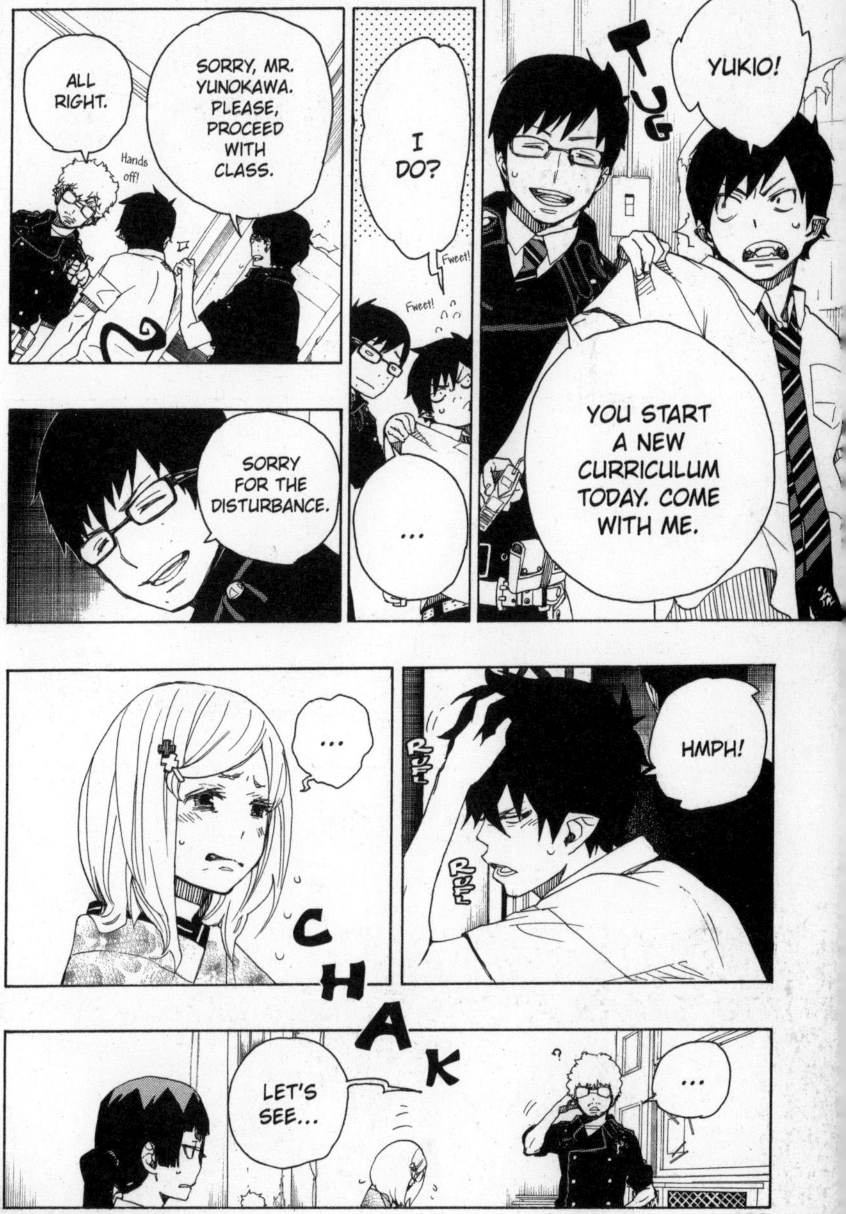
YUKIO!
TUG
YOU START A NEW CURRICULUM TODAY. COME WITH ME.
I DO?
Fweet!
Fweet!
...
SORRY, MR. YUNOKAWA. PLEASE, PROCEED WITH CLASS.
ALL RIGHT.
Hands off!
SORRY FOR THE DISTURBANCE.
HMPH!
RUF
RUF
...
CHAK
...
LET'S SEE...

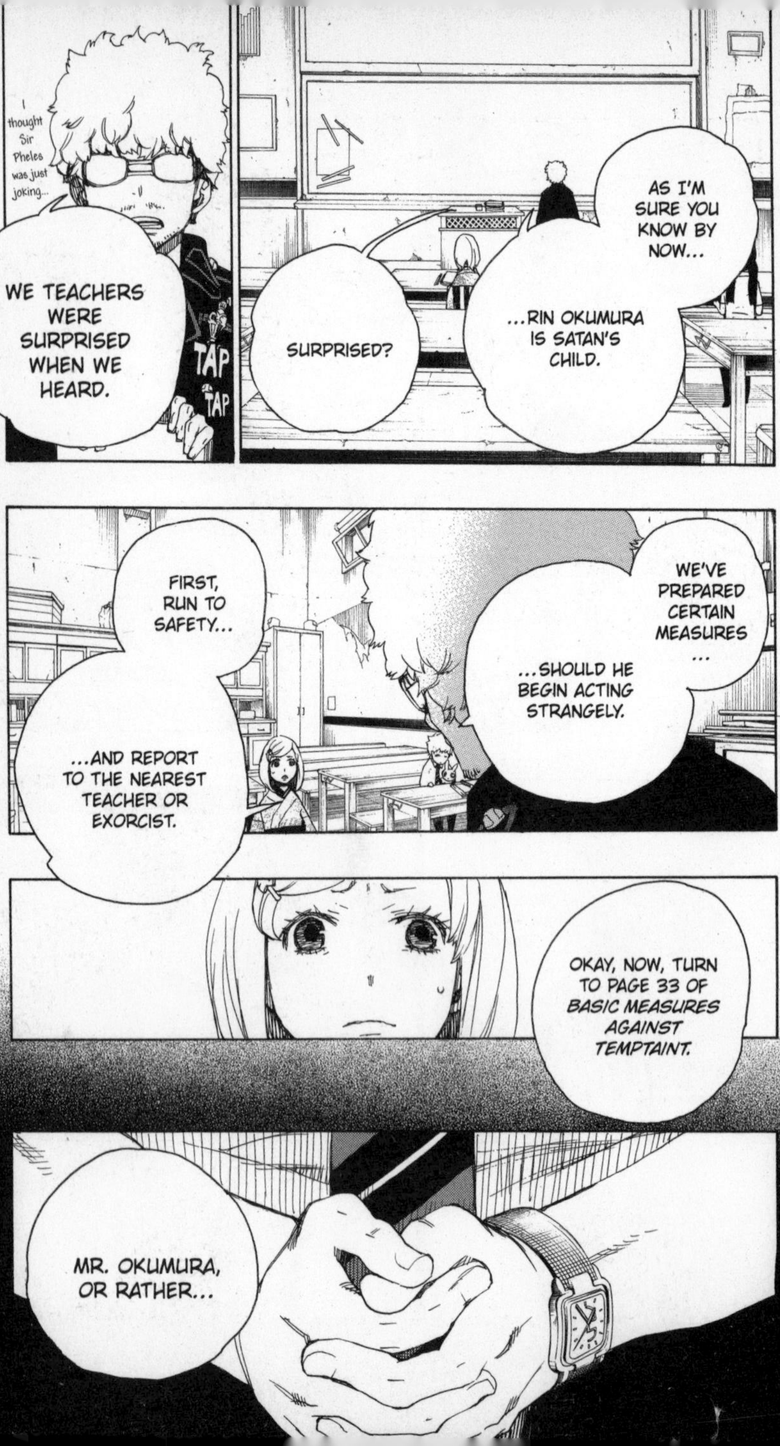
AS I'M SURE YOU KNOW BY NOW...
...RIN OKUMURA IS SATAN'S CHILD.
SURPRISED?
I thought Sir Pheles was just joking...
WE TEACHERS WERE SURPRISED WHEN WE HEARD.
TAP TAP
WE'VE PREPARED CERTAIN MEASURES...
...SHOULD HE BEGIN ACTING STRANGELY.
FIRST, RUN TO SAFETY...
...AND REPORT TO THE NEAREST TEACHER OR EXORCIST.
OKAY, NOW, TURN TO PAGE 33 OF *BASIC MEASURES AGAINST TEMPTAINT.*
MR. OKUMURA, OR RATHER...

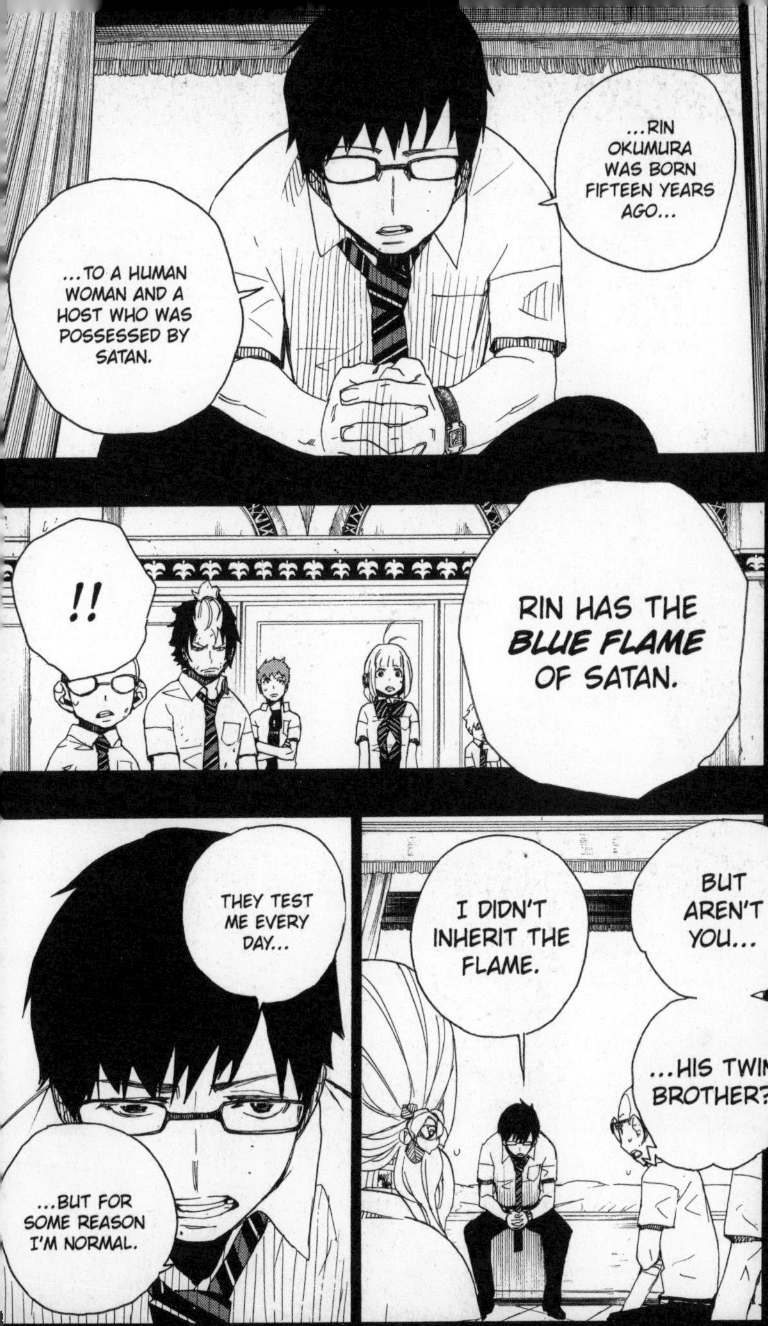
...RIN OKUMURA WAS BORN FIFTEEN YEARS AGO...
...TO A HUMAN WOMAN AND A HOST WHO WAS POSSESSED BY SATAN.
RIN HAS THE *BLUE FLAME* OF SATAN.
!!
BUT AREN'T YOU...
...HIS TWIN BROTHER?
I DIDN'T INHERIT THE FLAME.
THEY TEST ME EVERY DAY...
...BUT FOR SOME REASON I'M NORMAL.

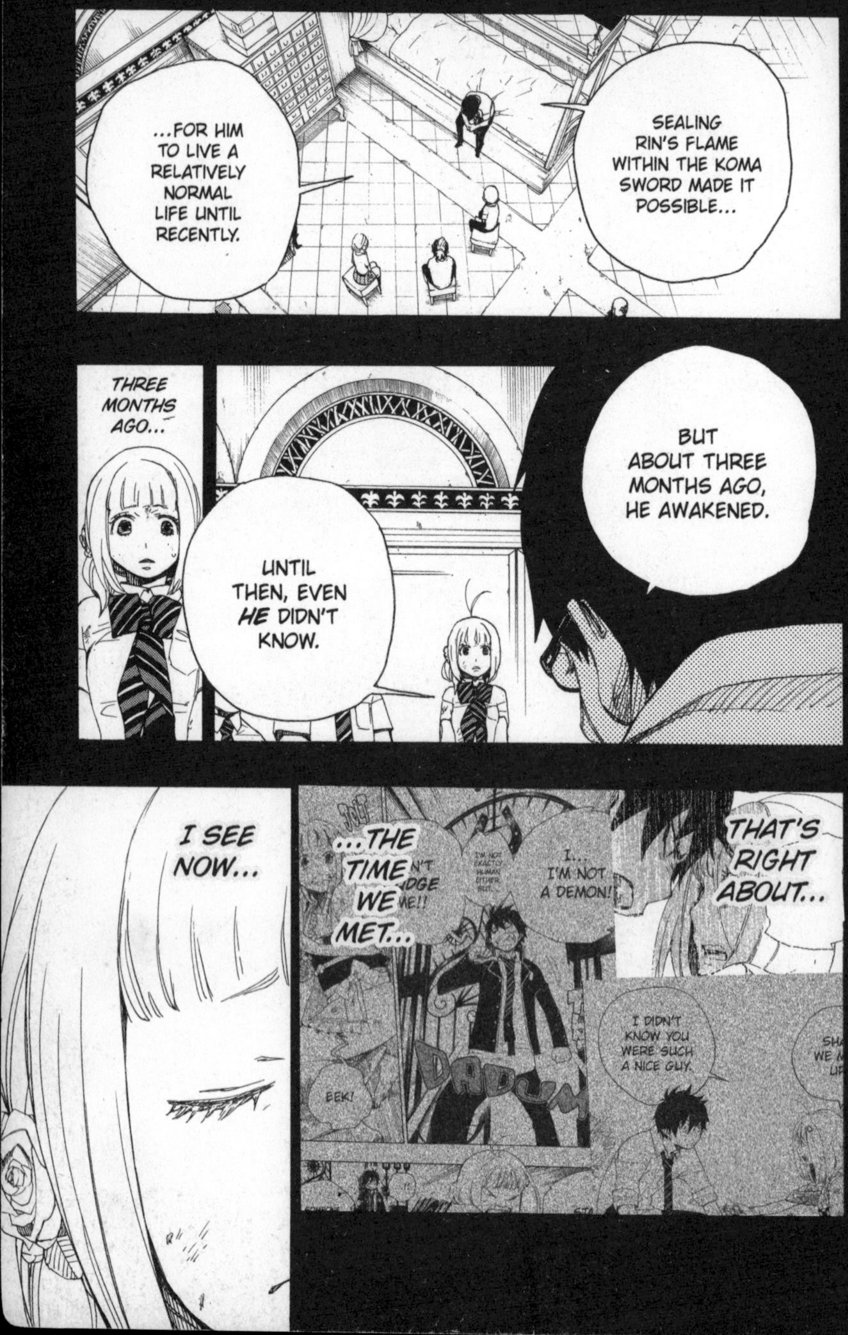
SEALING RIN'S FLAME WITHIN THE KOMA SWORD MADE IT POSSIBLE...
...FOR HIM TO LIVE A RELATIVELY NORMAL LIFE UNTIL RECENTLY.
BUT ABOUT THREE MONTHS AGO, HE AWAKENED.
UNTIL THEN, EVEN *HE* DIDN'T KNOW.
THREE MONTHS AGO...
THAT'S RIGHT ABOUT...
...THE TIME WE MET...
I... I'M NOT A DEMON!
I'M NOT EXACTLY HUMAN EITHER BUT...
I DIDN'T KNOW YOU WERE SUCH A NICE GUY.
EEK!
I SEE NOW...

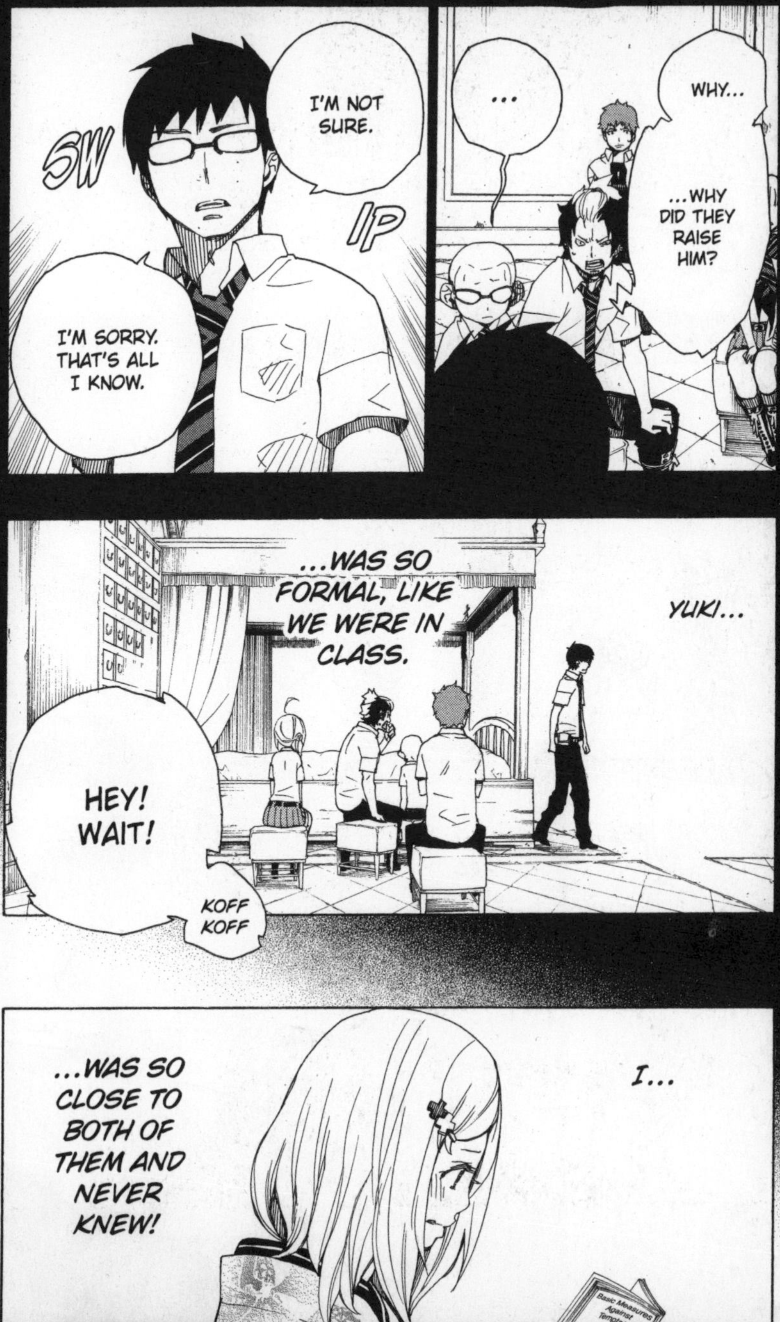
WHY...
...
...WHY DID THEY RAISE HIM?
I'M NOT SURE.
SWIP
I'M SORRY. THAT'S ALL I KNOW.
YUKI...
...WAS SO FORMAL, LIKE WE WERE IN CLASS.
HEY! WAIT!
KOFF KOFF
I...
...WAS SO CLOSE TO BOTH OF THEM AND NEVER KNEW!
Basic Measures Against

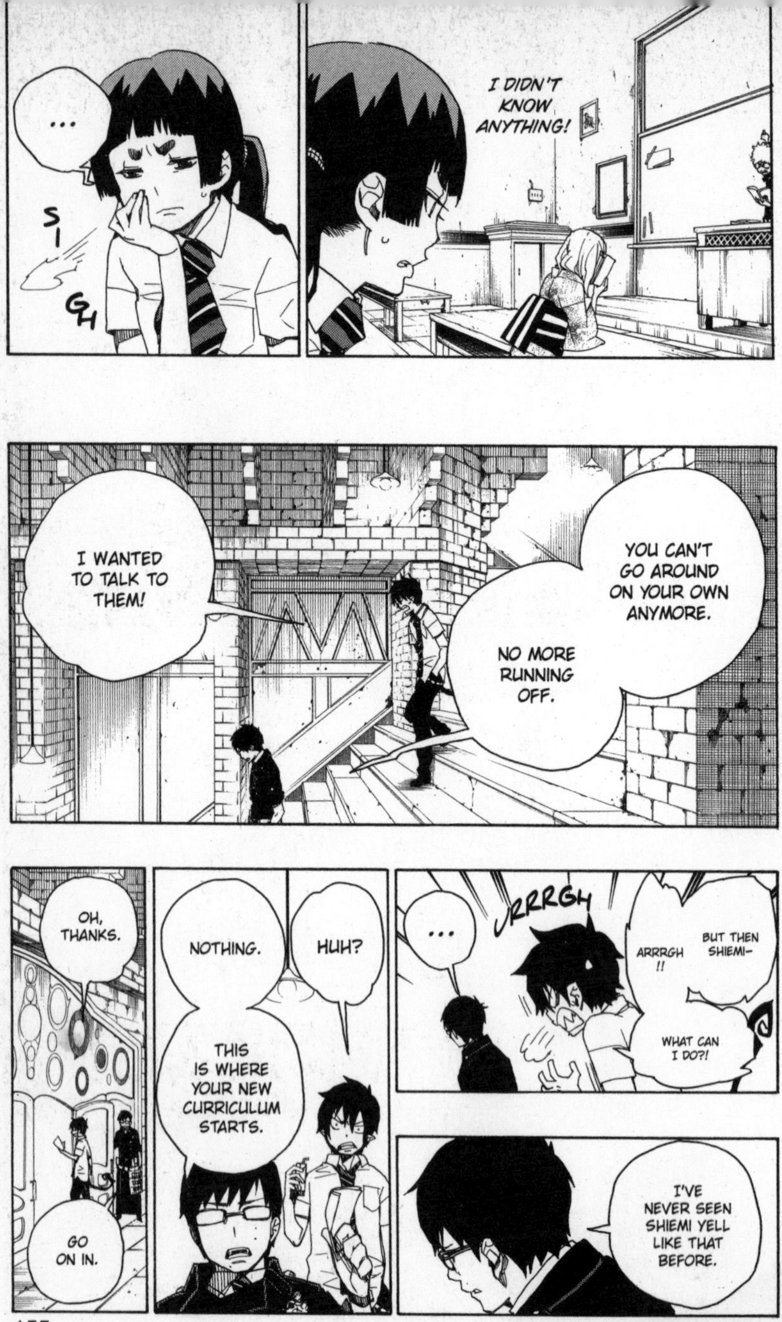
I DIDN'T KNOW ANYTHING!
...
SIGH
YOU CAN'T GO AROUND ON YOUR OWN ANYMORE.
NO MORE RUNNING OFF.
I WANTED TO TALK TO THEM!
BUT THEN SHIEMI—
ARRRGH!!
WHAT CAN I DO?!
URRRGH
...
I'VE NEVER SEEN SHIEMI YELL LIKE THAT BEFORE.
HUH?
NOTHING.
THIS IS WHERE YOUR NEW CURRICULUM STARTS.
OH, THANKS.
GO ON IN.

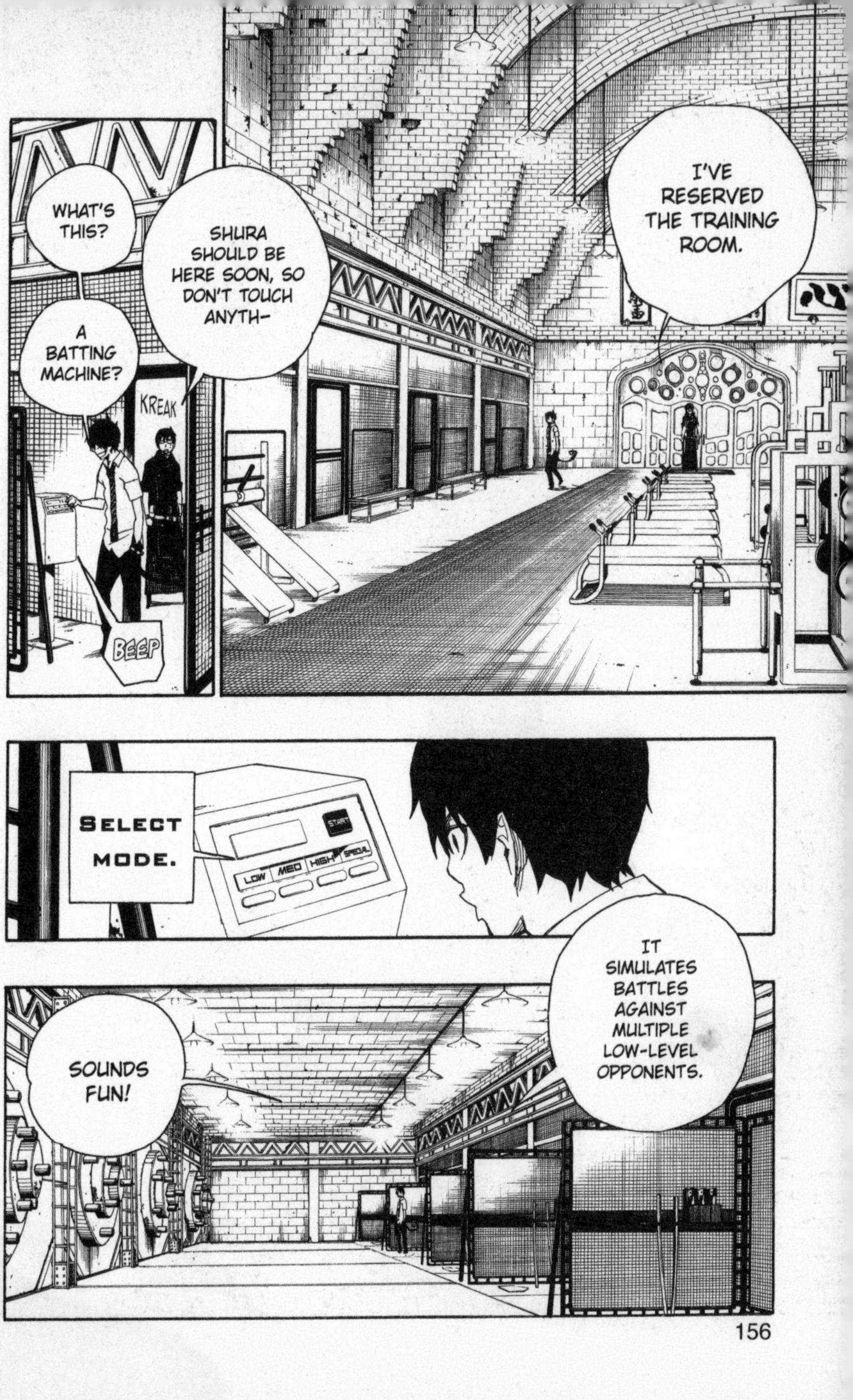
I'VE RESERVED THE TRAINING ROOM.
KREAK
WHAT'S THIS?
A BATTING MACHINE?
SHURA SHOULD BE HERE SOON, SO DON'T TOUCH ANYTH-
BEEP
SELECT MODE.
START
LOW
MED
HIGH
SPECIAL
IT SIMULATES BATTLES AGAINST MULTIPLE LOW-LEVEL OPPONENTS.
SOUNDS FUN!

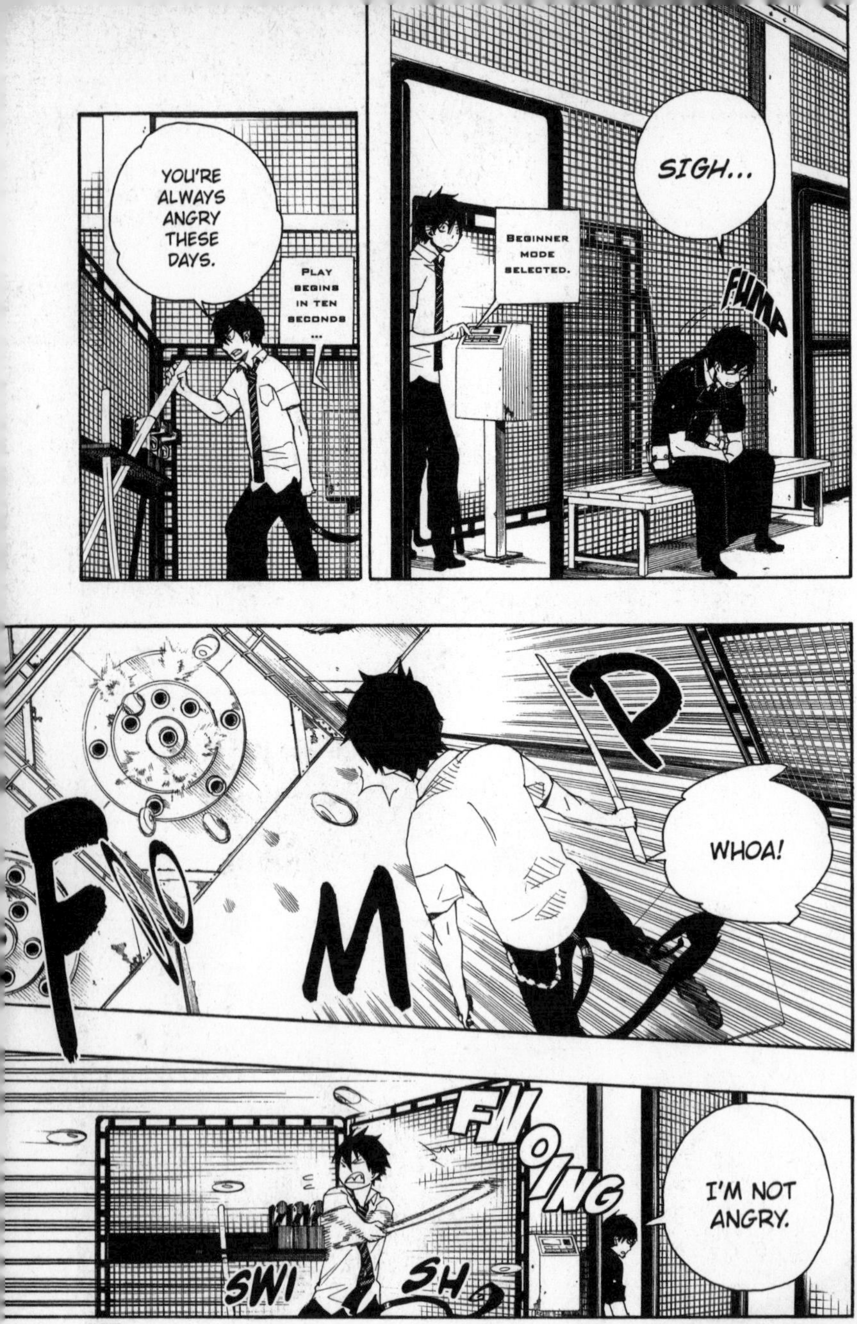
SIGH...
FUMP
BEGINNER MODE SELECTED.
YOU'RE ALWAYS ANGRY THESE DAYS.
PLAY BEGINS IN TEN SECONDS ...
WHOA!
FMP
I'M NOT ANGRY.
FWOING
SWISH

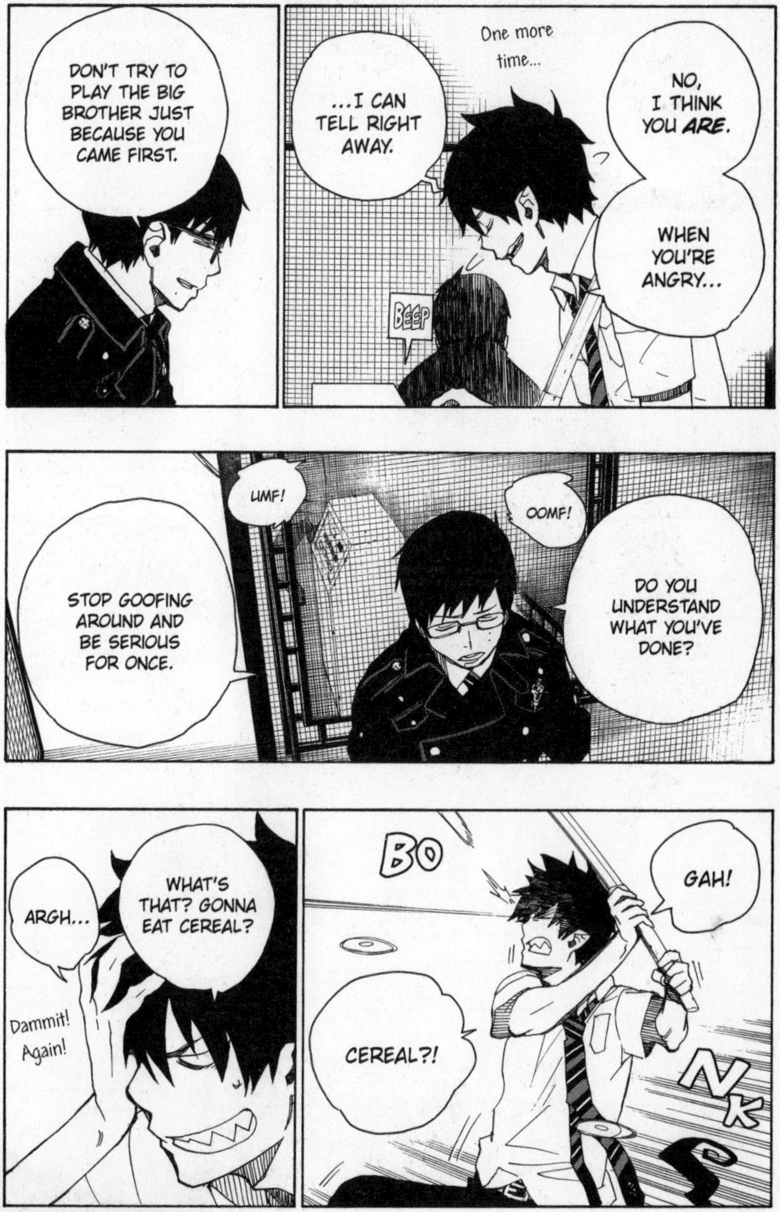
NO, I THINK YOU ARE.
WHEN YOU'RE ANGRY...
One more time...
...I CAN TELL RIGHT AWAY.
BEEP
DON'T TRY TO PLAY THE BIG BROTHER JUST BECAUSE YOU CAME FIRST.
OOMF!
DO YOU UNDERSTAND WHAT YOU'VE DONE?
UMF!
STOP GOOFING AROUND AND BE SERIOUS FOR ONCE.
GAH!
BO
NK
CEREAL?!
WHAT'S THAT? GONNA EAT CEREAL?
ARGH...
Dammit! Again!

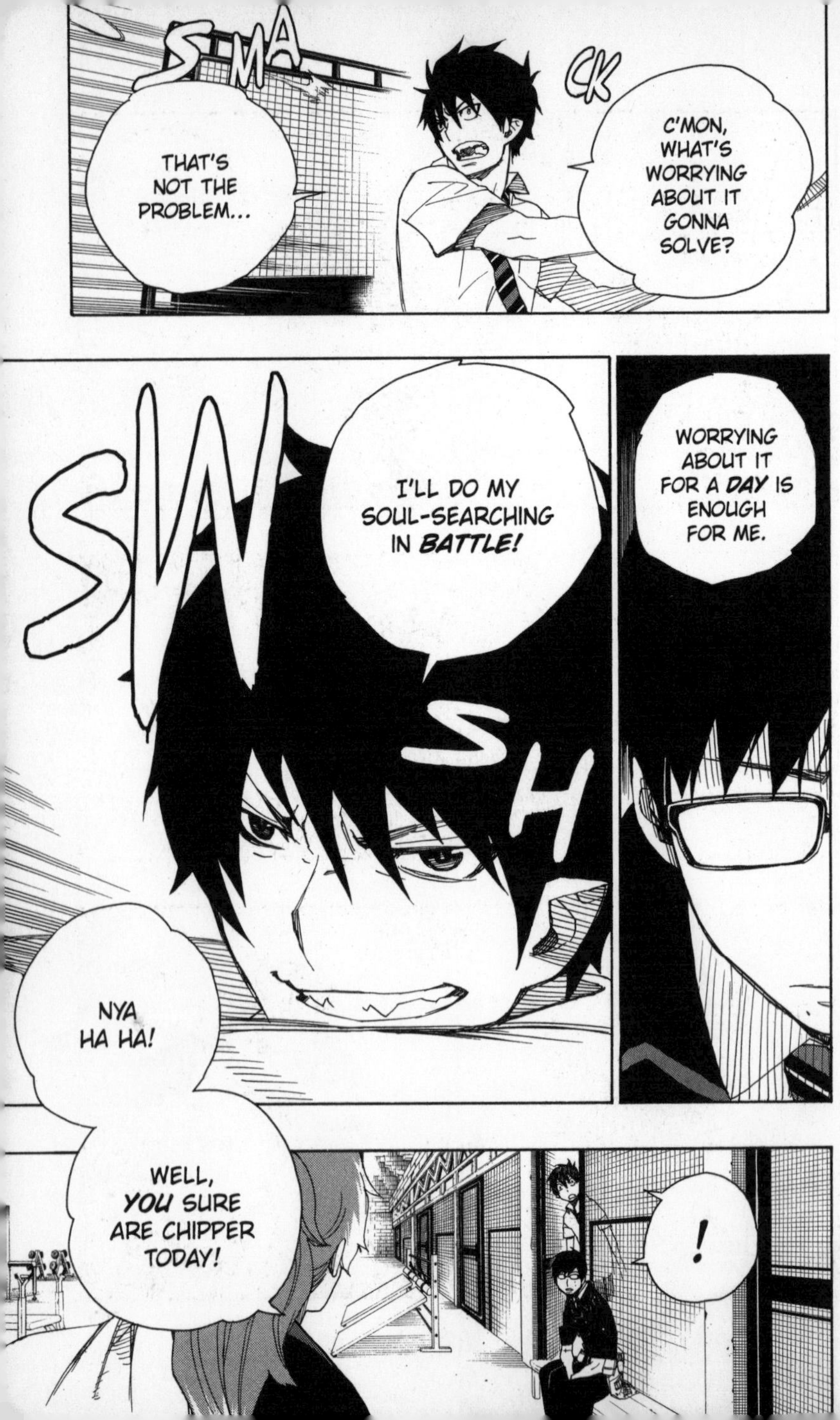
SMACK
C'MON, WHAT'S WORRYING ABOUT IT GONNA SOLVE?
THAT'S NOT THE PROBLEM...
WORRYING ABOUT IT FOR A *DAY* IS ENOUGH FOR ME.
SWSH
I'LL DO MY SOUL-SEARCHING IN *BATTLE!*
NYA HA HA!
!
WELL, *YOU* SURE ARE CHIPPER TODAY!

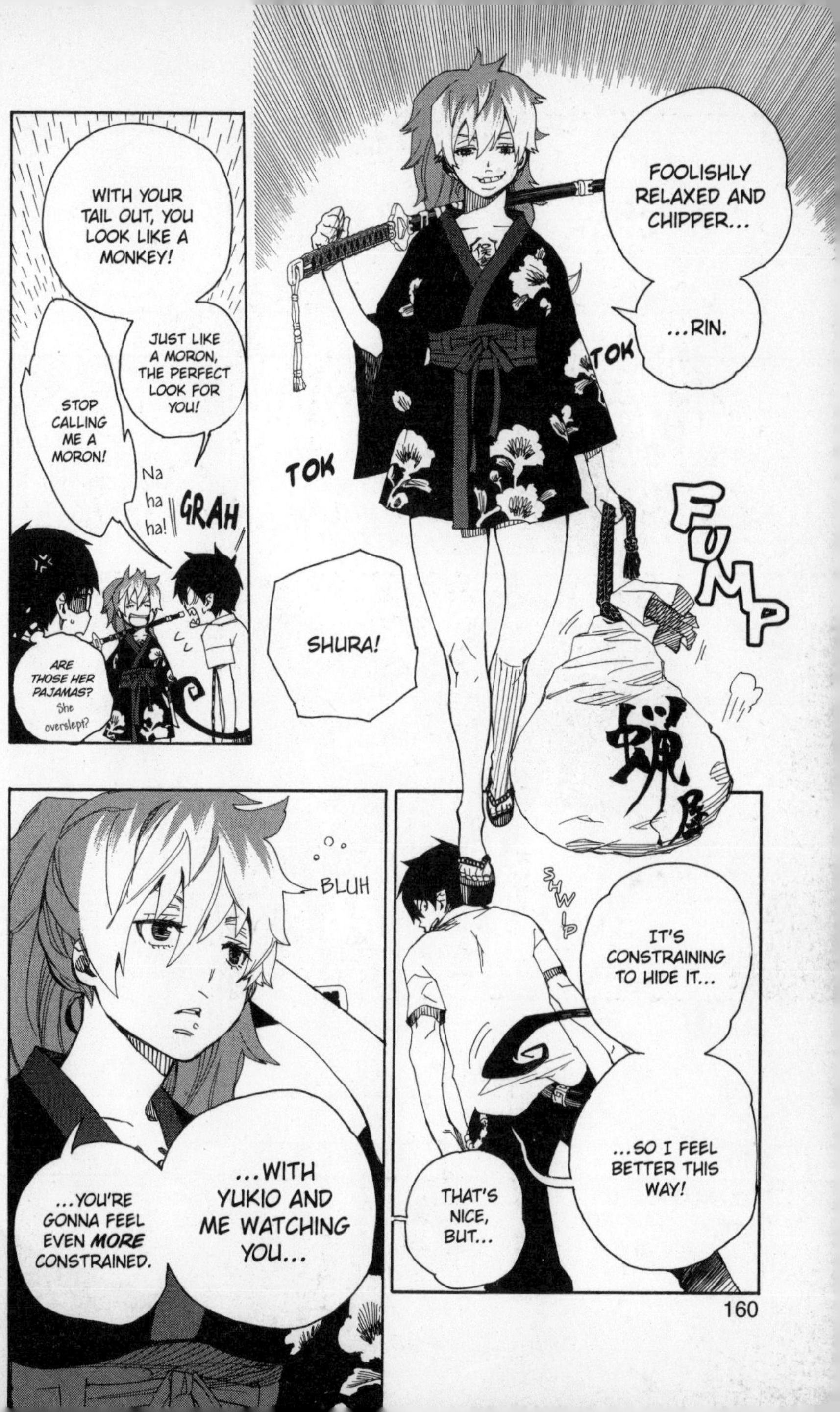
FOOLISHLY RELAXED AND CHIPPER...
...RIN.
TOK
TOK
FUMP
SHURA!
WITH YOUR TAIL OUT, YOU LOOK LIKE A MONKEY!
JUST LIKE A MORON, THE PERFECT LOOK FOR YOU!
STOP CALLING ME A MORON!
Na ha ha!
GRAH
ARE THOSE HER PAJAMAS? She overslept?
SHWIP
IT'S CONSTRAINING TO HIDE IT...
...SO I FEEL BETTER THIS WAY!
THAT'S NICE, BUT...
BLUH
...WITH YUKIO AND ME WATCHING YOU...
...YOU'RE GONNA FEEL EVEN MORE CONSTRAINED.

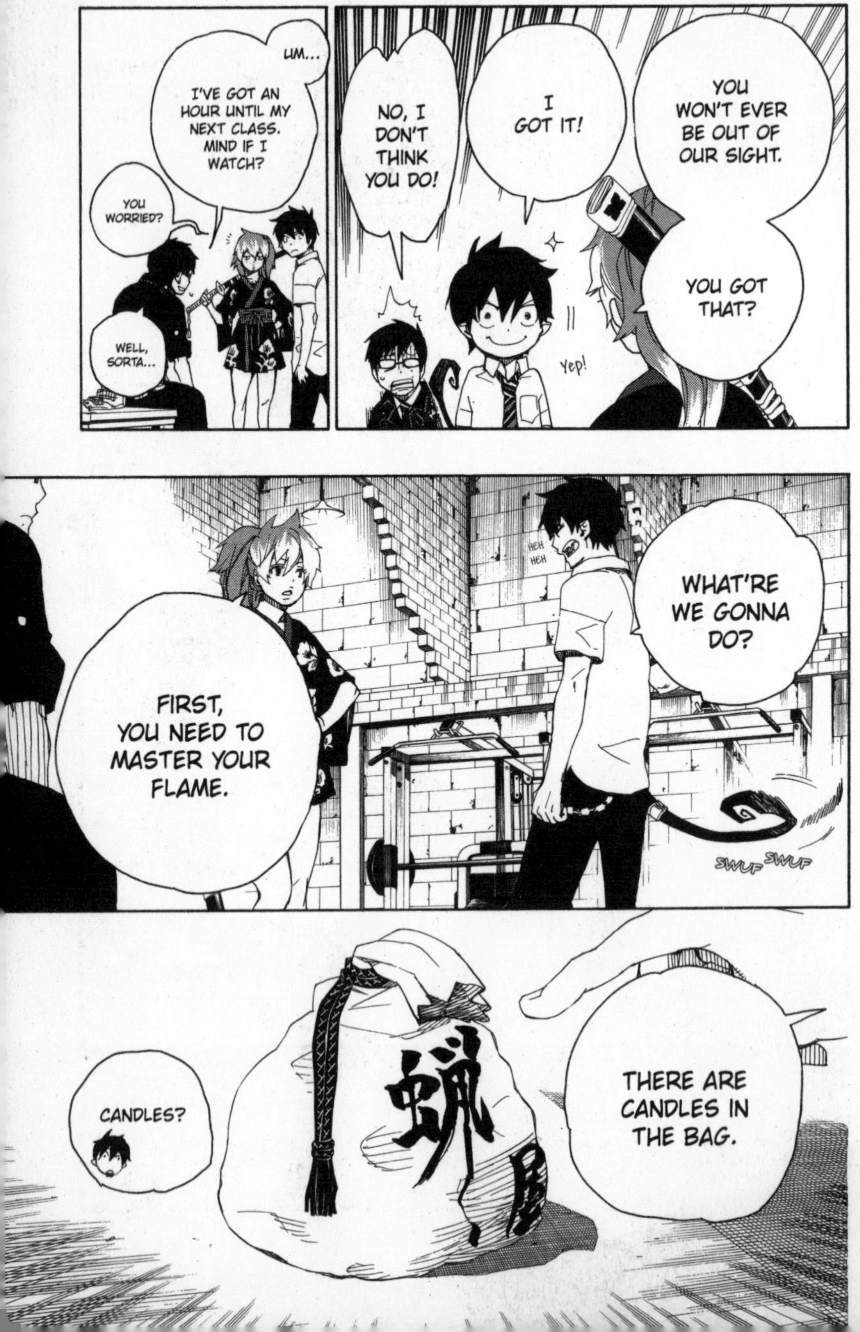
YOU WON'T EVER BE OUT OF OUR SIGHT.
YOU GOT THAT?
I GOT IT!
Yep!
NO, I DON'T THINK YOU DO!
UM...
I'VE GOT AN HOUR UNTIL MY NEXT CLASS. MIND IF I WATCH?
YOU WORRIED?
WELL, SORTA...
WHAT'RE WE GONNA DO?
HEH HEH
SWUF SWUF
FIRST, YOU NEED TO MASTER YOUR FLAME.
THERE ARE CANDLES IN THE BAG.
CANDLES?

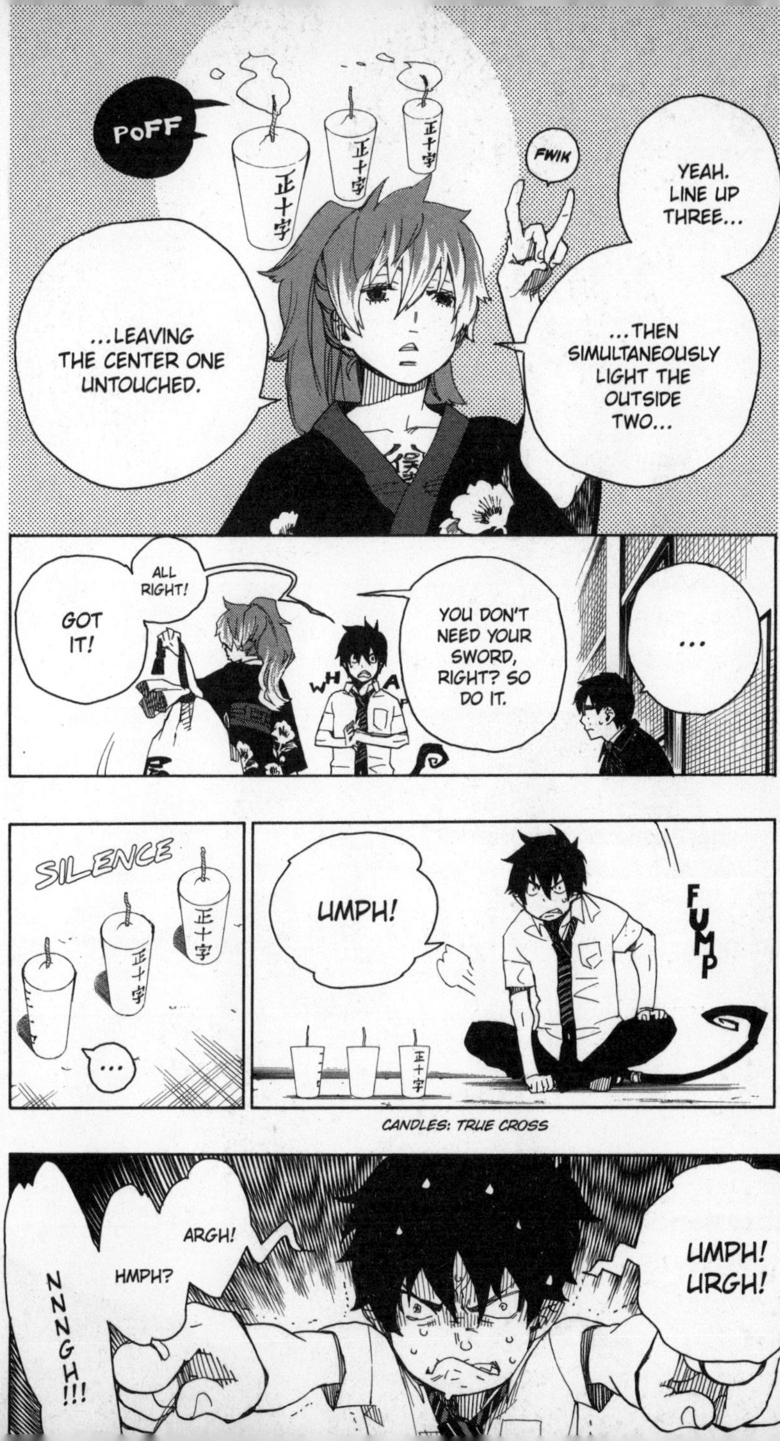
FWIK
YEAH. LINE UP THREE...
...THEN SIMULTANEOUSLY LIGHT THE OUTSIDE TWO...
POFF
...LEAVING THE CENTER ONE UNTOUCHED.
正十字
...
YOU DON'T NEED YOUR SWORD, RIGHT? SO DO IT.
WHAP
ALL RIGHT!
GOT IT!
FUMP
UMPH!
SILENCE
...
CANDLES: TRUE CROSS
UMPH! URGH!
ARGH!
HMPH?
NNNGH!!!

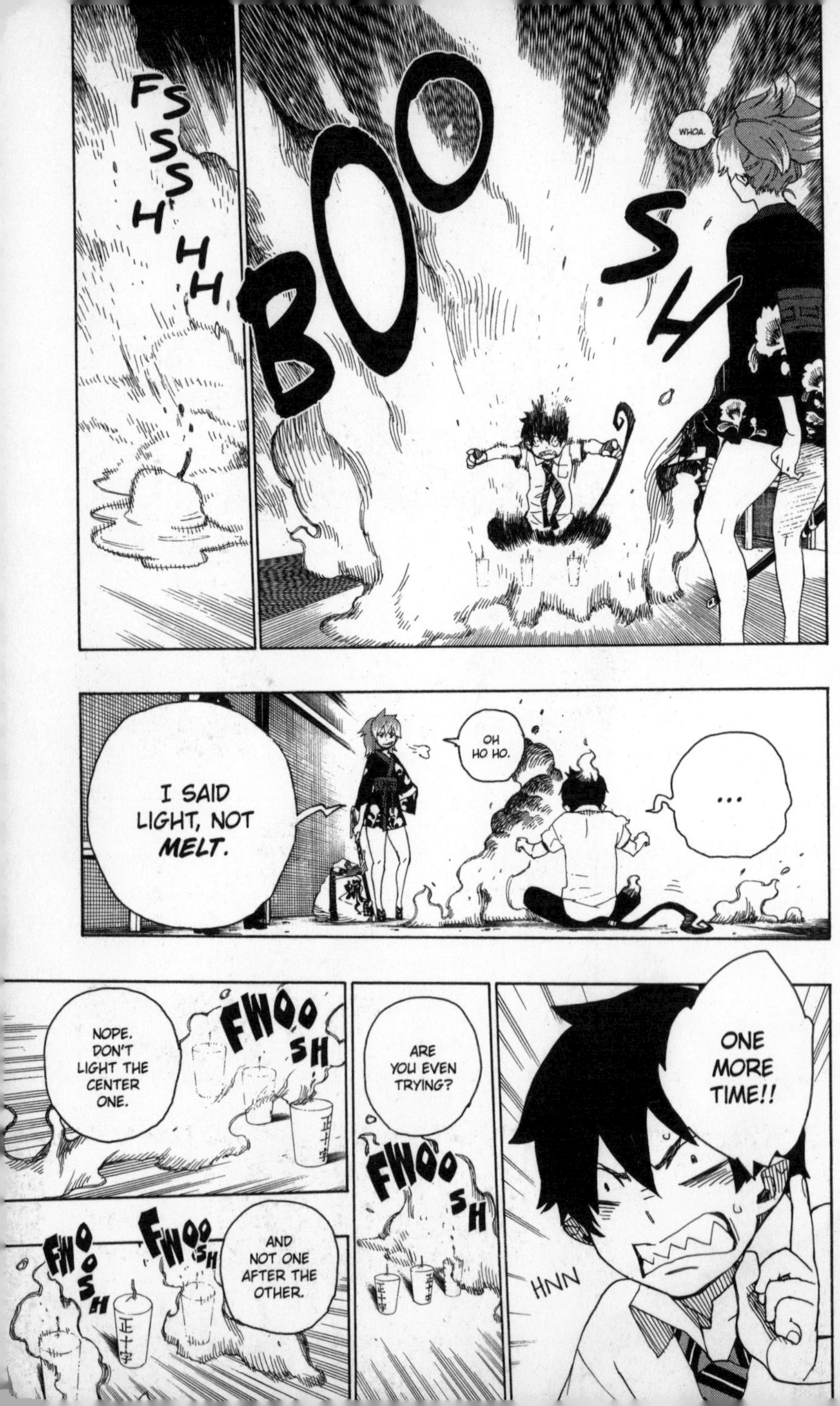
WHOA.
BOOSH
FSSSHHH
...
OH HO HO.
I SAID LIGHT, NOT MELT.
ONE MORE TIME!!
HNN
ARE YOU EVEN TRYING?
FWOOSH
FWOOSH
NOPE. DON'T LIGHT THE CENTER ONE.
AND NOT ONE AFTER THE OTHER.
FWOOSH
FWOOSH

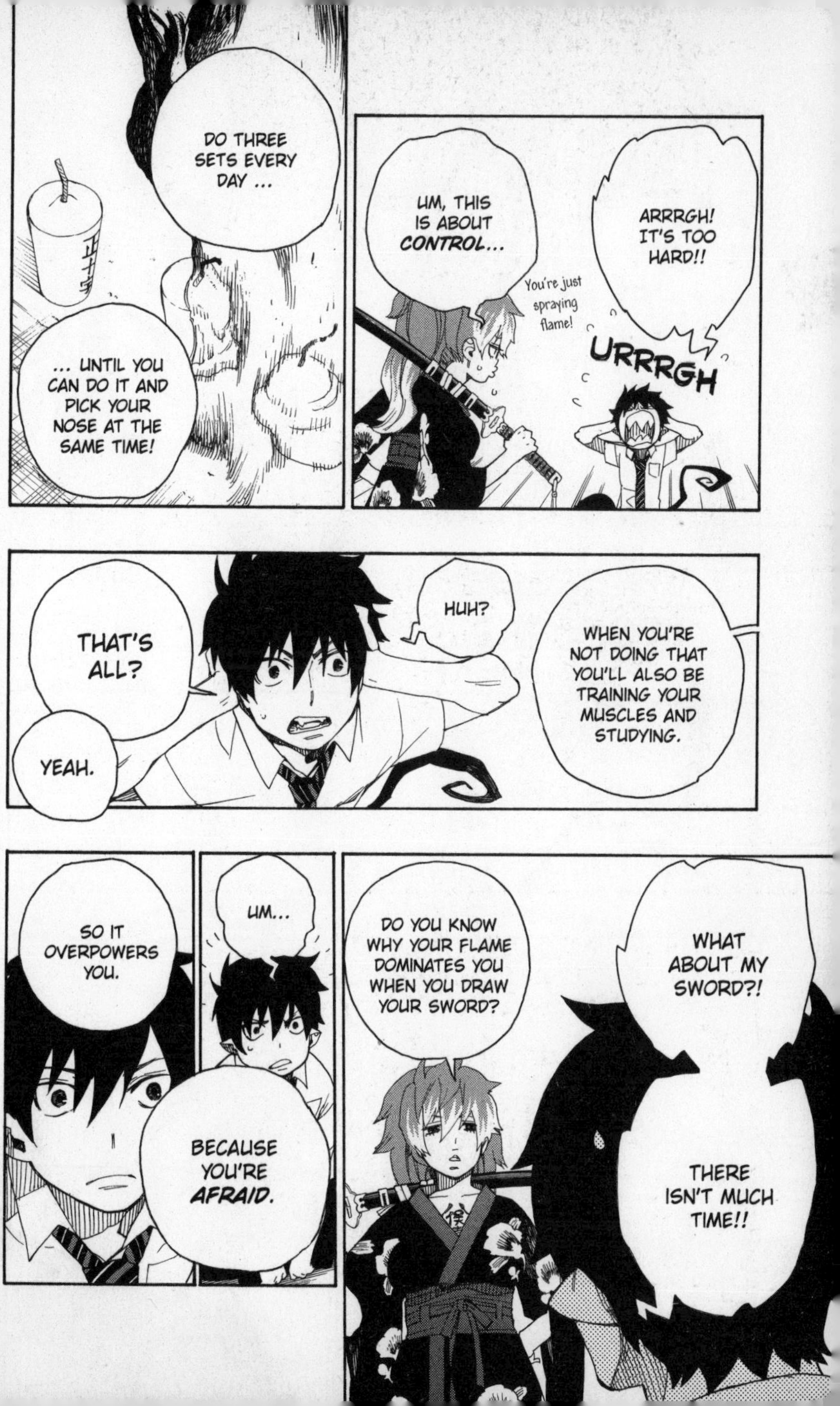
ARRRGH! IT'S TOO HARD!!
URRRGH
UM, THIS IS ABOUT CONTROL...
You're just spraying flame!
DO THREE SETS EVERY DAY ...
... UNTIL YOU CAN DO IT AND PICK YOUR NOSE AT THE SAME TIME!
WHEN YOU'RE NOT DOING THAT YOU'LL ALSO BE TRAINING YOUR MUSCLES AND STUDYING.
HUH?
THAT'S ALL?
YEAH.
WHAT ABOUT MY SWORD?!
THERE ISN'T MUCH TIME!!
DO YOU KNOW WHY YOUR FLAME DOMINATES YOU WHEN YOU DRAW YOUR SWORD?
UM...
BECAUSE YOU'RE AFRAID.
SO IT OVERPOWERS YOU.

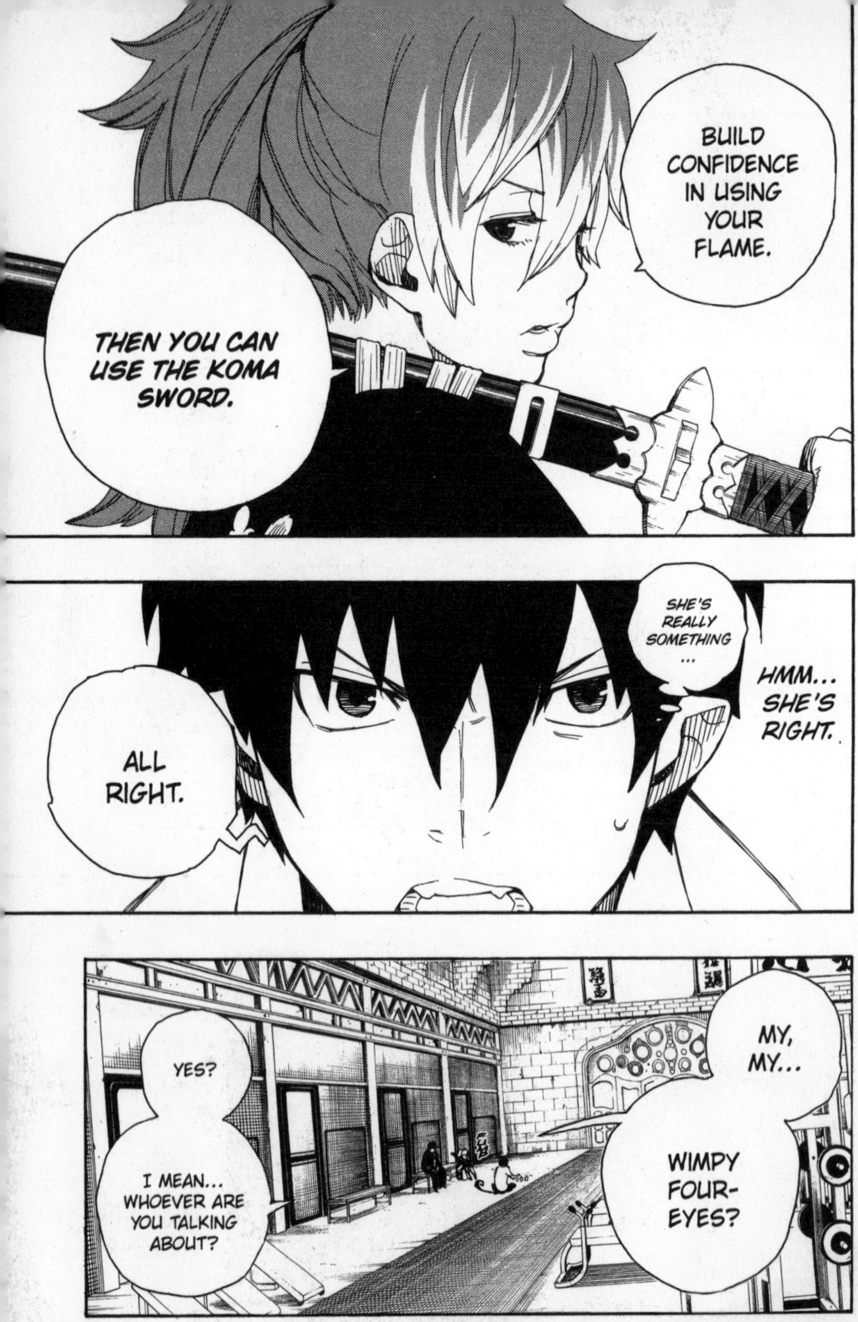
BUILD CONFIDENCE IN USING YOUR FLAME.
THEN YOU CAN USE THE KOMA SWORD.
HMM... SHE'S RIGHT.
SHE'S REALLY SOMETHING ...
ALL RIGHT.
MY, MY...
WIMPY FOUR-EYES?
YES?
I MEAN... WHOEVER ARE YOU TALKING ABOUT?

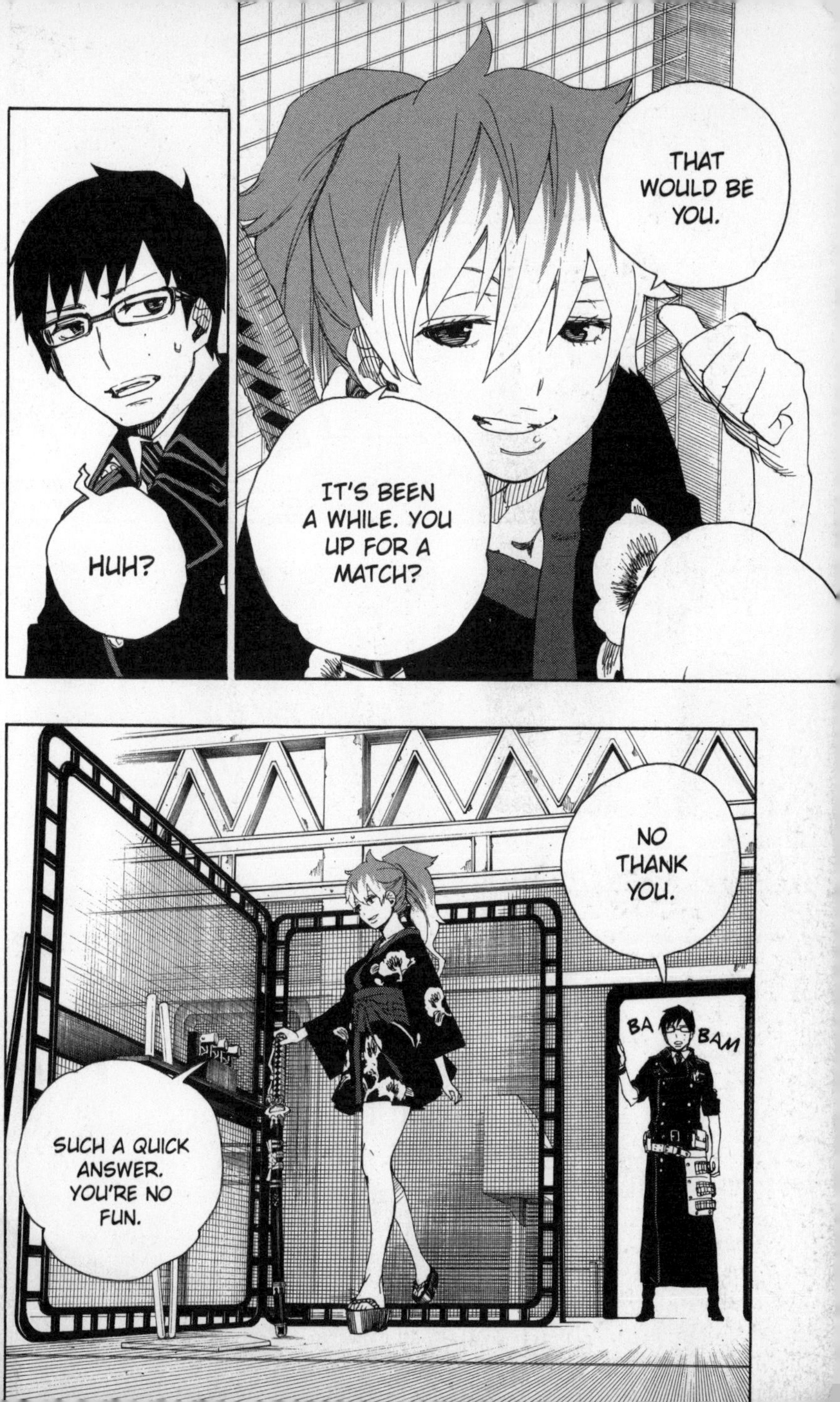
THAT WOULD BE YOU.
IT'S BEEN A WHILE. YOU UP FOR A MATCH?
HUH?
NO THANK YOU.
BA BAM
SUCH A QUICK ANSWER. YOU'RE NO FUN.

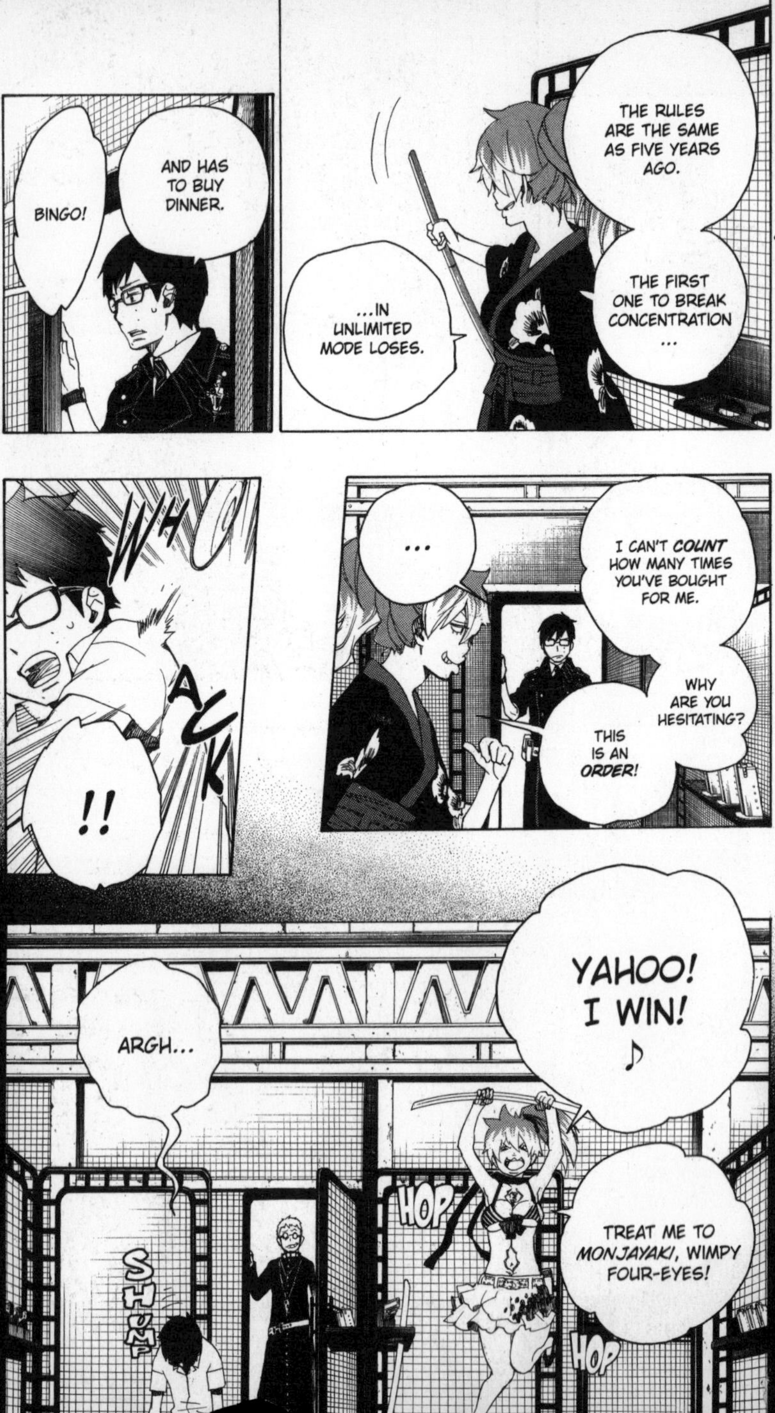
THE RULES ARE THE SAME AS FIVE YEARS AGO.
THE FIRST ONE TO BREAK CONCENTRATION ...
...IN UNLIMITED MODE LOSES.
AND HAS TO BUY DINNER.
BINGO!
I CAN'T *COUNT* HOW MANY TIMES YOU'VE BOUGHT FOR ME.
...
WHY ARE YOU HESITATING?
THIS IS AN *ORDER*!
WHACK
!!
YAHOO! I WIN! ♪
TREAT ME TO *MONJAYAKI*, WIMPY FOUR-EYES!
HOP
HOP
ARGH...
SHUMP

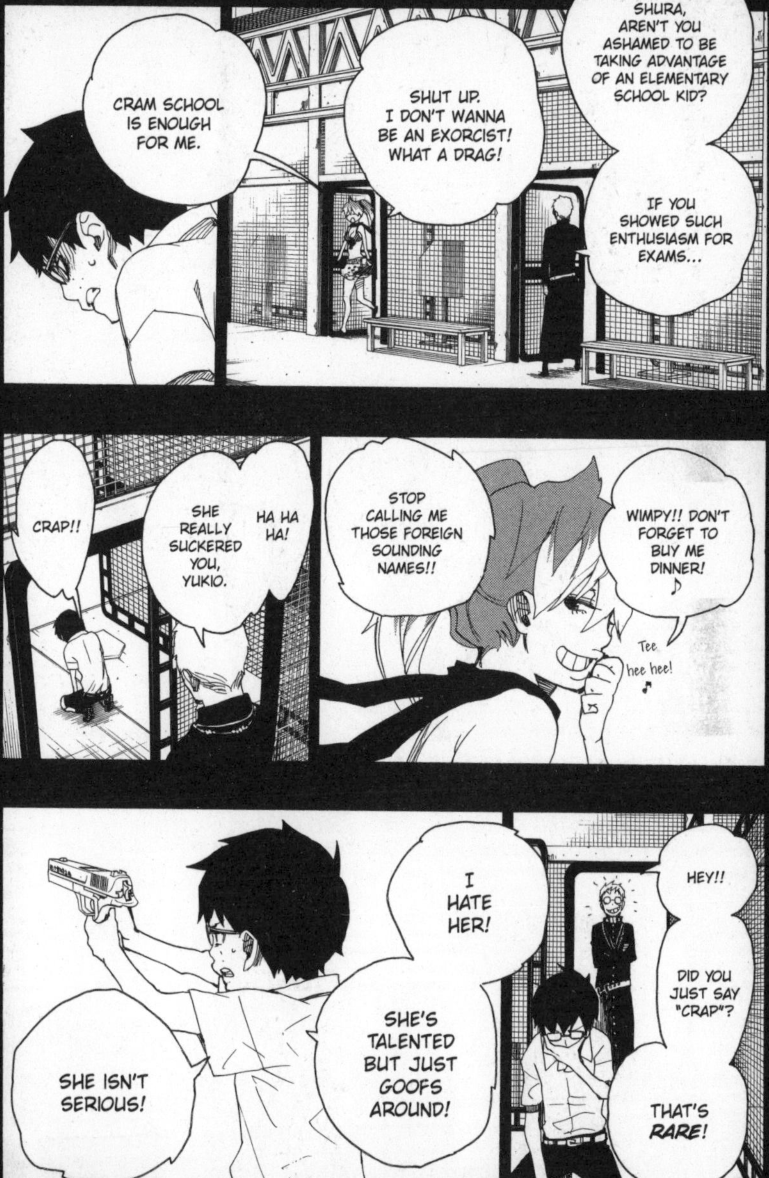
SHURA, AREN'T YOU ASHAMED TO BE TAKING ADVANTAGE OF AN ELEMENTARY SCHOOL KID?
IF YOU SHOWED SUCH ENTHUSIASM FOR EXAMS...
SHUT UP. I DON'T WANNA BE AN EXORCIST! WHAT A DRAG!
CRAM SCHOOL IS ENOUGH FOR ME.
WIMPY!! DON'T FORGET TO BUY ME DINNER! ♪
STOP CALLING ME THOSE FOREIGN SOUNDING NAMES!!
Tee hee hee! ♪
HA HA HA!
SHE REALLY SUCKERED YOU, YUKIO.
CRAP!!
HEY!!
DID YOU JUST SAY "CRAP"?
THAT'S *RARE*!
I HATE HER!
SHE'S TALENTED BUT JUST GOOFS AROUND!
SHE ISN'T SERIOUS!

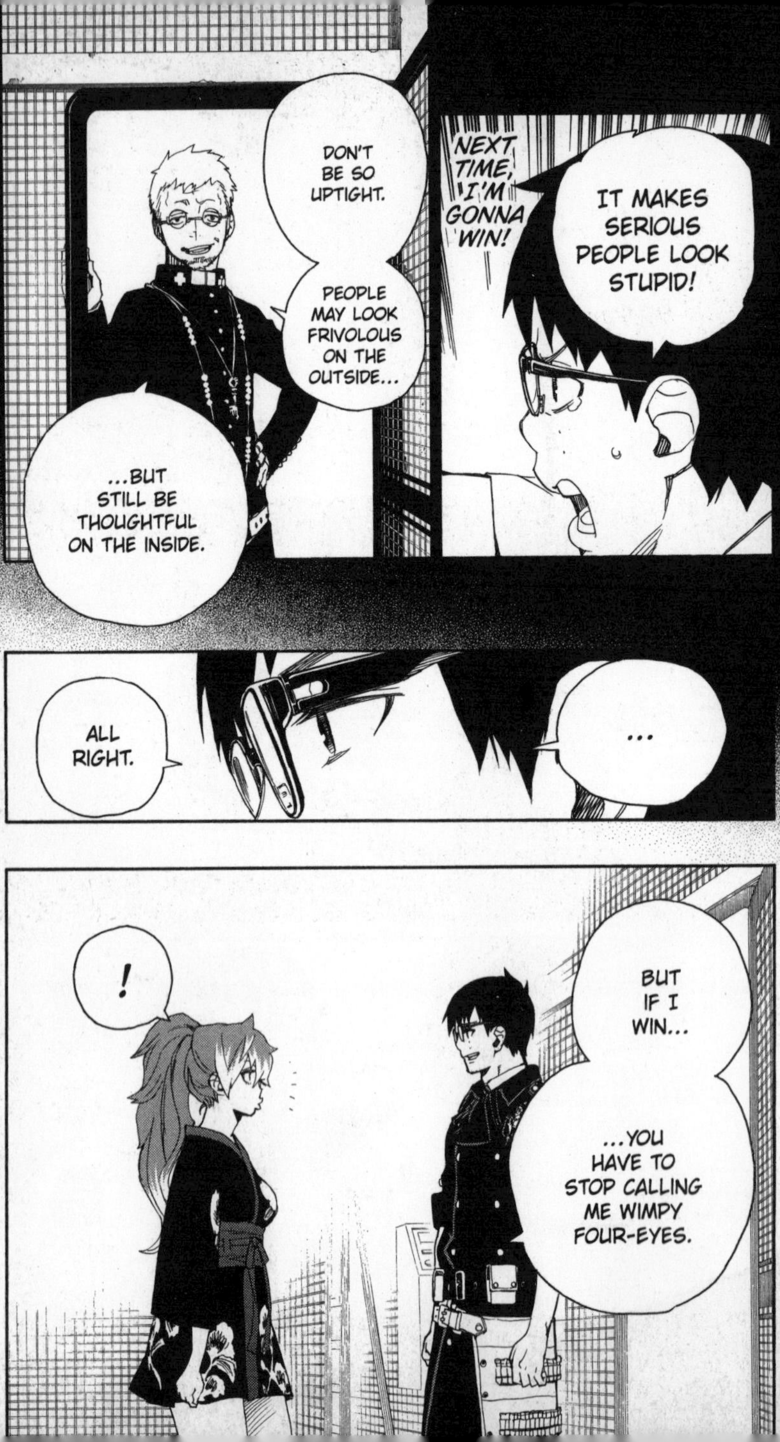
IT MAKES SERIOUS PEOPLE LOOK STUPID!
NEXT TIME, I'M GONNA WIN!
DON'T BE SO UPTIGHT.
PEOPLE MAY LOOK FRIVOLOUS ON THE OUTSIDE...
...BUT STILL BE THOUGHTFUL ON THE INSIDE.
...
ALL RIGHT.
BUT IF I WIN...
...YOU HAVE TO STOP CALLING ME WIMPY FOUR-EYES.
!

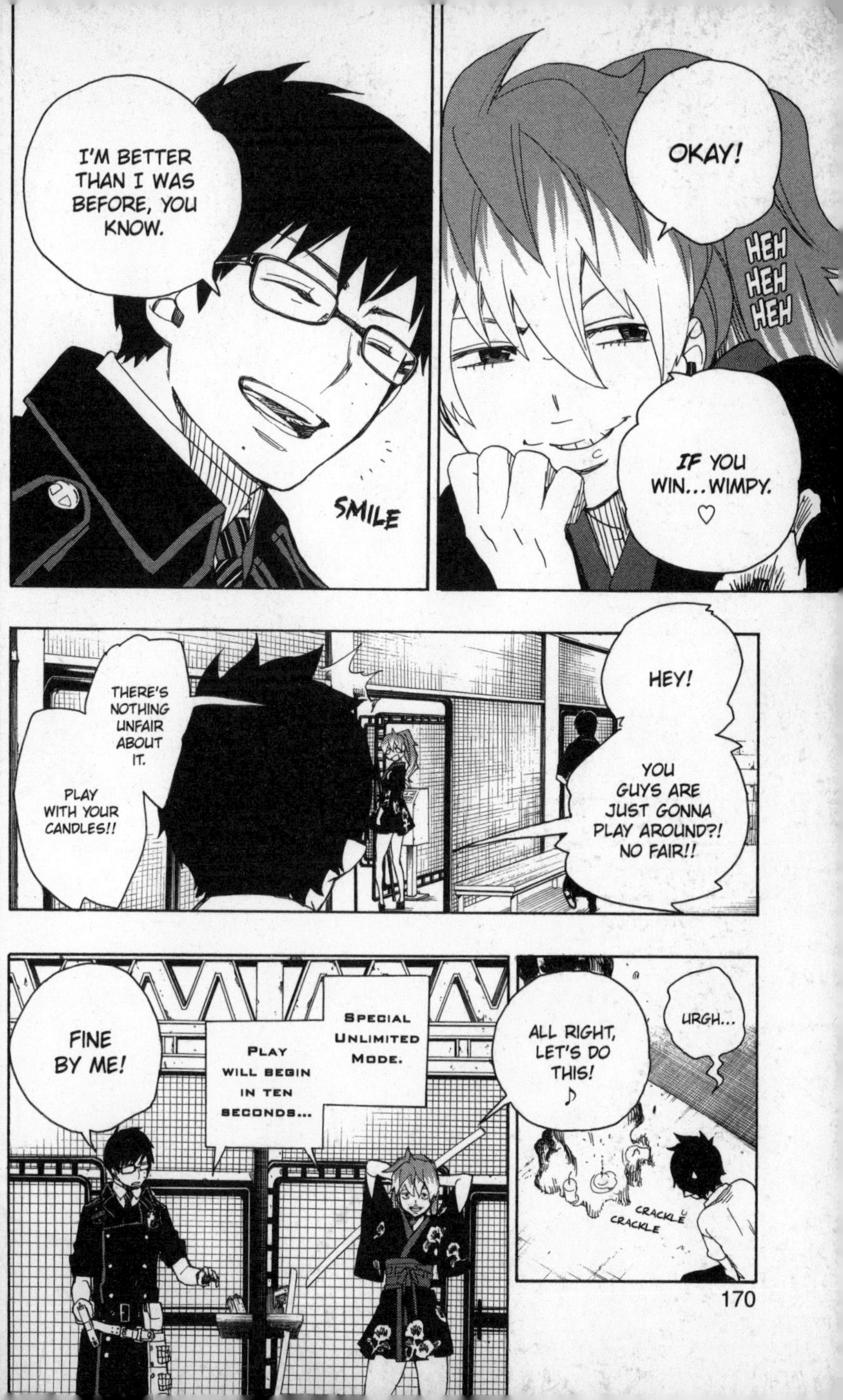
OKAY!
HEH HEH HEH
IF YOU WIN...WIMPY. ♡
I'M BETTER THAN I WAS BEFORE, YOU KNOW.
SMILE
HEY!
YOU GUYS ARE JUST GONNA PLAY AROUND?! NO FAIR!!
THERE'S NOTHING UNFAIR ABOUT IT.
PLAY WITH YOUR CANDLES!!
URGH...
CRACKLE
CRACKLE
ALL RIGHT, LET'S DO THIS! ♪
SPECIAL UNLIMITED MODE.
PLAY WILL BEGIN IN TEN SECONDS...
FINE BY ME!

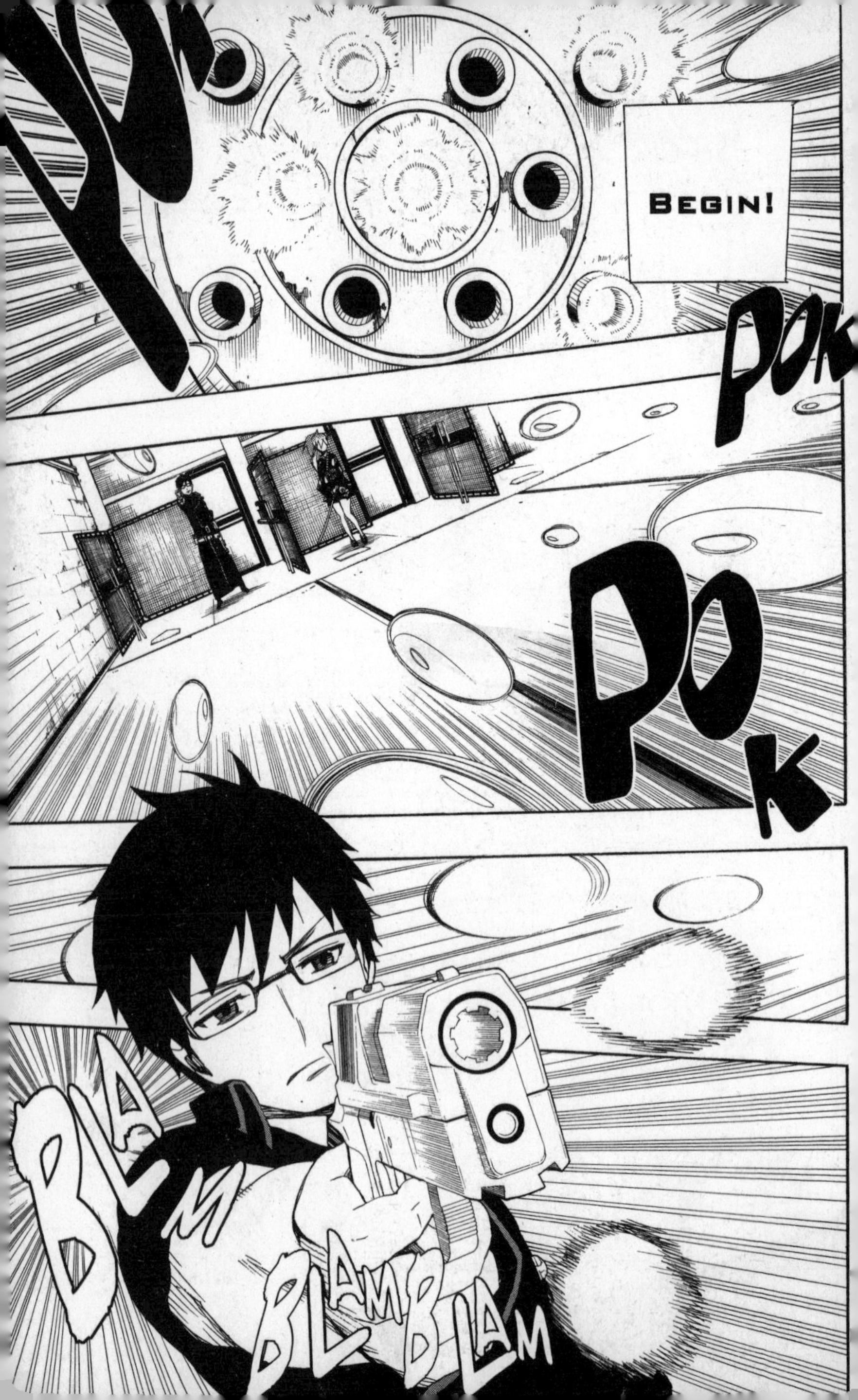

Begin!
POK
POK
BLAM
BLAM
BLAM

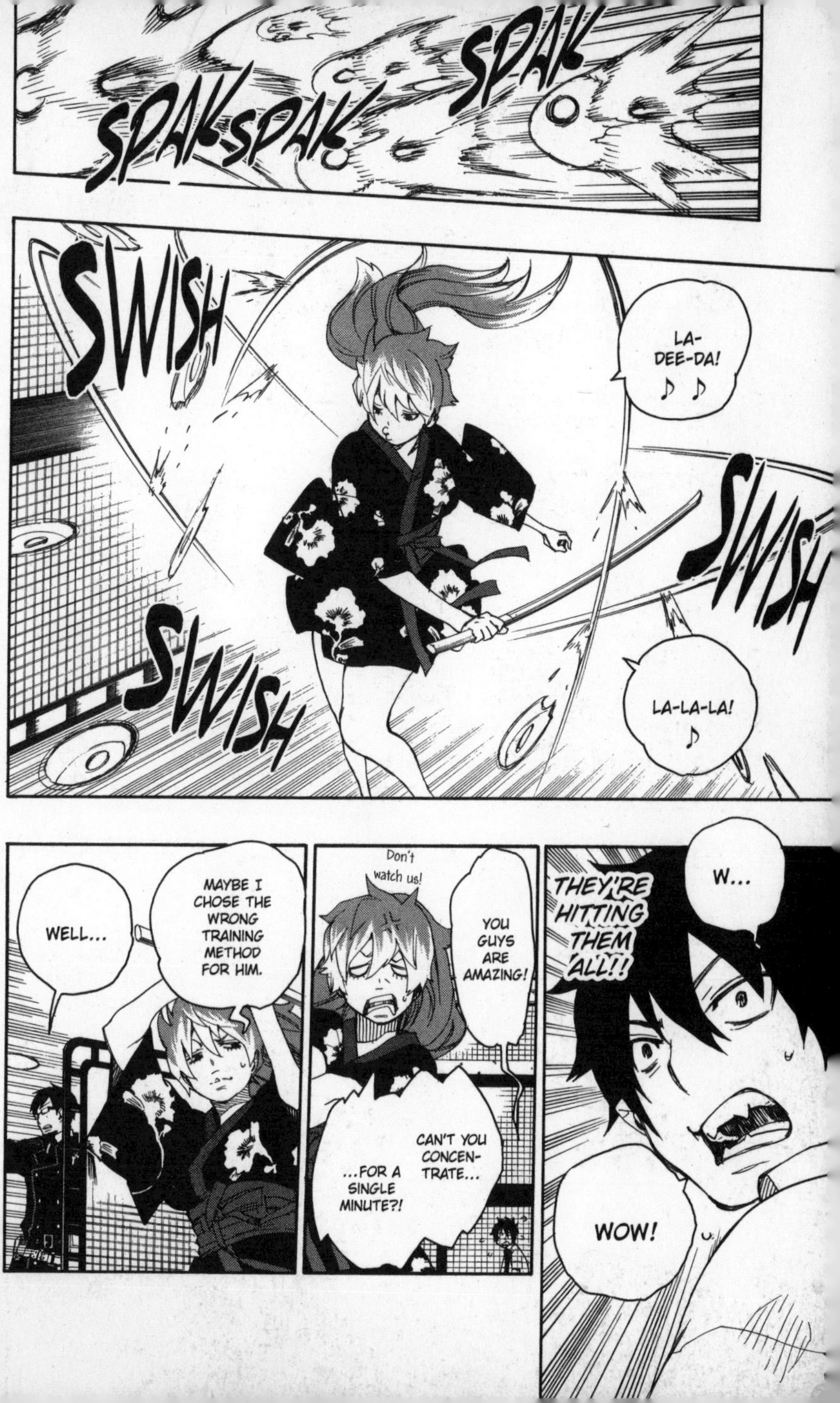
SPAK
SPAK-SPAK
LA-DEE-DA! ♪ ♪
SWISH
SWISH
LA-LA-LA! ♪
SWISH
W...
THEY'RE HITTING THEM ALL!!
WOW!
YOU GUYS ARE AMAZING!
Don't watch us!
CAN'T YOU CONCENTRATE...
...FOR A SINGLE MINUTE?!
MAYBE I CHOSE THE WRONG TRAINING METHOD FOR HIM.
WELL...

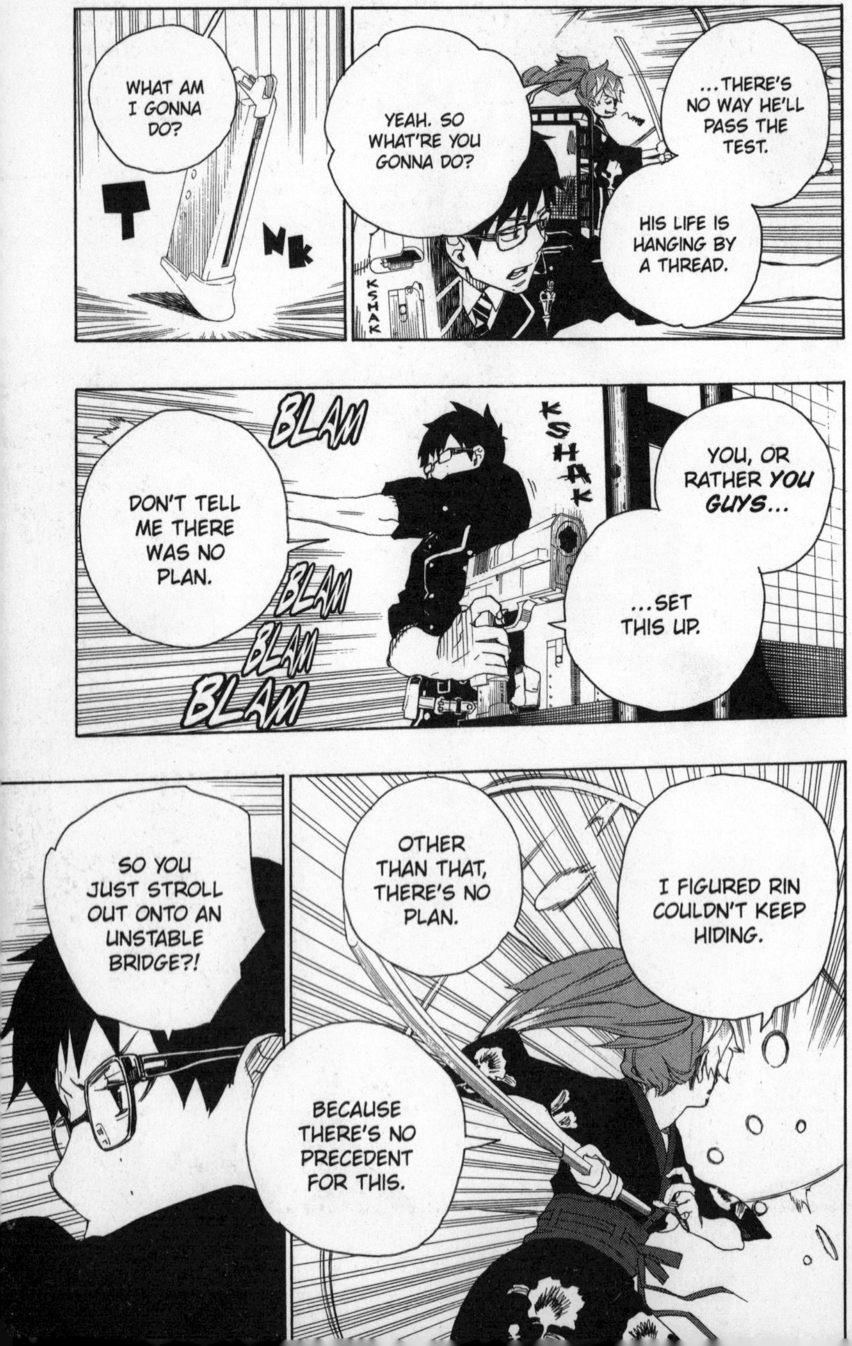

...THERE'S NO WAY HE'LL PASS THE TEST.
HIS LIFE IS HANGING BY A THREAD.
YEAH. SO WHAT'RE YOU GONNA DO?
KSHAK
WHAT AM I GONNA DO?
TNK
YOU, OR RATHER ***YOU GUYS***...
...SET THIS UP.
KSHAK
BLAM
DON'T TELL ME THERE WAS NO PLAN.
BLAM
BLAM
BLAM
I FIGURED RIN COULDN'T KEEP HIDING.
OTHER THAN THAT, THERE'S NO PLAN.
SO YOU JUST STROLL OUT ONTO AN UNSTABLE BRIDGE?!
BECAUSE THERE'S NO PRECEDENT FOR THIS.

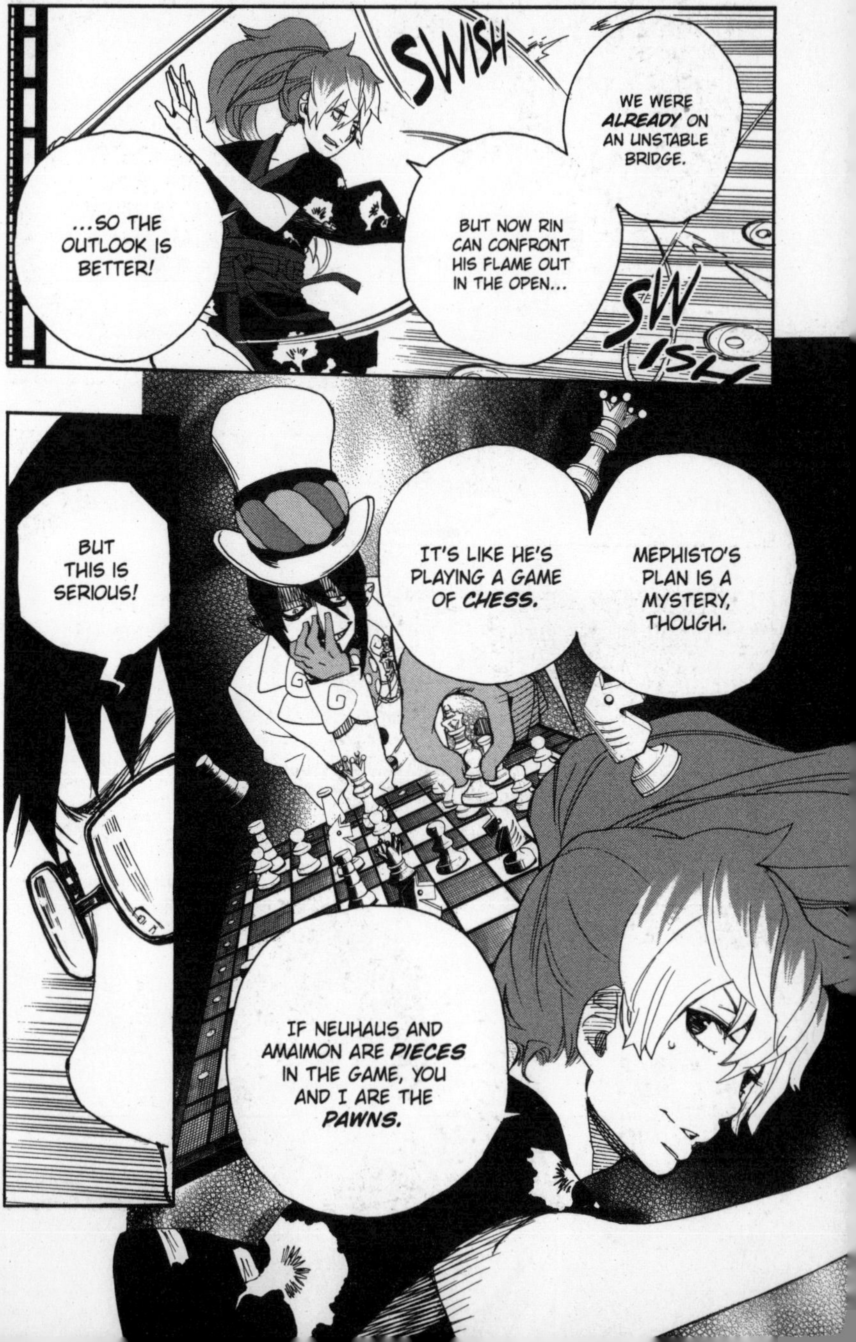
SWISH
WE WERE ALREADY ON AN UNSTABLE BRIDGE.
BUT NOW RIN CAN CONFRONT HIS FLAME OUT IN THE OPEN...
SWISH
...SO THE OUTLOOK IS BETTER!
MEPHISTO'S PLAN IS A MYSTERY, THOUGH.
IT'S LIKE HE'S PLAYING A GAME OF CHESS.
IF NEUHAUS AND AMAIMON ARE PIECES IN THE GAME, YOU AND I ARE THE PAWNS.
BUT THIS IS SERIOUS!

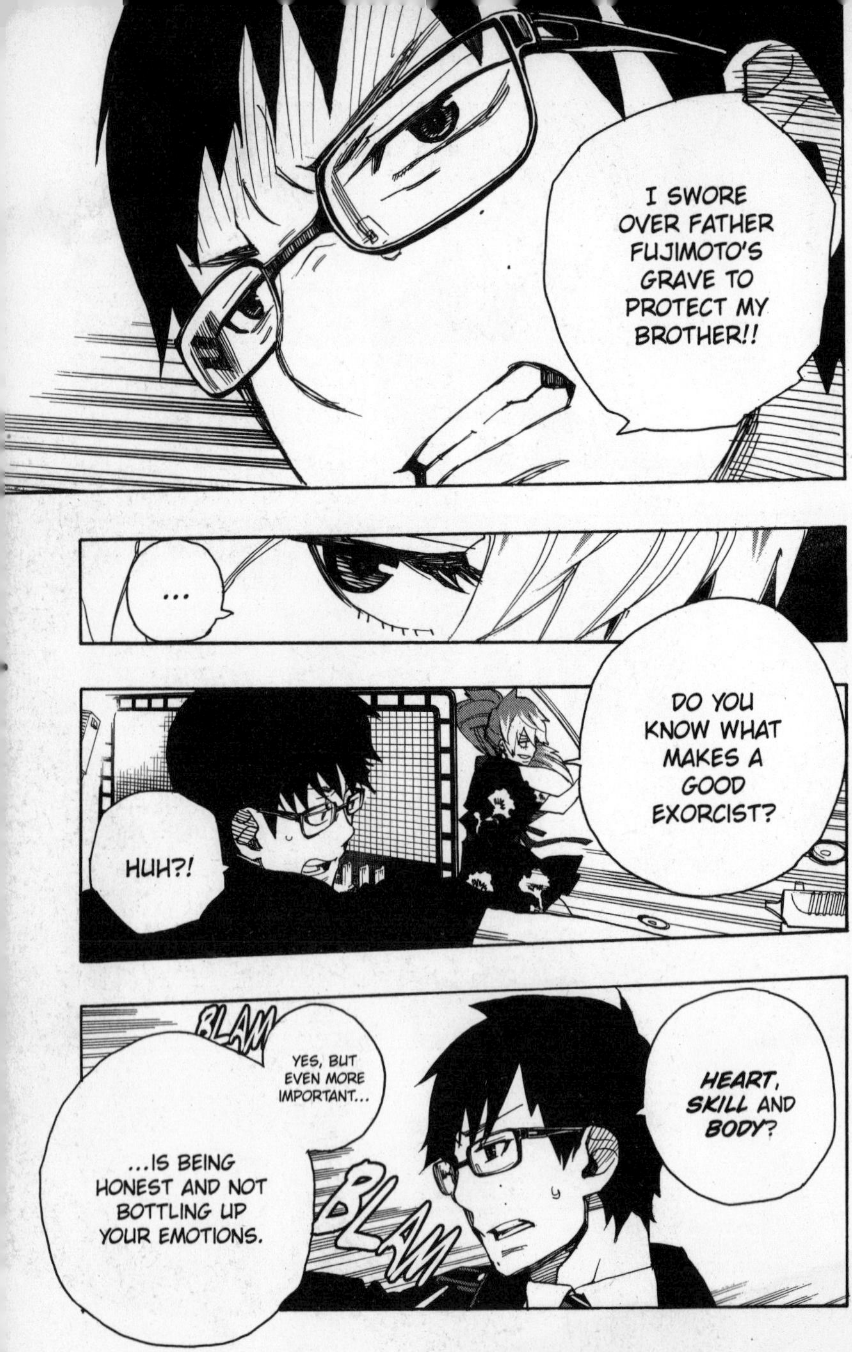
I SWORE OVER FATHER FUJIMOTO'S GRAVE TO PROTECT MY BROTHER!!
...
DO YOU KNOW WHAT MAKES A GOOD EXORCIST?
HUH?!
HEART, SKILL AND BODY?
BLAM
YES, BUT EVEN MORE IMPORTANT...
BLAM
...IS BEING HONEST AND NOT BOTTLING UP YOUR EMOTIONS.

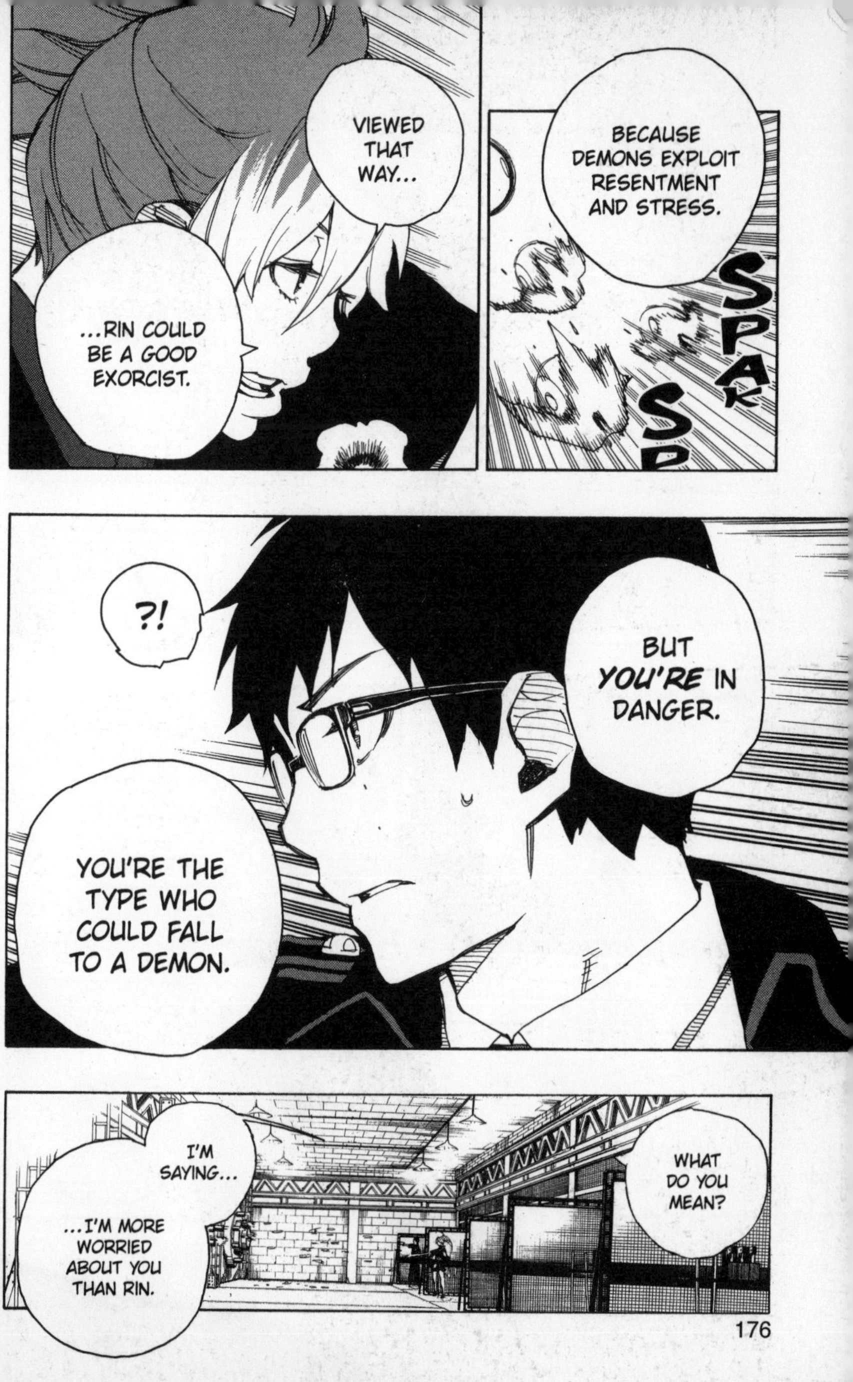
BECAUSE DEMONS EXPLOIT RESENTMENT AND STRESS.
SPAK
SP
VIEWED THAT WAY...
...RIN COULD BE A GOOD EXORCIST.
BUT *YOU'RE* IN DANGER.
?!
YOU'RE THE TYPE WHO COULD FALL TO A DEMON.
WHAT DO YOU MEAN?
I'M SAYING...
...I'M MORE WORRIED ABOUT YOU THAN RIN.

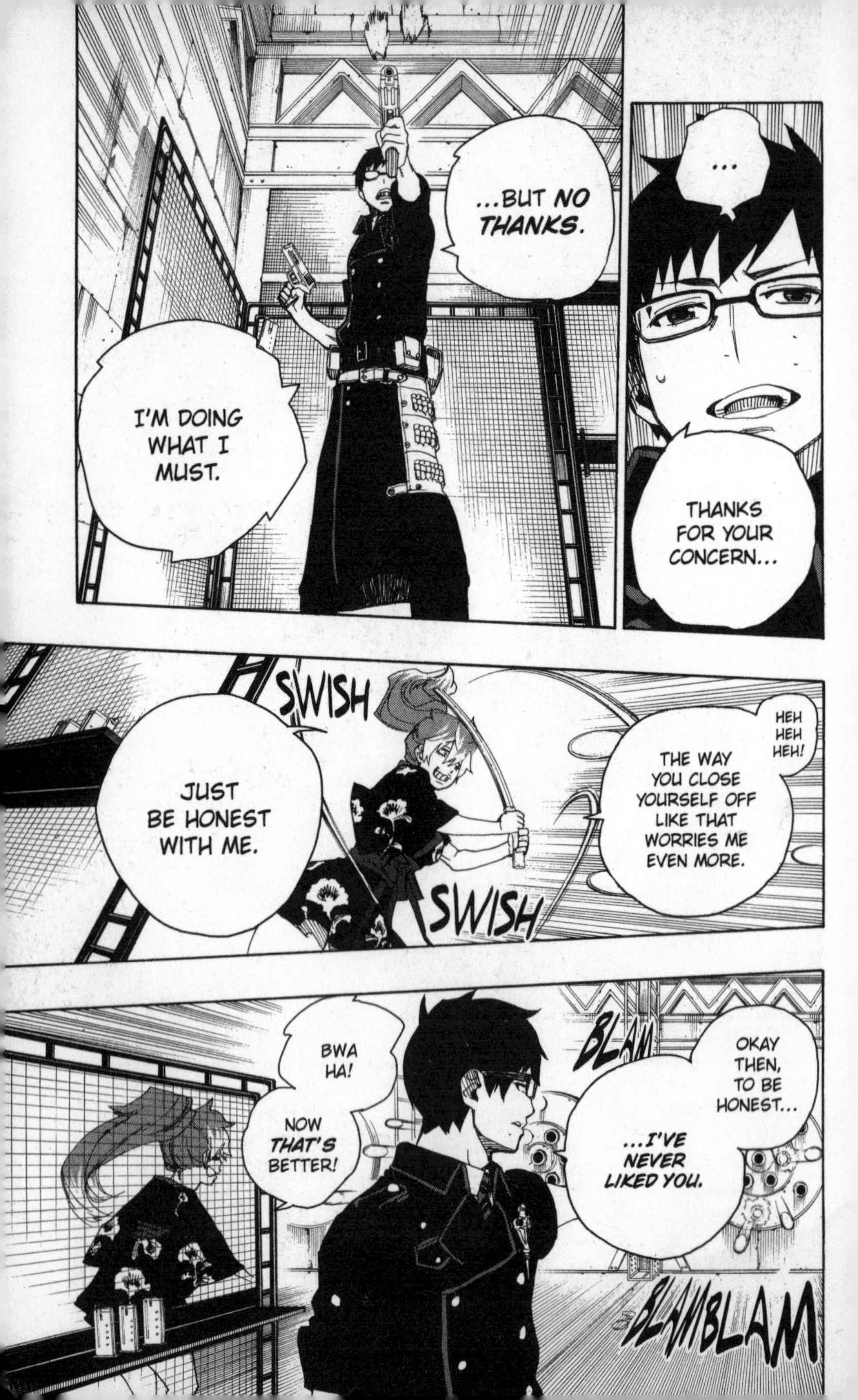
...
THANKS FOR YOUR CONCERN...
...BUT NO THANKS.
I'M DOING WHAT I MUST.
HEH HEH HEH!
THE WAY YOU CLOSE YOURSELF OFF LIKE THAT WORRIES ME EVEN MORE.
SWISH
JUST BE HONEST WITH ME.
SWISH
OKAY THEN, TO BE HONEST...
...I'VE NEVER LIKED YOU.
BLAM
BLAMBLAM
BWA HA!
NOW THAT'S BETTER!

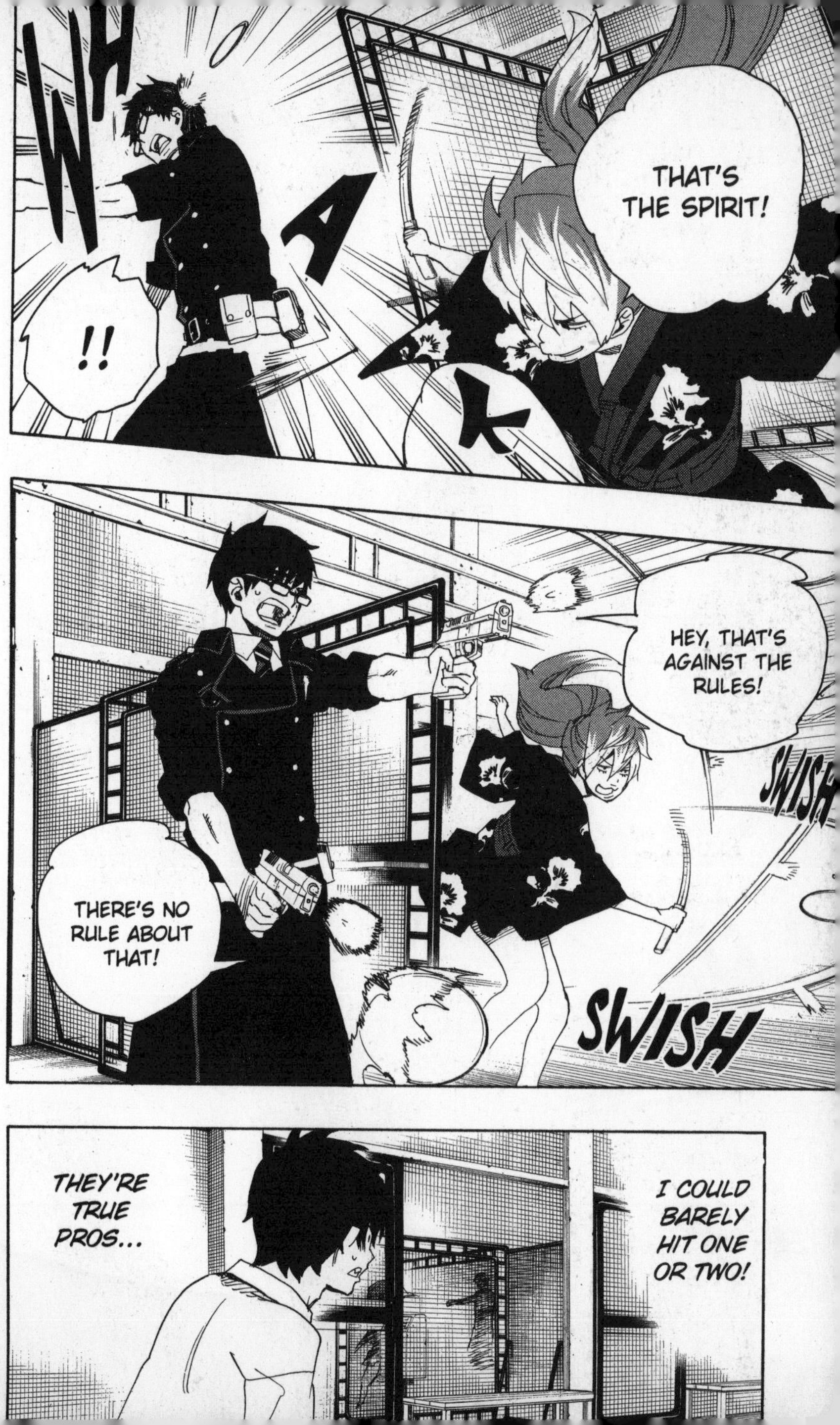
THAT'S THE SPIRIT!
WHACK
!!
HEY, THAT'S AGAINST THE RULES!
SWISH
THERE'S NO RULE ABOUT THAT!
SWISH
I COULD BARELY HIT ONE OR TWO!
THEY'RE TRUE PROS...

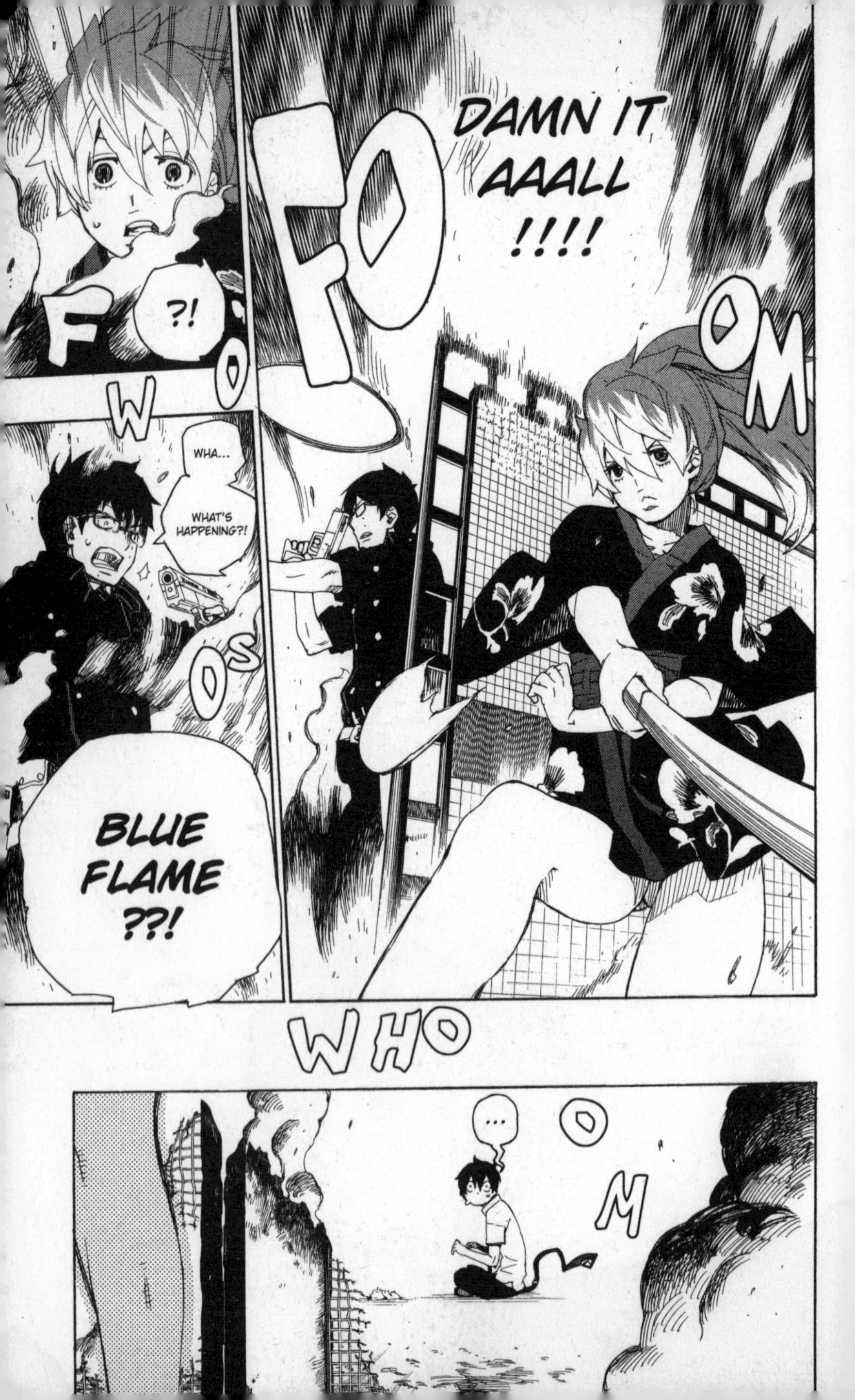
FO
DAMN IT AAALL!!!!
OM
?!
F
O
W
O
WHA...
WHAT'S HAPPENING?!
O
S
BLUE FLAME ??!
WHO
O
M
...

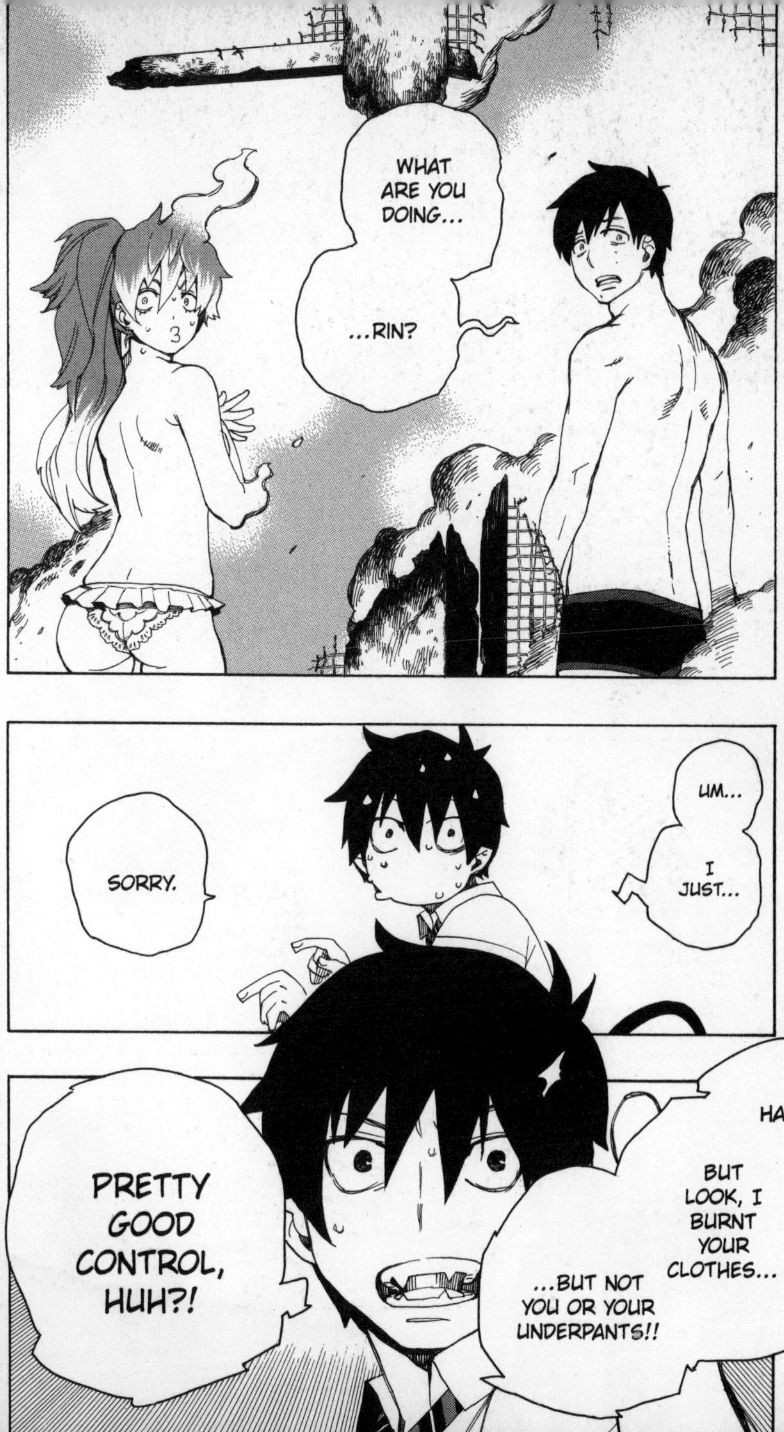
WHAT ARE YOU DOING... ...RIN?
UM... I JUST...
SORRY.
HA! BUT LOOK, I BURNT YOUR CLOTHES...
...BUT NOT YOU OR YOUR UNDERPANTS!!
PRETTY GOOD CONTROL, HUH?!

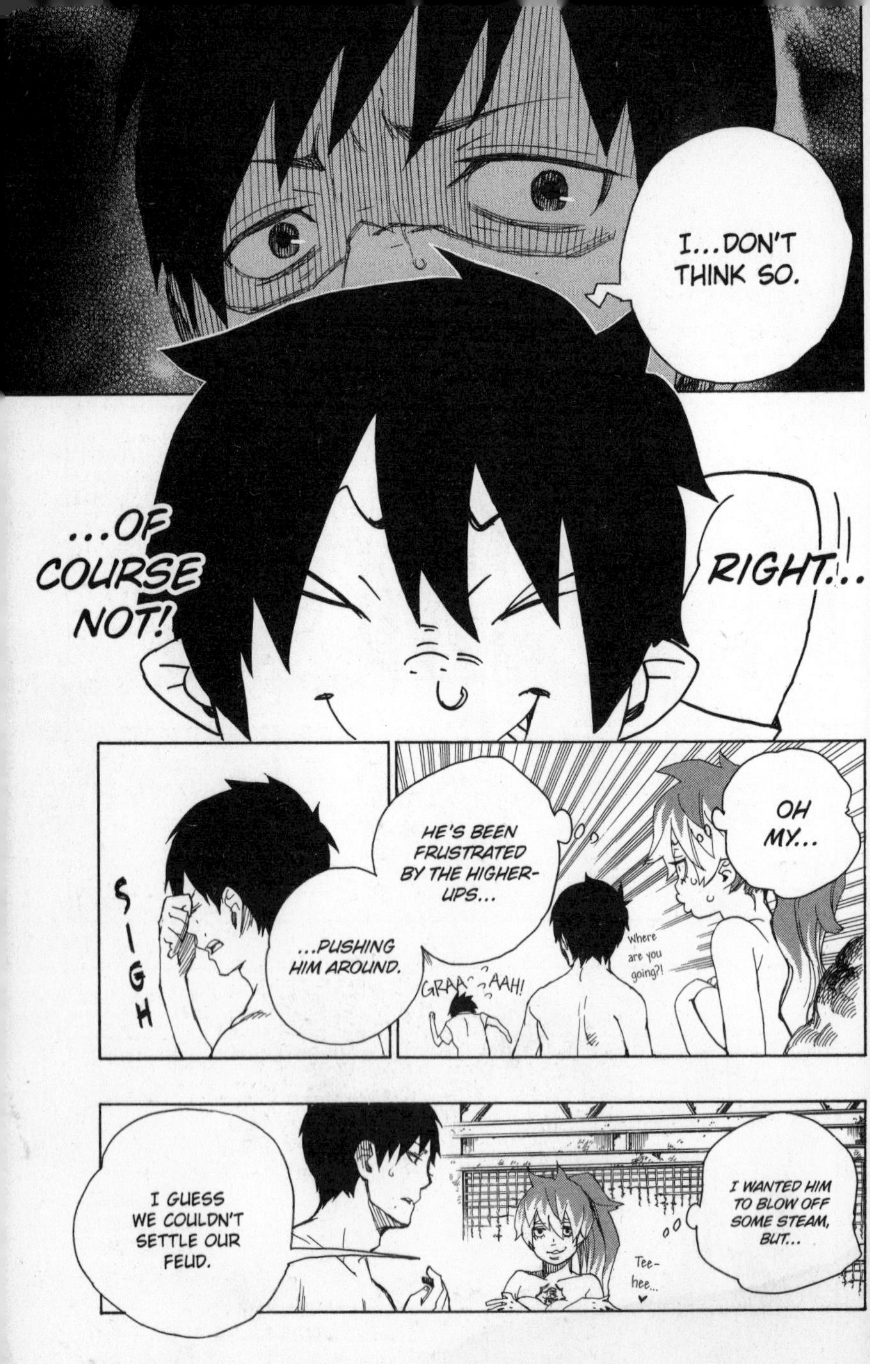
I...DON'T THINK SO.
RIGHT...
...OF COURSE NOT!
OH MY...
HE'S BEEN FRUSTRATED BY THE HIGHER-UPS...
Where are you going?!
GRAA AAH!
...PUSHING HIM AROUND.
SIGH
I WANTED HIM TO BLOW OFF SOME STEAM, BUT...
Tee-hee...
I GUESS WE COULDN'T SETTLE OUR FEUD.

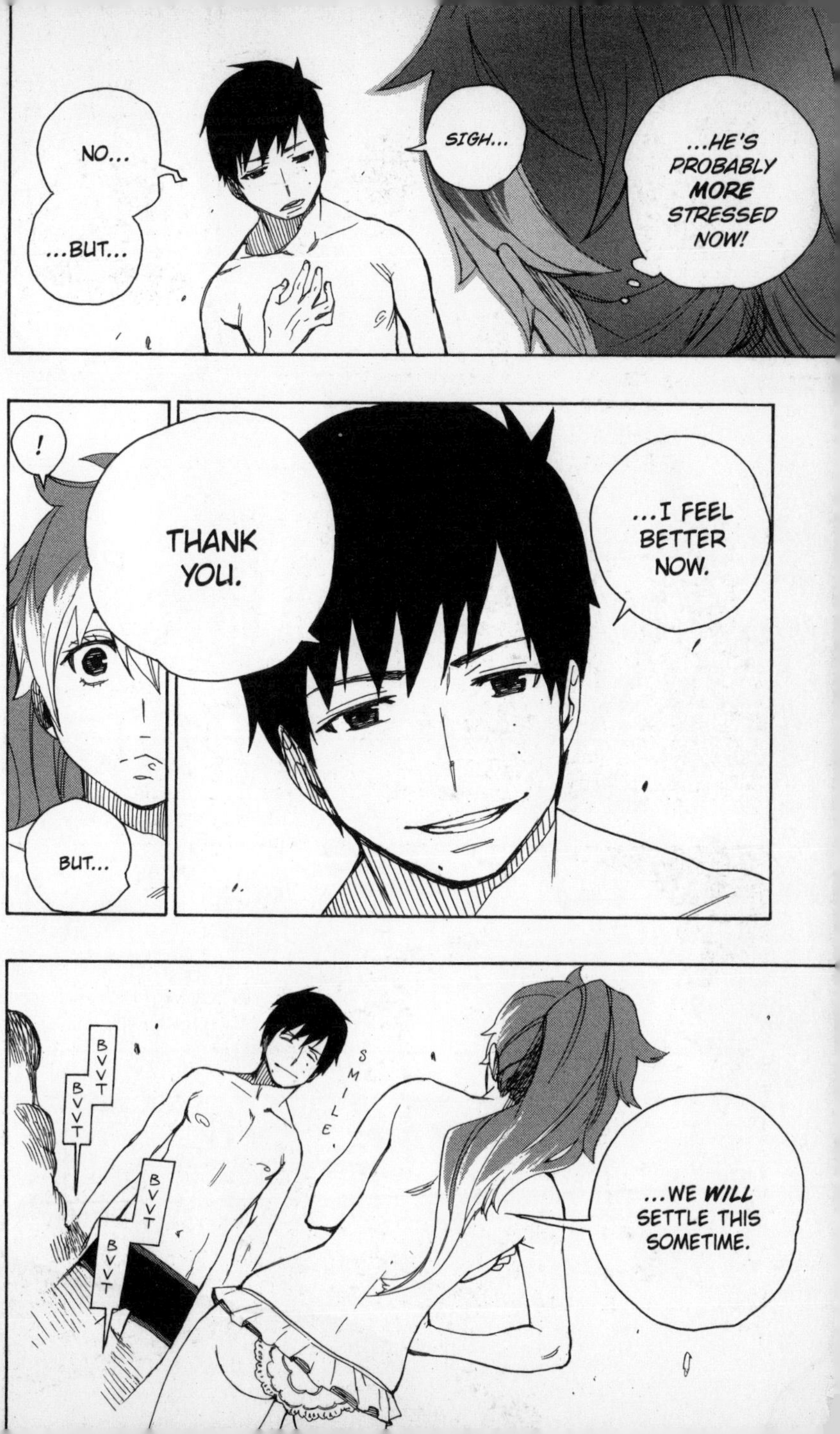
...HE'S PROBABLY MORE STRESSED NOW!
SIGH...
NO...
...BUT...
...I FEEL BETTER NOW.
THANK YOU.
!
BUT...
...WE WILL SETTLE THIS SOMETIME.
SMILE
BVVT
BVVT
BVVT
BVVT

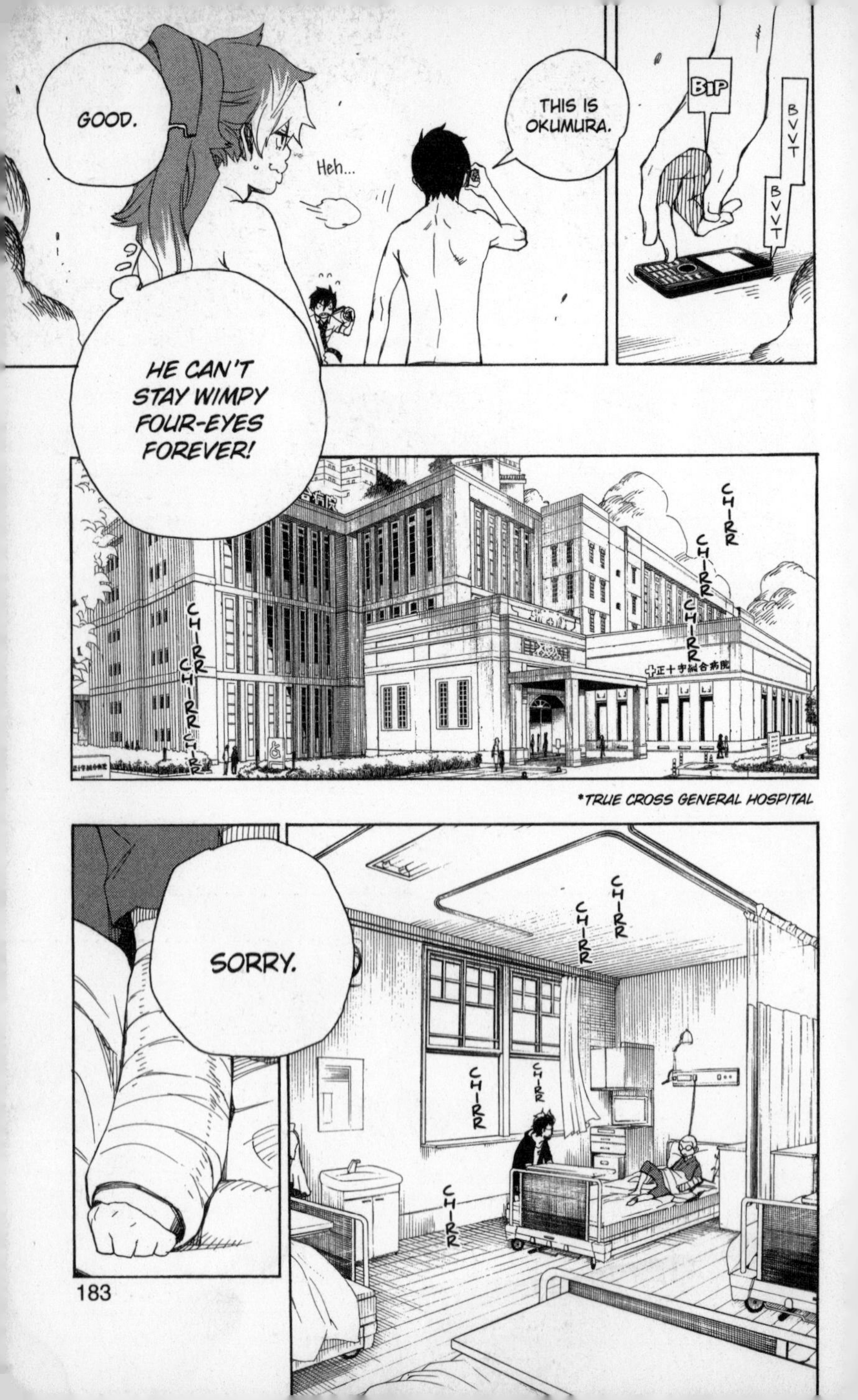
BIP
BVVT
BVVT
THIS IS OKUMURA.
Heh...
GOOD.
HE CAN'T STAY WIMPY FOUR-EYES FOREVER!
CHIRR
CHIRR
CHIRR
CHIRR
CHIRR
CHIRR
*TRUE CROSS GENERAL HOSPITAL
CHIRR
CHIRR
CHIRR
CHIRR
CHIRR
SORRY.

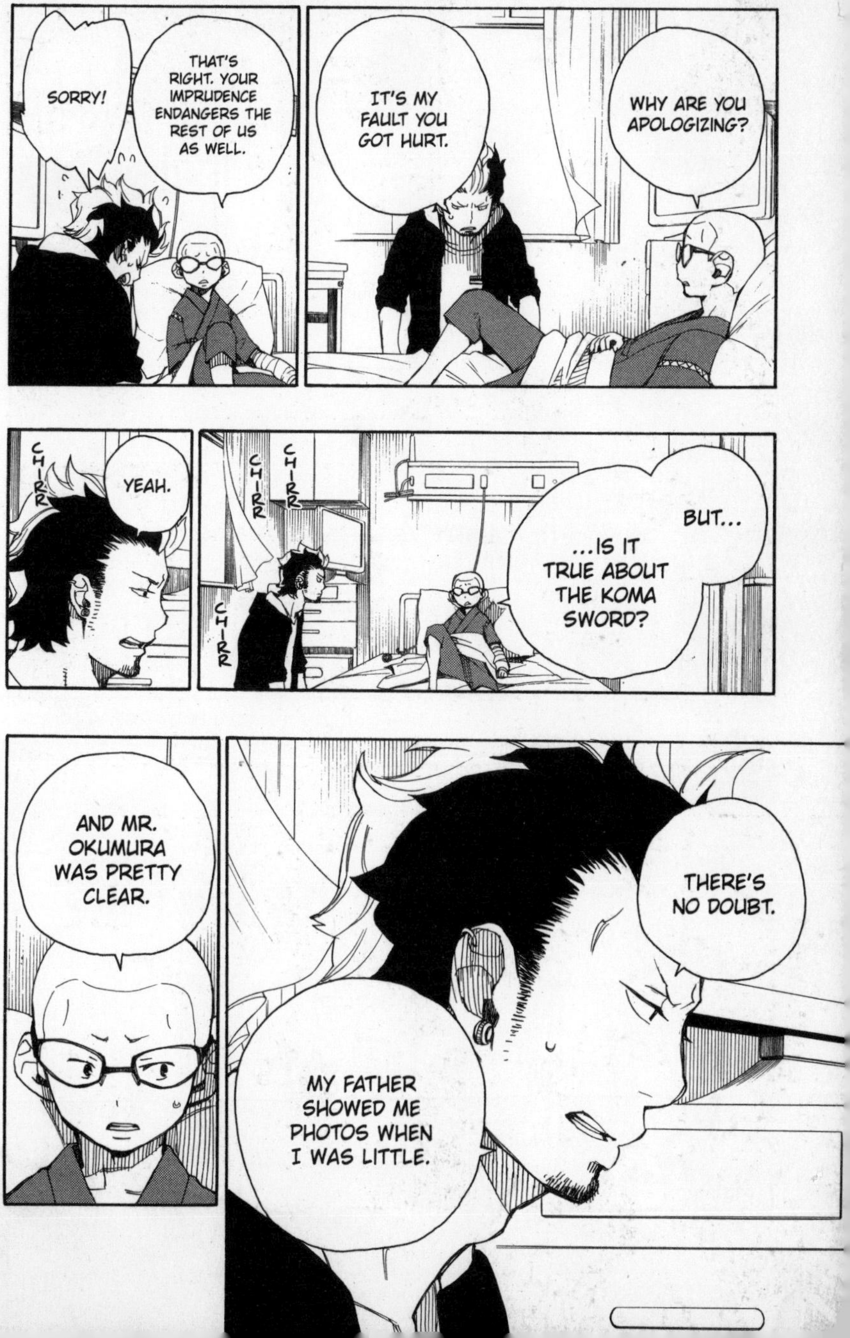
WHY ARE YOU APOLOGIZING?
IT'S MY FAULT YOU GOT HURT.
THAT'S RIGHT. YOUR IMPRUDENCE ENDANGERS THE REST OF US AS WELL.
SORRY!
BUT...
...IS IT TRUE ABOUT THE KOMA SWORD?
CHIRR
CHIRR
CHIRR
YEAH.
CHIRR
THERE'S NO DOUBT.
MY FATHER SHOWED ME PHOTOS WHEN I WAS LITTLE.
AND MR. OKUMURA WAS PRETTY CLEAR.

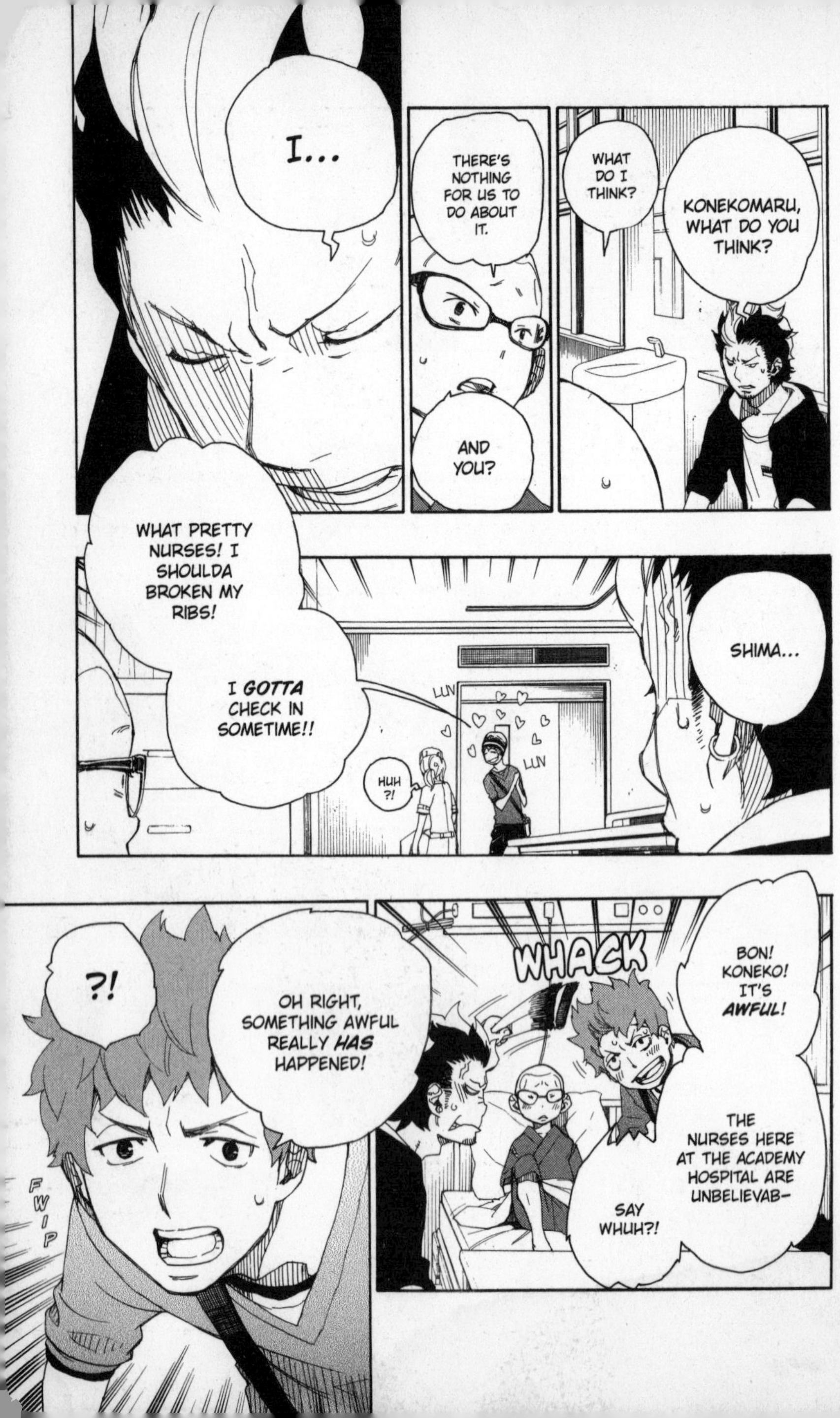

KONEKOMARU, WHAT DO YOU THINK?
WHAT DO I THINK?
THERE'S NOTHING FOR US TO DO ABOUT IT.
AND YOU?
I...
SHIMA...
LUV
LUV
HUH?!
WHAT PRETTY NURSES! I SHOULDA BROKEN MY RIBS!
I GOTTA CHECK IN SOMETIME!!
BON! KONEKO! IT'S AWFUL!
THE NURSES HERE AT THE ACADEMY HOSPITAL ARE UNBELIEVAB-
WHACK
SAY WHUH?!
?!
OH RIGHT, SOMETHING AWFUL REALLY HAS HAPPENED!
FWIP

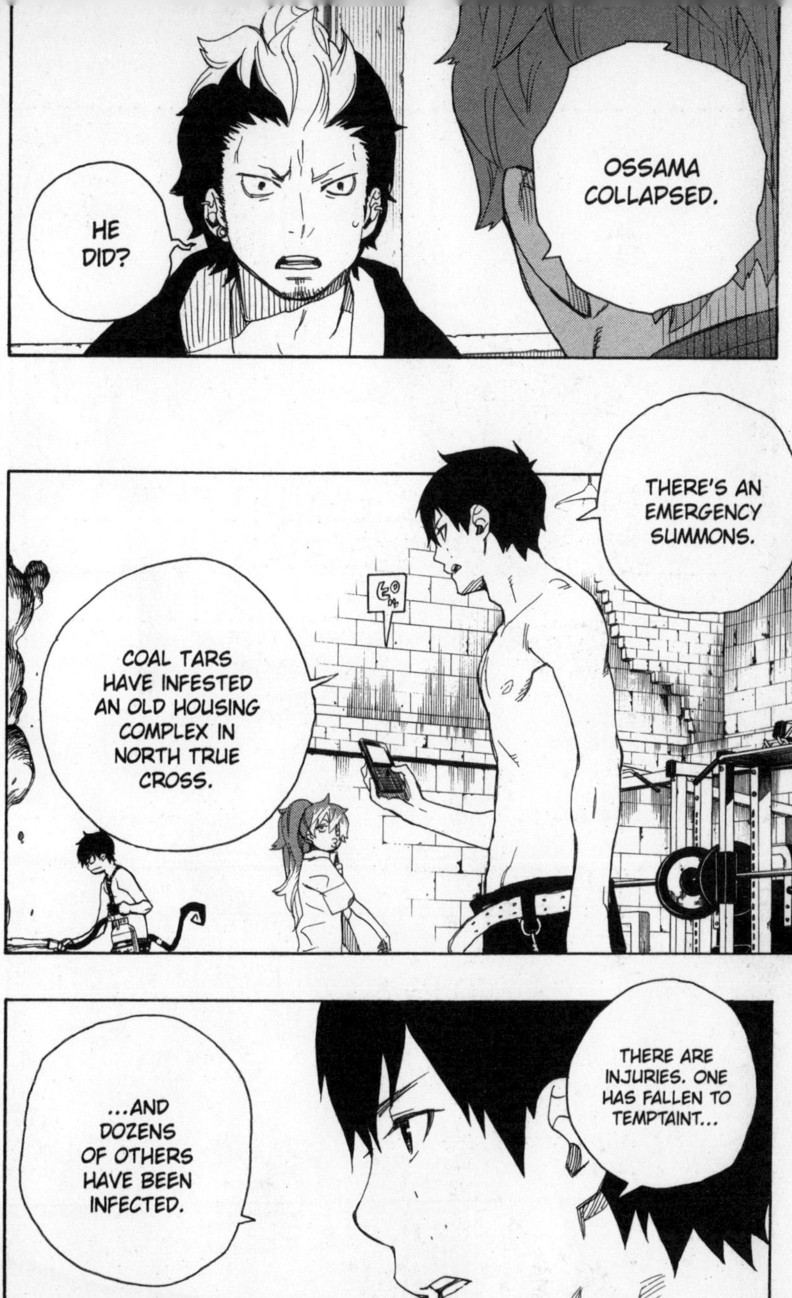
OSSAMA COLLAPSED.
HE DID?
THERE'S AN EMERGENCY SUMMONS.
COAL TARS HAVE INFESTED AN OLD HOUSING COMPLEX IN NORTH TRUE CROSS.
THERE ARE INJURIES. ONE HAS FALLEN TO TEMPTAINT...
...AND DOZENS OF OTHERS HAVE BEEN INFECTED.

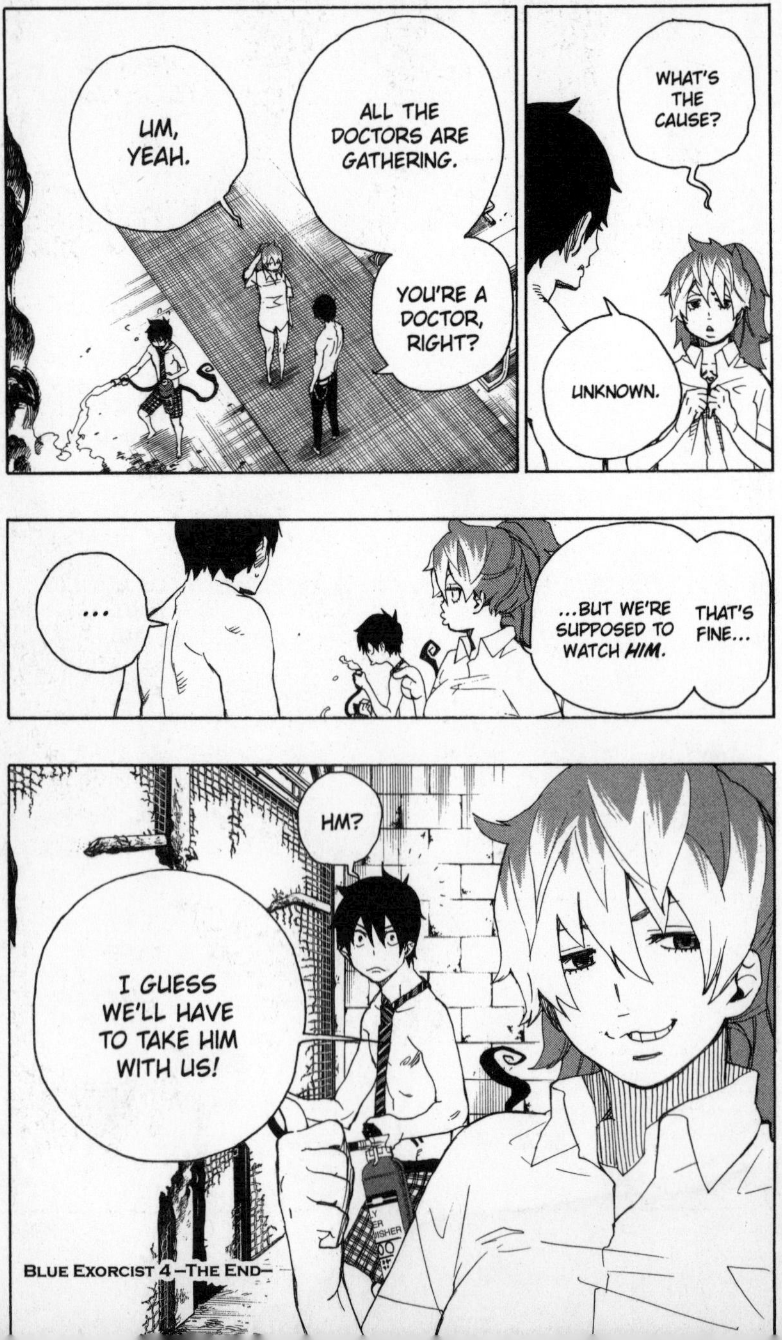
WHAT'S THE CAUSE?
UNKNOWN.
ALL THE DOCTORS ARE GATHERING.
YOU'RE A DOCTOR, RIGHT?
UM, YEAH.
THAT'S FINE...
...BUT WE'RE SUPPOSED TO WATCH HIM.
...
HM?
I GUESS WE'LL HAVE TO TAKE HIM WITH US!
BLUE EXORCIST 4 —THE END—

Blue Exorcist Chapter 15 Slackers

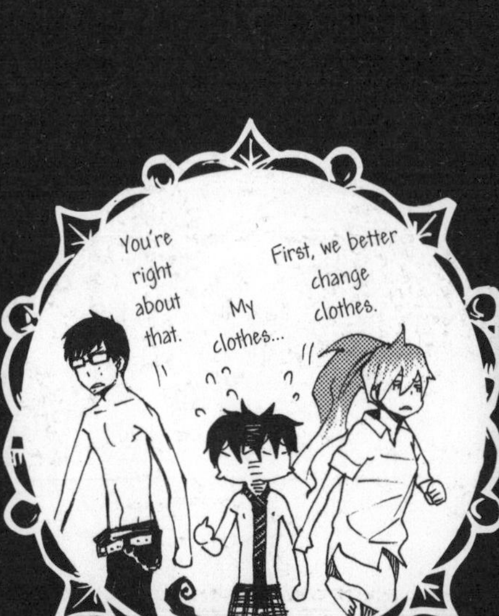
First, we better change clothes.
My clothes...
You're right about that.

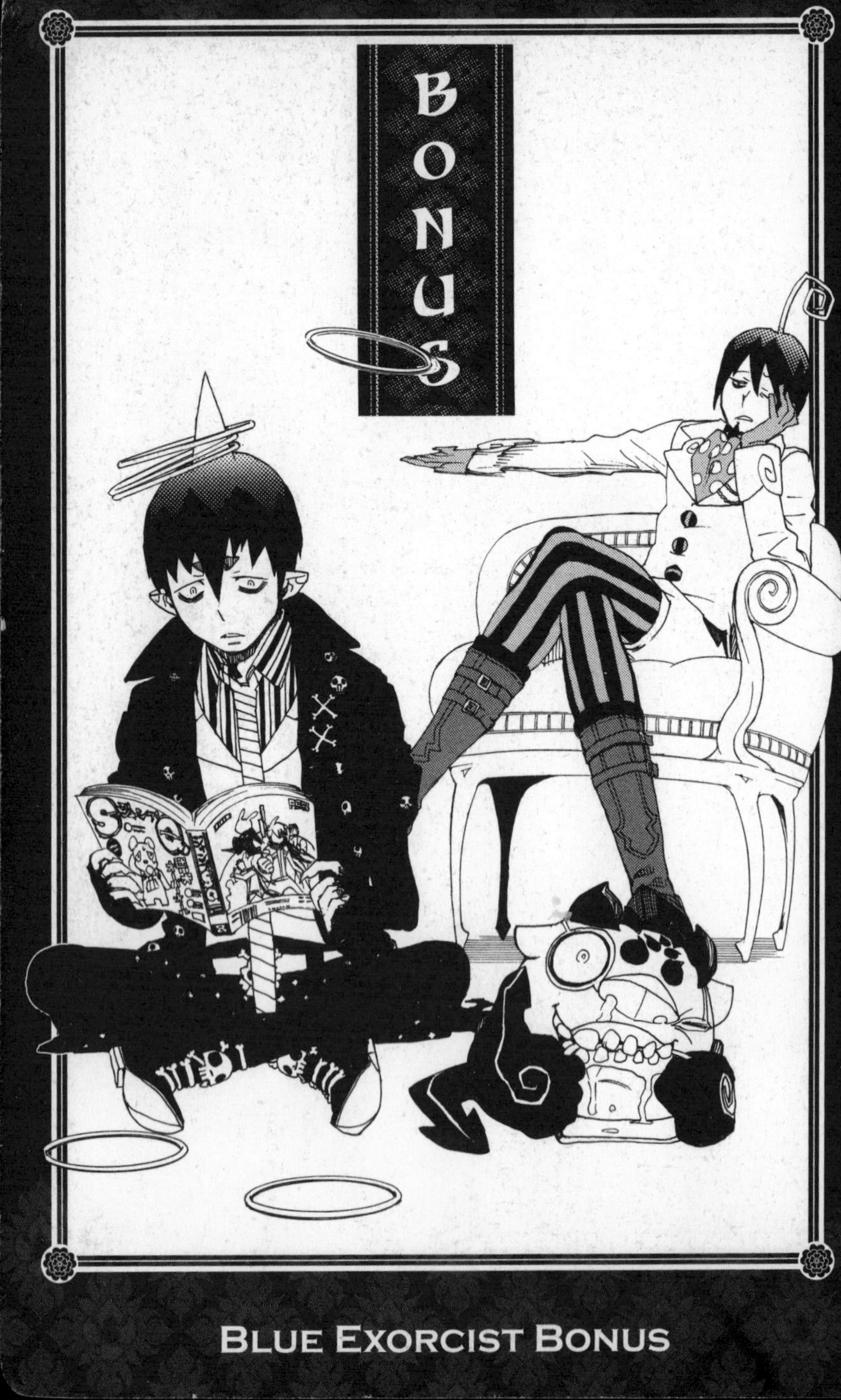
BONUS

BLUE EXORCIST BONUS

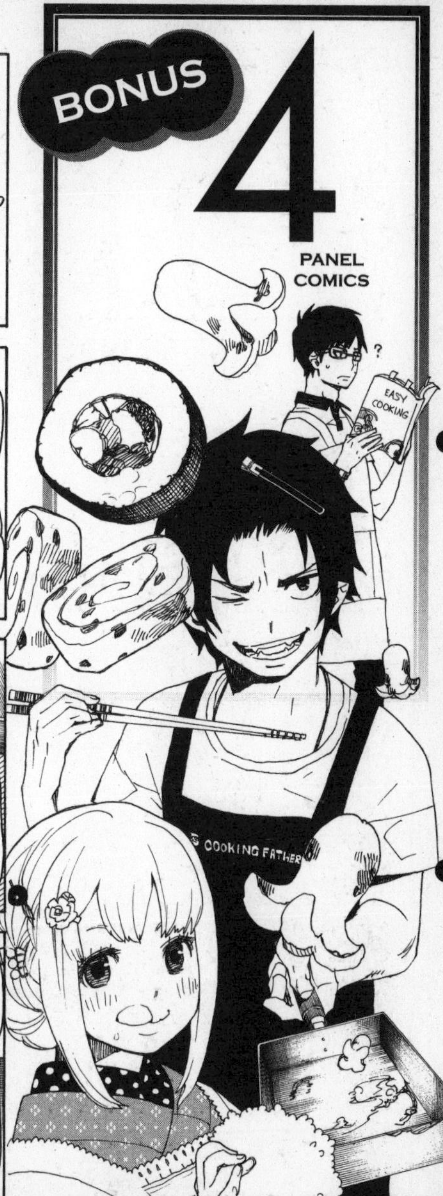
BONUS
4
PANEL COMICS
EASY COOKING
COOKING FATHER

IT'S AN UNFAIR WORLD!

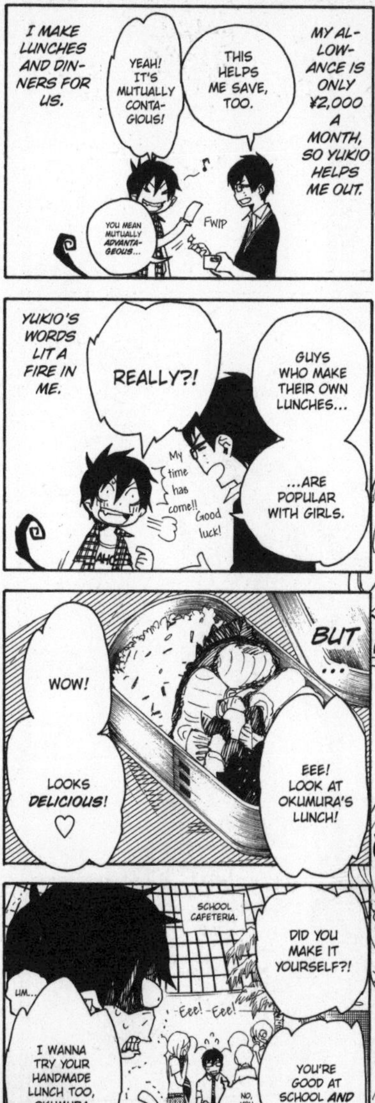
MY ALLOWANCE IS ONLY ¥2,000 A MONTH, SO YUKIO HELPS ME OUT.
THIS HELPS ME SAVE, TOO.
YEAH! IT'S MUTUALLY CONTAGIOUS!
I MAKE LUNCHES AND DINNERS FOR US.
FWIP
YOU MEAN MUTUALLY ADVANTAGEOUS...
GUYS WHO MAKE THEIR OWN LUNCHES...
...ARE POPULAR WITH GIRLS.
REALLY?!
YUKIO'S WORDS LIT A FIRE IN ME.
Good luck!
My time has come!!
BUT...
EEE! LOOK AT OKUMURA'S LUNCH!
WOW!
LOOKS DELICIOUS! ♡
DID YOU MAKE IT YOURSELF?!
YOU'RE GOOD AT SCHOOL AND COOKING!
SCHOOL CAFETERIA.
NO, YOU DON'T UNDERSTAND...
-Eee! -Eee!
UM...
I WANNA TRY YOUR HANDMADE LUNCH TOO, OKUMURA

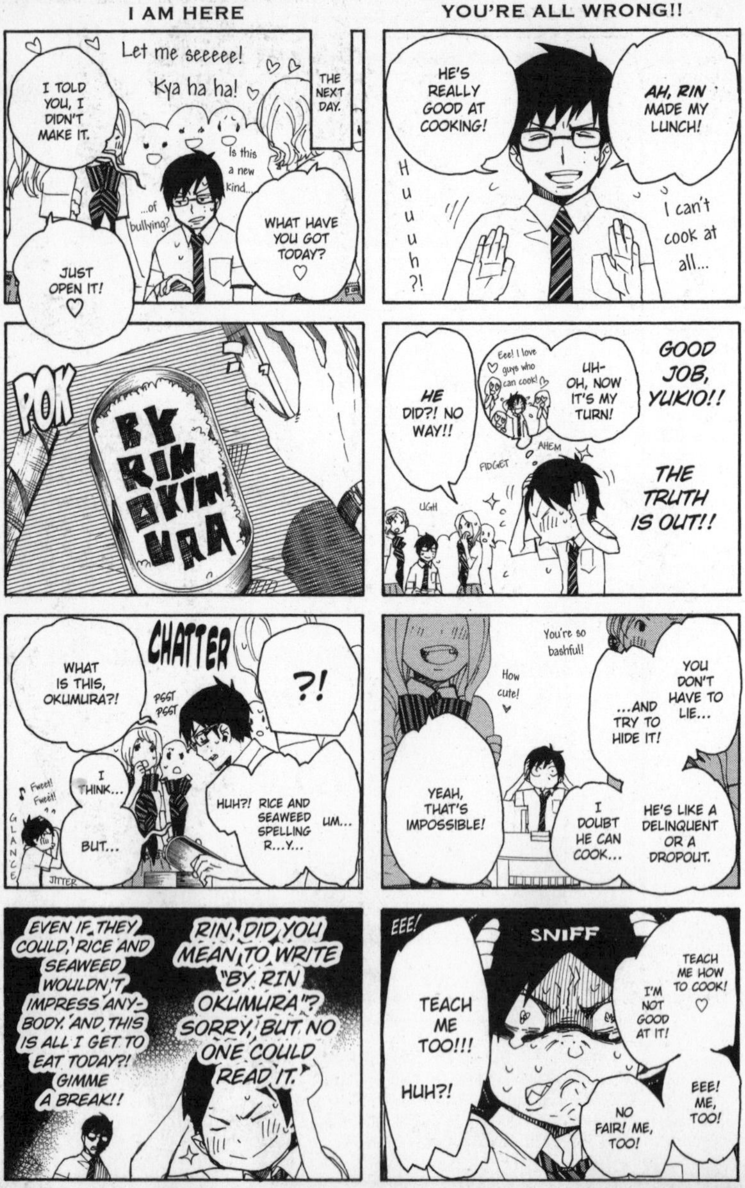
YOU'RE ALL WRONG!!
AH, RIN MADE MY LUNCH!
HE'S REALLY GOOD AT COOKING!
I can't cook at all...
Huuuh?!
GOOD JOB, YUKIO!!
UH-OH, NOW IT'S MY TURN!
Eee! I love guys who can cook!
HE DID?! NO WAY!!
AHEM
FIDGET
THE TRUTH IS OUT!!
UGH
You're so bashful!
YOU DON'T HAVE TO LIE...
...AND TRY TO HIDE IT!
How cute!
HE'S LIKE A DELINQUENT OR A DROPOUT.
I DOUBT HE CAN COOK...
YEAH, THAT'S IMPOSSIBLE!
SNIFF
TEACH ME HOW TO COOK! ♡
I'M NOT GOOD AT IT!
EEE!
TEACH ME TOO!!!
EEE! ME, TOO!
NO FAIR! ME, TOO!
HUH?!
I AM HERE
THE NEXT DAY.
Let me seeeee!
Kya ha ha!
I TOLD YOU, I DIDN'T MAKE IT.
Is this a new kind...
...of bullying?
WHAT HAVE YOU GOT TODAY? ♡
JUST OPEN IT! ♡
BY RIN OKIMURA
POK
?!
CHATTER
WHAT IS THIS, OKUMURA?!
PSST PSST
UM...
HUH?! RICE AND SEAWEED SPELLING R...Y...
I THINK...
BUT...
Fweet! Fweet!
GLANCE
JITTER
RIN, DID YOU MEAN TO WRITE "BY RIN OKUMURA"? SORRY, BUT NO ONE COULD READ IT.
EVEN IF THEY COULD, RICE AND SEAWEED WOULDN'T IMPRESS ANYBODY. AND THIS IS ALL I GET TO EAT TODAY?! GIMME A BREAK!!

EARLY DESIGN ILLUSTRATION

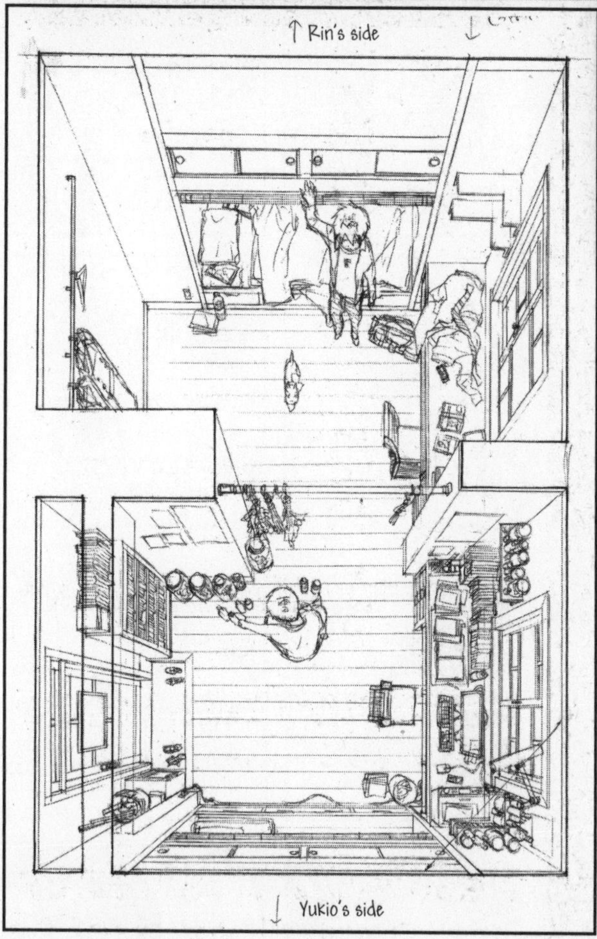
↑ Rin's side
↓ Yukio's side

I WANTED A BLEND OF EASTERN AND WESTERN STYLES. IN THE END, MY ASSISTANTS MADE IT A LITTLE WIDER AND CHANGED THE LAYOUT. I'M NOT TOO PRECISE ABOUT SUCH THINGS.

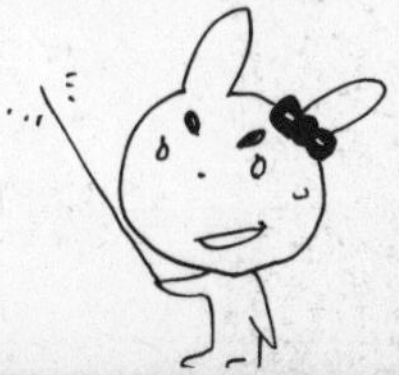

THE BLUE EXORCIST TEAM

Art Assistants

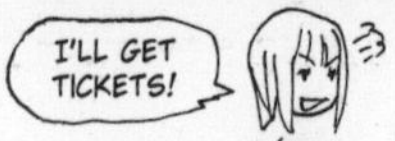
I'LL GET TICKETS!
Shibu-tama

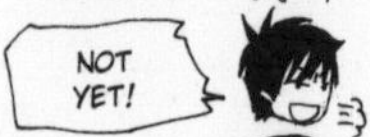
NOT YET!
Uemura-san

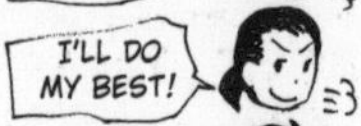
I'LL DO MY BEST!
Kamimura-san

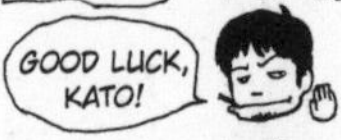
GOOD LUCK, KATO!
Kimura-kun

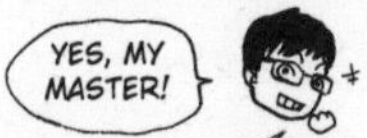
YES, MY MASTER!
Hayashi-kun

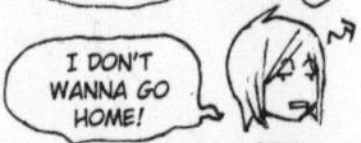
I DON'T WANNA GO HOME!
Kawamura-san

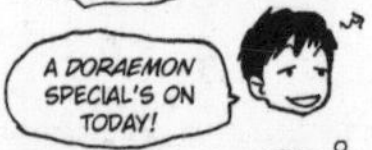
A DORAEMON SPECIAL'S ON TODAY!
Kimura-kun (Nori)

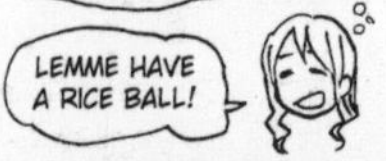
LEMME HAVE A RICE BALL!
Minotarosu

Editor

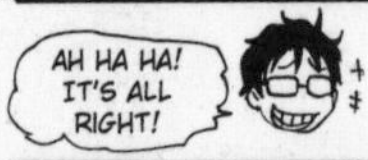
AH HA HA! IT'S ALL RIGHT!
Shihei Rin

Graphic Novel Editor

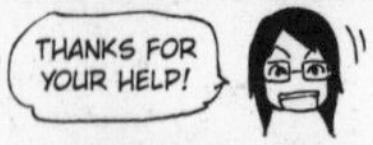
THANKS FOR YOUR HELP!
Natsuki Kusaka

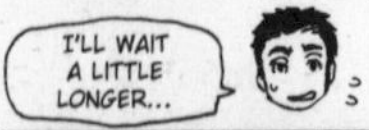
I'LL WAIT A LITTLE LONGER...
Ryusuke Kuroki

Graphic Novel Cover Design

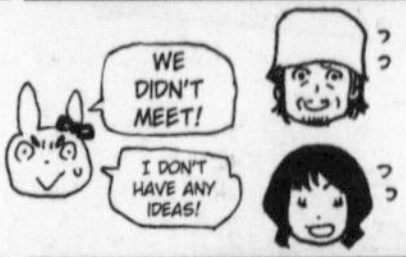
WE DIDN'T MEET!
I DON'T HAVE ANY IDEAS!
Shimada Hideaki

Tomoko Hasumi (L.S.D.)

Manga

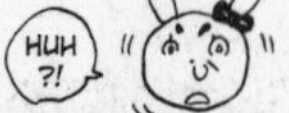
HUH ?!
Kazue Kato

(in no particular order)

(Note: The caricatures and statements are from memory!)

Be sure to pick up Volume 5!

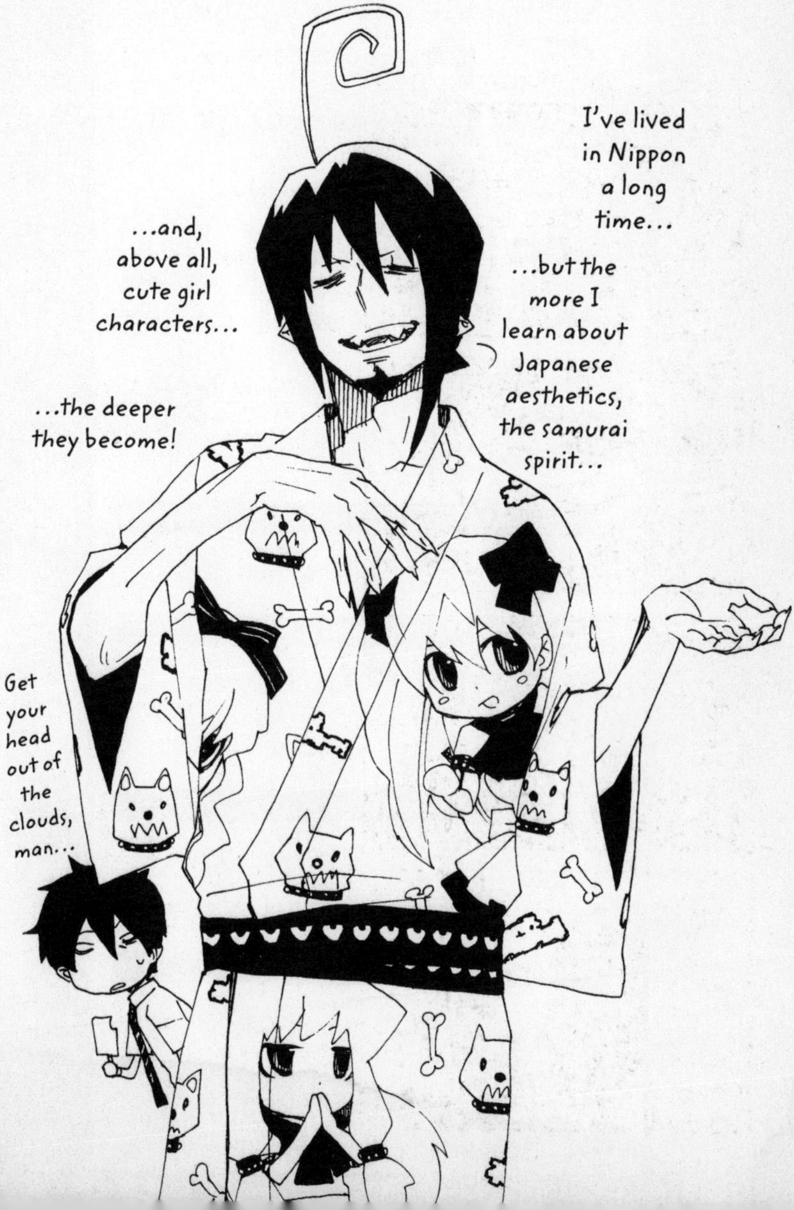
I've lived in Nippon a long time...
...but the more I learn about Japanese aesthetics, the samurai spirit...
...and, above all, cute girl characters...
...the deeper they become!
Get your head out of the clouds, man...

Mephisto's a Geek

Quasar Wave!!!!
BAM
MNCH
MNCH
Choco Chips
KO
WHAM
New Moon!!!!!
Gaaah!
KO!!
MNCH
MNCH
Choco Chips
WIN
Mmm, pretty good, bro.
Of course. I attack different than you do.
Regenerate
MNCH
MNCH
Choco Chips
It tastes really good!
Agh!
MNCH
MNCH
Gaaah?!! My custom-ordered “Mephisto Pink” wireless controller!!!!
GNAW
GNAW

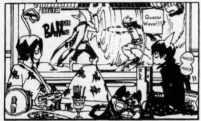

Robe: kanji for “demon”

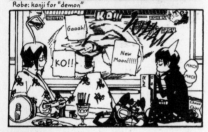

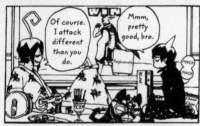

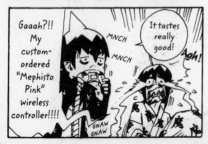

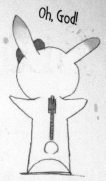

Oh, God!

KAZUE KATO

THANKS TO YOU READERS, HERE'S VOLUME 4! I ALWAYS WONDER WHAT TO WRITE HERE. I CAN'T THINK OF ANYTHING WITTY AT ALL!

FOR NOW, CHECK OUT VOLUME 4!

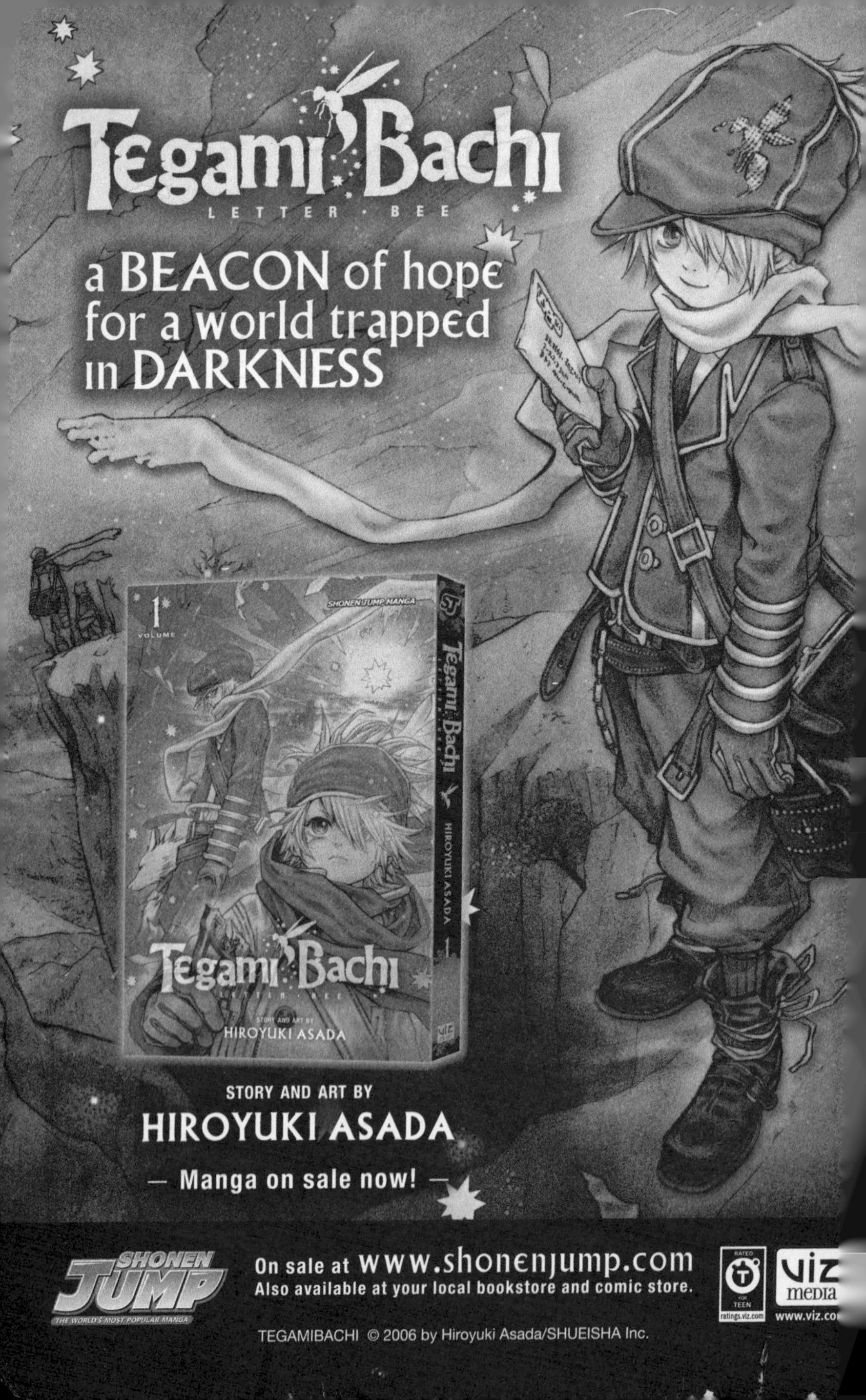
Tegami Bachi
LETTER • BEE
a BEACON of hope for a world trapped in DARKNESS
SHONEN JUMP MANGA
1 VOLUME
Tegami Bachi
LETTER BEE
STORY AND ART BY
HIROYUKI ASADA
STORY AND ART BY
HIROYUKI ASADA
— Manga on sale now! —
SHONEN JUMP
THE WORLD'S MOST POPULAR MANGA
On sale at www.shonenjump.com
Also available at your local bookstore and comic store.
RATED T FOR TEEN
ratings.viz.com
viz media
www.viz.co
TEGAMIBACHI © 2006 by Hiroyuki Asada/SHUEISHA Inc.

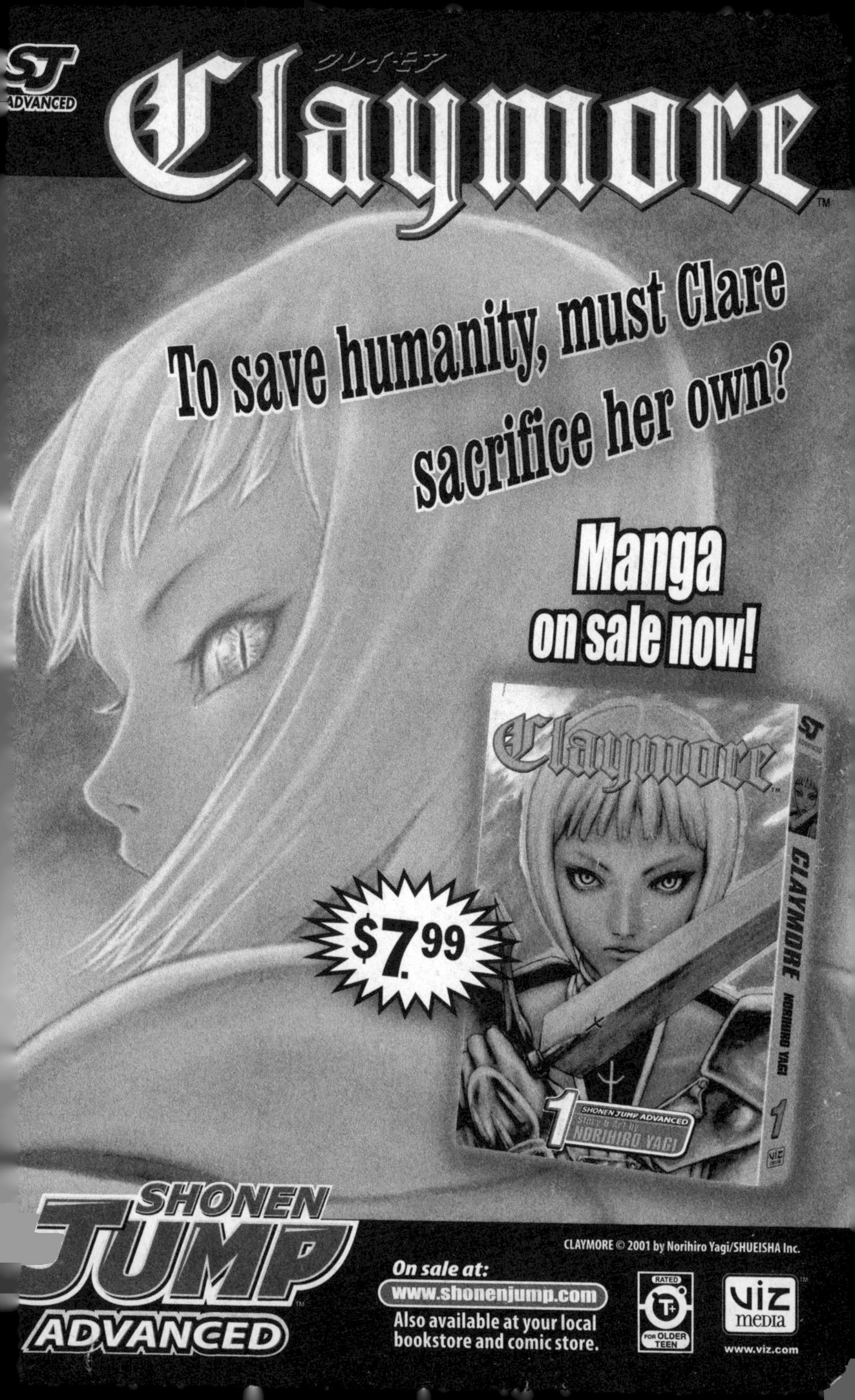

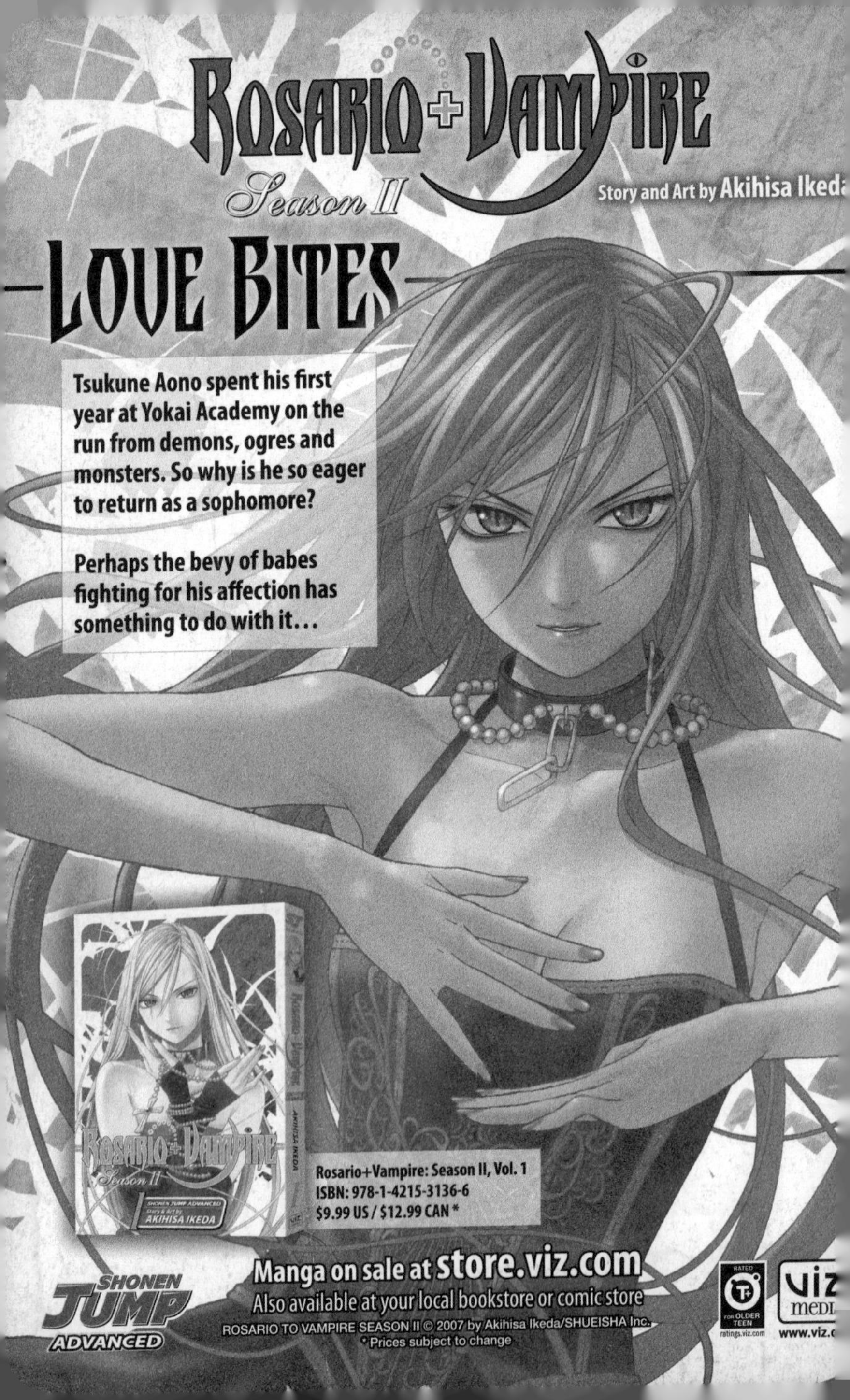

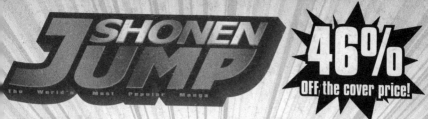
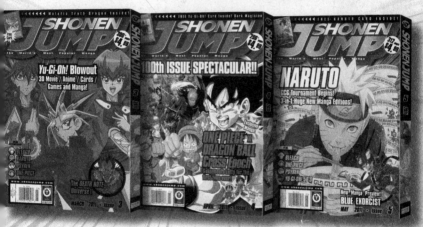
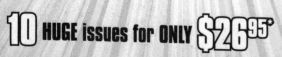

BLUE EXORCIST

BLUE EXORCIST VOL. 4
SHONEN JUMP ADVANCED Manga Edition

STORY & ART BY KAZUE KATO

Translation & English Adaptation/John Werry
Touch-up Art & Lettering/John Hunt, Primary Graphix
Cover & Interior Design/Sam Elzway
Editor/Mike Montesa

AO NO EXORCIST © 2009 by Kazue Kato
All rights reserved.
First published in Japan in 2009 by SHUEISHA Inc., Tokyo.
English translation rights arranged by SHUEISHA Inc.

The stories, characters and incidents mentioned in
this publication are entirely fictional.

Printed in the U.S.A.

Published by VIZ Media, LLC
P.O. Box 77010
San Francisco, CA 94107

10 9 8 7 6 5 4 3 2 1
First printing, October 2011

www.viz.com

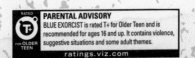
PARENTAL ADVISORY
RATED T+ FOR OLDER TEEN
BLUE EXORCIST is rated T+ for Older Teen and is
recommended for ages 16 and up. It contains violence,
suggestive situations and some adult themes.
ratings.viz.com

THE WORLD'S MOST
CUTTING-EDGE MANGA
SHONEN JUMP
ADVANCED
www.shonenjump.com

In the next volume...

ZWF
THAT BLUE FLAME CAN *KILL* PEOPLE!
LIKE MY GRAND-FATHER...

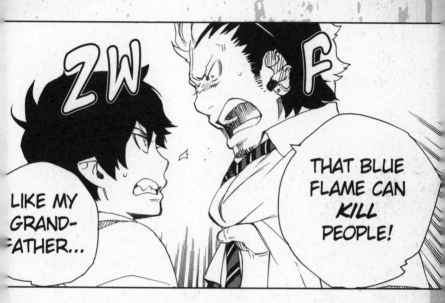

In the late Edo Period, a demon known as the Impure King killed thousands of people. After defeating the demon, the Knights of the True Cross kept its left eye safely sealed away on Academy grounds—but now someone has stolen it! Hearing the thief has taken a child hostage, Yukio and Rin go to help. The investigation and pursuit will lead Rin and his friends to Kyoto and involve them even deeper in a sinister plot! But will his friends' knowledge that Rin is the son of Satan drive a wedge between them?

Coming December 2011!